To Jeavey & Gull with wa...

THE ENGLISH
HIGHLAND CLANS

THE ENGLISH HIGHLAND CLANS

Tudor Responses
to a Mediaeval Problem

RALPH ROBSON

'Tynedale and Redesdale . . . These highlanders . . . run
together in Clangs as they term it, or Names.'

Gray's *Chorographia, anno* 1649

'Redesdale and Tynedale . . . The only allegiance of
the warriors of these wild regions was loyalty towards
their own clans.'

G. M. Trevelyan: *English Social History*

JOHN DONALD PUBLISHERS LTD
EDINBURGH

ISBN 0 85976 246 7

By the same author
  The Oxfordshire Election of 1754 (Oxford, 1949)

Phototypeset by Quorn Selective Repro, Loughborough.
Printed in Great Britain by Bell & Bain Ltd., Glasgow.

PREFACE

One problem facing English monarchs in the sixteenth century that did not always annexe the priority it deserved, concerned relations with Scotland. Integral to that problem was the state of affairs along their common frontier, any examination of which in its entirety would be tantamount to writing much of the history of Scotland and England over half a millennium. A more manageable alternative is to place under the microscope one district, typical up to a point but with peculiarities sufficient to justify special attention. For this the upland region formed by Tyne- and Redesdales seems well qualified, inasmuch as in documentation they protrude on the English side like mountains from their foothills. The extent to which to date they have been neglected by historians strengthens their claim.

The challenge presented by the wild community inhabiting the Middle Marches of the insecure frontier, dalesmen in winter and highlanders in summer, had been inadvertently fostered in the Middle Ages by authorities with quite other purposes in mind. Over a third of the present work is taken up with that long prelude, while most of what ensues will seek to explain how by 1500 these unruly clans were in a position to foment disorder in two quarters where the Tudor monarchy could least afford it, namely the North of England and what was still a foreign and hostile kingdom beyond.

The tools for dealing with a thorny problem that were at the disposal of the administration have to be displayed. Given that the King was *primum mobile* and the utilisation of the tools determined by the royal personality, this has largely to be a book about Henry VIII, during whose reign the crisis in the highlands apparently attained its apogee. On balance it is an often lenient potentate who emerges, more reconcilable with a popularity during lifetime than with a grisly reputation since.[1]

The fortunes of Tyne- and Redesdales were a barometer of Anglo-Scottish relations; their survival due to enduring enmity between the British nations; and their extinction to the Reformation, in so far as it created conditions for the unification of the dynamic little island under a Scottish sovereign. Despite the concentration upon one district of one realm, and to the extent that the relative poverty of Scottish archives permits,[2] this then is an essay in *British* history of which after all not a lot has materialised for the years before 1707. The final two chapters cover the period when England was ruled by Henry VIII's children, and during which the highlanders fell headlong into ruin. Owing to the lurid nature of the Elizabethan material this is the half-century upon which popular books about the area have lingered, exhibiting, however, scant awareness of the catastrophe that befell Tyne- and Redesdales.

We labour under three disadvantages. Firstly there is the over-dependence on sixteenth-century sources that afflicts many mediaeval historians. Secondly the documentation concerning the interval between the accession of Richard II and the death of Richard III is inadequate to that juncture's importance, necessitating more extrapolation than is desirable from prior and subsequent events. A third if minor hindrance has been the relative rarity, and inferiority to the Scottish, of Northumbrian ballads. None the less one can be fairly confident that the corporate personality of the English Middle Marcher will emerge from the shadows. Whatever the eschewal of romantic overtones, any description of the two dales in their heyday serves to recall an era when our countryside was more than a museum set in a park.

For continual encouragement and expert advice, spread over many years, I am deeply grateful to Mr. Clifford Davies, sometime Lecturer in History at the University of Glasgow, now Sub-Warden of Wadham, my old College; and also yet again to the late Dame Lucy Stuart Sutherland, Principal of Lady Margaret Hall. I am indebted, too, to the late Dr. W. H. Charlton of Hesleyside for courteous and enlightening corrrespondence; to Mr. R. M. Gard of the Northumberland County Archives for efficient assistance; and to my son Christopher Robson for devotedly producing the maps. The effigy of a Northern Horseman on the cover is reproduced by kind permission of Mrs Flora Fairbairn at the Border History Museum in Hexham.

I trust no confusion will arise due to compression into a short book of matter relating to many personages with repetitive surnames. Wherever in this respect I may have failed, reference to the Index at the end should help to clarify.

By way of footnote I have a private interest to declare in so far as among my paternal great-grandparents there was a Dodd and a Hedley, besides a Robson, all of them moss-trooping names of the Middle Marches. As Le Roy Ladurie once pointed out, significant forbears are not confined to the nobility; nor, one might add, a taste for the ancestral picaresque to Australians.

NOTES

1. G. R. Elton, *Policy and Police*, pp. 121 & 388–9.
2. Jenny Wormald, *Lords and Men in Scotland*, p. 1.

CONTENTS

MAPS

MAP 1

Stirling
Bannockburn
Falkirk
Firth of Forth
Pinkie
Dunglass
Pease Strait
EDINBURGH
Coldingham
BERWICK
KINGDOM OF SCOTLAND
S.E.M.
The Merse
Melrose
Flodden
Tweeddale
Kelso
E.E.M.
S.M.M. Jedburgh
Hawick
Coquetdale
Alnwick
Teviotdale
Otterburn
Warkworth
Redesdale
Felton
S.W.M.
Liddesdale
Nth Tynedale
E.M.M.
Kinmont
Bellingham
Morpeth
Caerlaverock
Solway Moss
Hexham
Tynemouth
Sth Tynedale
Newcastle
Solway Firth
CARLISLE
Allendale
Prudhoe
Penrith
DURHAM
Hartlepool
E.W.M.
Neville's Cross

Kendal

KINGDOM OF ENGLAND

Ripon
Boroughbridge
Sheriff
Hutton
Knaresborough
YORK
Stamford
(Losecoat Field)
85 miles
Towton

IRISH
SEA

NORTH
SEA

N

■ ■ ■ ■ ■ Anglo-Scottish Border   • • • • • • • Marches' Boundaries

S.W.M., S.M.M., S.E.M. Scottish West, Middle, East March

E.W.M., E.M.M., E.M.M. English West, Middle, East March

■ Major Centres   ■ Towns   ● Minor Settlements   ✕ Battles

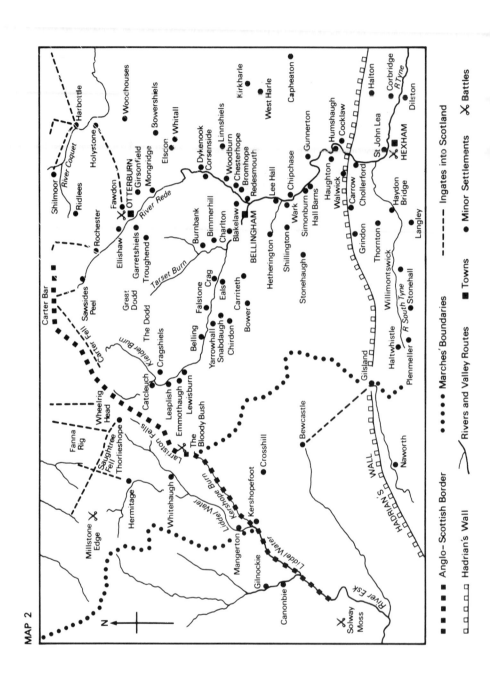

MAP 2

Anglo-Scottish Border

Hadrian's Wall

Marches' Boundaries

Ingates into Scotland

Battles

Towns

Minor Settlements

Rivers and Valley Routes

Harbottle
Shilmoor
Ridlees
Woodhouses
Holystone
River Coquet
Rochester
Fawdon
OTTERBURN
Girsonfield
Mongridge
Bowersheils
Whitall
Elscon
Kirkharle
West Harle
Capheaton
Ellishaw
Garretshiels
Troughend
River Rede
Dykenook
Corsenside
Linnshiels
Woodburn
Chesterhope
Bromhope
Redesmouth
Lee Hall
Chipchase
Gunnerton
Humshaugh
Cocklaw
St John Lea
Halton
Corbridge
R Tyne
Dilston
Carter Bar
Sawsides Peel
Great Dodd
The Dodd
Kielder Burn
Cragshiels
Burnbank
Bimmerhill
Charlton
Crag
Eals
Carriteth
Blakelaw
BELLINGHAM
Wark
Simonburn
Hall Barns
Haughton
Walwick
Carrow
Chollerford
Grindon
Thornton
Willimontswick
Haydon Bridge
Langley
Carter Fell
Wheelrig Head
Fanna Rig
Slaughtree
Thorlieshope
Catcleuch
Leaplish
Emmothaugh
Lewisburn
The Bloody Bush
Larriston Fells
Falstone
Belling
Yarrowhall
Snabdaugh
Chirdon
Bower
Hetherington
Shillington
Stonehaugh
Gilsland
Bewcastle
Naworth
HADRIAN'S WALL
Haltwhistle
Plenmeller
R South Tyne
Stonehall
Millstone Edge
Hermitage
Whitehaugh
Kershope Burn
Liddel Water
Crosshill
Mangerton
Kershopefoot
Gilnockie
Canonbie
Liddel Water
River Esk
Solway Moss

HEXHAM

N

PART I: THE ORIGINS AND EXTENT OF THE THREAT

CHAPTER ONE

The Norman Liberties of Tynedale and Redesdale

Royal commissions were convened in 1541 and 1551 under the chairman-ship of Sir Robert Bowes to consider the problems presented by what were roundly termed the 'evil people' of Tynedale and Redesdale. Among much else they declared that 'there be very few able men in all that country of North Tynedale,[1] but either they have used to steal in England or Scot-land[2] . . . They most praises and cherishes such as begin soonest in youth to practise themselves in thefts and robberies . . . nothing regarding the laws of God or the King's Majesty . . . The Redesdalers do likewise delight and use themselves in thefts and spoils as the Tynedalers do'.[3] That these reports remain in several respects a unique source for situations that had originated centuries before has to be confessed at the outset. Nevertheless the fact is sufficiently well attested that the twin communities — highlanders rather than dalesmen whenever the weather permitted — had endowed England with a Wild North as lawless as, and more enduring and authentic than the Wild West of the United States.

The first of three worlds they inhabited was determined by geography. Before the Union of the Crowns the Middle Marches of England confronted Scotland from the Cheviot Forest to Kershopefoot in Cumberland. The frontier sector of 400 square miles was bounded on the west by the Bewcastle and Larriston fells; on the east by the Watling Street; and on the south by Hadrian's Wall. Watered by the Rede and the North Tyne, it was a fair country, its burns stocked with otter, salmon and bull trout, its hills and woods with the red deer and black grouse, and its farms with flocks of sheep.

The northern part of Tynedale that is the present concern begins at Chollerford, on the barbarous side of the Roman Wall, where even nowadays a meadow looks like a forest clearing. Level nowhere for fifty consecutive yards, the road coils up past the pinewoods of Wark towards Bellingham, where barer hills have now been usurped by blackfaced sheep and the dwindling trees huddle about the young Tyne. Around Tarset the hills roll away like billows warmed only by the heather in its season. Beyond lie Falstone and the Cheviot sentinels, between which and the Kielder glens the arterial river loses identity in a network of capillaries. Staired down innumerable linns, these burns irrigate only mosses, fern and moorland grasses. The picture has recently been radically transformed, with the planting of the Kielder Forest and under the flood of a vast reservoir, but by the sixteenth century there was population to a breadth of up to three miles on either bank of North Tyne, hemmed in on all sides by the Waste.[4]

Leaping like Tyne Water from the Cheviots, the Rede mingles with her consort under a canopy of ash and willow, seven miles below Otterburn. Even the valley floor is 500 feet above sea-level, and June frosts are encountered along the heath-covered hilltops, which reach to 1500 feet. From them the view is of brown and forbidding moorland stretching into Scotland, striped bright green with limestone gairs, grazed like the rushes and mountain grasses by sheep. Between the hills lurk noisome peat-bogs called flow-mosses. Inside Redesdale horizons are closer than those in Tynedale, and the land tamer on each side of the high-road north under Carter Bar.

The two dales form an entity which the Redesmouth link confirms and an intervening ridge of wilderness strives vainly to undo. G. M. Trevelyan described them as jointly 'cut off from the rest of the world' from which they 'lived secluded'.[5] Moreover through a symbiosis lasting half a millennium the geographical came to reflect a social and political unity as well, so that a Bishop of Durham could allude to the 'territorium de Tynedale et Redesdale', and William Gray in 1649 to the twins as 'a *country* that William the Conqueror did not subdue'. Although the antiquarian was wrong about William I, his concept of a single territory in continual need of subjugation was valid enough. In their attempts to ensure that the highlanders harmonised better with their idyllic surroundings, Norman and Angevin rulers enlisted the aid of institutions both sacred and profane.

With the focus on an Age of Faith, Bowes' aspersion of godlessness has to be seriously examined. Technically the district was as ecclesiastically regular as Kent, forming part of the venerable Anglo-Saxon diocese of Durham. Redesdale broke down conventionally enough into the parishes of Elsdon, consisting of Elsdon, Monkridge, Otterburn, Rochester, Troughend and Woodside;[6] Holystone; and Corsenside. As for Simonburn, which engrossed North Tynedale, it was as extensive as many dioceses, necessitating within a radius of some six miles decentralisation to other chapels at Bellingham, which was the best attended, and Falstone, 'used for private masses at some times'.[3] Around 1300 an enormous £136 p.a.[7] was reckoned necessary to attract suitable incumbents to Simonburn, which made the right of presentation to the living, or advowson, a coveted property. After years of argument it was finally wrung from the Prince Bishop of Durham by Edward III in 1356,[8] but whether it was held in royal or episcopal hands seemed to make little difference. Amongst a score of parishioners who in 1313 had remained contumacious forty days in face of greater excommunication, figured besides some Dodds — the Surname is significant — the parish priest himself.[9] On the other hand, when in Henry VII's day another lot of excommunications were promulgated the Tynedale clergy were castigated as the most remiss in the Province of York, some of them unfrocked or even bogus; even those who *were* genuine, and in orders for as long as ten years, were unable to read properly the masses they intoned in ragged vestments, within defaced ruins, to the dishonour of religion. Redesdale chaplains were notorious for cohabitation with concubines.[10] That said, the Tyne- and Redesdalers clung to the sacraments, whether or not administered by the contemporary version of whisky priests, and when judged by the usual criterion of attendance at mass were good Catholics down to the Reformation and somewhat beyond. Like the Sicilian, highland society was as god-fearing as it was vicious, and no answers are to be found in paganism or impiety.

One respect in which conditions created by religious observance affected events in the highlands stemmed from the proximity of Hexhamshire, which abutted Tynedale on its south-eastern corner. Like the County Palatine of Durham, this ecclesiastical Liberty was one of several north of Trent that had been donated by pious Kings in fits of generosity or remorse to prelates such as, in this case, the Archbishop of York. Operative within the district was a right of sanctuary that stretched beyond the more usual forty days to a whole lifetime, and in a similar church fief benefited murderers to debtors in the proportion 60:40.[11] Given that Hexhamshire's borders with Cumberland and South Tynedale were longer than with the highlanders, without detrimental effect, it would be idle to suppose that this pool of 'grithmen', immune from prosecution, unsettled the highlanders through bad example. At the same time neighbourhood between those of like mind unquestionably left room for mutual stimulation. Indeed, although never so close, the relationship between Tynedale and Hexhamshire may have antedated that between the former and Redesdale. The Archbishop's Bailiffs were accused of taking bribes from robbers, probably out of Tynedale, in 1273,[12] while the first instances of tripartite collaboration involving the more remote Redesdalers dates from Henry V's reign.

The third of the worlds populated by the highlanders was the secular counterpart of the ecclesiastical structures aforementioned. Indeed the County Palatine occupied a position intermediate between the two concepts, in so far as the Prince Bishop was expected to be at least as valiant in defence of the Tyne valley as of a saintly disposition. *Alias* Honour or Soken, the military class of Liberty was sufficiently privileged to entice realistic Frankish barons into an uninviting north in order to consolidate against a foreign neighbour, no less than against unruly natives, what had been won by fire and sword. In 1075 Sir Robert de Umfraville, Lord of Tours and Vian, otherwise Robert-with-the-Beard, received from his kinsman the Conqueror a grant of the lordship, valley and forest of Redesdale *in comitatu*, that is to say as a shire in private hands, in succession to Mildraed, son of Akman, the former Anglian Lord, of whom alas no other trace survives.[13] Apart from a brief confiscation in the decade of Magna Carta, the illustrious Umfravilles retained the Liberty until 1436.

In its feudal guise Redesdale was the Barony or Head Manor of Harbottle, comprising in 1290 eleven members as follows: Otterburn, Monkridge, Elsdon, Garretshiels, Woodburn, The Leams, Troughend, Chesterhope, Lynshiels, Bromhope and Corsenside. In the sense that they were held as entities by individuals Monkridge, Chesterhope and Bromhope were at that time conventional manors, whereas The Leams, Troughend, Otterburn and Elsdon were fragmented into roughly equal tenements, one carucate being typical. Some very substantial holdings such as Leverwick, Winshiels and Snarisdelf (Raylees) were as big as some of the members,[14] the last-named being considered by Simon de Montfort in 1265 worth his service and a rent of sixty marks *per annum*.[15] Whether Snarisdelf depended on neighbouring Elsdon or Monkridge or whether, as seems likely, a tenant of such eminence would have held of the Head Manor direct, cannot be established.

With regard to Tynedale, the sole respect in which it assimilated to the Redesdale model, rather than conversely, was in the matter of Liberty status. For a century after the Conquest it was still being taken *de corpore comitatus*,[16] that is to say treated as an ordinary district of the shire of Northumberland. This, together with Cumberland, had been coveted by the Scots ever since Malcolm Canmore's victory over the northern Angles at Carham in 1018 had put them in mind of pushing the frontier south to the Tees and the Eden, thereby changing the British balance of power forever. At his accession Henry II decided in the light of previous intermittent warfare that the Scots had to be bought off as well as fought off. The price, conveniently nestling between Cumberland and Northumberland, and on the rim of Scotland, was to be Tynedale. Converted in its turn into a Liberty, it was traded to King William the Lion for renunciation of his designs on Northumberland in 1157,[17] but subsequently forfeited after his defeat at Alnwick. Restored to the Scots by the Convention of Falaise in 1175 against renewed renunciation of the county at large,[18] the Liberty was confirmed to them yet again by Henry III under the Treaty of York in 1237, which enlarged the disclaimer to cover Cumberland as well. Both Tynedale and the Honour of Penrith, thrown in for good measure, remained ultimately under English suzerainty,[19] although it was understandable that

Scottish judges in 1279 should have erroneously defined Tynedale as being outside the realm of England and in the realm of Scotland.[20]

In *its* feudal guise Tynedale was the Barony of Wark, consisting of nearly forty manors or fees held of the Liberty between the Tynes, and between the South Tyne and the Allen.[17][21] For fiscal and administrative purposes South Tynedale, the chief manor of which was Grindon between the two arms of the river; and North Tynedale remained associated down to Stuart times.[22] Thus Staworth Peel[23] and Plenmellor[24] were in the late Middle Ages still regarded as integral parts of the Liberty, though on or near the Allen. However, the respective populations of the north and south differed so radically as to render the link artificial, uneasy and ever more tenuous. So utter was North Tynedale's monopoly of problems that by the sixteenth century it had become common practice to refer to it as 'Tynedale' *tout court*,[25] which is why attention in the present work is concentrated upon it almost exclusively. In 1300 its members comprised: Bellingham, Charlton, Chirdon, Tarset, Wark demesne, Shitlington, Hetherington, Simonburn, Humshaugh, Haughton, Walwick (Grange), and Haughton Strother. In addition, though after the cession of Alston to Cumberland as far south in the Liberty as it was possible to go, Knarsdale possessed outlyers in the north.[26][27] By 1600 Hesleyside and Nunwick had been substituted for the three last-named.[23] In the earlier period a third tier of tenements depended on the manors as follows: a bondage in Charlton, a hamlet at Greystead, and holdings at Espleywood and Lewisburn on Tarset;[28] Hesleyside on Bellingham;[29] Nunwick on Simonburn;[30] and the hamlet of Snabdaugh on Chirdon.[28][31] In 1205 one third of Haughton was subinfeoffed to Knarsdale.[32]

If the two Liberties commended themselves to English monarchs either as a gift from a revered ancestor to a companion in arms, or as useful currency for barter, the 'royal franchises' surrendered in the grant to the Umfravilles,[13] and duplicated to the Kings of Scots constituted an exorbitant price. That the King of England's writ did not run endowed with a glorious independence the two lords in whom all shrieval and judicial powers were vested, and insulated both Liberties from such seminal acts as the Assize of Northampton and the Statute of Westminster. Far in the future, laws passed under Henrys V and VII for a *Gleichschaltung* of Tyne- and Redesdales with Northumberland and the remainder of England took years to become operative. This left the inhabitants till the very threshold of modern times answerable, more often than not, to two peculiar and in most respects inferior legal systems: the *Leges Marchiarum* for international litigation,[33] and baronial laws, part equity and part local custom, administered in the courts at Wark and Harbottle.

One upshot was that the Scots monarch for nearly 150 years governed Tynedale subject only to minimal restrictions: liability to limited homage for a fief of the English Crown; no licence to fortify castles or grant markets or fairs; and the obligation on his judges to bob the occasional genuflexion towards the Throne of England. Thus the judicial process could be set in motion only upon receipt by the Scottish Bailiff of articles of the Crown from English justices itinerant who had to halt on the Borders of Tynedale. Scots judges then proceeded with the trial of common pleas, and of even such pleas of the Crown as murder and robbery, though in accordance with English baronial and not Scottish law.[34] This was tantamount to enjoyment by the northern Crown of more authority in Tynedale than in its own equivalent, known as the Regality, where royal justices in eyre were not competent for the four pleas of the Crown.[35] There were two implications that are best illustrated by reference to slightly later history. Accounts to be rendered for Queen Philippa's agent in Tynedale for the years 1363–7 demonstrate how lucrative to her Scots predecessors such jurisdictional profits as fines and confiscations must have been.[36] More importantly, when shortly beforehand Tynedale offenders made their escape through Cumberland, it was Cumbrian men who were penalised because 'maufesours cannot be pursued within the franchise of Tynedale';[37] while in 1388 an Earl of Northumberland who snatched three fugitives within Tynedale was accused by its Lord, the Duke of York, of violating 'the privileges of his Liberty'.[38]

By and large, however, it was Lords of Redesdale who were more assertive of these. When in 1290 summoned by royal justices to hand over certain Redesdalers for trial, Gilbert de Umfraville, the redoubtable fifth incumbent, ordered the wanted men not to stir from their homes,[39] then proved at law his contention, disputed by Edward I, that the Conqueror's original grant empowered Gilbert's justices at Harbottle to try all pleas including those of the Crown. Furthermore he substantiated claims to the return of all the King's writs in Redesdale; all profits from litigation; all appointments to coroner or sheriff (sic); the chattels of fugitives; and discretionary power to waste the lands of felons[40]. It was centuries before he was given the lie: in 1509 all the foregoing privileges, plus the nomination of J.P.'s, were officially upheld,[41] as was in 1537 Redesdale's immunity from shrieval jurisdiction.[42] Meanwhile, like the grithmen and most modern Irish terrorists, highland malefactors could rely on the local authorities to shield them from extradition to face the laws of England. Even if cooperation *was* forthcoming at the whim of the Lord, the time it took to procure a writ from him afforded the quarry ample time to escape.[43]

NOTES

1. By the sixteenth century generally abbreviated to Tynedale. B(ritish) L(ibrary), Calig(ula) B VIII, fol. 63, 2/12/1541 *inter alia*.

2. BL.Calig.B VIII, fol. 106, 1551 (not 1542 as inscribed).

3. Ibid., fol. 63, 2/12/1541.

4. John Hodgson (*History of*) *Northumberland*, Part II Vol. III p. 21n.

5. G. M. Trevelyan, *The Middle Marches*, pp. 14–15.

6. Hodgson, *Northumberland*, Pt II Vol. II p. 83. There was a Norman church at Elsdon before it was rebuilt in 1400.

7. C. M. Fraser, (*History of Antony*) *Bek*, p. 110.

8. C(*alendar of*) C(*lose*) R(*olls*), 16/5/1356.

9. Reg(*istrum*) Pal(*atinum*) Dun(*elmense*), ed. Hardy in *Rolls Series*, Vol. I p. 291, 14/12/1313.

10. *Bishop Fox's Register*, ed. Surtees Vol. 147 p. 80, 1498.

11. (Rachel) Reid, (*The King's*) *Council in the North*, p. 14.

12. Hodgson, *Northumberland* Vol. III Pt I p. 37: '*Baillivi ejusdem Libertatis diversos latrones capiunt sed permittunt evadere pro pecunia*'.

13. *Ibid.*, Pt II Vol. I p. 5. There is no other evidence extant on the Anglican Soken. I see no reason to share Horace Round's belief that this charter was a forgery, or not based on an older document, simply because Richard de Umfraville got the number of 'greats' before grandfather wrong. Robert of that ilk was described as Lord of Redesdale in a Pipe Roll of 1130, while Gilbert Bataille's claim in 1207 that his ancestor had accompanied Robert to the Conquest is the earliest made on behalf of any companion of the Conqueror.

14. *Ibid.*, pp. 2, 6, 15 & 75.

15. Northumberland R(*ecord*) O(*ffice*), Swinburne MSS, 2/4, c.1185.

16. Hodgson, *Northumberland* Pt II Vol. III p. 16n.

17. Margaret Moore, *Lands (of the) Scottish (Kings in England)*. p. 21.

18. *Ibid.*, p. 4.

19. Maurice Powicke, *The Thirteenth Century*, pp. 586–7.

20. Moore, *Scottish Lands*, pp. 57–9.

21. BL, Add(*itional*) MSS, 32646 fol. 259, 7/11/1541.

22. P(*ublic*) R(*ecord*) O(*ffice*), S(*tate*) P(*apers*) 14 9A, 1604.

23. C(*alendar of*) P(*atent*) R(*olls*), 26/4/1387.

24. *Ibid.*, 8/3/1491.

25. PRO, SP I 152 fol. 150–3, 21/9/1539.

26. CPR, 3/5/1315.

27. Moore, *Scottish Lands*, pp. 40–7 & 129.

28. Cal(*endar of*) Inq(*uisitiones*) P(*ost*) M(*ortem*) Edward II, Item 751, 1326.

29. C(*alendar of*) D(*ocuments*) R(*elating to*) S(*cotland*), ed. Bain, Vol, II Item 168.

30. Moore, *Scottish Lands*, p. 44n.

31. *Cal. Inq.PM* Ed. II, Vol. VI Item 164, 5/9/1318.

32. Moore, *Scottish Lands*, pp. 41–2. Manorially related lands were not necessarily contiguous or even neighbouring.

33. See p. 158 below.

34. Moore, *Scottish Lands*, pp. 57–9. When Scots judges proceeded 'according to the law of England', it could hardly have been the Common Law, of which they would have had no knowledge.

35. Thomas Rae, (*The Administration of the*) *Scottish Frontier*, pp. 11–15.

36. Moore, *Scottish Lands*, pp. 83–7.

37. *Northern Petitions*, ed. Surtees, Vol. 194, p. 100, 1342.

38. CCR, 2/6/1388.

39. CDRS, Vol. II Item 1972, 1300/7.

40. Most felonies were pleas of the Crown. How he could ever have appointed a Sheriff is obscure. Hodgson, *Northumberland*, Pt II Vol. I, pp. 5 & 24–7.

41. CPR, 16/12/1509.

42. PRO, SP I 116 fol. 178–9, 2/3/1537.

43. M. H. Dodds, (*History of*) *Northumberland*, Vol. XV p. 154 ff.

CHAPTER TWO

A Taste of Prosperity in the Thirteenth Century

The closest that the English Middle Marches ever approached to a Golden Age coincided not only with Scottish rule over much of the territory, but also probably with the apogee of feudalism there.

The Liberty of Redesdale was held in grand serjeantry 'by the service of defending that part of the country for ever from enemies and wolves, with that sword which King William had by his side when he entered Northumberland'.[1] Traditionally the last wolf in England was killed in Redesdale, but it is more apposite that 'wolf' and 'bearer of the wolf's head' were mediaeval euphemisms for outlaw. Rated for taxation purposes at two and a half knight's fees,[2] Otterburn was the most important manor, and like Harbottle Castle retained by the Lord in his own hands, the sole exception being late in Edward I's reign. At that time, in what was tantamount to a bid to evade death duties, a failing Gilbert de Umfraville tried to make over Otterburn in name only to a henchman, in order to deprive the King of the forty marks to which he was entitled for wardship of the young heir. By and large Umfraville vassals in the major tenements seem to have been smaller fry than their counterparts in North Tynedale, but their rents or other dues heavier. In 1245 the tenures of over a third of them were military, typical being Lynshiels, Chesterhope and Bromhope, assessed at one-fifth, one-half and one-twelfth of a knight's fee respectively. Another class of tenure was by petty serjeantry, involving a service or gift in kind to the Lord. Carucates at Elsdon and Otterburn, and a parcel of twelve acres in Ravenshope, each went for an annual pound of pepper, and a tenement in Greensomehillslea for as much cumin. And as throughout Northumberland there survived, of Norse origin, a third tenure, less of a peppercorn, known as drengage, partaking of the military character of the first and the servile character of the second: a dreng resembled the working knight of Domesday Book. The manor of Monkridge was held on such terms. Lastly, among the few major tenements let to money rent around the mid-thirteenth century were Lower Leam (sixpence p.a.) and Little Leverwick (one shilling).

Hard to evaluate as these obligations may be, the signs are that those involved in the thirteenth century deemed their investment rewarding. To begin at the top, although the Umfravilles were substantially landed elsewhere they clearly regarded Harbottle, not Prudhoe or Ovingham, as their home: the first absentee Lord of Redesdale came after their time, towards the end of the fifteenth century. Gilbert in 1227 paid £100 for the relief and livery of his lands, while Simon de Montfort received enormous sums for the wardship of his heir, so there is no likelihood that the family would have needed to vegetate in a backwater. Moreover for a district sharing a frontier with a warlike and aggressive foreigner the ambience was amazingly peaceable. Had Redesdale been a cockpit of war, the King would never have insisted that fortifications formerly added by Richard de Umfraville be dismantled in 1225. Litigation in the Lord's court was as absorbed as any other in England with such routine feudal concerns as assises of novel disseisin and mort d'ancestor, or pleas of dower and distress.[3]

In 1244 500 acres of demesne land at Harbottle plus two mills were valued at £33½ p.a., and 200 acres and a mill at Otterburn at around £12¼;[4] in 1303 the whole Liberty and Otterburn were worth 500 and forty marks respectively.[5] By way of comparison, a skilled carpenter earned £4 p.a.,[6] and the Wark park-keeper 1½d. per diem,[7] whereas a year's week-work by a villein was valued at 30/-.[8] Mr. Maurice Keen's dictum that 'in the comparative peace of the late thirteenth century the Border counties had been assured of advancing prosperity'[9] would certainly then seem to apply to the old Liberty.

So long as Tynedale belonged to the King of Scots it was priced at one soar (i.e. yearling) goshawk delivered every Michaelmas at Carlisle Castle in token of fealty.[10] When in the hands of the Prince Bishop in 1292, it was held in free alms, involving surrender of nothing in particular.[11] Below tenant-in-chief one did not escape so cheaply. By 1300 those sitting in the manors or larger tenements were dubbed free tenants, antecedent to the later freeholders and often Anglo-Norman aristocrats, who owed suit and rendered services at the Wark court.[12] Tarset was held by one and a half knight's fees, but Simonburn more typically by fealty and homage, implying compulsory attendance on the Lord in battle.[13, 14] Till exempted from any military commitment in 1177, Haughton was held in drengage,[15] but thereafter with Humshaugh for one soar sparrowhawk. In 1325 Chirdon too was held in drengage, owing half a knight's fee and an annual sparrowhawk.[13, 16]

Under-tenants were liable to similarly miscellaneous dues. One-quarter of Hetherington manor was held by serjeantry in the shape of service within Tynedale of one archer in time of war,[17] whereas a twenty-four acre messuage was held in drengage,[18] as was the piece of Haughton detached to Knarsdale, together with the so-called Huntlands, in King John's reign. Here the under-tenant's obligation was pitched as high as two pairs of gilt spurs or two shillings, in addition to one soar sparrow hawk.[11] The vill of

Charlton was held in 1302 by Adam de Charlton for one-twentieth of a knight's fee.[19]

Enjoying similar continuity of lordship to Redesdale till the last decade of the century, and because for once in a way the two realms shared an interest in its tranquillity, Tynedale thrived. Far from being a recipe for anarchy, the feudalism of a Liberty still spelled orderliness and efficiency. That attempts were made so rarely to infringe the embargo on fortification — contrast the simultaneous obsession with castle-building on the Welsh Marches — is eloquent of a peaceful situation. When the Scots King licensed a tenant to embattle a manor-house in 1237 he nearly caused war,[20] and it was unprecedented when in 1267 Henry III as ultimate overlord permitted John Comyn to crenellate his manor-house in Tarset, enclosing it with a fosse and a wall of stone and lime.[21]

Lawsuits were preponderantly of a bucolic sort, as when in 1279 the Abbot of Jedburgh sued William de Bellingham for failure to erect fences near Hesleyside, so that the religious carthorses strayed in and became imparked. The two also wrangled about the pasturing of horses and cows, much as landowners in Sussex or Surrey might have done.[22] When Edward I rewarded Robert de Cottingham for years of devotion as a civil servant[23, 24] with the rich Simonburn living, the Bishop of Durham 'vexed' the new vicar regarding certain tithes and offerings.[25] Father Robert's everyday concerns were whether to buy park herbage for his beasts, and whether to negotiate with Ranulf Haughton about a ferry to cross the Tyne from Chollerton.[26] All very normal in a place not to be shunned, but of safe resort.

From time to time the Liberty or components were assessed in money terms which are of an impressive order of magnitude. The value of the whole was put at £116 p.a. in 1286–7[27] and at £108 in 1293;[28] the mercenary Bishop of Durham paid £400 rent for it plus five Cumberland manors in 1289.[29] Retrospectively from the next century the manors of Tarset, Thornton, Walwick and Henshaw were stated to have been worth 500 marks (£333) p.a.;[30] Tarset mill and park £46; Walwick manor, park and bondages around £35; and Emmelhope £6/13/4d. for grazing.[31] The figures are intelligible enough to explain why Tynedale was reckoned a piece of real estate fit for a King of Scots or Prince Bishop; or in 1311 as a gage of love from Edward II to Piers Gaveston[32] who did not however live long enough to enjoy it.[27]

What of the industry that underlay all this finance? According to Bowes, 'the soil and ground [of Redesdale] is not so fertile or commodious as Tynedale is'.[33] Unsuitable for wheat, the c. 90,000 acres of the old Liberty had on the other hand always been productive of oats and barley, and of pasture for horses, cattle and sheep. As for the workforce, in Sir Robert's estimation 'the inhabitants of Redesdale be much richer and live more upon the labour of the ground than Tynedale doth'. [34] More contemporaneous witness that game in abundance, too, was regarded as a ready food-source is attested by one item in a de Umfraville dowry in 1185, which made over to the lady and her new husband four hunting stations west of Rede, with 'right of pursuit with their men, dogs, horn, bows and arrows'. [35]

There is no reason to suppose that Bowes' description of Tynedale potential as 'a great number of good grounds both fertile and commodious for tillage, hay and pasture, the which truly . . . laboured . . . would sustain . . . a good number of people in truth' [33] had been any less valid three centuries previously. Where in its southern reaches the North Tyne was broad, there was arable in plenty, though more meadow even within the demesne of some manors. On the way north expanses of moorland, heath and near-mountain came to predominate. Forest and, where tamed, parkland was everywhere, with lots of pasture for cattle, horses and sheep except on the Border itself.

Venison abounded in woods around Wark, Tarset and Walwick. When in 1290 the Lord's deputy took twenty-seven bucks around Wark, they were of such quality that 64/- was spent on carriage to Westminster; [36] next year Edward I arranged through him a present of two bucks and four does; and in 1306 twelve stags were forwarded to the royal household. [37] Outside the parks rights of vert or chase and venison were conferred that overrode manorial ownership. Chases for the red deer known as Huntlands were scattered overall, the hunting of which belonged to the Comyns [38] and not the Prats, ensconced as they were in the manor called Huntland. Freedom to hunt one's own demesne had to be procured through a separate grant, as in 1307 by a Swinburne of free warren over Simonburn, extending to game of all kinds. [39] Whenever the Liberty was in royal hands, the King hunted regardless of even the Comyns, [40] but more likely out of an ancient claim to hunt anywhere in the realm than *qua* Lord. There was also fish, some of which was presumably farmed salmon. In 1286 Robert de Lisle, Lord of Chipchase just over the stream from the eastern edge of the Liberty, paid sixpence to the Manor of Wark for a stank or breeding-pool between dams, sited on the river nearby. [41]

Besides animal protein the forest yielded timber, regarding which the Lord again exercised overriding rights. Had John Swinburne not purchased a grant of reasonable estovers, he would in 1279 have been unable to fell from the Wark woods or his own manor of Haughton. [89] Other of the Lord's income derived from the forge at Wark, and also the mill, to preserve which in 1264/5 he spent 10/- on altering the water-course. By 1300 the mill rated £10 p.a.[42] As in addition weaving was carried out at Wark,[43] most of the essentials for normal life were present.

Upon this favourable economic picture were superimposed European trends to which, despite being an obscure part of the most backward country in western Christendom, the Northumbrian uplands conspicuously conformed.[44] The century saw the widespread introduction of demesne farming through the installation of bailiffs, and the two Liberties benefited from this consignment of management to wholetime professionals. One hundred years before the practice had ceased elsewhere of farming out most royal manors to rapacious sheriffs, bailiffs in 1158[45] and 1174[46] were accounting to their Edinburgh master for the management of Tynedale lands not subinfeoffed. With Umfravilles more on the spot, they waited longer to acquire such agents, who were however in post by 1274, without any hint of innovation.[47, 48]

Being textile-based, the contemporary commercial revolution enhanced the terms of trade for such pastoral areas as the Northumbrian hinterland, even though their coarse fleeces were less prized than those from farther south.[49] Tyne- and Redesdalers could only have benefited from a surge in the export of wool to clothe expanding populations at the outset of the century, as indeed from a disproportionate increase in meat prices towards its close. Amongst markets founded to lubricate the effects of the revolution around the highlands[50] were one at Thornton in 1221[51] and another at Haltwhistle in 1307, coupled at the latter venue with three-day fairs every May and December.[52] Corbridge market was similarly a place of common resort.[53] Within Tynedale itself there was at Bellingham a Saturday market and a fair every St. Cuthbert's Day, known to Bowes as of long standing.[33] The Umfravilles exacted tolls from annual fairs and weekly markets at Elsdon and Harbottle, and presided over their own mercantile courts of pie powder.[54, 55] Thus the network for the transfer of meat and wool down to Newcastle and Hartlepool was comprehensive.

The demographic background was a spurt in population throughout Europe between 1100 and 1314, the initial effect of which on agriculture was stimulating, in so far as marginal lands were now brought under the plough. Given the expanse of heathland, no districts offered more scope than Tyne- and Redesdales. The drive was boosted by a universal tendency to replace with money rents the slavish and hence half-hearted week-work. By 1300 nearly all services within Wark manor had been thus commuted,[56] which aligned Tynedale at any rate with the more progressive parts of England. Her temporary divorce from that realm commencing in the mid-twelfth century may have helped its villeins to preserve this gain. The inflation that supervened shortly after withdrawal motivated English landlords through erosion of rent-values to reimpose week-work. It being axiomatic that week-work spelled serfdom, lawyers generally busied themselves to demonstrate that most leaseholders were still serfs at law. Such lawyers however had no access to the court at Wark, within whose barony villeins tranquilly continued to defray the long-term rents recognised as the badge of free status.[57] In 1325 a bondage tenant in the manors of Snabdaugh and Charlton, for example, rendered none of the ancient labour services on the demesne, but still paid rent for his toft and twelve to thirty acres.[58] That the Scottish regime did not react identically with that farther south to inflationary pressures may be attributable to the high proportion within Tynedale of marginal lands to which tenants had to be enticed, and to the fact that the care of sheep was not labour-intensive.

The favourable impression is enhanced by the high percentage of free tenants as compared, say, with the Liberties of Penrith and Huntingdon, likewise in Scots hands.[59] Besides fulfilling any duties of drengs or serjeants to which they were liable, such tenants paid rents that must have been related, like national taxation, to the fractions of knight's fees by which they held.

Inasmuch as Redesdale remained a domestic affair of the Umfravilles, of which national Treasuries took no such cognizance as they did of Tynedale, the situation in the older Liberty is, through dearth of records, more obscure. What can safely be stated is that when stock was taken at the end of the Middle Ages the proportion of free tenants within the Manor of Harbottle was far higher than within the Manor of Wark.[60] A curious feature, furthermore, is the use of the label 'sokmen' for certain tenants in Redesdale, a term employed elsewhere in England to describe rent-payers who had managed to vindicate their freedom against the lawyers' onslaught aforementioned.

Every situation accumulates its contradictions, and the level of prosperity attained by the rural economies of the two dales in the thirteenth century was no exception.[61] Nationwide from 1200 onwards, the beneficial increase in population began to press upon the means of subsistence. That in Tynedale at least the right to tenure through rent had been upheld was all very well, but in response to land hunger those rents could be put up, as the surviving English ones were, together with all manner of feudal fines. Alexander III's valedictory gesture was to treble the rents from Wark and Grindon manors between 1285 and 1286.[62] His forge and mill at Wark were monopolistic sources of income,[7] and it is unlikely that his episcopal successor paid £10 p.a. for the use of Bellingham mill without substantial dividend.[63]

Available statistics[60] relevant to the capacity of local agriculture to sustain extra charges are unsatisfactory inasmuch as they fail to distinguish between meadow and pasture held privately and in common, and worse still date from no earlier than 1600.[64] Consolation has to be sought in the recurrent phrase 'from time immemorial', and in the slow rate of change in agrarian communities even after commencement of the age of enclosures. This late evidence suggests that in Redesdale 60% and in Tynedale 20% of acreage comprised arable and pastures held by individuals in several strips known as winter ground, lowlands or infield; and that the rest consisted of common land, shared out among specific groups, and variously dubbed the highlands, the waste, the summer grounds, or the outfield.

Basic was the infield/outfield system characteristic of the Old English homeland in North West Germany and of parts of Scotland. The infield tenements were located on the alluvial valley floors or the lower slopes of hills, and even here the raising of livestock loomed large. After the Spring sowings, in a cycle that has come to be known as transhumance, the inhabitants trooped out to pass the summer in the outfield with their beasts. The task of a Lord's deputy was to superintend the movement, and to fine any lagging behind one noble, lest they be tempted to steal from neighbours during absence.[65] Not until the infield hay was ready to mow did the community, at a second signal from the deputy, descend home again.[66]

Now the infield/outfield system was notorious for drastic overcropping and progressive impoverishment, probably aggravated in the highlands by a rudimentary collectivisation: within the infield each man sowed with barley, and reaped and mowed his own ground, yet consumption was communal 'without either stint or number', hardly an incentive to hard work. Possibly too, if the position in 1620[65] is anything to go by — a not entirely fantastic proposition — then a sizeable minority possessed no stake in the arable at all, being left to till 'barren heath, high cold mountains and desert wastes, so that in ten miles of ground there will not be ten acres of arable'.[60] The last people to meet increased rents, such tenants would have swelled the landless proletariat encountered all over England by 1300, and like all men on the loose represented a standing threat to law and order.

Two Rolls survive of Pleas held at the Court of Wark at the end of the century, with disquieting elements already present. The first dates to 1279,[22] when Alexander III still ruled. The prevalent themes are naturally murder, assault, and sudden death. More peculiar were frequent allusions to gaol-breaks from Wark and Simonburn prisons, a phenomenon often associated with organised criminal fraternities; and the alacrity with which non-Common Law judges sanctioned settlements out of court for felony, despite having execution, mutilation and outlawry in their repertoire. The second dates from 1293, when Tynedale was back in England.[67] Thomas

Robson is stabbed by the householder whose house he is burgling; townships including Chirdon, Tarset and Charlton are reprehended for a poor turn-out at the decapitation in Bellingham of William Robson, who has killed the miller's daughter with an axe; and John Dodd and others of a robber band from Bellingham and Shitlington are indicted for murder. Though not the surnames, the offences might have cropped up anywhere in the kingdom, but the prominence of gangs rather than lone criminals is exceptional.

More ominous were episodes in which some Redesdalers provided tools in crime for a great man. In July 1267 Gilbert de Umfraville sent 'one hundred of the King's enemies, including outlaws of Redesdale' to eject William Douglas from his manor of Fawdon near Girsonfield. They stole money, jewellery and weapons to the value of £100,'applied fire' to the Douglas family, and nearly beheaded the eldest son. William was then confined in Harbottle with another son.[68] Subsequently Gilbert falsely accused William of treason but had himself to stand trial for the son's murder. He then 'put himself at the head of his Redesdale subjects as a great captain of spoilers, ready at his word to go out on any errand of violence or outrage'.[69] Many inquisitions on the Hundred Rolls show this de Umfraville to have extorted money by menaces, and taken from robbers hush money of up to 100 marks at a time.[70, 71] In 1283, William de Umfraville, a close enough kinsman to have acquired Elsdon manor and imprudently assumed that mercantile rights had been ceded along with it, complained that when at the Thursday market he had 'erected a pillory and tumbril and other things belonging to such franchise', they had been knocked down by Gilbert and twenty-four henchmen with names like Fitzforester, Ponder and Le Fever, as well as less ephemeral ones like Harle and Reed; in addition they had assaulted and wounded many traders.[54, 72]

Both as Prince and, from 1272, King, Edward I had enough experience of Gilbert de Umfraville's irregularities to exert continual, sometimes illegal, and not uniformly successful pressure upon him, scotching the Lord's plans for castle-extension;[56] confiscating over his head in 1265 the Redesdale lands of an alleged traitor;[73] and in 1275 distraining his bailiffs' property for ignoring a shrieval percept.[47, 48] Once Tynedale had reverted completely to England on Alexander's succession by the Maid of Norway in 1289, the Plantagenet resolved to put in his own man. He approached the problem with a Scottish precedent in mind, wherein their King, necessarily an absentee, had consigned the government of Tynedale to a deputy or senior bailiff. Apart from an interval between 1273 and 1278[74] the post had been held since 1268 by William Swinburne of West Swinburne,[75] treasurer to Queen Margaret of Scotland. His immunity from Sheriff's tourns may have been of especial interest to a legalistic Edward I.[76]

What sprang to the royal mind was his servant Antony Bek[77] — soldier, diplomat, Prince Bishop and, one is bound in fairness to add, scoundrel. His style at first was 'Keeper of the King's Land of Tynedale',[78] a title destined to adhere for centuries to the Lord's deputy, but in a different capacity. Bek paid rent for the Liberty, first to the Maid's family,[79] then a smaller one, eked out with his disreputable prayers, to John Balliol, in 1293 Edward's candidate for the Scottish Throne.[80] Finally, when the client rebelled against his master, the King confirmed the Bishop as Lord of Tynedale in his own right, for the even less onerous rent of frankalmoign.

Bek's performance was scandalous. When in 1300[81] he was defied by Prior Hoton of Durham, whose convent he had pawned for £5000, he sent Hugh de Wales, his Bailiff in Tynedale, with 'fourteen-score men of North Tynedale, enemies of the Lord King', all archers with as many from Weardale, to besiege the Priory for nine weeks. Beyond declaring the assailants to be satellites of Satan, the Archbishop of York did not intervene. Finding the blockade ineffective, the besiegers battered down the gates and forcibly replaced Hoton by Bek's nominee, Prior Luceby. After three days of torture by the Bishop's agents, 'during which no mass nor matins were said', Hoton managed to escape and eventually to plead his case in Rome before Boniface VIII, who ordered his reinstatement and the suspension in his turn of Antony Bek. The Bishop's only response was to send back the Tynedale archers, who smashed up the cloister and refectory and made off with £300 out of the Prior's treasury, together with linen and silver vessels. Soon afterwards a new Pope reversed the decision of the last and even appointed Bek Patriarch of Jerusalem, with precedence over the Archbishop of Canterbury, surely one of the Papacy's most comical acts. Disillusioned with his former favourite, the old King in 1306 ejected him from the Liberty,[82] and only in the year of the Bishop's death was he briefly reinstated as Lord by Edward II.[83] It was in vain that Bek's successors strove repeatedly to regain Tynedale in 1315, 1329 and 1346. All they salvaged was the advowson of Simonburn.

Inasmuch as Edward II was a nincompoop, the lessons to be drawn from the Prince Bishop's abuse of power remained for the time being latent. Obviously, however, it had been eloquent of the unacceptability of an 'independent' Lord of Tynedale. Also, given the fact that the Lord in view of high rank would always be an absentee, and the inevitability of a resident deputy like Hugh de Wales, it was essential that that official should stay in the monarch's pocket. The 'Keeper' moreover should unlike the first so-named be as nearly as possible indigenous to Tynedale. Such was Alexander III's sensible choice in William Swinburne who from 1256 held lands inclusive of Haughton dependent on Knarsdale of the Prats, and from 1273 manors in both South and North Tynedale.[84] What could not yet have been inferred was the absence of guarantee that even an ideally qualified Keeper would be dutiful to the Crown. One need only reflect that in terms of travel-hours Tyne- and Redesdalers were more remote from London than the Falkland Islands nowadays,[85] to the detriment of effective control.

Simultaneously, from its different departure point, Redesdale too was heading towards Keepership. With its powerful Lord normally in residence, there was patently less need for the institution of a senior and singular bailiff — as distinct from the several bailiffs who were farm managers. Nevertheless as a great nobleman the Umfraville had often to be absent on his own or the King's business, with the outcome that even he eventually came to require a right-hand man. Such an official was definitely in existence by 1294 when the incumbent John de Harle of Hatherwick in Monkridge, and of West Harle just outside the old Liberty, pursued a suit at law in his official capacity against the de Lisles of Woodburn regarding Troughend. In 1298 the Bailiff (sic) of Redesdale, probably the same man, conducted an inquest on lands held in free marriage at Elsdon of the late Gilbert de Umfraville.[86] John's estate was assessed at £15 p.a., while his namesake and probable heir was a substantial enough gentleman to be included in a list of knights returned into Chancery in 1324.[87] Two years later Sir Roger Mauduyt, during an Umfraville minority, became the first man on record to be dubbed 'Keeper of the lands and castles of Redesdale'.[88]

NOTES

1. Hodgson, *Northumberland*, Pt II Vol. I pp. 5 & 61.

2. Peasants, (*Knights & Heretics*), ed. R. H. Hilton, pp. 136–172 *passim*. A knight's fee was the amount of land required to maintain a fighting knight in the field for sixty days p.a., reckoned to lie between seven and twenty-four hides in the poorer North of England. An exaggeration at the time of the Conquest, this area by 1300 accorded more with reality, due to inflation and the elaboration of equipment.

3. Hodgson, *Northumberland*, Pt II Vol. I pp. 11, 15, 17, 19, 20, 27, 62 & 108 for these two paragraphs.

4. *CDRS*, Vol. I Item 1667.

5. *Ibid.*, Vol. IV Item 1790.

6. Peasants etc. p. 71.

7. Moore, *Scottish Lands* p. 86.

8. Peasants etc. p. 72. From time to time in this work sums of money are quoted for which, if only because of utterly different standards of living, it would be absurd to attempt any conversion to modern equivalents. That said, multipliers of 2000 and 300 for 1300 and 1600 respectively would give not too misleading an

impression. Cf. Lawrence Stone, 'The Fruits of Office', in *The Economic & Social History of Tudor and Stuart England*, ed. Thirsk.

9. M. H. Keen, (*England in the*) *Later Middle Ages*, p. 80.
10. Moore, *Scottish Lands*, Introd ix–xii & pp. 1–12.
11. C. M. Fraser, *Bek*, pp. 62 & 90.
12. Moore, *Scottish Lands*, pp. 40–7 & 129.
13. *Cal. Inq. PM Ed II*, Vol. VI Item 164, 5/9/1318.
14. *Ibid.*, Item 751, 1326.
15. Moore, *Scottish Lands*, pp. 44–7.
16. *Cal. Inq. PM. Ed II*, Vol. VI Item 693, 20/3/1325.
17. *Ibid.*, *Ed I*, Vol. II Item 665, 28/6/1287.
18. *Ibid.*, Vol. III Item 47, 1291.
19. *Ibid.*, Vol. IV Item 166, 1300.
20. Moore, *Scottish Lands*, p. 58.
21. CDRS Vol. I Item 2463.
22. *Ibid.*, Vol. II Item 168, 18/11/1279. A full version was published in London 1858 by the Archaeological Institute of Gt. Britain and Ireland. Hereinafter referred to as *Iter of Wark*.
23. *Reg. Pal. Dun.*, Vol. IV pp. 20–7, 1305.
24. CCR, 15/10/1305.
25. Ibid., 26/3/1310.
26. Moore, *Scottish Lands*, p. 22.
27. Hodgson, *Northumberland*, Pt III Vol. II p. 394.
28. CDRS, Vol. II Item 665, 6/4/1293.
29. CPR, 20/2/1290.
30. CDRS, Vol. III Item 512, 15/11/1316.
31. *Ibid.*, Item 993, 20/10/1329.
32. *Ibid.*, Item 214, 28/5/1311.
33. BL, Calig.B VIII fol. 63, 2/12/1541.
34. Ibid., fol. 106, 1551.
35. Northumberland RO, Swinburne MSS, 2/4, c.1185.
36. Moore, *Scottish Lands*, pp. 25–6.
37. CDRS, Vol. II Item 510, 1306.
38. Moore, *Scottish Lands*, pp. 25 & 44–7.
39. *Cal(endar of) Chart(er) R(olls)*, III 84, 1307.
40. CDRS, Vol. II Item 510, 1306.
41. Moore, *Scottish Lands*, p. 22.
42. *Ibid.*, p. 8.
43. *Cal. Inq. PM Ed II*, Vol. V Item 501, St. Luke's Day 1314.
44. D. C. Coleman, *The Economy of England (1450–1750)*, p. 27.
45. CDRS, Vol. I Items 62–64.
46. *Ibid.*, Item 113.
47. *Northumberland De Banco Rolls*, ed. Surtees, Vol. 158 Item 167.
48. *Ibid.*, Item 248.
49. *Arch(aeologea) Aeliana*, Vol. XLIII, Fourth Series p. 243 ff. (J. B. Blake).
50. (Margaret) Spufford, *Contracting Communities*, p. 61.
51. CDRS, Vol. I Item 809.
52. CCR, III 88.

53. CPR, 18/1/1331.

54. *Ibid.*, 28/5/1283.

55. *Cal. Inq. PM Hen VII*, Vol. I Item 971, 30/5/1494.

56. Moore, *Scottish Lands*, pp. 83–7.

57. Peasants etc., pp. 58, 74, 182 & 189.

58. *Cal. Inq. PM Ed II*, Vol. VI Item 693.

59. Peasants etc., pp. 71 ff. & 91 ff.

60. PRO, SP 14 9A, 1604.

61. J. A. Tuck, in *N(orthern) H(istory)*, Vol. XXI p. 41.

62. Palgrave (*Documents*), Introd. p. v.

63. Moore, *Scottish Lands*, p. 8.

64. However, my main reliance has been on R. A. Butlin, 'Northumberland Field Systems' (*Agricultural Review* Vol. XII).

65. PRO, E(Exchequer) 134, Michaelmas 1621.

66. *Agrarian History (of England and Wales*, ed. H.P.R.) Finberg, Vol. IV p. 22.

67. CCR, p. 309, 3/2; p. 313, March & 11/12/1293. CPR, 20/3/1293.

68. CDRS, Vol. I Item 2452.

69. Hodgson, *Northumberland*, Pt II Vol. I p. 26.

70. CPR, 23/10/1275.

71. *Ibid.*, 3/7/1304.

72. *Ibid.*, 16/5/1285.

73. Hodgson, *Northumberland*, Pt III Vol. I p. 105.

74. CDRS, Vol. II Item 146, 1278.

75. *Ibid.*, Vol. I Item 2625.

76. *Ibid.*, Item 2495. 1268.

77. C. M. Fraser, *Bek*, pp. 55, 62, 67 & 91

78. CPR, 5/6/1291.

79. *Ibid.*, 27/8/1290.

80. *Cal. Chart. R.*, Vol. II p. 456 1294.

81. I have accepted C. M. Fraser's dating (*Bek*, pp. 130–164), though at variance with that in *Reg. Pal. Dun.*, Vol. IV pp. 20–7.

82. *Northumbrian Petitions*, ed. Surtees Vol. 176 p. 42, 1307.

83. CPR, 27/5/1308.

84. Moore, *Scottish Lands*, pp. 42–3.

85. As late as the sixteenth century a letter took five days to reach the Borders from London.

86. *Cal. Inq. PM Ed I*, Vol III Item 461, 2/8/1298.

87. Northumberland RO, 542/26.

88. CDRS, Vol. III Item 884, 9/6/1326.

89. *Rot(uli) Parl(iamentorum ut et Petitiones et Placita)*, I 194A, 1279.

CHAPTER THREE

Disaster in the early Fourteenth Century

Part of the story so far has been concerned with Scottish ambitions to acquire estate in England. The process went into reverse in 1291, when a dispute about the succession to the northern throne was referred to Edward I, prompting him to reactivate an English claim to the suzerainty of all Scotland. The first phase of the resultant War of Independence, from 1296 till 1307, left him seemingly victorious; William Wallace a defeated hero; and both of them dead. As to the role that must inevitably have been played in the transactions by the Tyne- and Redesdale highlanders, all that can safely be asserted is that Antony Bek, Lord of Tynedale, fought with distinction at the Battle of Falkirk.[1]

Just before the accession of Edward II, a new and eventually triumphant phase of the Scots resistance was initiated by Robert the Bruce. Chiefly as archers, the Tynedalers were in the thick of the ensuing struggle, with the Redesdalers engaged too, though less conspicuously. In 1306 a force of 300 archers under three captains left Tynedale for Carrick and Glentrool in Galloway to serve for twenty-four days under Sir Geoffrey de Mowbray, who was hunting King Robert: they received £66 between them for the operation and may have helped to defeat him at the Battle of Methven. A year later Robert de Barton, Keeper of Tynedale, together with his predecessor Hugh de Wales, again joined Mowbray with a like force, as many that is as Westmorland contributed, and half again as many as Cumberland.[2] Six months later Roger Heron of Ford, by then Keeper of Tynedale, joined yet another expedition against the Scottish leader in Galloway.[3] Shortly afterwards Robert, sixth Lord of Redesdale and second Umfraville Earl of Angus, was named Lieutenant of Scotland,[4] while kinsman Sir Ingelram became Warden of Carrick, of which the Bruce was Earl, with forty men-at-arms.[5] In August 1309, preparatory to an invasion that did not materialise, Bek was commanded by Edward II to bring 200 from North Tynedale and 300 from Durham to Newcastle in October.[6] In the Spring following the 'Warden of Scotland' was commissioned, not for the first time, to raise men-at-arms and foot from the whole north including the Franchise of Tynedale,[7] which was apparently functioning not only as a source of troops but also as an attack route; one hundred Hexhamshire men bound for Roxburgh in 1311 were among the users.[8]

In the opposite direction King Robert now began to employ the same high road, already familiar to the Scots from the Wallace years when the Earls of Atholl and Menteith had ravaged Redesdale and Tynedale.[1] After a reconnaissance of Tynedale via Harbottle and Redesmouth in 1311,[9] the Bruce in 1312 drove through it into the Bishopric with a great army, levied £2000 in danegeld and a promise of 'free transit and return whenever he wished to ride farther into England'.[10] By carrying the war thus into the enemy's rear King Robert contrived to beleaguer the English strongholds in Scotland, and by 1314 felt strong enough to lay siege to Stirling. On Edward II's arrival with a relieving army he destroyed it piecemeal at Bannockburn. Among other casualties were the Lord of Redesdale, taken prisoner while 'fighting mightily with the vaward',[11] and Sir Ingelram, at first believed slain but in fact likewise captured.[12, 13] As for Keeper Roger Heron, he was in 1317 to receive the large sum of £148 to compensate himself and the Tynedalers for horses lost in the battle.[14]

There is, then, every reason to suppose that the highlanders played a regular part against the Scots in their War of Independence, and shared fully in the final defeat. At this point it becomes convenient to pause, and ponder the threats and blandishments to which as frontiersmen they must surely have been subjected during hostilities. In considering whether their loyalty to England had been unalloyed, we have to concentrate on their upper classes, partly because there is no choice, but largely because in a feudal order of society above all others there was a temptation, nay compulsion, to conform with the example set by one's betters.

The key to Redesdale's attitude during the war lies in the unchallengeable dominance of the Umfravilles who in the fourteenth century added direct control of Monkridge to that of Harbottle, Otterburn and much of Elsdon. They were at pains to ensure that no other family ever obtained more than a toehold, the nearest to an exception being the de Lisles with substantial tenements at East Woodburn and Troughend between 1250 and 1440, but their centre of gravity was elsewhere, at Chipchase and Felton. The Batayles of Linshiels, with lands scattered around Otterburn and Elsdon, stayed under the Umfraville thumb. Simon de Montfort never had leisure to turn his stake into an interest, but the bad grace with which after his fall the young Lord of Redesdale, at the Crown's insistence, transferred Snarisdelf to Sir William Swinburne, Alexander III's faithful henchman in Tynedale, might indicate a no very welcoming disposition towards Scottish intruders either.

In fact, although peers of Scotland from 1244, and with the notable exception of Sir Ingilram, who sided with the enemy until 1308, these Umfravilles had always in their loyalties been impeccably English. Odonel, third son of Robert-with-the Beard, was one of The Lion's captors at Alnwick. Richard, third Lord of Redesdale, was Lionheart's Captain of Acre and creditably opposed to King John, who seized his sons as hostages and sequestrated Redesdale and his other lands for ten years. Husband of the Countess of Angus in her own right, his successor Gilbert was celebrated at his death in 1244 as 'guardian and chief flower. . . [and] matchless ornament of the North of England' — why is no longer ascertainable, but certainly the distinction accorded him on state occasions bespoke a real eminence.[15] If somewhat of a villain, who deserted his guardian before the Battle of Evesham, the fifth Lord, likewise Gilbert, fought valiantly against Welsh, French and Scots in the last quarter of the century, and assumed an important role in William Wallace's downfall. The mainly honourable family chronicle was destined to continue.

What led to the relative undoing of Tynedale was that at the higher echelon the War of Independence was a civil war between Normans. The pinnacle, moreover, had long been adorned not by trusty Umfravilles but by a foreign potentate, and a situation in which immediate and ultimate overlords had been two intermittently warring monarchs still unsettled the allegiance of the Tynedale gentry.

A minority was explicitly Scottish in its sympathies. Thus John Prat of Knarsdale and Haughton was declared a rebel, his estates forfeit, in 1315.[16, 17] In three other families one member would lean to one nation, and another to the other. Most notable of these were the Comyns of Badenoch, kinsmen of the Earls of Atholl, and pretenders to the Throne of Scotland. From early in the twelfth century they had held Walwick, Thornton, Henshaw and Tarset, a fief which by 1329 would come to be known collectively as the Talbot lands.[18] Having dropped his claim to the Crown on marriage with John Balliol's sister, Sir John Comyn lost his lands for supporting his brother-in-law against Edward I. In 1296, however, upon swearing fealty to the latter he recovered them again. Meanwhile his son, the Red Comyn, had invaded Cumberland with a Scots army, had been captured at Dunbar, and then had been imprisoned in the Tower of London. Subsequently he was briefly to replace Wallace as leader, but after submission to England he was murdered in a church by the Bruce. Red Comyn's son fell at Bannockburn for the English. In half his Tynedale lands he was succeeded by David Strathbogie, Earl of Atholl, who was in 1335 to join an invasion of Scotland, sponsored by the English, in an attempt to recover his inheritance there.[19]

The allegiance of the East Swinburnes wobbled no less. They held Humshaugh, Simonburn and portions of Haughton in 1291;[20] Knarsdale with northern outlyers from 1315;[16, 17, 27] and Chirdon from 1325.[22] They were also tenants of the Comyns in Espleywood and Lusburn.[23] For steady adherence to Edward II during hostilities Sir Robert Swinburne acquired Knarsdale after confiscation from the 'disloyal' Prats.[17, 21, 24] Ten years later he was given Chirdon as well,[22] and in 1322 was named inspector of munitions in the castles and towns of Cumberland, Westmorland, and the Liberty of Tynedale.[25] By contrast Adam, his son or younger brother, rode with Scots invaders, burning and plundering in Cumberland and Northumberland, with particular detriment to Hexham Priory. In due course his lands were seized, and he himself was captured and imprisoned by Antony Bek. Upon release in 1297 he switched allegiance and fought in Scotland for Edward I, by whom he was eventually designated Sheriff of Northumberland. Having in 1318 with some prudence rejoined the Scots and thrown in his lot with an egregious English traitor, Sir Gilbert Middleton, he forfeited his Tynedale lands yet again.[26, 27] Hence in the aftermath of Bannockburn the Swinburnes could well have been in action against one another. Adam's daughter Barnaba, Lady Stirling, inherited his fickle temperament, regaining his lands in 1327 by re-submission to England, then losing them again through another about-turn.[28] It was not until 1358, after another apostasy, that she was reconfirmed in her Tynedale lands, together with nephews Widdrington and Heron of Ford, who between them entered into Haughton, Humshaugh and Simonburn. Heron, incidentally, had to meet a fine of 270 marks to clear his ancestor Adam Swinburne's name of complicity with the Scots.[29]

Like the Comyns of mixed Saxon and Norman descent,[30] the de Ros's of Wark Castle and Plenmellor in Tynedale, and Haltwhistle, were the third shaky family. For ushering in the marauding Earls in 1295, and subsequent misdemeanours Robert de Ros was deprived in 1302 as 'an enemy and rebel to the King'.[31] Having lived down a similar reputation,[32] his close kinsman William was rewarded in 1301 with Wark Castle for services in Gascony,[31] and in 1308 came to share the Lieutenancy of Scotland with Robert de Umfraville, the new and sixth Lord of Redesdale.[4]

Aware that Tynedale was rotten with treason, Edward I in 1297 commanded the then Bailiff to require all free tenants to swear fealty, and 'to take into the King's hands for rebellion' the tenements of defaulters.[33] Shortly after Bannockburn the Lanercost chronicler recorded that the Scots occupied both North and South Tynedale and 'Tynedale did homage to the King of Scots'.[24] That disaffection towards England centred around the Manor of Wark rather than the Manor of Grindon is attested by the reaction of South Tynedalers, in whom a distaste for their unsavoury neighbours along the north river was now fortified by reluctance to become Scots. When King Robert granted his vassal William de Soules the Lordship of all Tynedale, the men of a dozen manors south of the river first bought immunity from the 'seigneurie' with an enormous 35-lb weight of silver; then petitioned Edward

II for inclusion within the shires of Cumberland or Westmorland.[34] Clearly the boons of belonging to a Liberty could be purchased at too high a price. They had more luck with their petition to the Scots than with that to the English, bent on the recovery in its entirety of a Liberty that was strategically placed, and the private property of the monarch. When late in the century the Earl of Cambridge was to become Lord of Tynedale, the manors under his direct control indiscriminately included some in South Tynedale, as well as at Bellingham, La Leye (i.e. Leehall) and Chirdon.[35]

From the miseries that now engulfed the highland area for years to come, the collaboration with the enemy of a section of her population brought no more relief to Tynedale than the red banner of the Umfravilles to Redesdale, for all its golden cinquefoil and orle of crosses. Between 1315 and 1350 the nation as a whole touched its nadir, successive disasters being aggravated by the over-population bequeathed from the thirteenth century. So bad were the harvests, particularly in 1315 and 1321, that the price of wheat quintupled in six years. Resultant famine was compounded by a typhoid epidemic, a rinderpest in 1319, and a murrain among the sheep in 1321, all of which except the first afflicted the pastoral north most heavily of all. In Scotland and therefore probably in the adjacent Liberties, the dearth had begun five years earlier. The surge in grain prices was naturally more extreme in the north than elsewhere and not offset by commensurate rises in the price of meat. As for wool, there occurred between 1315 and 1322 a huge drop in exports from the Northumbrian hinterland out of Newcastle and Hartlepool.[36]

What made conditions worse in the far north in general and the two dales in particular was that here the red and white horses of the Apocalypse were ridden as well. Until checked at Halidon Hill and Neville's Cross, the Scots gave any English within reach as little quarter as Cromwell ever gave the Irish. Within the technical limitations of an age without bombs or artillery, but assisted by the timber construction of most buildings, the Bruce's armies devastated as far south as the Ridings, but most effectively along the Borders. Since one Andrew Harcla, later Earl of Carlisle and even for a space Lord of Tynedale,[37] managed to stabilise the Cumbrian front, it was northern Northumberland that bore the brunt of an assault which was unremitting between 1315 and 1331, [38, 39] excruciating till 1323, and thereafter sporadic till the threshold of the fifteenth century.[40]

After Bannockburn the Scots stormed and dismantled Harbottle Castle,[7] which their Earls had failed to accomplish in 1295. One beneficiary from forty tuns of wine distributed by Edward II in 1319 among the Northumbrians who had suffered most, was William Harle of Redesdale.[41, 42] Further royal bounty was forthcoming in 1328 when Gilbert de Umfraville, quaintly described as 'king's yeoman', had an expensive minority curtailed to make up for losses in the family estates,[43] exemplified by the dive to a paltry 2/- of the annual value of what was crisply termed the 'site' of Otterburn manor.[44] Despite recent defeat, the Scots in 1336–7 scoured the old Liberty yet again.[45] In 1344 Elsdon parish petitioned the King to forgo the ninth they owed in taxes because the enemy had destroyed their crops and other goods, and lifted their cattle.[46] So shattered was Harbottle still that in 1351 de Umfraville was permitted to ward Redesdale prisoners at Prudhoe, right outside the Liberty.[47]

Tynedale's fate ran in parallel. Appointed Keeper in 1315, Antony de Lucy was sent in to pick up the pieces and recover any property he was able from the lands of the King, the Comyns and 'others who have deserted the King and adhere to his enemies'.[48] In so far as the invader had taken draught oxen from the ploughs, burned corn, and even, as in Tarset, cut down the fruit trees, the good national harvests of 1316–7 passed the far north by.[49] In the latter year a great swarm of Scots again plundered Tynedale,[50] while as those hardest hit two other recipients of Edward II's vinous bounty were Roger of Simonburn and Robert de Milneburn (i.e. Milburn).[41] The extent of spoliation after twelve years of warfare is reflected in an inventory of the Comyn alias Talbot lands in 1325 — Walwick and Tarset manors destroyed; hopes (i.e. small cultivated valleys) at Tarset, Emmel, Carriteth, Kielder and Thorneyburn reduced in annual value from sums as high as £26/13/4d. down through 13/4d. to nil; acre values down from twelve through four pence to nil; only one of fourteen 20-acre bondages in Charlton, and ten of thirty-eight acres in demesne near Tarset still farmed. Meadows were no longer mowed and the recurrent epithets are 'waste' and 'tenantless': in other words the inhabitants had died or fled.[18, 51, 52] When in 1336 sundry of these lands were allocated to one de Impiton the rents were remitted in view of 'his losses in wars with the Scots'.[53] As for the Liberty at large, it was assessed during de Harcla's fleeting enjoyment at a mere knight's fee, less than some of its members in bygone years.[37] In 1344 Simonburn and Knarsdale parishes joined with Elsdon in protesting an inability to surrender the ninth of sheaves and sheep required of them because of the plunder endured at enemy hands.[46]

Out of the desolation engendered by the incursions arose demoralisation and anarchy throughout the Borders.[27] The modicum of collaboration with the foe long detectable in Tynedale now filtered to lower social strata, spreading to Redesdale and beyond. In 1317, while the second Umfraville Earl of Angus was still a captive in Scotland, his Keeper Sir

Roger Mauduyt captured at Redepath Richard Middleton, kinsman of the rebel chief, together with his band of English renegades and Scots. Not merely did disaffected Redesdalers spring the prisoners but they subsequently sold Middleton to Edward II for an extravagant £100;[50] in 1326 they were to perform a similar feat over again, with the loss to the Keeper this time of ransoms to a total of £20.[54] Meanwhile the Earl of Richmond had in 1319 complained that men from Tynedale and Durham had vandalised Catterick and five other of his Yorkshire manors, removing property and several of his bondsmen to hold for ransom;[55] and in 1322 that a dozen of them had burgled his castle at Bowes, from which they had purloined his personal armour, moneys for rent and valuable wines.[56] On the latter occasion their leader was a William Tailboys, already probably seised of Northumbrian lands,[57] and whose descendant would one day inherit all Redesdale from the Umfravilles. In 1327 some Reeds and other Redesdalers stole sixty horses, forty head of cattle and £100-worth of moveables from their Keeper Mauduyt *vi et armis*.[58] In 1340 Edward III exhorted the Lord of Redesdale amongst other magnates 'to put down the evildoers who infest the passes and woods in Northumberland, make prisoners and rob and slay my lieges.'[59] In 1343 Cumbrians and Northumbrians denounced to the Lords of Redesdale and Tynedale and the ecclesiastical Sokens 'disturbers of the peace from the said Lordships . . . [who] . . . come daily with armed force into those counties . . . and who . . . being confederates of the Scots daily perpetrate homicides, pillages, firing and innumerable other evils'.[60] Around the same time, the now adult seventh Lord of Redesdale was joined in commission with Lords Neville and Percy to investigate offences by desperadoes out of Tynedale and Hexhamshire.[61]

Although most of the foregoing persons would have savoured punishment, until Halidon Hill at any rate the government tended perforce towards clemency, being in the shadow of defeat inclined to woo back the drifters, vagrants and worse to their allegiance. In an order of the day in 1316 Edward II commiserated with the intolerable oppressions to which his lieges on the Borders had been exposed, '*tum per homicidia, tum etiam per rapinas et incendia*'.[62] In 1324 Roger Heron, probably still Keeper of Tynedale, was told to clasp back into allegiance all 'who through poverty or other urgent necessity have adhered to the Scots'.[63] Even under Edward III the Sheriff of Northumberland had to proclaim that 'men of Tynedale and neighbouring parts' wanting to attend Corbridge market 'may do so without any fear of arrest by reason of trespass . . . in the time of war between the late King and the King of Scots'.[64] One way and another highland offenders were faring far better than the Earl of Carlisle, who, having been rewarded with Tynedale for saving Edward II's throne at Boroughbridge in 1322, met the horrible death of a traitor soon afterwards for making terms with King Robert identical with those accepted before long by the English King himself.[65, 66]

NOTES

1. C. M. Fraser, *Bek*, pp. 74–6.
2. CPR, 19/3/1307.
3. *Ibid.*, 27/5/1308.
4. CDRS, Vol. III Item 46, 21/6/1308.
5. *Ibid.*, Item 47, June 1308.
6. C. M. Fraser, *Bek*, p. 222.
7. CDRS, Vol. III Item 137, 10/4/1310.
8. *Reg. Pal. Dun.*, Vol. IV p. 95, 1311.
9. *Arch. Aeliana*, Vol. IX p. 230.
10. *Priory of Hexham*, ed. Surtees Vol. 44 App. lix, 1312.
11. Hodgson, *Northumberland*, Pt II Vol. I p. 29.
12. CDRS, Vol. III Item 373, 22/7/1314.
13. *Ibid.*, Item 374, 24/7/1314.
14. *Ibid.*, Item 584, 1317.
15. Hodgson, *Northumberland*, Pt II Vol. I pp. 6, 11, 15, 18, 20, 24, 25, 27, 31, 61, 100, 135 & 171 for these two paragraphs.
16. CPR, 3/5/1315.
17. CDRS, Vol. III Item 1045, 28/11/1331.
18. *Ibid.*, Item 993, 20/10/1329, which speaks of 'lands being in the custody of Richard Talbot by the King's grant'. I have been unable to discover anything else about this Lord of Eccleshall's connexion with Tynedale.
19. *Foedera* (*Conventiones Litterae inter Regis Angliae et alios quosvis*, ed. Rymer), Vol. II Pt 2 p. 1175, 1341.
20. Moore, *Scottish Lands*, p. 43.
21. CDRS, Vol. III Item 464.
22. *Cal. Inq. PM Ed II*, Vol. VI, Item 693, 20/3/1325.
23. *Ibid.*, Item 751, 1326.
24. (*Chronicle of*) *Lanercost*, App. lix 219, 229 & 230, 1314–5.
25. CPR, 10/12/1322.
26. CDRS, Vol. II Items 963 & 1183, 1297–1300; Vol. IV Items 389 & 392, 1297, and Item 2, 1357–8.
27. J. A. Tuck in *NH*, Vol. VI p. 29 ff.
28. CDRS, vol. IV Item 4, 1357/8.
29. CPR, 20/12/1358.
30. *Cal. Inq. PM Ed II*, vol. V Item 396, St. Scolastica 1312.
31. *Ibid.*, *Ed I*, Vol. IV Item 1335, 12/12/1302.
32 *Ibid.*, Vol. III Item 1795, 1299.
33. *Ibid.*, Item 1764, 1297.
34. *Rot. Parl.*, I 293b.24/7/1314.
35. CPR, 8/2/1374.
36. Peasants etc., pp. 6 & 88–110 *passim*. In 1326 Newcastle was one of

fourteen staples for the export of English wool. After a temporary loss of status it became so again in 1353. Cf. an article by J. B. Blake in *Arch. Aeliana*, Vol. XLIII (Fourth Series).

37. *Cal. Chart. R III*, 19/6/1322.
38. CDRS, Vol. III Item 435, 24/5/1315.
39. CCR, 20/4/1358.
40. For the best summary Jean Scammell 'Robert I and the North of England', in *E(nglish) H(istorical) R(eview)* Vol. lxxiv pp. 387–403.
41. CCR, 8/7/1319.
42. *Foedera*, Vol. II p. 378, 1319.
43. CPR, 3/11/1328.
44. CDRS, Vol. III Item 978, 31/3/1329.
45. (Cadwallader) Bates, (*History of*) *Northumberland*, p. 149.
46. CPR, 19/10/1344.
47. *Ibid.*, 22/2/1351.
48. *Ibid.*, 16/12/1315.
49. *Peasants etc.*, p. 114.
50. CDRS, Vol. III Item 539, 22/2/1316.
51. *Ibid.*, Item 886, 24/7/1326.
52. CCR, 17/10/1383.
53. CPR, 28/3/1336.
54. *Ibid.*, 20/2/1327.
55. *Ibid.*, 15/2/1319.
56. *Ibid.*, 18/5/1322.
57. Within fifteen years he indisputably was (CPR, 5/11/1337).
58. CDRS, Vol. III Item 948, 20/2/1328.
59. *Ibid.*, Item 1334, 8/5/1340.
60. CPR, 28/1/1343.
61. Moore, *Scottish Lands*, p. 67.
62. *Foedera*, Vol. II p. 292, 1316.
63. *Ibid.*, p. 556, 1324.
64. CPR, 18/1/1331.
65. *Foedera*, Vol. II p. 502, 1323.
66. *Ibid.*, p. 528, 1323.

CHAPTER FOUR

Stabilisation under King Edward III

The preoccupation then was with first aid to, not castigation of, the stricken districts. As a private Liberty, Redesdale was largely left to its own devices, or more accurately to those of Mauduyt who contrived to remain in charge long after 1328 when the young Gilbert de Umfraville came of age. With an effrontery that did not pass uncensured, the Keeper in 1329 married the dowager Countess of Angus, securing thereby direct control of dower lands around Elsdon, Woodburn and Harbottle.[1, 2] It was therefore to a temporarily reduced inheritance that the young master entered in 1331.[3] Even in 1343 commissions were still being addressed to Gilbert de Umfraville or 'such as supplies his place',[4] and in 1351 Mauduyt was still being asked to account for stewardship of the inheritance,[5] upon which Sir Roger did not finally relinquish his grasp until 1368.[2] All the same it was probably he who saved the patrimony from ruin. As early as 1317 he had recruited 'mounted men' for the 'repulse of the Scots', and protected Tynedale's flank against such as the Middletons.[6] Once the Umfraville Earl was back home, the Keeper acted as his right-hand man in the posting of royal garrison-men at Harbottle and Prudhoe Castle.[7] By the time of Robert de Umfraville's death in 1326, the old Liberty was self-sufficient enough for Mauduyt to spare another force of horsemen for Prudhoe.[8] In the prelude to Halidon Hill it was to him, as to Sir Roger Heron, that King Edward applied for intelligence about enemy movements.[9] As for his protégé, the seventh Lord, he was to figure in the fullness of time among the victorious generals at Neville's Cross.[10] Still freely spoken of in 1343 as the Lord's deputy,[11] Keeper Mauduyt provokes speculation with regard to the nature of his relationships both with his master and stepson, and with his unruly charges.

Concerning his own Tynedale, the King's immediate policy was to ensure that it did not leave his hands except to those who were extensions of himself. Hence between 1328[12] and 1336[13] Sir John Darcy, a best friend and confidant, was the incumbent, to be followed by two members of the royal family: Queen Philippa[14] and son Prince Edmund, as Earl of Cambridge in 1373[15] and Duke of York in 1387.[16, 17] In no sense underkings like the Umfravilles, even the last two were to enjoy life tenures only.

In the dark twenties the men of Tynedale were regularly mustered, showing that control up to a point was never lost. Senior officers involved were somewhat miscellaneous. After Sir Robert Swinburne's inspection of weapons in 1322,[18] William de Felton, 'king's yeoman', arrayed all fencible Tynedalers, preparatory to joining the King with them in 1324;[19] while in 1344 for Neville's Cross they rallied to Aymer, Earl of Atholl,[20] relict of the Comyns and lord of the Talbot lands.[21] However, the norm to which the system was approximating was a muster headed by the Keeper, such as Thomas de Featherstonehaugh[22] who in 1326 'assessed them to arms . . . with power to punish any found rebellious in this behalf'.[23] Robert Ogle, who was Keeper by 1335, shared royal commendation with five of the highest in the land for prowess at Neville's Cross,[24] to which he was presumably accompanied by the men of Philippa's personal demesnes in Tynedale, who had been specifically omitted from Atholl's command.[20] That, on the other hand, no record survives of musters by Alan del Strother, Keeper during the Queen's last seventeen years, is hard to explain away, unless one can postulate a period of quiescence during the French wars.

The royal interest manifested in Tynedale one way or another seems to have had some beneficial effect. By the autumn of 1335 the Talbot lands had recovered enough gloss for the Earl of Atholl to be at pains to retrieve them,[25] though this may have had something to do with his recent failure, in common with the similarly 'disinherited' Gilbert de Umfraville, to recover Scottish estates by force of arms.[26] Tarset demesne had increased eightfold in acreage since 1325; Chirdon bondages were back in cultivation and like the several neighbouring 'hopes' recovered their peacetime values.[27] For the Liberty at large the Queen deemed it reasonable to pay John Darcy £1000 in 1337,[14] a sum that would have made the same sort of impression on contemporaries as two millions on us today. Simonburn and other Tynedale tenements headed the list of lands which William Heron of Ford reckoned worthwhile to redeem in 1358 for over 260 marks (c.£177).[28] At Philippa's death the head manor at Wark rated only a modest £40 p.a., but La Leye alias Leehall, Bellingham and half of Chirdon hope all between ten and twelve pounds, harking back to before the trough of 1325; while a package in which the Talbot lands bulked large changed hands for a respectable £760.[29] For Redesdale, regrettably, being less of an affair of state, no comparable touchstones are extant for the first half of Edward III's reign.

This steady if modest recovery was consonant with national economic trends which were tending to offset the effects of chronic warfare upon northern upland farmers. Ceasing to grow around 1340, the English population after the Black Death went into decline for over a century, a development which despite reactionary counter-measures favoured the underdog. Grain prices slumped as wages soared, so that luxuries came within the ambience of a dwindled peasantry. Most important of these was meat, much to the profit of Border shepherds, already in a valued profession because not labour-intensive.[30]

Nevertheless this mild revival in no way addressed the fundamental problem of national defence in a vital sector. Pure highland air, to which the black rat preferred noisome towns, had furnished a fair protection against bubonic plague, but could not defend against the Picts and Scots. For military reasons Tyne- and Redesdales had suffered as marked a depopulation as the rest of the country. For purposes of scorched earth the Border counties were evacuated on the eves of both Halidon Hill and Neville's Cross. Thus in 1333 the inhabitants, 'from within the Liberties as well as without', were licensed to move 'with their goods, property and animals into the southern parts, wherever they please in our forests, pastures and wastes'. Sheriffs as far south as Notts and Derby were commanded to cooperate.[31] Then in 1345 they were not merely invited but ordered, with a Scottish offensive imminent, to drive their herds down to the Forest of Galtres, where the Sheriff of Yorkshire would offer them every amenity.[32] It may be assumed that nowhere would these decrees have been put into effect with more enthusiasm than in the two secular Liberties, given their proximity to the enemy. In fact, discovering the more tranquil inland more to their taste, such of the Salvayns, Le Parkers, Dynants, Battays, Boles, Cokedeans and Teckets of Tynedale; and Aslakebys, Harelaws, Batailles, Fitzwilliams, Fitzforesters and Ponders of Redesdale as had not previously been wiped out by the invader — a common enough fate on the English Borders between 1315 and 1330[33] — never returned home. When superimposed upon the emptying of such manors as the Talbot lands during the twenties, and the disappearance into Scotland of the equestrian Prats, de Ros's and Comyns, this all amounted to English highland clearances on a considerable scale.

The vacuum had to be filled, and in a businesslike way. After Bannockburn a new type of soldier known as the hobiler first appeared, it having struck Andrew Harcla that a lancer or archer mounted on a fell pony was well fitted to catch, keep up with, or for that matter decamp from, the nimble Scottish flying columns. Primarily a mounted infantryman, the hobiler, though shielded by basic body-armour himself, was unhampered by the coverlet of mail or stuffed leather which clad the horse of the man-at-arms. Whereas the English armies that were shortly to win dazzling victories on the French plains abandoned the hobiler after Crecy, he remained among the Border hills dominant till well on in the sixteenth century. As early as 1316 Antony de Lucy was garrisoning Staworth Pele in South Tynedale with fifteen men-at-arms and forty hobilers,[34] and it was with a like mix of heavy and light horsemen that Mauduyt assailed the raiders in Tynedale soon afterwards,[6] and that the Umfraville strongholds were manned in 1322.[7] Five years later hobilers were the staple of the force with which Edward III invaded Scotland in his first campaign as King.[146] In 1336 the troops with which de Lucy joined the Duke of Lancaster,[35] and others raised throughout Northumberland by the Lord of Redesdale,[36] consisted of men-at-arms, archers, foot-soldiers and hobilers 'ad pugnandum potentes'. Twenty years later Robert Ogle went to the assistance of Wardens of the Marches 'with men-at-arms, hobilers and archers, as many as he could'.[37]

So far as Tyne- and Redesdales were concerned there were two groups from which the hobilers were to be drawn. Firstly there were those who returned home after the diaspora, among whom were prevalent bearers of four family names in the larger, and two in the older Liberty. Charltons, Milburns (*alias* Milneburn or Midelburne), Dodds (*alias* Todds) and Robsons (*alias* filii Roberti) had been resident in Tynedale since at latest 1279.[38] Indeed a Charlton claimed in 1297 that a great-great-grandmother had possessed lands in nearby Gunnerton.[39] That Charlton is site of an old manor in Tynedale, and that a Dodd Hill overlooks the Falstone argue indigenous origins. In a society in which the father-son bond counted for so much, the Robson patronymic is strangely unique, inspiring such legends as that it originated with bastards of Robert-with-the-Beard;[40] or that the eponymous ancestor was the Uncle Hroethbert whose runic tombstone was unearthed, appropriately enough, at Falstone. The Dodds, too, have been shoved back into the Dark Ages by Northumbrian folklore, which retails that in the seventh century one Eilaf was changed into a fox for having stolen cheese from monks guarding St. Cuthbert's corpse, 'from which day all the race of Eilaf bore the name of Dodd or Tod, which in the mother-tongue signifies a fox'.[41] All four of these surnames recur in North Tynedale with intensifying frequency from the late fourteenth century onwards. Bearers of ancient surnames who returned to Redesdale were the Harles and Reeds who had been in residence since at latest 1283.[42, 43, 44] One can be moderately confident that the Harles who were prominent in the Otterburn area throughout the fourteenth century,[45, 46, 47] having in 1360 redeemed for £10 lands there forfeit for rebellion with Scots,[48] were identical with the later, dominant Halls. Still side by side in the eighteenth century, though with Hall to Harle in a proportion 35:1,[49] both spellings due to the long 'a' vowel were pronounced the same by Northumbrians, added to which Redesdalers have always been noted for inability to manage even the effete English 'r'. Reeds were established at Troughend in place of departed Buttycombes by 1440.[50]

The steadfastness of these survivors still left appreciable gaps which on military grounds could not have been tolerated. The hypothesis is inescapable, though not proveable, that there was a second group comprising those of whom there is no record of previous residence. Yet again the historian is bedevilled by compulsory reliance on evidence from two lifetimes ahead, but muster rolls from Henry VIII's reign would suggest that many incomers carried the names Hunter, Stamper, Wilkinson and Yarrow into Tynedale; and Pott, Forster, Dawge and Fletcher into Redesdale.[51] Most important of all immigrants into the latter, however, would seem to have been Hedleys from Umfraville's woods on the south bank of the main Tyne,[52] in the service of that family in 1244,[53] but not demonstrably resident in the Liberty till 1397.[54] Although again there is no proof, some form of partial plantation is indicated. It has been myopically objected to me that such a concept would have been organisationally beyond the government of Edward III, but in fact the Norman Conquest itself had involved plantation, which from the era of the Frankish invasions had been of the very essence of feudalism. Within a mere fifty years of the settlement envisaged here, the Duke of Bedford was in an ironic turnabout to allocate Norman lands to English captains and their retinues, in return for a defensive obligation.[55]

How was the first group emboldened to sit tight and the second — if the hypothesis is correct — to settle in so precarious an environment? The problem resolved itself, here as in other parts of the Borders, into devising means to enable humble but able-bodied men to arrive on the battlefield accoutred as hobilers. Under the old system of tenure, based on the knight's fee and discredited by defeat, the only men who could normally afford equestrian gear were the free tenants, too few in number to erect a dyke against the Scots of requisite dimensions. Mr. J. A. Tuck has already spoken of the militarisation of Northumbrian society that took place in the fourteenth century,[26] and, with the reservation that even the former system had been essentially military too, it is the contention here that in Tyne- and Redesdales at any rate the change assumed the form of a large-scale conversion of tenures, coinciding broadly with the breathing space in Anglo-Scottish hostilities in the period 1357–1377. The moment was propitious inasmuch as, with land at a discount owing to depopulation, the national consciousness was growing accustomed to greatly improved conditions of tenure.[56] In contemplation of the revolution in which the mewed sparrowhawks, soar goshawks, and pounds of pepper vanished into the void with the Teckets and Batailles, the historian is up against a problem more familiar to the geologist or archaeologist, in so far as *what* happened may be gauged and *when* within narrow margins, but *how* is a matter for informed conjecture.

During the Queen's tenure as Lady of Tynedale existent rights at the manorial level were not tampered with, so that in 1358 William Heron of Ford routinely inherited the lion's share of the Swinburne properties.[57]

However, Philippa's death and succession by an inexperienced Prince in 1373 was a precipitant, since King Edward began immediately to display interest, commissioning the Keeper, Adam del Strother; the Prior of Hexham; and Heron of Ford and Chipchase, as a major land-holder, 'to make inquisition in the Liberty of Tynedale touching the values of the King's manors, lands and rents'.[58] Subsequently the Keeper was assiduous in supplementing the list by confiscations 'due to forfeiture of war', as of Bellingham meadows and Chirdon in 1374,[59] and of La Leye *alias* Leehall and other of the Abbot of Jedburgh's properties 'for time out of mind', in 1377.[60] The King's intention behind all this activity was to establish 'which of [these tenements] he can grant in fee, for life or otherwise',[58] a transaction that most probably involved a new tenurial basis, which cannot however be finally proved without the Wark manorial rolls that no longer exist. With regard to members of Wark out of royal hands, the old system persisted unimpaired for the present, there being no interference with Heron of Ford's entry in 1375 into Bellingham, to which his title was unflawed.[61]

Even if the foregoing theory as to the date and circumstances of the tenurial conversion is erroneous, and although the lateness of detailed evidence exhibits the new system only in advanced decay, as to its salient characteristics there is no room for doubt. An historian so distinguished as Dr. Joan Thirsk has likewise had to draw conclusions about the Middle Ages from reports written under the Stuarts.[62]

Every recipient of Tynedale lands reallocated under the new dispensation held of the Manor of Wark as tenant-in-chief of the Crown, with whose agent the Keeper he exclusively dealt. There were two classes of such tenant, superseding the seven present in the twelfth century, none of whom had held *in capite*. The more numerous and lowlier were the customary tenants, and even they enjoyed privileges far beyond those of copyholders, whom they otherwise resembled. 'They challenge to hold their tenements by title of tenant right,paying their rents to the Keeper for his own use . . . and serving in field on horse or foot for the defence of the Border lands, in which many of the inhabitants have lost their lives . . . The tenant may sell his tenant right or any part thereof, without reference to the Lord',[63] in which respect and in his complete testamentary freedom he excelled the common run of customary tenants. He paid no fines on death or alienation, so that conversion to tenant right of their tenures was understandably a prime demand of rebellious northern peasants in 1536.[64] Under James I the size of a customary tenement averaged between one and two hundred acres. While no exact inferences can be drawn from this as to fourteenth-century acreages, the fact remains that there existed a closer resemblance in population density between 1350 and 1600 than between either and the sixteenth century.

One can assume that most of the highlanders held many times over the fifteen acres reckoned necessary to support a peasant family in northern Europe during the fourteenth,[65] but that the land was of below average quality. The rents paid by customary tenants to the Keeper at Whitsun or midsummer, and at Martinmas,[66] were low at their inception, because of the conditions prevalent at their probable period of origin: the fourteenth century witnessed a collapse in land values so severe throughout England, and so protracted that within two hundred years it was to obliterate 98% of the nobility that had survived foreign and civil wars.[67] An additional reason for pitching rents on the Borders even lower than elsewhere was as the bribe to stay put already discussed. On the other hand according to the unique and late evidence available rents could be moved up and down, and were not fixed by immutable custom as, for instance, in County Durham.[65]

Perhaps a ninth of the whole in the Jacobean Liberty, the other class of tenant, namely the freeholders, were even better placed: 'They hold their land of His Majesty, as of his manor of Wark, by knight service . . . at the command of the Keeper to serve in field on horse or foot for the defence of the Border lands in as strict a manner as any of the customary tenants'[66] '. . . and to defend the dale called Tynedale from thieves and wolves'[68] '. . . The heir comes into court to take out his fine'.[66] Otherwise inheritance was by word of mouth only or by indenture, admittance in the court never being called for.[68] Acreage was huge, up around the 4000 mark. Rents were so negligible that, on reclassification as a freehold, Henry Dodd's customary tenement had its rent cut to one-fortieth.[66] The fine or gressum to which on death or alienation a freeholder was subject was less of a peppercorn, amounting on occasion to three years' rent, but did not become a major irritant until after 1517 when excuses were found for levying it with increasing frequency.[69]

The distinction between the two categories of tenant-in-chief was of class rather than caste. Even the customaries came of the lineage of the radknights of Saxon antiquity, the drengs, the twelfth-century vavasors, or the working-knights of Domesday.[70] Already under the earlier Plantagenets a given individual could hold in different tenures so that around 1300 Adam Charlton, who sat in Hesleyside by the fragment of a knight's fee,[71] had also been a bondage tenant in Charlton.[72] After the conversion the tenurial divergence was much narrower: Roger Widdrington of Cartington Castle and John Hall, gentleman of Otterburn, were each in 1620 customary tenants as well as freeholders.[68]

The Umfravilles had as much interest in the stability and defensive posture of Redesdale as the Crown in that of Tynedale, and *a posteriori* it is likely that the surviving inhabitants were in the fourteenth century offered similar or even higher bribes to dig themselves in, and to persuade incomers to move in. In respect of the old Liberty there is extant what is lacking in respect of the larger, namely evidence bearing on the actual conversion. An *inquisitio post mortem* in 1494 on the estate of Robert Tailboys, till recently Lord of Redesdale, records that 'in the said Manor [of Harbottle] there are divers free tenants holding their tenements there . . . who were wont anciently to pay 40/8½d . . . in Lent and . . . in autumn equally; 9 lb pepper and 9 lb cumin; but in the time of war between England and the Scots [i.e. quasi-permanently] they shall pay no rent . . . but give their help together with their Lord there to keep the Vale of Redesdale . . . from plunderers, enemies and robbers.[73] By the time of the Jacobean surveys the state of both categories of tenant in each Liberty had become so like that of those in the other, that all the surveyors had to do with relevant documentation was to substitute Harbottle and Redesdale for Wark and Tynedale respectively, or *vice versa*. Statistical profiles, however, were not interchangeable. In the old Liberty the proportion of freeholders and customary tenants had come to be as narrow as 2:1, with the individual tenements of both classes of similar size. Freeholders' rents were even more nominal than in Tynedale: in 1604 one hundred of them remitted a total of £5½ for 25,000 acres, about a tithe of the amount paid by customaries for the same area.[66] In contrast with Tynedale, a whiff of villeinage persisted even into the seventeenth century. Redeshead, a summer pasture used by Reeds, 'as their ancestors time out of mind have used the same customarily', owed to the lord of the manor ploughing services as well as rent as late as 1620.[63, 68] The extent to which all these features had generated from fourteenth-century seeds can only be guessed at: the sole difference as to which there is certainty is that in the earlier period the Redesdale tenants did not hold *in capite*.

The possible repercussions of the hypothetical injection of prosperity during Edward III's last years are best examined in two fields, the first indirectly, the second directly connected with national defence. So far as internal security was concerned, the situation manifested no radical lawlessness even before Philippa's death. Most offences appear to have been fiscal in character, relating to taxes and customs levied to pay for glorious but futile wars in France. Between 1358 and 1360 the men of Tyne- and Redesdales and Hexhamshire defaulted on their share of the tenths and fifteenths, and in the wool subsidies, for which their representatives were summoned to account before the Exchequer. The Archbishop of York backed their case for non-appearance inasmuch as 'all their country was at war so that they dared not leave home'.[74] Subsequently three collectors were appointed for each dale,[75] although one half of the dues were forgiven.[76] In 1371 North Tynedale merchants were prosecuted in Chancery for avoidance of customs in

smuggling wools and hides through Berwick into Scotland.[77] The incentive
was that though North Eastern wool fetched, for example, only eight marks
per sack in 1343, as against fourteen for that of the Midlands, it was liable
to identical export duties.[78]

Obstructiveness on the part of officialdom within the Liberties had
persisted. In 1362 the King had reason, albeit illegally, to command his
Wardens of the Marches to punish Keepers who had refused to surrender
alleged malefactors.[79] The indignation which this aroused may be gauged
from the response to a writ of *Quo Warranto* in 1344 by the seventh Lord of
Redesdale, who declared that 'no ancestor of his ever held his court to deliver
from the said Liberty before the justices of the Bench at Westminster'.[45] On
the other hand the Queen was understandably more conscientious. With the
King's Bench at her elbow she never wanted for expert advice in the choice
of judges to despatch into her remote fief.[80] Whatever rearrangments her
widower may have made regarding the tenurial base produced no immediate
benefits. On the contrary 'the commons of the Tynedale franchise' were soon
petitioning that under the Earl of Cambridge's regime no justices were being
appointed to try pleas of the Crown, as well as civil actions, and that this
neglect had brought them to the point of destruction.[81] That nothing had
changed much even by 1388 is suggested by a rebuke from this same Duke
of York to the Earl of Northumberland as royal Warden, who having entered
Tynedale to snatch three fugitives had acted 'contrary to the privileges of my
Liberty'.[17]

Nor did the putative tenurial conversion have any immediate effect
in the military sphere either, for the Scots did pretty much as they
pleased. In 1371 the Court of Chancery ordered the manorial court at
Wark to forward papers for 'an inquisition what evildoers and breakers
of the peace at Falstone in Tynedale slew John Robson of Tynedale,
Adam Robson and Thomas Robson . . . and who by deceit took Roger
del Spence, the King's liege man at Charlton in Tynedale and delivered
him to the King's enemies of Scotland . . . who after knowingly harboured
the said evildoers'.[82] The unprecedented concern at a high level, together
with Spence's royal connexion, suggests that the victims may have been
among the dragon's teeth that we surmise to have been lately sown within
the Liberty, with the additional implication that a tenurial conversion may
have commenced even before Philippa's death. In 1379–80 the Redesdalers
were paying fifty, and the Wark neighbourhood twenty marks in annual
tribute to the Scots, and jointly bewailed that they were suffering more in the
alleged truce than in full-blown warfare.[83] Observing that by the year 1500
the Tyne- and Redesdalers would have come to be rated an essential part of
national defence, Mr. J. A. Tuck has contrasted the absence from the first

Earl of Northumberland's '*retinencia . . in bello Scotico*' of the surnames that would indicate their presence in 1385. Yet the fact is that four Halls and two Dodds — in the form 'del Hall' and 'Tod(de)' respectively — not to mention three Robsons and a Reed, do indeed figure on that roll, though without territorial affiliation;[84] but in any case most highlanders as Liberty-dwellers would not normally have mustered under a mere manorial lord, however exalted his station. That they took no part in the Battle of Otterburn on their very doorstep in 1388 is frankly unbelievable. Just before the Scottish victory, which mopped up all the English remnants in Teviotdale, two-thirds of Otterburn manor plus Harbottle were assessed at a mere £5 'by the destructions of the Scots',[85] to which properties was attributed a scarcely higher rating in 1392.[86] In 1404 Otterburn 'fortlet' was pronounced to be in no better condition.[87, 88]

If, as there is reason to suppose, it was Edward III who was instrumental in the tenurial conversion that demonstrably took place, then he was too canny a soldier and lawyer to expect other than long-term fruits. In the drive to establish within the twin Liberties as many viable fighting men as feasible, the Crown followed by the Umfravilles admitted a privilege and indulged a practice which in conjunction generated a unique situation.

It was laid down that any tenant convicted of treason or felony should not forfeit his estate in the normal way, which meant that after the offender's execution it would pass smoothly to other frontiersmen within the family. Statutes enacted early in the next century to quash what had already come to be regarded as an outrageous anomaly remained dead letters.[89] Though according to one optimistic theory the exemption was void for crimes committed outside the Liberty itself,[68] a Jacobean Lord of Tynedale for one ignored that saving grace in asserting that 'this pretended inhumane (sic) custom, contrary to law and reason . . . makes them so desperate in their courses that they will adventure their lives with any that oppose them, and neither fear the danger of the law nor care for their landlords'.[90] Indubitably here was a privilege that any English baron might envy.

The practice aforementioned was the introduction, or more likely toleration with regard to tenant right, of the custom of partible inheritance or gavelkind, to wit the division of a tenement among all sons. More widespread than English lawyers since the thirteenth century had ever cared to admit,[91] it was unusual nevertheless, aligning the highlanders with the ceorls of Alfred's reign.[92] One corollary of this device to breed soldiers was that no woman could inherit, a deprivation recognised as sufficiently exceptional to elicit comment at regular intervals between 1580 and 1649.[66, 93, 94] More serious still, as among the poor whites of South Africa, was the fragmentation of holdings: 'if a man have issue ten sons, eight, six, five or four, and sits on a holding of six shillings rent, every son shall have a piece of his father's holding'.[95] In the fourteenth century the practice entailed no hardship owing to the great extent of tenements and thinness of population; in most of the fifteenth, too, the highlands were not beset by the agrarian stagnation due to universal smallholding that afflicted England between the accessions of Henry IV and Edward VI. That notwithstanding, a progressive deterioration was inevitable.[96]

Whereas in Redesdale gavelkind was rigorously applied, in Tynedale there were limitations.[97] There a widow enjoyed a third part, and whenever a customary tenant died intestate the next heir, albeit female, automatically inherited. Gavelkind was regarded as a convenient option rather than an obligation, for many willed at least the major part to eldest sons.[66] Freeholders had no such choice in either Liberty, their freeholds being regulated through primogeniture at the two manorial courts.[68]

The combination of partible inheritance with immunity from confiscation stimulated the growth of what were already, or in process of becoming, kin-groups, for which in English since the early sixteenth century the Celticism 'clan' has become normal usage, but which was not apparently adopted by the highlanders themselves till after the advent of the Stuarts.[94] Regrettably there has to be the usual over-reliance on late witness, but it is clear nevertheless that the raw materials were the families whose labels will already be familiar. 'They stand most by Surnames', wrote Bowes in 1551, 'whereof the Charltons are the chief, and in all services or charges imposed upon that country the Charltons, and such as are under their rule, be rated for one half of that country; Robsons for a quarter; and the Dodds and the Milburns for another quarter . . . Redesdale (likewise) standeth much by Surnames, of which . . . the Halls be the greatest and most of reputation . . . and next to them the Reeds, Potts, Hedleys, Spores, Dawges and Fletchers.'[98] In Redesdale there is no evidence for geographical grouping, but in Tynedale the Charltons tended to bunch around the Middle reaches of the North Tyne, the Robsons on the wilder ground towards its source, and the Milburns along the banks of the Tarset burn.[99] All but the last three cited by Bowes qualified as Head Surnames, but by 1539 half the population belonged to the minor clans,[100] and in 1528 there were as many Fletchers as Potts in Redesdale.[101]

As to the origin of these kin-groups there is some mystery. According to Scottish experts, it was in the fourteenth century that similar cousinly aggregations came into existence north of the Border as defensive organisations to contain the effects of ceaseless warfare,[102] and Tyne- and Redesdales were unquestionably in important respects outcrops of Scotland rather than

England. On the other hand, when viewed in isolation several features of the English clans were of surprisingly primitive appearance, so that a mere six lifetimes ago they still exhibited characteristics encountered nowhere else in the realm for a thousand years.[103] Furthermore, it will already be plain that all the surnames except Hedley appertaining to the major clans were well established in the Liberties by the thirteenth century, which is as far back as one can go with Saxon surnames. Finally, extended families already in being would have stood a better chance than any conventional families of surviving the havoc after Bannockburn, and of being on hand when any redistribution of lands occurred.

Whatever its antiquity, the Surname was no empty abstraction, and in contemplating it one need not be abashed by the retrospective nature of the evidence, because changes in family structures move as slowly as the glacier. Governments saddled the Surname with the corporate responsibilities of the 'maegth' in King Ethelred's codes,[104] and advisedly since, in the words of G. M. Trevelyan, 'The Halls, Reeds, Hedleys, and Fletchers of Redesdale; the Charltons, Dodds, Robsons and Milburns of North Tynedale were the real political units in a society that knew no other organisation'.[105]

Clanship shaped agricultural method, the staff of life. With Surnames in Tynedale at least tending to colocation, they must habitually have shared out crops from the same infield. When in the operation of transhumance they moved from valleys to uplands, it was by Surnames. 'They shiel together by Surnames . . . They pay their part of the summer farm for that they are descended of such a Surname or race of men, to whom such a summering belongeth', the exploitation of Redeshead by the body of the Reeds being a case in point.[106] Each component family shieled in its tiny cabin on the hillside, where the beasts of the whole Surname were turned loose to graze without distinction.[107] That the beasts were communally owned is unlikely, but Mr. Finberg's opinion that transhumance fortified the clan spirit is irrefutable.[108]

In a bid to save a namesake from the gallows in 1597 three hundred of the Halls were to offer 140 head of cattle and field work for life.[106] Whenever despite such endeavours a malefactor *was* executed, those of his Surname lent less timely support through vendetta on the plaintiffs, 'as though they had unlawfully killed him with a sword'.[98] Even in 1649, by which time things had simmered down, antiquarian Gray could write of Tyne- and Redesdales that 'if any two be displeased, they expect no law but bang it out bravely, one and his kindred against the other and his . . . This fighting they call their feids, a word so barbarous that I cannot express it in any other tongue'.[94] Scottish parallels and Anglo-Saxon precedents abound. Thus Dalrymple alluded to 'deadlie feid, nocht of ane in ane or few in few, but of thame ilk ane and al, quha ar of that familie, stock or tribe, how ignorant sa evir they be of the inure',[109] while Old English law right down to Alfred's day had largely been framed to curtail its grisly incidence.[99, 104] The custom still flourished sufficiently in 1558 for government to seek to ban it throughout Northumberland,[110] and in 1596 for Burghley to ascribe the downfall of the English clansmen to 'deadlie feud, the word of enmity on the Border'.[111]

Each Surname consisted of several graynes,[98] in defining which no help is forthcoming from their posterity, who confuse with the Surname.[112] It appears to have been a family with cousinly ramifications resident upon a neighbourhood of farmsteads. Whereas it is clear that it might contain ten able-bodied men,[113] and that for example the Charltons of Hesleyside and Bellingham belonged to the same one, where one grayne ended and the next began is no longer detectable. Early in the sixteenth century there were four Robson graynes,[114] while the tally of Charlton graynes fluctuated inexplicably between three and five in the space of seven years.[115, 116]

Each grayne had a chieftain called a heidsman, whose badge of office was residence in the chief house, which in the case of freeholds descended by primogeniture. In view of the equal division of lands by gavelkind, it is harder to arrive at the truth in the case of the customaries. Under James I it was to be ruled that primogeniture should decide ownership of the chief house even here,[68] but this probably prevailed only *ceteris paribus*, so that whenever one brother of whatever age was clearly the most capable, then as in the Scottish Lowlands[117] the heidship along with the chief house would pass to him. Thus brothers Henry and John Robson were to cohabit at Falstone farm,[118, 119] each with his sons, but though the former and elder survived till 1541[120] at earliest, he had been eclipsed by John for the previous five years. Besides the Tynedale bastles, massive examples of chief houses were Otterburn Tower and Troughend Pele. Faced with the problem of repetitive surnames that Welsh villagers solve occupationally and Vikings and Bulgars patronymically, these heidesmen adopted 'by-' or 'to-names' which were either descriptive, sometimes boisterously, or incorporative of the chief house. It was thus that Eddy Dodd of the Crag avoided confusion but he apparently did not have other kinsmen living under the same roof. Henry and John of the Falstone, Prat and Jerry Charlton of the Bower, and Hector and Edward Charlton of Hesleyside were all to be awkwardly coexistent. Within each Surname there was normally one grayne and chief house of acknowledged supremacy, with that of the heidsman to match. Such were the Halls (*alias* Harles) of Otterburn, the Reeds of Troughend, the Charltons of Hesleyside, and the Robsons of the Falstone. Other graynes, shorter of wealth, influence and durable masonry, enjoyed from time to time a more ephemeral eminence, when the incumbent heidsman happened to be a man out of the common run.

Though even these heidsmen never vied with the chieftains of the Scottish Lowland clans, who were to become Earls and Dukes in the fullness of time, 'heidsmen and gentlemen' was a hackneyed jingle in Tudor Northumberland.[121] No-one who could lead 500 mounted men into Scotland might properly be described as a member of the lower classes. Often styled 'laird', the heidsmen discharged the dual duties of Anglo-Saxon lordship: they were military leaders, and they stood surety for the behaviour of their juniors, who thereby escaped the stigma and danger of King Athelstan's 'lordless man of whom no law can be got.' The murkier side of this patronage was that divers heidsmen preserved a facade of respectability, which they employed to shield errant clansmen from their deserts. 'There be some that have never stolen themselves', declared Bowes, 'which *they* call true men, and yet such will have rascals that steal . . . whom they do reset [i.e. harbour] and will receive part of the stolen goods . . . [They] labour to the officers . . . to acquit and discharge the thieves from just correction.'[98] They were probably also the 'master thieves' who in 1649 were accused of taking 'sawfey money' from the pillaged for the return of their stolen cattle.[94]

For better and for worse a patriarchy that fused leadership with the blood-tie stamped a fabulous *esprit de corps* on a society that had been fostered with a military purpose in mind. In any case it is a reasonable surmise that the forbears of the Tyne- and Redesdalers included the Bellingas of the Anglian conquest, of whom several place-names are redolent and which denote 'highlanders' or 'highlandsmen', by which they were habitually known as late as the seventeenth century. Long settlement breeds a local patriotism beyond kindred, and according to Bowes 'they would not assent to leaving Tynedale . . . for their delight is much in the great numbers of their country, thinking themselves of more power and strength thereby';[122] 'they would rather be poor there than rich anywhere else'.[98] Bellingham was the capital of their Lilliputian realm where they not only purchased bread, ale and other provisions, but where the whole body of them assembled whenever they had 'any matter or cause to treat and commune of amongst themselves'.[122] There was some parallel between these meetings and the Wark court on the one hand, and the folcgemot and Hundred Court of the Anglo-Saxons on the other, especially as the last-named was supervised by the King's reeve *alias* Keeper, and frequently assumed the name of a royal manor.[123]

Links between Surnames were military as well as consultative, inasmuch as they commonly operated in 'friendships' or 'bands' — or as the Scots less graciously termed it, 'gangs'[124] — comprising members of several. Hence a

Warden's reference in 1559 to the 'bandsmen' of Tynedale, an early variant of bandits.[125]

Finally the sense of separateness as a territory received every encouragement from compatriots, who took for granted that if any Tynedaler settled outside the Liberty he would provide a safe house to which fellow-highlanders would resort for shelter and concealment of loot. In consequence 'true countries' were loth to have such 'outparters' dwelling among them. In 1495 it was laid down that no land outside the Liberty might be let to any Tynedaler, unless two forty-shilling freeholders would be bound by recognizance to the King in the sum of £20.[126]

Due to the hegemony first of the Umfravilles, then of the Halls *alias* Harles, Redesdale society tended to be more monolithic than that of the sister dale. In 'envying the stranger' the Redesdalers were long renowned for the mistrust that was counterpart to their own corporate solidarity.[113] The sentiment was heartily reciprocated: any fellow of a Newcastle guild risked a fine of £20 for taking apprentices from either Liberty.[127]

Symptomatic of the treatment of the clan-based societies almost as foreign powers, whenever an official desired to parley with the inhabitants their representatives were convened under safe-conduct to the frontiers of the Liberty, like so many delegates to an armistice conference. Chollerford[128] and Hexham[129] were customary venues. This was one of the 'old liberties of that country' which in the sixteenth century the highlanders still 'proudly claimed and used'.[98]

Lastly, an ostracism to which both were subject reinforced the bond between the two dales, who settled the not infrequent mutual thefts through their Keepers, assisted by their wisest heidsmen 'after the manner of redress between England and Scotland, and they will not seek further lawful remedy'.[98] Such moots out of court usually took place at the Three Pikes, a mile north-west of the Carter Fell,[66] symbolising a relationship so intimate that outsiders seldom distinguished at all between the two clan aggregations. Thus the Robson in Bulleyn's play, written in the year of Shakespere's birth,[130] was depicted as a native of Redesdale rather than of his ancestral Tynedale.[131]

The infusion of prosperity which hypothetically took place in the fourteenth century through danger money, eventually produced not only a threat to law and order that had not been planned, but also formidable defences in depth, that had. As so often, one has to fall back on evidence from the sixteenth century, fortunately however before the art of war along the Borders had been transformed, prior to disappearance altogether.

What was the manpower involved? Figures available suggest a sharper

increase in highland population than might have been expected from the
slump, followed by a slow climb-back, in that of England at large between
1300 and 1550. Around the former date Tynedale had fielded two or three
hundred men,[132] a force of the same order as that of the County Palatine;
by the end of the period Bowes would comment on 'the great number of
wild people inhabiting in the same countries, which be no fewer than 1500
of active and able men upon horseback and foot',[122] with Tynedalers in a
slight majority in so far as Redesdale's population, though more numerous,
contained fewer able-bodied men.[121] In an age when Norwich and Bristol
had 15,000 inhabitants, these numbers represented a force thrice as great as
the Duke of Norfolk generally mustered;[133] half again as many as the Earls of
Cumberland and Westmorland jointly, or the Prince Bishop singly; as many
as Henry Percy from all his Border domains;[134] about the same as Middlesex
and rather more than Cornwall.[135]

Crucial was the proportion of hobilers, or light or Northern Horsemen
as they came to be called in Tudor times. Common to the Marchers of both
kingdoms, the highlanders' stock mounts were shaggy ponies of thirteen
hands and without iron shoes, to cope with uneven and slippery terrain.
The Tyne- and Redesdalers were by absurd ordinances forbidden horses worth
more than a noble (i.e. 6/8d.) in the reign of Henry VII,[136] or 50/- in the
inflated days of James I,[137] *except* against the Scots. That many Tynedalers
took their military status seriously enough to go fully armed even to church
can be gathered from the terms of the late fifteenth-century excommunications. It was because the little hobblers, not they themselves, wore no armour
that they were known as the 'licht' horsemen, since the rider was accoutred
in jack and knapeskull or sallet.[136] The first was a sleeveless tunic of quilted
leather, often iron-plated fore and aft;[138] the second a steel bonnet with or
without a peak; and the third a globular headpiece, with or without a vizor,
of which the underpart curved outwards behind.[139]

The standard weapon was a Scottish lance: evidence for its length
is inconclusive — one reference to six ells seems far-fetched — but it
probably equalled twice the height of a tall man.[140] Swords were also
carried.[141] Belatedly the footmen came to share the English addiction to the
long bow, so that the Tynedalers started a big fray in 1575 with a shower
of arrows as well as abuse.[142] However, it would have been the less lethal
Scottish short bow with which they did Antony Bek's dirty work in 1300.
Though a Borderer's garb and armoury were quaint enough to be donned as
fancy dress for Henry VIII's court revels,[143] these centaurs were serviceably
equipped from the late fourteenth century onwards. The highlanders in
particular, even when past their best, were extolled by Camden as 'notable
light horsemen', and by an Elizabethan Warden of the Marches as superior to

their neighbours as 'knowing the mosses, more nimble on foot, and some keep sleuth [i.e. trail] hounds to serve the country'.[144] Able to subsist indefinitely on ewe's milk, in mobility they vied with the ancient Tartars.[138]

In the static mode they were entrenched in a fashion that owed as much to nature as to art. Sir Robert Bowes spoke of 'such strengths naturally fortified as well by reason of mosses and morasses . . . and of banks and cleughs of wood, wherein of old time for the more strength great trees have been felled and laid so overthwart the way . . . it will be hard for strangers having no knowledge thereof to pass thereby in any order, and specially on horseback . . . The houses . . . of Tynedale is much set upon either side of the said river . . . and by the brooks . . . Surely the heidsmen of them have very strong houses, whereof for the most part the utter . . . walls be made of great swar [i.e. heavy] oak-trees strongly bound . . . together with great tenors of the same [and] thick mortressed . . . A great number of the houses [are] set so together in one quarter that a fray or outcry made at one house may warn all the residue . . . both men and women, that the said country will be shortly thereby warned and assembled'.[122] These 'bastles [i.e. bastilles]', of which what remains of Falstone Farm is a massive extant example, were not dwarfed by the modest castles in or near the Liberty of which Haughton, Simonburn, Wark-on-Tyne, Chipchase, Hesleyside and Tarset still stood tall in the fourteenth century.[98]

Whereas the Tynedale strongholds merged with the hillsides, the classic Border peles of Redesdale stood out against them but were no easier to assail. Built about a well-staircase defensible with a single sword-arm, pierced with shot-holes, and crowned with a beacon like a naval crow's nest, Otterburn Tower, the fourteenth-century Vicar's pele at Elsdon, and the like could be sixty feet high and forty square, with walls five feet thick. Three stories over a vaulted basement, the entrance secured by an iron 'yett' (i.e. gate), the Redesdale strongholds scorned any mediaeval artillery to which they were accessible.[145]

NOTES

1. *CDRS*, Vol. III Item 932, 16/8/1327.
2. *CCR*, 24/9/1368.
3. *CDRS*, Vol. III Item 1037, 3/10/1331.
4. *CPR*, 28/1/1343.
5. *CCR*, 24/2/1351.
6. *CDRS*, Vol. III Item 539, 22/2/1316.
7. *CCR*, 11/5/1322.
8. *CPR*, 3/9/1327.

9. *CDRS*, Vol. III Item 1057, 11/8/1332.
10. Hodgson, *Northumberland*, Pt II Vol. I pp. 37–9.
11. *Northern Petitions*, ed. Surtees Vol. 194 p. 100, 1342.
12. *CPR*, 24/12/1328.
13. *Ibid.*, 13/10/1336.
14. *CCR*, 18/3/1337.
15. *CPR*, 23/4/1373.
16. *Ibid.*, 26/4/1388.
17. *CCR*, 2/6/1388.
18. *CPR*, 10/12/1322.
19. *Ibid.*, 27/8/1324.
20. *CDRS*, Vol. III Item 1438, 12/7/1344.
21. *CCR*, 17/8/1330.
22. *CPR*, 7/5/1329.
23. *Ibid.*, 16/4/1320.
24. *Foedera*, Vol. III p. 91, 1346.
25. *Ibid.*, p. 920, 1335.
26. J. A. Tuck, in *NH*, Vol. XXI pp. 38 & 49, and vol. XXII p. 78.
27. *CCR*, 7/8/1330.
28. Hodgson, *Northumberland*, Pt III Vol. II p. 325.
29. *CPR*, 8/7/1373.
30. D. C. Coleman, *Economy of England*, p. 34.
31. *Foedera*, Vol. II Pt 2 p. 856, 1333.
32. *Ibid.*, vol. III Pt 1 p. 62, 1345.
33. M. H. Keen. *Later Middle Ages*, p. 80.
34. *Northumbrian Petitions*, ed. Surtees Vol. 176 p. 25, 1316.
35. *Foedera*, Vol. II Pt 2 p. 936, 1336.
36. *Ibid.*, p. 1030, 1338.
37. Northumberland RO,ZSW 1/68, 28/7/1356.
38. *CDRS*, Vol. II Item 168, 18/11/1279. Iter de Wark.
39. *Ibid.*, Vol. IV Item 392.
40. A theory put to me forty years ago by the late Mr. Herbert Honeyman, Secretary of the Newcastle Society of antiquaries.
41. (Edward) Charlton, (*Memorials of*) *North Tynedale (and its Four Surnames)*, pp. 8–9.
42. *CPR*, 28/5/1283.
43. *Ibid.*, 16/5/1285.
44. J. A. Tuck, *NH* Vol. III p. 29 & Vol. VI p. 27 does not push back the Surnames far enough, e.g. the earliest Reed he can find is in a bond *anno* 1400.
45. *CPR*, 24/10/1344.
46. *Ibid.*, 1/10/1348.
47. *Ibid.*, 2/2/1350.
48. *Ibid.*, 20/11/1360.
49. Redesdale Pollbook for 1710.
50. Northumberland RO, 542/21, 1440.
51. *L(etters) and P(apers), Hen(ry) VIII*, IV(2) no. 4336, 6/6/1528.
52. *CPR*, 7/2/1276.

53. CDRS, Vol. I Item 1667, 1244.

54. CPR, 16/2/1397.

55. Cf. Anne E Curry, *The First English Standing Army*, p. 187. The settlers were visualised as a garrison to be supplemented by field armies raised contractually in England.

56. M. H. Keen, *Later Middle Ages*, pp. 387–9.

57. CPR, 20/12/1358.

58. *Ibid.*, 5/10/1373.

59. *Ibid.*, 8/2/1374.

60. *Ibid.*, 5/3/1377.

61. (W. Percy) Hedley, (*Northumberland) Families*, Vol. 2 p. 48 ff.

62. Peasants etc., pp. 21 & 35.

63. PRO, E 134, Michaelmas 1621.

64. (J. M. W.) Bean, *The Estates (of the) Percy (Family 1416–1537)*, p. 65 & S. J. Watts, in *NH*, Vol. VI p. 66.

65. Spufford, *Contracting Communities*, p. 62.

66. PRO, SP 14 9A, 1604.

67. Spufford, *op cit.*, pp. 71–2. Paradoxically, a period of national economic depression (1333–1425) was studded with brilliant English victories.

68. PRO, E 134, Easter 1619 No. 13.

69. Bean, *Percy Estates*, pp. 64 & 67.

70. Peasants etc., pp. 145 & 158–9 (Sally Harvey) & 2.

71. *Cal.Inq.PM Ed I*, Vol. IV Item 166, 1300.

72. Moore, *Scottish Lands*, p. 41n.

73. *Cal.Inq.PM Hen VII*, Vol. I Item 971, 30/5/1494.

74. CCR, 20/4/1358.

75. CPR, 20/4/1360.

76. CCR, 10/7/1360.

77. CPR, 11/12/1371.

78. *Arch. Aeliana*, vol. XLIII (Fourth Series), p. 243 (J. B. Blake).

79. *Foedera*, Vol. III p. 645, 1362.

80. Northumberland RO Swinburne MSS, 2/34, 18/11/1364.

81. *Northumbrian Petitions*, ed. Surtees Vol. 176 Item 105 p. 127.

82. CCR, 13/4/1371.

83. *Northern Petitions*, ed. Surtees Vol. 194 Item 113, 1379–80.

84. in *NH*, Vol. XXI p. 51, quoting BL, Rot.Cot. XIII 8.

85. *Cal.Inq.PM Rich II*, Vol. XVI Item 470, 25/5/1386.

86. *Ibid.*, Item 1083, 1390.

87. CPR, 20/3/1404.

88. *Cal(endar of) Inq(uisitions) Misc(ellaneous in Chancery)*, Item 233, 28/9/1403.

89. See p. 58 below.

90. PRO, SP 14 109, 1619.

91. (*Essays in the) Economic and social History (of Tudor and Stuart England)*, ed. Joan Thirsk, pp. 70 & 77–8.

92. (Sir Frank) Stenton, *Anglo-Saxon England*, p. 314.

93. *Calendar of Letters and Papers relating to the Affairs of the Borders* (henceforth CBP), Vol. II Item 268, 18/5/1596.

94. William Gray, *Chorographia (or a Survey of Newcastle upon Tyne)*.

95. CBP, Vol. I Item 50, 2/5/1580.

96. See p. 70 below.

97. S. J. Watts, in *NH*, Vol. VI pp. 69–70 contends that gavelkind was not present in Tynedale at all, rejecting the witness of such contemporary experts as Sir Robert Bowes, Lord Eure, and Sir John Forster.

98. BL, Calig B VIII fol. 106, 1551.

99. J. A. Tuck, in *NH*, Vol. VI pp. 27–8 disbelieves in any such grouping in Tynedale either.

100. PRO, E 36 Vol. 40 fol. 29, 29/3/1539.

101. *LP*, IV(2) no. 4336, 6/6/1528.

102. Thomas Rae, *Scottish Frontier*, p. 5 & J. A. Tuck in *NH*, Vol. III p. 29.

103. *Agrarian History*, Finberg, Vol. IV p. 9.

104. Stenton, *Anglo-Saxon England*, p. 312.

105. (G. M.) Trevelyan, *(English) Social History*, p. 153.

106. CBP, Vol. II Item 763, 24/9/1597.

107. Cf. Camden's *Britannia*, cit. A. L. Rowse, *England of Elizabeth*: 'as it were the ancient nomads, a martial kind of men who from April into August lie out summering . . . with their cattle in little cottages here and there, which they call shiels and shielings'.

108. *Agrarian History*, Vol. IV p. 23.

109. Thomas Rae, *Scottish Frontier*, p. 10.

110. BL, Harl. 643 fol. 241, 17/4/1558.

111. CBP, Vol. II Item 245, 1/4/1596.

112. Thus a clock donated to Bellingham Town Hall in the last century was said by subscribers to have come from the four 'graynes' of Tynedale.

113. CBP, Vol. II Item 652, 8/6/1597. In 1583 graynes of Liddesdale Elliots comprised six to eleven able-bodied men each, sons or brothers to the heidsman.

114. BL, Calig B III fol. 6, 20/5/1524.

115. PRO. SP I 47 fol. 25, 28/2/1528.

116. Ibid., 96 fol. 169–173, 15/9/1535.

117. Thomas Rae, *Scottish Frontier*, p. 6.

118. PRO, SP I 157 fol. 50–1, 13/1/1540.

119. BL, Royal MSS 7 cxvi fol. 140–2, 22/1/1540.

120. *LP*, XVI no. 780, c.30/4/1541.

121. BL. Calig B VIII fol. 128, 1551.

122. Ibid., fol. 63, 2/12/1541.

123. Stention, *Anglo-Saxon England*, pp. 294–7.

124. Thomas Rae, *Scottish Frontier*, p. 7 'companies of wicked men coupled in friendship by reason of their surnames, or near dwelling together'.

125. C*(alendar of)* S*(tate)* P*(apers)* F*(oreign Series of the Reign of Elizabeth)*, anno 1865, no. 299, 19/11/1559.

126. (Edward) Hughes, *North Country Life (in the Eighteenth Century)*, p. xv.

127. M. H. Dodds, *Northumberland*, Vol. XV p. 156.

128. PRO. SP I 136 fol. 161–4.

129. BL, Add. MSS, 24965 fol. 126, c.3/12/1523.

130. (William) Bulleyn, *(A) Dialogue*.

131. By the end of the sixteenth century there were in fact plenty of Robsons in Redesdale.

132. See p. 22 above.

133. *LP*, XIX(1) no. 273, end March 1544.

134. *Ibid.*, XI no. 580, c.8/10/1536.

135. *Ibid.*, IV(1) no. 972, c.27/12/1524.

136. Bishop Fox p. 80. 1498.

137. (Howard) Pease, *(The Lord) Wardens (sic) of the Marches (of England and Scotland)*, p. 43.

138. BL. Calig.B VII fol. 236, 1/7/1525.

139. G. Macdonald Fraser, *The Steel Bonnets*, p. 86 ff., and *OED*.

140. *LP*, XII(1) no. 843, 6/4/1537.

141. 'The Rookhope Ride', in F. J. Child, *(English and Scottish Popular) Ballads*, p. 179.

142. 'The Raid of the Reidswyre', in Pease, *Wardens of the Marches*, p. 133.

143. *LP*, VIII(1) no. 666, 5/5/1535.

144. *CBP*, Vol. II no. 650, 6/6/1597.

145. (Godfrey) Watson, *(The Border) Reivers*, p. 97 gives a useful summary on peles, barmkins and bastles.

146. A. E. Prince, 'The Importance of the Campaign of 1327', in *EHR* Vol. L (1935), p. 299.

CHAPTER FIVE

The Percy Connexion in the Fifteenth Century

Unless it is credible that the militarily-organised kin-groups sprang fully armed from Zeus's head in the reign of Henry VIII, from which most direct evidence derives, then the chief houses soon after the conversion of tenures began to jostle the manors. Nevertheless, although their monopoly had been infringed, feudal elements continued to flourish alongside the clans, and often in the same individuals. Thus the ancestor of John Dodd, who occupied Dally Castle around 1600, would have paid rent for his tenant right to the King's Keeper and not, say, to a Swinburne lord of Chirdon on which Snabdaugh hard by Dally had always depended.[1] Other tenants-in-chief were freeholding heidsmen like Charlton of Hesleyside, while Hall (alias Harle) of Otterburn, not yet tenant-in-chief, was lord of a member manor as well as a Head Surname man. Like miniature Dukes of Argyll such men relished the dichotomy in their prestige. Once Redesdale had ultimately assimilated to the status of its twin, its freeholders, having subsequently lost that cachet again, left their new lord in no doubt that to be a tenant of the Duke of Norfolk's grandson was a poor substitute for tenancy in capite.[2]

That said, the feudatories with the most influence in the highlands had no family links with the Surnames at all. Just as their forerunners the free tenants in the thirteenth century had rubbed shoulders with pretenders to the Throne of Scotland, so these men counted earls in their ranks,[3] hobnobbing in some sense with whom was not calculated to breed a meek and submissive temper in the remainder. On the threshold of the fifteenth century there were three tenants-in-chief in particular whose fortunes were associated with those of the highlanders. The first was Heron of Ford and Chipchase, tied in with the Tynedalers; the second was the Lord Umfraville, ruler of Redesdale; and the third was Henry Percy, Earl of Northumberland, with interests in both Liberties.

By the time William Heron of Ford died in 1427 the Tynedale holdings of the family consisted of Chipchase, on the rim of the Liberty and acquired in 1348;[4] Haughton, Humshaugh and Simonburn in 1358;[5, 6, 7, 8] Bellingham in 1375; and Thornton. The inheritance surpassed that of the Comyns in the Talbot lands, which was why one Lord of Redesdale thought it worthwhile to concoct an abortive scheme to rob William's son John of the succession.[9, 10] Already the Heron estates were split between Chipchase on the one hand,[4] Ford and the rest on the other, but the two wings of the family were to stay on cordial terms for another 150 years. However, in dealings with third parties a violent streak was in evidence from time to time, as when in 1363 they had clubbed together to murder a Sheriff of Northumberland.[11]

As for the Umfravilles, their brilliance had as yet lost little of its sheen. Thus Sir Gilbert, ninth Lord of Redesdale, shared in the glamorous triumphs of Henry V, whose crowned helmet he had the honour of holding on a halberd during the celebratory banquet for Harfleur, and whose van he led in the advance to Agincourt.[12] Sir Robert, his uncle and despite bastardy successor in due course, was Vice-Admiral of England under the first Lancastrian Kings, but as doughty by land as by sea, worsting the Scots in three Border frays around 1400, with such booties as to attract the sobriquet of Robin-mend-the-Market. The death in 1436 of the great warrior was thus lamented by a faithful retainer:

> Of sapience and verray gentilnesse,
> Of liberal herte and knightly governaunce,
> Of hardiment, of trouthe, and grete gladnesse,
> Of honest mirthe withouten greviaunce,
> Of gentille bourdes [i.e. jests] and knightly dalliaunce,
> He hathe no make [i.e. equal], I dare right well avouwe,
> Now he is gone, I may nought gloss him nowe.[13]

The Norman had become a paragon among Englishmen, much as Wallace and Bruce among Scots.

It was on balance sad that he was the last of the Umfravilles, his nephew Gilbert having lost the will not merely to reproduce, but even to govern Redesdale. Having succumbed to the prevalent obsession with France, he was defeated and killed under the Duke of Clarence by a predominantly Scottish army at Baugé in Anjou in 1421. Victories like Verneuil were still to come, but this all the same was the first notable English defeat in close on a century of continental warfare, and sounded a knell.[14] Meanwhile, in the absence of *l'oeil du maître*, Redesdale still languished in the doldrums, a miserable relief of under £7 being paid for it in 1436 by the Umfravilles' successor as Lord.[15] The writing had been on the wall for the old family since Otterburn, when not they but the Percys led the English to defeat.[16] When the Crown sought a guardian for the young Gilbert de Umfraville, Henry Percy called Hotspur was given the election over Sir Robert's head.[17] It was this son of the first Percy Earl, too, who took revenge for Otterburn on Homildon Hill in 1402.

The suppression of the Umfravilles was symptomatic of the progressive intrusion of the most famous of all Northern Houses. By 1309 these descendants of Louis IV of France had established a Northumbrian bridgehead within the Barony of Alnwick,[18] and by 1500 the list of their manors would be breathtaking.[19, 20] In the meantime the vast territorial base had attracted power to a cumulative degree. Created Earl of Northumberland by Richard II in 1377, the third Lord Percy speedily came to look upon the North East as part of the family jewels. Growing awareness of this proprietary attitude left the King with misgivings that he sought to assuage through the appointment of John of Gaunt for two spells as Lieutenant in the North; and through the elevation to the Earldom of Westmorland of the head of the rival House of Neville. However, the only permanent setback sustained by the Percy Earl was the loss of his lands in Roxburghshire pursuant to the Scots' success in the intervening eighties.[21]

Given the nationwide spread of Percy interests, it would be idle to pretend that events in the two Liberties could ever have been a vital matter to them, but they could not ignore them either. It was not just that four of their biggest manors — Rothbury, Corbridge, Prudhoe and Ovingham — were within striking distance of Tyne- and Redesdales. More importantly, these Earls of Northumberland in the century after 1373 acquired more and more lands within the highlands themselves, so that when their fiefs came to be inventoried at their downfall many years later the chief surveyor in trepidation responded thus to the Lord Privy Seal: 'Your Lordship wroght (sic) unto me that I should go through all the lands of the Earl of Northumberland . . . Sure, if we shall peruse all, we must into Tynedale and Redesdale', in which eventuality 'we [must] be the better accompanied'.[22]

In 1381, through marriage to the Lady Maude, née Lucy and the widow of Gilbert de Umfraville, the first Earl inherited a third part of Redesdale, including the manor of Monkridge[23] and Otterburn Tower. Despite the allegedly still parlous state of the Liberty, Hotspur at the end of the century considered it practical to pay a bailiff eighty marks a year to manage these estates.[17] A century later the family also annexed Fawdon, where of olden time the Douglases in their English days had come to grief. In 1436, moreover, the second Earl was in effect strengthened by the replacement of the Umfravilles by the Tailboys, already Percy vassals in three Northumbrian manors;[24] on friendly terms with the Herons of Ford;[4] and unlike their predecessors unthinkable as rivals to the Percys. Because Sir Walter Tailboys spent as much time as he could in ancestral Lincolnshire, he appointed 'Roger Widdrington his lieutenant in Redesdale and constable of Harbottle . . . as well for war as for peace . . . dwelling in his proper person with his mesnie and household within the donjon of the said castle'.[25] Thereby the pattern of *de facto* Keepership instituted by Roger Mauduyt perceptibly hardened, and the presence of a professional manager — and the reference to war means that he was more than that — no doubt conduced to an upturn in prosperity which by 1462 had brought back the assessment of the fief to a respectable 100 marks *per annum*.[26] Given the Earl's substantial interests in the old Liberty, such economic improvement furnished an additional reason for gratification at the demise of the Umfravilles.

As for Tynedale, the Percys started in 1373 to absorb the Talbot lands, tenure of which gave them a foothold at both the top and bottom of the dale. The first step was a payment of £760 for the wardship pending marriage of the Atholl heiress, with custody of her Northumbrian tenements;[27] the second was Hotspur's outright acquisition, probably through purchase, of the Tynedale part of the patrimony in 1399.[28, 29] Since at some time during the fifteenth century the Herons came to hold Chipchase of the Earl[19] and were always faithful to their lord, the two branches of the family between them guaranteed the Percys secure bases alongside both Tynedale and Redesdale. Furthermore in 1444 John Heron of Chipchase became Sheriff of Northumberland and in 1455 Keeper of Tynedale,[4] no mean henchman to have. To sum up, by the time the fourth Earl became Edward IV's Warden of the Marches it was estimated that one-tenth of his total income, to wit £100 p.a., was derived from his Tynedale estates.[30]

Any attempt to weigh up the relationship between the great family and the highlanders involves some consideration of the former in its two fifteenth-century roles, firstly as lofty members of the Establishment. Although by no means invariable, the Percys' most durable loyalty was to the House of Lancaster: the first Earl and his redoubtable son Hotspur helped usurper Bolingbroke to the Throne as Henry IV; the second died for Henry VI at First St. Albans; Lord Egremont, a cadet, fell at Northampton; and the third Earl at Towton for the same cause. The extent to which their highland tenantry attended them, or were even present under other leadership on these battlefields is a matter for pure speculation. Concerned almost exclusively with the top layers of society, contemporary witness is silent on the subject from the time of Otterburn till that of Flodden, so that when acting within the law the clansmen cast only fleeting shadows. For all the intrusion of the Earl of Atholl in the previous century,[31] one would assume that they followed into legitimate battle not the Percys, but the Lords of their Liberties; and that, for example, the Tynedalers formed part of the 700 or 800 men for whom the Earl of Cambridge drew wages from Richard II, in the last quasi-feudal muster in English history. There is, however, no trace on that occasion in 1385 of an Umfraville or his Keeper among the admittedly incomplete list of tenants in chief.[95]

Now it could hardly have eluded Percy notice, in this their more public-spirited mood, that through intermediary of a government midwife a small monster had been brought to birth on the Middle Marches; or, at best, that a community made desperate by long harassment was becoming alive to the military power that had been somewhat thrust upon it. After banishment with his grandfather under Henry IV, the second Earl was redeemed from Scottish exile by Henry V in 1416 and summoned back to rule the Borders as Warden. In the precarious position of a young man newly reconciled, he could scarcely have been enraptured with the nationwide reputation for brigandage which the upland region was fast gaining. Rendered impotent through warfare and plague, the decimated commons of the northernmost counties in 1421 petitioned Parliament that many inhabitants had been 'destroyed by numerous robbers and felons called Intakers and Outputters[32] dwelling in the Franchises of Tynedale, Redesdale and Hexhamshire, against which malefactors they possessed no remedy, in so far as the said Liberties and Franchises are exempt from shrieval jurisdiction ['severez de guildable'] and the King's writ does not run'. The plea made to Parliament seven years before was repeated, namely that on pain of a fine now quintupled to £100 Lords of Liberties be commanded to prosecute such offenders forthwith,[33] a protest amplified by King Henry himself, who forwarded to the chamber a sheaf of complaints against the highlanders that had been laid on the steps of the very throne.[34]

No less embarrassing to the second Earl as Warden were further acts of violence perpetrated by the Tyne- and Redesdalers while he was serving Henry VI. One of his minor offices was the Stewardship of Knaresborough in the North Riding, where in 1441 his clients declined to pay customary tolls to the Archbishop of York for attendance at Ripon Fair. The Primate's response was to arrange for them to be terrorised by 200 men from his Hexhamshire tenantry and from Tynedale, currently still on cordial terms. Behaving as it was strangely said like the garrison of a besieged town, the visitors threw Ripon Fair into confusion, demanded of the townsmen with menaces sixpence to a shilling a day and 'bouche of court (i.e. rations)', and challenged the Knaresborough men to battle: 'Would God their knaves and lads of the Forest would come hider, that *we* might have a fair day on them!' Disappointed when the quarry did not put in an appearance, but reinforced with a hundred rascals from Beverley and York, the travellers resolved to sack Boroughbridge instead, from which they were headed off by Sir William Plumpton, a Percy vassal with a large force. The town was saved but the incident damaged relations between the Archbishop and the Earl.[35] Finally, as a vexatious distraction when Henry Percy had a fresh war with Scotland on his hands, he was in 1445 ordered to prosecute 'the evildoers, robbers and highwaymen dwelling in the Lordships of Tynedale and Redesdale, county of Northumberland, who mutilate, rob and slay the people thereof'.[36]

Like the highlanders themselves — now brigands, now defenders of the realm — the Earls of Northumberland could be as ambiguous as Jekyll and Hyde. Possession of the Talbot lands gave them a line into the heart of the clan community through the manor of Charlton, held of Tarset by one-twentieth of a knight's fee.[28, 29] In the middle of Tynedale, upriver from Bellingham and on the opposite bank from Hesleyside, Charlton was the ancestral seat of the chief grayne of the clan so named, as far back at least as the late thirteenth century.[37] Since it was still in the hands of the restored Percys in 1604,[3] and Charlton of Hesleyside (and Charlton) seems always to have been a throughgoing Percy vassal, the manor's omission from Mr. Bean's list for 1538 is puzzling.[38] However that may be, the Earls' connexions with the clans from an early stage went beyond the Charltons. Indicative of rapprochement was personal intervention by the first earl in 1397 to procure pardons, in respect of felonies committed before the Feast of the Purification, for Henry Dodd of Thorneyburn, and Robert his brother from Tarset;[39] and in respect of those dating to before the last Christmas, for Robert Hedley of Redesdale.[40] The fact is that there were grounds other than the territorial nexus for a growing familiarity between the great family and the Surnames. Conducive to a meeting of minds was that the Percys were as addicted as the latter to the vendetta, which the Earls pursued for generations with the Scottish Douglases and the English Nevilles: according to one theory it was a clash at Stamford Bridge in 1453 between Percys and Nevilles that provided the detonator for the Wars of the Roses.[41] When in that frame of mind, or whenever the Earls found themselves on the wrong side of the law, a temptation hard to resist was the proximity of a body of fierce clients, with a record as intimidators reaching back to Edward I; and who furthermore had virtually been subsidised for standing to arms at short notice. Because when the Percys found themselves, as it were, in opposition they could usually rely on the highlanders to rally to the Blue Lion rampant, it is in the three periods of the fifteenth century during which the Earls fell into royal disfavour that their relations with the Tyne- and Redesdalers will repay examination.

The first period lasted for the thirteen years after 1403 when, having proclaimed the restoration of Richard II, Hotspur was checkmated at the Battle of Shrewsbury. Although pardoned, his father was stripped of all office; of lands including his third of Redesdale;[17] and before long even of his titles. Since among others the Duke of York, Lord of Tynedale, was bidden in 1405 to levy fines on 'certain of the King's lieges lately in insurrection in the company of Henry, late Earl of Northumberland and wishing to seek the King's peace',[42] involvement of Tynedalers can be assumed. It was not long before the dispossessed Earl took refuge over the Border, whence in 1408 he was slain in a sortie, leaving the young second Earl a fugitive in Scotland but, to quote Rachel Reid, 'the efforts of his adherents, aided by the Scots of the Merse and the men of Tynedale, Redesdale and Hexhamshire to restore the Percys . . . kept the North in turmoil'.[43] The highlanders' contribution took the form of raids by marauding bands upon the farmsteads and market towns of those whom they chose to regard as ill-disposed towards the Earl's claims.[44] Shortly after Henry V's accession, they were singled out for denunciation by his inaugural Parliament in 1414 as 'large numbers of men from the Franchises of Tynedale, Redesdale and Hexhamshire', who not only committed 'many murders, treasons, homicides and robberies and other crimes' against the commons of Northumberland, but also aided and abetted Scots with counsel and comfort to abduct and hold the same for ransom. Not for the last time the remedy proposed was that for offences outside the Liberties the inhabitants be subjected to the Common Law: their lands outside the Liberties should be confiscated by the King, and those inside by the Lords or their Keepers, who for non-compliance ought to be fined up to £20.[33] Had the statute not remained a dead letter, the highlanders would have forfeited their most cherished privilege, but simultaneously the defensive system of the Middle Marches would have been undermined, which is why things were left exactly as they were.

What imparted a distinctive flavour to the second period, broadly the sixties, was the behaviour of the Tailboys Lords of Redesdale. William, who succeeded Walter in 1444 at the age of twenty-three,[45] was clearly more at home in their adoptive county than his father had been, so that familiarity with the lawless clans may go some way towards accounting for his lifestyle. However that may be, he proceeded to demonstrate what mayhem could be created with the armed power of the Liberty behind him. By 1447 he had been implicated in enough murder for the Duke of Suffolk's intimacy with him to have contributed largely to the discrediting of the Beaufort clique about Henry VI; while in 1450 he was accused in the House of Commons of having instigated the 'greatest riot in history', though at Westminster not in Northumberland. So gross had his offences become by 1459 that, despite impeccably Lancastrian credentials, room could be found for him in a list of twenty-five predominantly Yorkist persons attainted as 'universally throughout the realm famed and noised, known and reputed severally for open robbers, ravishers, extortioners and oppressors of the King's liege people'.[46]

Being each lord and vassal to the other, the Percys and Tailboys were members one of another to a peculiar degree. The third Earl had meanwhile been consolidating Lancastrian power in the north, where at the Battle of Wakefield in December 1460 he and his other chief henchman, John Heron of Ford, had helped cut down the Duke of York himself 'with great despite and cruel violence'.[47] The fleeting effect of this battle and of that shortly afterwards at Mortimer's Cross was to leave the kingdom divided between Henry VI and the Duke's heir, Edward IV, north and south of Trent respectively. Having done the Percys the signal service of recapturing Alnwick Castle for them, William Tailboys was appointed its captain at around the time the fourth Earl succeeded the third.[48]

Their enjoyments were short-lived, inasmuch as in March of that same 1461 Edward IV won a seemingly conclusive victory at Towton, where William Tailboys fought[45] and Heron of Ford died.[49] Given the spread of their estates, they were about as likely to have come to the field without the Redesdalers, and perhaps some of the Tynedalers as well, as without an arm and a leg. In a bid to make himself as much master in the North as in the South, it was natural enough at this juncture that the triumphant Edward should have assigned a high priority to the extirpation root and branch of the Percy establishment in Northumberland. His scheme was to supplant the Earls with attendant Herons and Tailboys by Sir Robert Ogle, rare among Northumbrian gentlemen as a Yorkist, and one of a mere eight knights advanced to the peerage for service to the new monarch. By stages Lord Ogle received Redesdale and Harbottle, which had been confiscated from the Tailboys;[50, 51] Ford and the Tynedale manors of the late Heron, posthumously likewise attainted of high treason,[52] coupled with an injunction to the beneficiary 'to seize Roger Heron the heir and keep the same';[49] and consequent upon the committal to the Tower of London of Henry Percy himself, the Talbot lands, valued at £10 p.a.[26] In the event Ogle found his resources overstretched and allowed this final item to drift away, first to the Duke of Clarence,[52] then to John Neville, to whom the King had lately consigned the Percy earldom.[53]

It was in fact the Nevilles who at the Battles of Hedgeley Moor and Hexham in 1464 put the finishing touches to the campaign against the old order in Northumberland. According to a story which it is not necessary to believe, but which inspired a bad contemporary song[54] and a well-known pre-Raphaelite painting, the Lancastrian Queen Margaret[55] and Prince of Wales were after Hexham rescued by one of the robbers with whom the woods were plausibly reputed to be infested. Allegedly she addressed her saviour thus: 'Man thou wast born under a lucky star. After all the wrong thou hast done, a chance is now given thee of doing a good deed that shall never be forgotten. It is to turn thee from thine old way of life that I, the wretched Queen of England, am fallen into they clutches'.[56] Meanwhile another fugitive from the battle, Sir William Tailboys, had taken refuge either among his Redesdale tenantry, or in North Tynedale, but was before long captured 'in a close place' farther to the east.[57] Much of the Queen's war-chest of £3000 was found in his possession, and he was subsequently beheaded at Newcastle. Through an Act of Attainder his heir was, in addition, shorn of such estates as had evaded the Ogles.[58, 59] Yet again, William's Redesdale vassals could scarcely have avoided participation in the disastrous campaign; that their Tynedale comrades had so been is directly attested by a letter from the King to the Archbishop of York in 1466, empowering him to readmit to the King's peace all those indicted of treason within the Liberties of Tynedale and Hexhamshire.[60, 61] From 1476 there is also extant a petition from the Prior of Hexham to Morton, later Cardinal Archbishop of Canterbury, in which a juxtaposition of grievances might be taken to suggest the highlanders had been employed to extort funds for the Lancastrian forces: the prelate speaks of the 'great necessity that we stond in at this time', both from 'the four hundred mark, aforetime lent unto Dame Margaret, late Queen of England' and from 'subtraction of our cattle by the thieves of Tynedale'.[62]

Whether Tailboys involvement in the second period of Percy estrangement from authority terminated with the Earl's imprisonment is a matter of opinion. By 1467 the alienation of the Nevilles from Edward IV was beginning to create opportunities for the dispossessed family to hit back, the upshot being in July 1469 nearly simultaneous risings[63] in the East Riding under Robert Hilliard, who assumed the *nom de guerre* of Robin of Holderness; and by 'northern men',[64] always a designator for Northumbrians rather than Yorkshiremen, under Robin of Redesdale. The former was crushed by John Neville, parvenu Earl of Northumberland, because outspokenly for the Percys; the latter he admitted to the South, because its aims were better disguised and on the calculation that the army of 20,000[65] constituted more of a threat to Edward IV than to the Nevilles. In fact such kinsmen of theirs as the Yorkshire Conyers did take part, with a share in the subsequent victory at Edgecote in Oxfordshire, which heralded a precarious couple of years for the King. However, during an interlude when the Yorkist King was briefly back in the ascendant, the Nevilles, despite the aid of his brother Clarence, failed to prevent the release of Henry Percy, who by March 1470 had been restored to his earldom. His rapprochement with the King was due to a common hostility to Warwick the Kingmaker, chief of the Nevilles, and to the lesson taught the monarch by Edgecote, that it was easier to rule the North with the goodwill of the Percys.

The identity of Robin of Redesdale has become as much matter for speculation as the Dark Lady of the Sonnets. Although the confusion among the welter of authorities is complete,[66] the favoured hypothesis, enshrined in the *Dictionary of National Biography* and in the standard work on the reign by Mr. Charles Ross,[67] but based ultimately on a chronicle by a nearly contemporary Cambridge don,[65] is that the nickname masked the identity of one of the Conyers brothers, who in the period 1469–70 latched on to any rebellion that was going. One is in short expected to believe that on just one of these four occasions[68] a Yorkshire gentleman, whose acknowledged status was as head of the Neville interest in its Richmondshire stronghold, would have needed to assume a *nom de guerre*, essentially a stratagem for one who out of obscurity seeks to cut a dash. Still less likely is that, striving for popular acclaim in a perilous enterprise, he would have plucked out of the air a title associating him with an area viewed with suspicion by inhabitants of the North Riding.

Whilst we are ignorant of the true identity of Robin of Redesdale, we do know who he ought to have been. On the analogy of Robert-with-the Beard, Robin-mend-the market and Robin of Holderness, it would appear likely that in a Christian age the bearer would never have renounced his baptismal name: thus the candidacy of Sir John and Sir William Conyers can be dismissed *ab initio*. Furthermore, with simultaneous risings by two Roberts in the same region, and both in the Percy cause, it would be natural that to avoid confusion each would append to his forename his place of origin, definitely Holderness in the one case, and logically Redesdale in the other. What advantages would the sobriquet Robin of Redesdale annexe as compared with Robert plus conventional surname? Firstly there was the glamour attaching to the name Robin Hood, still sufficiently alive for the Hexhamshire balladeer to have referred to Margaret's rescuer as 'of Robin Hood his race'.[54] Secondly, if conjecturally, it might be expected that so familiar a place-name would be better calculated to lure Redesdalers, and possibly Tyndalers too, out of the far north on an expedition. Now the sole individual satisfying the conditions implicit in the foregoing, and entitled anyway to call himself Robin of Redesdale, was Robert Tailboys, descendant of the first Robert de Umfraville, one of whose aliases had been Rob o' Redesdale; son-in-law of Sir John Heron of Chipchase,[69] and as such doubly conversant with the ways of Tyne- and Redesdales; and rightful heir of William Tailboys, Lord of Redesdale deceased. And assuredly, in the light of Robert Tailboys' connexions and grievances, no-one had more cogent motives for leading an insurrection against Edward IV, having lost his father on the scaffold; his own estates, like those of his friends the Herons of Ford, having been confiscated; and the Earl he looked upon as liege lord imprisoned and similarly disinherited.

There is one further coincidence lending marginal support to what is admittedly no more than a tentative theory concerning the identity of Robin of Redesdale. During the year following his revolt Lincolnshire, ancestral seat of the Tailboys, intrudes upon this narrative for the only occasion in the 500 years preceding the Pilgrimage of Grace. Thus when the Northern men were actually on the march to Edgecote they had been substantially reinforced out of Lincolnshire.[70] Then, around February 1470, men of the county rose again, this time against Edward IV's local standard-bearer, Sir Thomas Burgh, who had grown fat at their expense. On this second occasion the soldierly King advisedly took the field in person, duly carrying the day over 30,000 men. Once again Robert Tailboys should have had every motive for being of their number: not only was he closely related to Lord Welles, the ringleader,[71] but the Percy restoration that had got under weigh in October had not been accompanied by his own, so any marriage of convenience with the Nevilles could well have persisted into the second uprising. Through cession of their lands in Kesteven and Lindsey, pursuant to the attainder, the Tailboys had in fact been the biggest losers in the county to Sir Thomas.[72, 73] Finally, just as we suspect in the person of Robert Tailboys a denominator common to the two insurrections, so contemporaries, too, seemed aware of a connexion: Edward's victory was not in the usual way labelled with some such place-name as Stamford, but dubbed Lose-cote field, an obvious play on the name Edgecote.[74]

It must be none the less emphasised that the sparse records make no mention of the heir to Redesdale, which is hard to explain away merely on the grounds of the obsession of Yorkist chroniclers with the turpitude of Clarence and Warwick.[75] Of course, if the hypothesis were correct as to the identity of Robin of Redesdale, then mention of that individual would have done as well. That this, too, is missing is however less surprising since such a *nom de guerre* would have rung no bells with East Anglians.

In the interregnum between September 1470 and June 1471, during which Henry VI resumed his rule, commissioners *de waliis et fossatis* were appointed to defend the East Coast against Edward IV, who had taken refuge in Holland. Mr. Charles Ross has remarked[76] that 'never had commissioners of array for national defence been placed in the hands of so few,' yet room for Robert Tailboys was found among that select band alongside such notables as the Duke of Clarence, the Earl of Oxford and the Marquis Montacute[77, 78] — surely a tribute to recent military prowess as well as to sound Lancastrian politics. When shortly afterwards Edward IV tried to land in the area in question, he was driven off and disembarked in Yorkshire instead, whence he improbably sprang to win crowning victories at Barnet and Tewkesbury. Robert Tailboys' rehabilitation continued apace in spite of the Yorkist restoration. Notorious as was Edward IV for beheading foes in the heated aftermath of battle, he was equally well-known for indulgence towards any that escaped the instant axe. Even if this did not apply in Tailboys' case — let no questions be begged — what *was* applicable was that as a strong legitimist the monarch was always loth to see heirs of good family lose their inheritance.[79] In the decade 1471–81 this servant of Lancaster and the Percys successively filled every public office in Lincolnshire,[69, 80, 81] which he clearly preferred to Northumberland as place of residence.

In that county where Sir Robert all the same retained substantial interests, the King consolidated the work interrupted in 1470. On reversal of his father's attainder in 1472, Tailboys became Lord of Redesdale as well as titular Earl of Kyme.[25, 82] Both branches of the Herons were resuscitated: Sir Roger was to die peaceably as squire of Ford in the early eighties, to be succeeded by John, a minor, while his cousins had Chipchase back in their hands before 1477. The fact that the new John Heron of Chipchase was grandson to the original Lord Ogle[83] may have consoled the baron's progeny for abrupt ejection from lands enjoyed for a bare decade.

The third period during which the Percys' power was curbed, with repercussions around the two Liberties, occurred in Henry VII's reign. This attack was the most insidious and conclusive of all.

In few fields did the policy of the first Tudor lack for Yorkist precedents. Thus after the reconciliation the fourth Earl had been generously treated by Edward IV, who entrusted him with the Northumbrian Wardenries,[84] while subsequently Richard III not only confirmed the appointment but also made him Bailiff *alias* Keeper of Tynedale,[85, 86] indicative of the degree to which the link between Earl and clansmen was appreciated. None the less the brakes *were* applied, albeit subtly. Had Henry Percy played a more active role at Barnet and Tewkesbury, he might have inspired greater confidence. The upshot was that during the reign of the elder Yorkist the Earl had to share vice-royalty with the younger,[87] and after Gloucester's accession with the Council of the North that he had left behind to watch his interests.[88] Before that, Edward IV had in the time-honoured fashion allocated Tynedale to his uncle the Earl of Essex, 'to hold by fealty only, without fine or fee, except 20/4d. only'.[89] Nor was the scope for royal intervention in the old Liberty curtailed, given that its Lord, who had as likely as not been Robin of Redesdale, now acted as an absentee. The position of his bailiff, in this case one Richard Musgrave,[90] became in consequence firmer than ever, a tendency which the succession to the Lordship of George Tailboys, an idiot, did nothing to nullify.[91]

At his accession Henry VII was determined that the fourth Earl should be allowed to live down neither former abandonment of the Lancastrian cause, nor duplicity on Bosworth Field, where he had held off till it was obvious who was going to win. At the same time the King realised that, in the delicate circumstances of 1485, the House of Percy was indispensable both as stabiliser in the North and as bulwark against Scotland, and therefore, like Henry V and Edward IV before him, judged it opportune to release the Earl from the Tower and restore him to lands and offices.[92, 93] After four years the sovereign felt sufficiently sure of himself to take advantage of an opportunity that either offered itself, or was of his own machination, when Henry Percy was assassinated by a royal forester. The resultant long minority was exploited to set clamps on the huge inheritance. Not till late in life was the fifth Earl invited to officiate in the Border Wardenries, long reckoned the family's perquisite, and he was to be dancing irrelevant attendance on a King miles away in France while the invader was being crushed at Flodden in his native Northumberland.[94]

NOTES

1. PRO, E 134, Michaelmas 1622.
2. PRO, SP 14 109, 1619.
3. Ibid., 9A, 1604.
4. Hedley, *Families*, Vol. II p. 48 ff..
5. CDRS, Vol. IV Item 2.
6. *Ibid.*, Item 4.
7. CPR, 20/12/1358.
8. Moore, *Scottish Lands*, pp. 44–7.
9. CPR, 12/5/1439.
10. CCR, 12/11/1439.
11. J. A. Tuck, in *NH*, Vol. VI p. 36.
12. (A. H.) Burne, (*The*) *Agincourt War*, pp. 46 & 54.
13. Hodgson, *Northumberland*, Pt II. Vol. I, pp. 48–58.
14. Burne, *Agincourt War*, p. 153 ff..
15. Hodgson, *Northumberland*, Pt II Vol. I p. 61.
16. (Edward) Miller, *War in the North* (*The Anglo-Scottish Wars of the Middle Ages*), pp. 3 & 19.
17. CPR, 20/3/1404.
18. *Foedera*, Vol. II p. 99.
19. *Cal. Inq. PM Hen VII*, Vol. III, 12/4/1489.
20. And for the enormous power of the Percys (and Nevilles) by 1397, see Keene, *Later Middle Ages*, p. 295 ff..
21. J. A. Tuck, in *NH*, Vol. III pp. 27–52 *passim*: 'the most powerful

Border family from 1363 onwards'. With unconvincing iconoclasm, it has become fashionable in some quarters to dispute this verdict.

22. PRO, SP I 121 folios 169–170, 26/6/1537.

23. Hodgson, *Northumberland*, Pt II Vol. I pp. 45 & 100.

24. (M. E.) James, *A Tudor Magnate (and the Tudor State)*, p. 21n.

25. *N(orthumberland) and D(urham) Deeds*, p. 21 Item 8, 6/4/1438.

26. CPR, 28/1/1462.

27. *Ibid.*, 8/7/1373.

28. *Ibid.*, 17/11/1399.

29. Bean, *Percy Estates*, p. 8.

30. *Arch. Aeliana*, Vol. XI p. 184.

31. See p. 32 above.

32. The former presumably being a receiver of stolen property and the latter an organiser of raids.

33. *Rot. Parl.*, IV 21A, 1414.

34. Hodgson, *Northumberland*, Pt II Vol. I p. 60.

35. Plumpton (*Correspondence*, ed.) Camden Society, Vol. IV pp. liv–lvii, and *History of Northumberland*, Vol. III Pt I (Hexhamshire), p. 41.

36. CPR, 19/12/1447.

37. Charlton, *North Tynedale*, p. 12.

38. *Op. cit.* p. 110.

39. CPR, 15/2/1397.

40. *Ibid.*, 16/2/1397.

41. (R. L.) Storey, *(The End of the) House of Lancaster*, p. 27.

42. CPR, 26/4/1405.

43. *Op. cit.*, p. 39.

44. Moore, *Scottish Lands*, p. 14.

45. Hedley, *Families*, Vol. II p. 5.

46. *Rot. Parl.*, V 357.

47. *Ibid.* 477, 1461.

48. (Charles) Ross, *Edward IV*, p. 147.

49. CPR, 2/5/1461.

50. *Ibid.*, 20/2/1462.

51. *Rot. Parl.*, 598B, 1467/8.

52. CPR, 10/8/1462.

53. *Ibid.*, 1/8/1464.

54. 'A song made in Edward IV his time of the Battle of Hexham', of which there are two copies in the Bodleian.

55. In *Arch. Aeliana*, Vol. XXX (Fourth Series) pp. 59–61, Dorothy Charles argues that the Queen had left England in the August before the battle, but accepts the likelihood of an encounter between her and a robber at some time after Towton, in which case western Northumberland would seem as appropriate a venue as any.

56. Bates, *Northumberland*, p. 198.

57. Charles, *op. cit.*, p. 68.

58. (E. F.) Jacob, *(The) Fifteenth Century (1399–1485)*, p. 539.

59. *Rot. Parl.* V 477, 1461.

60. Hodgson, *Northumberland*, Pt III Vol. II p. 386.

61. *Rot. Parl.*, V 311, 5/7/1466.

62. *Priory of Hexham*, ed. Surtees Vol. 44 cv, 1474.

63. Ross, *Edward IV*, p. 126 & Appendix IV tends to the opinion that Holdernesse was sandwiched between two spurts by Redesdale.

64. (Edward) Hall, *Chronicle* (*being the Union of the two Noble and Illustre Families of Lancaster and York*), *passim* especially p. 273.

65. (John) Warkworth, *Chronicle* (*of the first thirteen years of Edward IV*, ed. Camden Vol. 10), p. 6.

66. Ross, *op. cit.*, p. 126: 'Contemporary narrative accounts are meagre, confused and contradictory and both the character and chronology of these rebellions remain obscure'. He goes on to say (App. IV) that this is reflected in the confusion among modern authors, giving examples.

67. *Op. cit.*, p. 128.

68. '*Patronage (Pedigree and Power)*', ed. (Charles) Ross, pp. 37–42, being an article by A. J. Pollard on the Richmondshire gentry.

69. J. C. Wedgwood, *History of Parliament* (1439–1509), p. 834.

70. Ross, *Edward IV*, pp. 139–140.

71. *N & D Deeds*, pp. 219 & 223.

72. CPR, 1461 –7, pp. 151 & 3711.

73. An article by R. L. Storey in *Nottingham Studies*, XIV (1970), p. 72.

74. Ross, *Edward IV*, p. 138.

75. *Ibid.*, Appendix V.

76. *Ibid.*, p. 157.

77. John Neville had been raised to the Marquisate as compensation for relinquishment of the Earldom of Northumberland.

78. CPR, 3/2/1471.

79. Cf. Keen, *Later Middle Ages*, p. 501 & M. A. Hicks, in NH, Vol. XX, pp. 24 & 32.

80. CPR, *Commissions of the Peace 1467–75*, pp. 620–1.

81. *Ibid.*, 7/3/1472.

82. *Rot. Parl.*, VI 18A.

83. Hedley, *Families*, Vol. 2 p. 45 ff..

84. Reid, *Council in the North*, p. 46.

85. CPR, 7/1/1486.

86. Reid, *op. cit.*, p. 60.

87. Ross, *Edward IV*, p. 200 ff.

88. Reid, *op. cit.*, Chapter III at large.

89. CPR, 16/7/1474.

90. *N & D Deeds* p. 221, 1483.

91. CPR, 15/5/1499.

92. *Ibid.*, 11/3/1477.

93. *Rot. Parl.*, VI 344, 1485.

94. M. E. James, *Tudor Magnate*, pp. 3–36 *passim* and N. A. Hicks, in NH, Vol. XIV p. 78.

95. N. B. Lewis, 'The Last Mediaeval Summons of the English Feudal Levy', in *EHR* Vol. lxxiii (1958), p. 2 ff.; S. Armitage-Smith, *John of Gaunt*, Appendix 2; J. J. N. Palmer, 'The Last Summons of the Feudal Army in England', in *EHR* Vol. lxxxiii (1968), p. 771 ff..

CHAPTER SIX

A Foretaste of Anarchy under Henry VII

The measures taken by Henry VII to fill the vacuum he had engineered in Northumberland were redolent of downgraded priorities. It was Baron Darcy, an individual more remarkable for religious fervour than anything else, whom the King's successor was to find as Warden of the Northumbrian Marches on assuming the Crown.[1] So thin was officialdom on the ground that in 1495 it fell to the Bishop of Durham to array the men not only from his County Palatine, but also from 'the King's Lordships of Redesdale (sic) and Tynedale'.[69] Although an excellent soldier, Lord Dacre of Gillsland, who became at one stage Constable of Harbottle and virtual Keeper of Redesdale, was greatly weakened by the enormous bonds for good performance wrongfully[2] extracted from him during the reign, portions of which were retained even after discharge of the apposite obligations.[3] For all his bravery Dacre was in any case no substitute for a war lord like Henry Percy whose power, baleful on occasion, had worked on the whole as a factor against anarchy.

As the discipline and cohesion imposed by the Earls of Northumberland wore off, vassals such as the Collingwoods, the Ratcliffes of Dilston, the Horseleys of Scrainwood, the Widdringtons, and the Swinburnes of Capheaton forsook a dying planet for the royal sun. In 1510, for instance, Sir Edward Ratcliffe became without Percy intervention one of the Lieutenants of the Middle Marches, with special responsibility for Redesdale, receiving £35 p.a. for his pains.[4]

Gentry of this class were joined by others like the Ogles who, though in no discernible feudal relationship, had been similarly vulnerable hitherto to the Percys' sheer social presence. Most notable of these were the Fenwicks who clustered around the middle reaches of the Wansbeck, halfway between Redesdale and Morpeth,[5] and whose forbear Sir Henry had supported the then Earl against the Nevilles in 1453.[6] Like, say, the Charltons of Tynedale,[7] the Fenwicks lived fairly close together and were prone to squabble among themselves. On the other hand there were more gentlemen among them than in the Tynedale Surname or the Halls *alias* Harles of Redesdale. In the first quarter of the next century the Fenwicks would be worth over £150 p.a. between them and could field one hundred horsemen, including Sir John of Stainton worth forty marks p.a. and with twenty horseman; Sir John of Wallington £100, with forty; and Anthony of Longshaws twenty marks, with twenty–one at least being rated 'a true toward gentleman'.[8] In 1321 Sir John Fenwick had been Sheriff of North-umberland,[9] while around July 1509 Sir Roger set a pattern for those of his surname when paired with the aforementioned Ratcliffe as Lieutenant and virtual Keeper of Tynedale.[1] The hallmark of the Fenwicks from the fourteenth century onwards had in a word been loyalty to the Crown, so that in its last quarter John of Gaunt, as Richard II's Lieutenant in the North, was driven to rely disproportionately on that extended family, through lack of any territorial base in their part of the country.[10] The trouble was that the Fenwicks, for all their royalism,[11] had more than their share of incompetents and black sheep.

Other gentry such as the Shaftoes of Bavington, the Erringtons, the Herons of Chipchase and Ford, and the Lisles of Felton and Woodburn in Redesdale,[12] as well as the Ridleys of Willimontswyke — who alone apparently were not Percy vassals, but subject to tug or repulsion from their neighbours — became unpredictably eccentric in their orbits. For much of the time they too assumed office under the Crown. Thus in 1491 Nicholas Ridley succeeded the defunct Earl himself as Bailiff alias Keeper of Tynedale, with the lordship of Plenmellor as wages.[13] Meanwhile by 1489, even before John Heron of Harbottle had entered into his inheritance as heir to Sir Roger of Ford,[14] he had been serving Sir Robert Tailboys as his lieutenant in Redesdale. No mere farm-manager this to a bunch of manors, but bound under penalty of £500 to prosecute felons and evildoers and prevent criminal intercourse between Redesdalers and Scots.[15] In other words Heron's obligations were to the King as well as the landlord, so that he was patently opposite-number already to the Keeper of Tynedale; his appointment was made substantive in 1494.[16] In post until death in action in 1497, he was specifically described thirty years later, when terms had become standardised, as having been 'Keeper of Redesdale, if but short time', prior to replacement by brother William upon the latter's succession to Ford. Before replacement in *his* turn by the incompetent Ratcliffe, Sir William[17] was in 1500 addressed by the Bishop of Durham, Richard Fox, in a precept to catch some wretched witch, as 'capitanus de Redesdale', without any glance at the Tailboys at all.[18] Such appointments were after all only to be expected out of a class on which the Tudors relied elsewhere for justices of the peace.

More significant, however, were gentlemen of the same stripe — often the same individuals — who on occasion yielded gratefully to temptation. That some of the Herons, for example, performed efficiently as Border officers cannot palliate their familiarity in his time with William Tailboys, or the notoriety as a brigand of John of Crawley, Sir Roger's acknowledged bastard.[14] One of the bonds illegally wrung from Lord Dacre during Henry VII's reign had been framed to ensure the good behaviour of Sir William Heron.[3] While such gentry could from time to time aspire to the lustre of treason, they were more commonly to become implicated in the more humdrum business of criminal association.

The more inoffensive accepted the highlanders as part of the landscape or weather, regrettable, but impossible to do anything about. A Bishop of Carlisle once confided to a Lord Chancellor: 'The gentlemen seeth them which did rob them and their goods and dare neither complain of them by name, nor say one word to them. They take all their cattle and horses, their corn as they carry it to sow or to the mill to grind; and at their houses bid them deliver what they will have, or they shall be fired and burned'.[19] Blackmail was regularly paid 'whereby gentlemen's goods were spared and poor men's spoiled',[20] and passive acceptance of protection money shaded into downright cooperation. Richard Fox in 1498 berated the foremost men in the region, not excluding royal justices, for sheltering and abetting Tyne- and Redesdale thieves, 'either under excuse of an indemnity, or from friendship and alliance, or because bribed'.[21] Such aspersions continued to echo into the next century, when the cover provided for highland marauders by complacent landowners was stigmatised as the ruin of Northumberland,[8] while cadets of good family vied with predatory heidsmen in wildness and oppression of the poor.[20] Lord Burghley would be assured that Northumbrian gentlemen often preferred to bargain with thieves than to surrender them to justice.[22] The most radical step that a gentleman might take was to assume the leadership of such malefactors, which not infrequently happened.

First among the reasons why the highlanders were receptive to overtures from disaffected gentry was that they were by no means exempt from the countrywide deference towards the upper class, to members of which they looked for organisation and thrust, supplying muscle in exchange. Secondly there were the economic trends that characterised the period 1470–1550. Cloth exports trebled, and as a rule prices of wool certainly, and of meat probably, outstripped those of grain;[23] there was furthermore a brisk demand for hides in Germany, still the main source of European silver. By and large, then, the pastoral uplands should have continued to thrive, but there were qualifications. Neither Liberty was proof against the national tendency for rents and fines to increase,[24] nor against the doubling in the price of consumer goods relative to wages.[25] Despite the tenurial conversion Redesdale in particular did not maintain the burst of recovery discernible in the mid-fifteenth century. At the death of Sir Robert Tailboys in 1494 the value of his lands there was set at no more than twenty marks p.a., held of the King by one quarter of a knight's fee; Harbottle Castle and Otterburn Tower were written off as valueless, as were 200 messuages because 'no profit can be taken therefrom on account of the Scots'. Hard to interpret as on balance the statistics are, our putative Robin of Redesdale obviously deemed insufficient to lure him out of Lincolnshire 3000 acres of meadow valued at between a halfpenny and one penny an acre; 1000 acres of arable and 300 acres of woodland worth 6/– each; 25,000 acres of pasture worth 20/– p.a. in all; and twenty cottages at threepence each.[26]

One factor to attenuate prosperity was demographic. In the two centuries after 1470 the national population was to double. In both Liberties, especially Redesdale, the tendency had been additionally promoted by the toleration of partible inheritance, which in a vicious circle population growth made more arduous to operate. 'There be more inhabitants within either of them', wrote Browes, 'than the said countries may sustain to live truly, for upon a farm of a noble [i.e. 6/8d.] rent there do inhabit in some places there three or four householders, so that these cannot upon so small farms without any other craft live truly', with the result that 'the young and active people, for lack of living, be constrained to steal and spoil continually either in England or Scotland', 'the great occasion of the disorder of both those countries'.[27, 68] More modernly, G. M. Trevelyan in his work on the Middle Marches has spoken of a 'great surplus population . . . in North Tynedale and Redesdale . . . which had to find its subsistence by raiding outside the valley bounds'.

With the awe of the Percys removed by Henry VII they were more inclined than ever to bring into play those peles and bastles that 'stood alone . . . upon strong and inaccessible cleughs, morasses, woods or suchlike desolate . . . places, whereunto they have heretofore used to convey all their spoils and preys'.[28] Indicative of truculence spread over many years was a rebuke from the perceptive Richard Fox in 1498 to 'the infamous and blatant robbers of Tynedale and Redesdale, about the crimes of which they had been boasting in taverns and other public places, and in which they had been bringing up their offspring . . . shifting their plunder of cattle and moveables back into the highlands by night or day'. Having waited on the Bishop in the Galilee of Durham Cathedral,[21] a Charlton, three Milburns, three Robsons and five Dodds received conditional absolution in due course at Norham Castle on September 25th. As a first-class civil servant Fox was uneasily unaware that affairs in the highlands were getting out of hand, and therefore laid down that the offenders except against the King's enemies were to wear no weapons longer than a cubit, especially in church, where they were to talk to no-one but the priest.[29] Just before Henry VII's death the clansmen bore out the Bishop's worst fears that, as in the days of his predecessor Antony

Bek, they were at the disposal of anyone rich and unscrupulous enough. A dispute having erupted about harbour dues between the municipality of Newcastle and the Prior of Tynemouth, 'five hundreth persons . . . riotously . . . with spears, glaives [i.e. swords], bows and arrows by the exhortation of the said Prior assembled together at Tynemouth . . . and with them in company great number of the inhabitants of Tynedale and Redesdale to whom . . . the . . . riot was committed. The Prior gave wages sixpence a day . . . that the said misdemeaned persons by his commandment should have murdered the mayor and aldermen . . . And so in harness . . . daily rode about . . . Newcastle by the space of six days . . . and . . . imprisoned [many of the inhabitants] . . . at Tynemouth . . . The said Prior said, though they killed one hundreth of the caitiffs dwelling in Newcastle, he should be their warrant . . . The inhabitants . . durst not for dread of their lives go to their ships at Shields . . . but kept them close within the walls . . . as though they had been assieged with enemies'.[30]

Over against Scotland, too, the withdrawal of Earls of Northumberland for nearly half a century removed a restraint. Because each party favoured Lancaster and was hostile to a House of Douglas that challenged the Stuarts for the Throne of Scotland, no less than the Percys for the Forest of Jedburgh,[31] Kings James II and III were more often than not on good terms with the Earls in the fifteenth century. Now that the highlanders were off the leash, their craving for plunder could be as well satisfied north as south of the Border, so it becomes appropriate at this point to examine the attitude of the Tyne- and Redesdalers to the foreign neighbour.

To begin with, he was foreign only in a technical sense. So far as the London housewife was concerned, the Robson in the old play was indistinguishable from a Scot in accent and demeanour, and he in fact belonged to the Anglo-Scottish fraternity that produced the Border ballads, and which in Mr. Rae's sensible view formed a peculiar entity, separate from either kingdom.[32] Specifically with the English highland clans in mind, G. M. Trevelyan observed that 'like the Homeric Greeks the Borderers were cruel and barbarous men, slaying each other like beasts of the field, but high in pride and honour and rough faithfulness'.[33] Common to all members of that society was the zest for the chase, which animated young highlanders in their misdeeds as much as a compulsion to make ends meet.[27] Or the concern for decorum of Barty Milburn of the Pele who, on catching sight of men sent to kill him, cried out to his wife: 'Wife, bring me out a clean sark; it sall never be said that the bluid of the Milburns ran doon upon foul linen'.[34] Or the jealousy for reputation of a namesake of the Combe, who was as sedulous as any Red Indian with his scalps to bring back as trophies the swords of two slain pursuers.[35] For all Borderers alike life was a ceremonious as well as a bloody business, and for the common run of Englishmen the inhabitants of the two Liberties were not merely a race apart, but Scots rather than English, men 'whom the neighbouring Scots have rendered yet more hardy, sometimes inuring them to war, and sometimes amicably communicating their customs and way of living'.[36]

What fortified the impression were family ties with adjacent parts of Scotland. Resident in Teviotdale were pockets of Robsons,[37] Potts[38] and Halls *alias* Harles, whose settlement was probably attributable to dispersal during the War of Independence, when some of the last-named at least had thrown in their lot with the rebel Gilbert de Middleton.[39] Without recognised heidsmen, and therefore 'broken men and every man's prey', they nevertheless preserved a connexion with southern kinsfolk meaningful enough to affect behaviour. It was the prominence of Halls and Robsons in a Scottish incursion in the next reign which made the English Warden suspect that family loyalties could transcend those due to the realm, since at that particular time Tynedale was never in better order.[40] Conversely when Robsons of Fawslaw and Plenderleith were attacked by Tynedalers, the Robsons alone of all the Head Surnames had the delicacy to abstain from the invading force.[41]

Of more perennial importance was the relationship with neighbouring Liddesdale, a deep, narrow and well-wooded glen hemmed in by low, blunt hills. Rising in the Cheviots with its twin fork of Hermitage Water, the Liddel for one third of its twenty miles marks the frontier between England and Scotland. Within the isthmus formed by the stream before merging with the Esk, the fields belonged to Canonbie Priory, which like a hinterland of meadows to the east and south along the Esk was almost till the Union of the Crowns debatable between them. Hence the name Threaplands (from the verb 'threap': to argue) by which the 7000 acres were known to the Borderers.[42]

In several respects this dale between the Middle and West Marches of Scotland[43] was a mirror-image of Tyne- and Redesdales, inasmuch as it too was populated by a tribe who were by season dalesmen or highlanders, and who derived mainly from four Head Surnames. Thus the Head or northern reaches of Liddesdale was occupied by the Elliots around Thorlieshope; by the Croziers of Riccarton; and by the Nixons. The more numerous Armstrongs predominated in the south from Mangerton all the way to Gilnockie. Like their English neighbours, they were in the late Middle Ages governed by a Keeper appointed by their King, but more often a nobleman and independent of intermediate officers than southern counterparts. Just as the Redesdale Keeper's deputy, when he had one, was Constable of Harbottle, so the

Liddesdale Keeper's was *ex officio* Captain of the Hermitage, a moat-girt tower on the green flats, the most daunting and ancient in Scotland. Whereas the English dales were Liberties, so Liddesdale was a Lordship, the owner of which in Tudor times was the Earl Bothwell, often Keeper as well. To the more intermittent influence of such Earls as Maxwell, there were parallels in Tyne- and Redesdales too. Again, like Tynedale, the Lordship had undergone a mediaeval sojourn in the other realm that had loosened without severing the ties of allegiance. What made these yet flimsier was that three of the Surnames had immigrated from the south between 1230 and 1376, and could still be regarded as 'evil Inglis' three centuries later.[44]

Liddesdale was tricky to get into[45] and as replete as the English highlands with such hide-outs as the Tarras Moss.[44] It also was bursting with population[46] and it would not be long before it was credited with a thousand horsemen.[44] All the same the proximity of the Threaplands offered outlets for expansion not available to its English neighbours. Despite the presence in the south thereof of the Grahams, another warlike clan marginally more Scots than English,[47] the Armstrongs were to commence infiltration in 1518.[48] The other solution open to the Liddesdalers was rapine in England and Scotland.

Resembling one another in nature, predicament and style, the people of the three dales tended to draw together. Since North Tyne and Liddel Heads were less than five miles apart, and there were seven well-trodden paths east and west,[49] the Larriston and Caplestone Fells and the Kershope Forest never prevented the Elliots and Robsons from visiting each other or even intermarrying.[50] That the legendary grave of the Cowt of Kielder, a Tynedale giant slain in the fourteenth century, should have lain in a barrow outside Hermitage Castle symbolised intertwined fates, if not invariable friendship. Nationality still counted enough for the Liddesdalers never to achieve or to seek the link with the others that welded Tynedale to Redesdale. Nevertheless in his day Bowes would justifiably deplore 'that unlawful confederation that tendeth alway to the spoiling and destruction of the true subjects of both the said realms . . . if Your Majesty . . . do not prevent . . . the malignity of their said evil purposes. Their countries are of great strength, lying so near together that one of them may aid in time of their necessities . . . the other. This makes them so proud and bold that they dread nor be in obedience unto any officer or laws'.[45]

Yet in spite of the affinities, and similar to Czechs and Slovaks, the Tyne- and Redesdalers on the one hand, and most Scottish Marchers on the other, were mutually obnoxious. The Robson in the play was outraged at the housewife's mistake.[51] For all their Liberty's sojourn as a pendant in Scotland's ear, the Tynedalers were never looked upon by the

Scots or themselves as anything but Englishmen. As for the Redesdalers, *their* Englishry was never queried even by their compatriots. Whereas on private errands the highlanders despoiled neighbours of either nation with a fine impartiality they were never anywhere but in the English ranks when it came to a formal battle. With the larger dale it had not always been so, given the capricious loyalty of the manorial lords there during the War of Independence. However, owing to the elimination of the more dubious Anglo-Normans; the ravages endured at the hands of the Scots invaders; and the tenurial conversion, the change of heart had been complete.

Certainly there was ample scope for hostility in the fifteenth century, because of the claims to suzerainty over Scotland that England continued to advance. The warfare that bubbled up between them from time to time never ended in a definitive peace, only in a renewal of truce.[52] Whereas the English were lamed by the terminal stages of the Hundred Years' War, then by the Wars of the Roses, the Scots under James III and IV forged ahead in military power. In the period 1460–4, taking proper advantage of Edward IV's distractions in establishing his supremacy over Lancaster, James III acquired Berwick as a bribe from the latter, and Roxburgh, last English stronghold in Scotland, by force of arms.[53] The natural consequence was a widespread English sentiment that any blow at the Scots must have some merit in it, which meant that the highlanders were free to disrupt any truce with impunity from their own authorities. In 1475, for example, the Scots King rebutted a complaint from the English Warden about Liddesdale with a *tu quoque* that 'in lik wiss oure liegis ar richt complaintewss of Inglismen duelland within Tindaile and Riddisdaile, quhilkis daili makis depredacionis and herschippis upon oure liegis'.[54] It was just such charge and counter-charge that entangled Scotland in the war of 1480–4 during which she again lost Berwick as well as, more temporarily, her capital city to the later Richard III.[55]

Long after renewal of the truce, in March 1494, Scottish commissioners including Walter Kerr of Cessford and the Abbot of Jedburgh; and English commissioners including the Baron Dacre, John Heron of Ford Keeper of Redesdale, and namesake of Chipchase presumably Keeper of Tynedale, met and jointly endorsed a complaint from the Prior of Canonbie and other Scots against two Charltons, two Dodds and two Robsons, with accomplices 'for the taking away of certain kie, on horse, certain sheep and geit, and burning of their sheep and destroying of goods'.[56] Possibly this incident was one of the provocations that led James IV in 1496 to declare war against Henry VII in support of Perkin Warbeck, and to harry Northumberland.[57]

Thereafter a new phase in Anglo-Scottish relations was broached in which King Henry schemed to placate the King of Scots by the gift of the Tudor Princess Margaret in marriage. Suddenly the highlanders' non-cooperation, from being tolerable, became totally unacceptable. In 1498, when already in trouble with Richard Fox, a score of Redes- and Tynedalers under William Hedley *alias* Weykspear were accused by the Sheriff of murdering Scots in breach of the armistice, and commanded to surrender at Berwick within three days, on pain of outlawry and death and — in contravention of the theory concerning a Liberty's privileges widely current[58] — forfeiture of property like ordinary felons. 'The Surnames of Charltons, Reeds, Hedleys, Robsons, Milburns, Dodds, Hunters and Fenwicks, resident in Tynedale and Redesdale' were enjoined to surrender within three days any of the wanted murderers they were harbouring.[59, 60]

More grave was an event arising out of operations in the recent war, which had been confined to the East marches, and during which the then Heron of Ford had been slain at Duns.[17, 61] While the circumstances are unknown, they were plainly such as to bequeath to the next Redesdale Keeper and other Herons a deadly feud against Sir Robert Kerr of Caverton, one of the Cessford branch, James IV's favourite and his Warden of the Middle Marches. At a day of truce John Heron of Crawley, bastard brother to the successive Keepers, with accomplices Starhead and Lilburn, ran Sir Robert through with a lance. By promptly outlawing Crawley and Starhead, who had taken to their heels, and by handing over the Keeper, William Heron of Ford, as a hostage, Henry VII limited the damage. For the time being James IV was mollified, but not so the new Kerr of Cessford, who despatched henchmen into England to kill Starhead and bring back his most distinctive feature in a bag.[62]

Scots historians appear vague as to the date of the Kerr murder, but create an impression that it shortly preceded King Henry's death, jeopardising the amity cemented by the royal marriage in 1503.[63] On the other hand the weight of circumstantial evidence from the English side indicates the turn of the year 1500/1501, leaving room for the conjecture that this was why the betrothal was so protracted. Thus having in the autumn of 1500 been confirmed in his Keepership,[64] Heron of Ford in January 1501, with his Chipchase cousin, incurred sequestration of lands for some serious misdemeanour.[65] In 1504 the pair were pardoned for some still unspecified offence,[66] as in 1506 was Edward Musgrave, heir to the late Robert Tailboys' Bailiff of Redesdale, for connivance in some act with all three Herons.[67] It was most probably this clemency that rankled with the King of Scots, but whether the original conspiracy matured in 1500 or 1508, these peals of thunder in Henry VII's reign presaged a storm, the eye of which stood over the two Liberties and which were to reverberate into Edward VI's time.[68]

NOTES

At this point the *Letters and Papers, Foreign and Domestic, of Henry VIII* become a staple source. However in many instances, for accuracy's sake, the original MSS have been consulted, in which case the date of the document has been suffixed to the BL or PRO reference to facilitate identification in the Calendar.

1. Patent 1 Henry VIII, p. 2 m. 13, 18/6 & 9/7/1509.
2. Ross, *Edward IV*, p. 339.
3. LP, I(1) (First Edition) no. 380, July 1509.
4. LP, I(1) (Kraus) no. 485.26, 10/5/1510.
5. *N & D Deeds*, p. 60, 10/8/1456.
6. Bean, *Percy Estates*, p. 96.
7. See p. 170 below.
8. PRO, SP I 45 fol. 101–7 & (1–3) P. S., 2/12/1527.
9. *N & D Deeds*, p. 52, 8/6/1321.
10. J. A. Tuck in NH, Vol. III p. 40.
11. *Ibid.*, Vol. VI p. 33.
12. Evidence that most of the aforementioned gentry held of the Earl is contained in M. E. James, *Tudor Magnate*, pp. 4–27 *passim*.
13. CPR, 8/3/1491.
14. Hedley, *Families*, Vol. 2 p. 45.
15. CDRS, Vol. IV Item 1556, 12/2/1489/90.
16. *N & D Deeds*, p. 221, 1494.
17. BL, Calig. B VI fol. 401, June 1525.
18. *Bishop Fox*, p. 129, 1500.
19. LP, III (2) no. 2328, 17/6/1522.
20. PRO, SP I 179 fol. 151, June 1543.
21. *Bishop Fox*, p. 80, 1498.
22. CBP, Vol. II Item 292, 2/7/1596.
23. D. C. Coleman, *Economy of England*, pp. 35–7 & 48–9.
24. *Peasants* etc., p. 213.
25. Coleman op. cit., p. 21.
26. Cal. Inq. PM Hen. VII, Vol. I Item 971, 30/5/1494.
27. BL, Calig. B VIII fol. 63, 2/12/1541.
28. PRO, SP I 152 fol. 150–3, 21/9/1539.
29. *Bishop Fox*, p. 110, 1498.
30. Star Chamber Proceedings Henry VIII, Bundle 20 no. 2, 1510.
31. Bean, *Percy Estates*, p. 7.
32. Thomas Rae, *Scottish Frontier*, pp. 4 & 10.
33. *Social History*, pp. 154–5.
34. Pease, *Wardens of the Marches*, p. 22.
35. Watson, *Reivers*, p. 119.
36. Camden's *Britannia*, p. 847.
37. Pease, *op. cit.*, pp. 102 & 174.
38. LP, III (2) no. 1883, 19/12/1521.
39. CPR, 20/11/1360.
40. PRO, SP I 70 fol. 232–5, 23/8/1532.

41. PRO, SP 49 5 fol. 29, December 1541.

42. (D. L. W.) Tough, *Last Years (of a Frontier)*, p. 23.

43. Thomas Rae, *Scottish Frontier*, p. 23. Though officially it lay in the Middle Marches, there was always a tug towards those of the West, with which it had more of a geographical affinity.

44. (R. B.) Armstrong, *(History of) Liddesdale*, Vol. I pp. 10, 64, 123, 145–6, 175–180 & Appendix D.

45. BL, Add, MSS 32646 fol. 259, 7/11/1541.

46. Tough, *op. cit.*, p. 183.

47. Pease, *Wardens of the Marches*, p. 60–2 & Macdonald Fraser, *Steel Bonnets*, p. 60 ('originally Scottish').

48. Armstrong, *Liddesdale*, p. 210.

49. Tough, *op. cit.*, p. 29.

50. Thomas Rae, *op. cit.*, p. 11. Despite punitive legislation on security grounds marriages across the line were commonplace from end to end of the frontier.

51. Bullein, *Dialogue*.

52. N. Macdougall, *James III. (A Political Study)*, p. 213.

53. A. Grant, *Independence (and Nationhood)*, pp. 32, 33, 50 & 52.

54. CDRS, Vol. IV App. I nr. 24, 14/7/1475.

55. Jenny Wormald, *Court (Kirk & Community, Scotland 1470–1625)*, p. 6 & Macdougall, op. cit., pp. 143–155.

56. CDRS, Vol. IV App. I nr. 34, 26/3/1494.

57. P. Hume Brown, *(History of) Scotland*, Vol. I p. 248 ff.

58. See p. 51 above.

59. CPR, 26/11/1498.

60. CDRS, Vol. IV Item 1649, 1498.

61. Andrew Lang, *(History of) Scotland*, Vol. I p. 370 & P. F. Tytler, *(History of) Scotland*, Vol. II p. 119.

62. George Buchanan, *(History of) Scotland*, Vol. II p. 246.

63. Hume Brown, *op. cit.*, Vol. I p. 261 & Tytler op. cit., Vol. II p. 135, who merely says 'in the time of Henry VII'.

64. CPR, 29/8/1500.

65. Ibid., 26/1/1501.

66. Ibid., 15/4/1504.

67. Ibid., 22/4/1506.

68. BL, Calig. B VIII fol. 106, 1551 (not 1542 as inscribed).

69. CPR, 22/3/1495.

CHAPTER SEVEN

The Heyday South of the Border

With the accession of the prodigious young Henry VIII the landscape becomes better illuminated. Because successive ministers had to keep lately Yorkist England beyond Trent in their sights, and were diligent archivists, wealth of documentation replaces mediaeval dearth and the need for bridging hypotheses recedes. Not merely does the historian move out of the fog into the daylight but in all probability there is actually more to see. During the thirteenth and fourteenth centuries feudalism had provided an efficient enough command structure to afford fair protection for life and property along the Borders against inward foes. As for the intermittent disruption attributable to the Wars of the Roses, it was no more marked in that region than in other parts of the realm. However, it took Edward IV and his Tudor successors many decades to impose a substitute for the old system, so that the predatory highlanders were by 1500 catching authority on the hop between the loosening of one grip and the tightening of another.

The first of three factors that conditioned their raids was seasonal, in so far as nights were longest, horses and cattle in peak condition for riding and driving between Lammas (1st August) and Candlemas (2nd February), before the oats gave out.[1] The second was geographical: there were no Cheviots, nor unfordable rivers, nor — till enclosures late in the century — hedges and fences, to hinder the eager drover. Countless bridle paths out of Redesdale and a decent road between Carlisle and Newcastle gave free range into the coastal plain, along the valley of the Tyne, or south into Hexhamshire and Durham, yielding a beaten zone between forty and eighty miles from home. The third was social, since the highlanders felt most self-assured when led by renegades from the knightly class, bold 'to guide ye o'er yon hill so high, and bring ye all in safety back, if ye'll be true and follow me.'

The behaviour of the Tyne- and Redesdalers during the first third of the reign was denounced continually. Ruthall, Bishop of Durham, bewailed the 'extreme impoverishment' of his tenants due to their depredations in 1511,[2] and by 1517 reckoned a thousand bills outstanding against them.[3] Upon acquisition by Wolsey of the See of York in 1514, it was to learn that his lordship of Hexham was a prime target, the robbers' intimacy with their old partners there having worn very thin. The worst years for plunder were

1515,[4, 5] 1516[6] and 1522, with up to a hundred sturdy thieves present in the abbey town every market day,[51] quite apart from accomplice Nixons and Elliots out of Liddesdale. Food shortages due to rinderpest and bad weather made robbery doubly attractive in these early twenties, and according to the Bishop of Carlisle none but castle-owners were safe to within eight miles of Carlisle, as well as in Northumberland.[7] By September 1523 the Earl of Surrey, who rated the Redesdalers the worst of the lot,[8] described the north country as nearly ruined by all their rapine.[9]

Especially disquieting was the widely-held belief in connivance farther up the social scale. Thus it was alleged that old Sir John Heron of Chipchase, county Sheriff in 1494, had conferred in 1514 with suspect heidsmen James Dodd,[9, 10] Christie Milburn and Tom Charlton of Carriteth as to how best to conceal their loot.[11] Nine years later Sir William Lisle and other gentlemen were accused of releasing scot-free Halls and other highlanders caught red-handed.[12] Less plausibly it was even rumoured that Baron Dacre of Gillsland and Sir Roger Fenwick, the very Warden General and his Tynedale Keeper respectively, were similarly implicated.[4]

All such mayhem was viewed from afar by the Court with mounting indignation, only fuelled when the Cardinal added further to his collection of benefices with the Prince Bishopric in 1523. The sufferings of his tenants and consequent inability to pay their rents wrung his heart, while according to Surrey the King likewise was 'marvellously discontented with the robberies and murders committed by the men of Tynedale and Redesdale',[8] singling out for particular condemnation the collaboration of the gentry as doers and receivers.[13] Yet apart from a few hangings[9] no punitive measures material-ised, and for two reasons. To deflect criticism of their own competence both Dacre and the Marquis of Dorset, during a spell as Warden, consistently played down the scale of the threat until April 1524.[14, 15, 16] Still more to the point, England was in the middle of a war with Scotland and the highlanders were urgently required at the front.[17]

Crime has always perturbed governments less than rebellion, for which in the sixteenth century systematic resistance rather than politics was the infallible criterion. Having fallen out with Dacre and the Fenwicks in a dispute over Plenmellor, Sir Nicholas Ridley in the autumn of 1523 sent a headstrong kinsman, Will of that ilk, from South into North Tynedale to stir up trouble.[18, 19] The malice aforethought was obvious enough for both King and Cardinal to voice extreme displeasure. Around him the young gentleman proceeded to gather a little staff comprising the Charlton heidsmen of Hesleyside, Bellingham, Shitlington and the Bower[20, 21, 22] — a clique to which, as will become apparent, it is appropriate to allude as the

Hesleyside Band; Tom Charlton of Carriteth;[23] and Percy Green, identifiable only as 'arrant thief and traitor'.[24] 'Chief captain of all our thieves and rebels', Ridley soon had a force of 400 men, half from Tynedale,[25, 26] the residue from Gilsland, Bewcastledale and to a minor extent Redesdale.[23, 27] In November Keeper Sir Ralph Fenwick was chased out of Tynedale with eighty men at his back.[25, 28]

By the summer of 1524 the war with Scotland was winding down so that Dacre now had no alternative but to bestir himself, imparting several hefty kicks to the hornets' nest. Ridley scooted into Liddesdale,[26] to be greeted and reinforced by some 600 of the Armstrongs and their allies.[23, 29] When the Scots government angling for peace began to bear down on Liddesdale, Ridley and his English summered in the Waste,[38] where they kept the prisoners who had accrued to the whole confederacy,[29] which was tightly enough organised to scorn the close season in an intensive campaign. Travelling from Newcastle, the Bishop of Carlisle had to effect a sixty-mile detour in order to reach his diocese,[52] while Wolsey was apprised of the 'extreme ruin and desolation' 'through great and huge robberies and felonies' that had befallen his own.[27] Between March and October 1525 the marauders carried fire and sword all over Durham and Northumberland,[29, 30, 31] 'riding in bushments [i.e. large bands] with banners displayed',[23] regarded in the sixteenth century as the very hallmark of rebellion. Within Tynedale a royal garrison was obliterated[31] and Fenwick put yet again to ignominious flight.[32] It was late autumn before the commotion suddenly subsided, after bombardment from every weapon in the arsenal of a Cardinal who was also first minister. For all that the sources reveal, Ridley vanished like a wraith.

Significant of a degree of sophistication was an attempt by the highlanders in parallel with this exertion of brute force to implicate the Warden General, who had been summoned to London in October 1524 to account for the competence and honesty of his stewardship. Henchmen of the dispossessed Percy Earl and regarding the Cumbrian baron as an interloper, the heidsmen of the Hesleyside Band put in circulation a story that 'they did nothing sithen the departure of the Lord Dacre but that it was his pleasure and commandment', and that they would have some good jokes ('bourdes') to tell their 'master' on his return;[33] meanwhile Sir Christopher Dacre would notify them whenever plans were made against them.[34] Though the disinformation was swallowed by the justices in eyre[23] and the Warden's very deputies, his severity towards the highlanders during the previous year served to clear him in the longer run.

Two parties had by and large remained unexpectedly aloof from the turbulence. The first was Redesdale,[35] bearing out a confidence expressed in them by Dacre in 1523.[36] The prime reason for their quiescence was contentment with the Warden and their Keeper, Heron of Ford, in marked contrast with the Tynedale attitude towards *their* two officers. Sir William remained on good enough terms with the dominant Hall clan to go bail for their members from time to time,[37] and was instrumental in laying Percy Green by the heels in Redesdale, which he would hardly have done without their cooperation.[22]

The second party to remain uncompromised during the crisis was Heron of Chipchase, perhaps because a Percy vassal not above a little business with the robbers in the past. Certainly Lord Dacre's satisfaction with Sir John's military performance declined sharply during the current war, and Heron waited till he was out of the way before joining with the Sheriff of Northumberland in two parleys with the highlanders,[35, 38] and even embarking on a stint as Keeper of Tynedale. What had kept him straight nevertheless was relationship by marriage with the baron, and by blood and professional association with cousin of Ford whom he joined in a declaration at the outset of the revolt that they would not 'flytt' from Dacre.[39]

There ensued a lull of two years between eruptions. Utterly cowed, Tynedale was described as 'in such good stay, train and quietness of good rule, as the like thereof hath not been seen'.[40, 41] Debility was aggravated by intensifying economic depression between 1525 and 1528, characterised by foul weather and cattle disease,[49] with the result that in Redesdale, for example, 'horsemeat and all other victuals be very scarce and extreme dear'.[42]

However, there was still the odd rumble from the slumbering volcano, if only because population pressures within the two dales became more unbearable than usual. In the 1527–8 winter it was seriously proposed to the Cardinal that they should be partially evacuated 'since there be a greater number of inhabitants . . . than truly may be sustained in the same'.[43] For most of the inhabitants, on the other hand, the preferred solution for hunger was still that of the predator.

Thanks to the reluctance of their rulers to meddle with them, Liddesdale had not been quelled like the Tynedale ally. Indeed the four great clans there were enjoying one of their rare spells of harmony,[40] and to them repaired malcontents out of Teviotdale, as well as fugitive Charltons of Shitlington and Dodds from Tynedale.[24] Between the Springs of 1526 and 1527 there were many prisoners taken for ransom and damaging sorties south under Armstrong leadership,[40] one of which into Hexhamshire, however, was bloodily discomfited.[44]

A new focus for disaffection stood already in the wings. Formerly Constable of Alnwick and Captain of Wark-on-Tweed, Percy vassal Sir William Lisle of Felton, fifteen miles down Coquet from Harbottle, began from a distinguished military career to drift into banditry at around the same time as Will Ridley, though their paths do not seem to have crossed. Possession of East Woodburn, in the Lisle family since Henry II's reign at least, made a Redesdaler of him, as well as a familiar of the nearby Halls. It was during the winter of 1523–4 that Sir William first brushed with the law, when he insulted the Sheriff of Northumberland who was trying to recover some stolen cattle from him, and also threatened to pluck the Cardinal by the nose.[45]

In August 1526, after a Star Chamber trial, Lisle and his heir Humphrey were gaoled for murder, robbery and sedition in Pontefract Castle,[41] where their companions included some Tynedale prisoners.[45] As Sir William had once virtuously complained about their behaviour,[40] there may have been initial diffidence, likely however to have been speedily overcome by a shared ferocity and intimacy with Redesdale, and the lure of Lisle's gentle birth. Soon afterwards father and son were shifted to Newcastle gaol where next summer they were joined by the Armstrongs netted in Hexhamshire.[44] In a marvellously coordinated move at the end of June 1527 the prisoners overpowered the gaolers and opened the gates to forty horsemen from all three dales, with whom they rode away north-west towards Mangerton; meanwhile a messenger from the Borders reached Pontefract, from which the Tynedale men absconded in their turn.[46]

Lisle, this 'wild and ungracious man more given to cruelty than to any goodness', lost no time in proclaiming himself 'captain of the thieves of both nations inhabiting the Borders',[47] notably 'the thieves and evil-disposed men both of Tynedale and Redesdale'.[44] Consternation at the revival of a threat deemed over and done with prompted the authorities to set a price of a hundred marks on his head.[47] Sir William's chief strength, like Ridley's, depended on men like the Dodds and the Charltons of Shitlington[48] and the Liddesdalers,[41, 47] but now there was a sprinkling as well of Redesdale Hedleys,[46] and renegade Ogles and Fenwicks who were more of his own class. There were also 'women and other simple persons' who acted as his spies.[42] That said, the majority of the highlanders were still sufficiently chastened to furnish no more than the water for the insurgents to swim in.

The leader's headquarters were wherever he happened to be at the time, migrant between the Threaplands, Ewesdale, Liddesdale and, during the harvest, back home at Felton.[42, 46] To the highlanders' customary hunting grounds in Hexhamshire and Durham[44] he added the coastal lands between Coquet and Aln, including Alnwick itself, which he knew better than they. Wolsey was of course the greatest loser. Among many others Sir William Ellerker, Sheriff of Northumberland, saw his properties at Humshaugh,[41, 47] Widdrington,[49] and Lynton burned and plundered of horses by the score, and his servants taken for ransom. However, a plot to ambush and kill Ellerker himself miscarried.

The revolt collapsed in January 1528 with the submission of Tyne- and Redesdales in the second week,[43] and the slaying of Will Charlton of Shitlington and the surrender of the Lisle family in the third.[53] That the duration of the rampage had been confined to a single raiding season was due in part to a burst of Scottish collaboration;[49, 50] in part to Lisle's fatal homesickness for Felton;[42] but above all to the appointment at Christmas 1527 as Northumbrian Warden of Sir William's liege lord, the sixth Earl of Northumberland, in a signal confession by the government that the North could not yet be ruled without the tremendous feudal influence of the House of Percy.

From hindsight of what impended it is once again worth looking at what had been the conduct of Heron of Chipchase. Unlike Ridley, Lisle had after all been as devoted to the eclipsed family as Heron himself. Moreover Sir John had flaunted his contempt for the new men who had ruled the Middle Marches in the interregnum between Dacre's departure and the recall of the Earl.[35] *Prima facie* it must have seemed suspicious that Heron should have abruptly resigned his Keepership shortly after Lisle's rebellion began.[54] The old gentleman's behaviour nevertheless remained unexceptionable. He had no reason to love a man whose first lawless act had been to help himself to the cattle of kinsman Roger Heron of Meldon.[45, 59] An attempt by Liddesdalers to round up sheep from Chipchase, during which several of the raiders were killed, indicated that the insurgents had been given no grounds for supposing that Sir John was a sympathiser.[55] Just before he died he was to be foreman of the jury that, in September 1535, found yet another true bill for treason against the incorrigible Sir Humphrey Lisle, who alone of his family had escaped judicial dismemberment.[46]

The next few years were relatively uneventful for the highlanders, too chastened and too involved in legitimate warfare to provoke ripples; but momentous for the nation as a whole, now embarked on faltering but irrevocable steps to detach her from the Roman Catholic Church. Symbolic were the hounding to death of Cardinal Wolsey and his replacement as first minister by a thoroughly secular Thomas Cromwell.

This dignitary was intent upon the abolition of the Liberty and the Cloister as strongholds of the Old Order. With regard to the former a statute of 1535 decreed that all such lapse progressively to the Crown. The local implications in western Northumbria were enormous, affecting Hexhamshire and Durham, destined for forfeiture in the forties, and of course the two robber dales. With regard to the monastic target, Hexham

Abbey, bastion of what was religiously the Roman Wall, was scheduled for immediate dissolution. Spearheading the assault was Sir Reynold Carnaby, whose father William was squire of Halton north of Corbridge; business acumen rather than strong nerves ran in the family. Prior to his demolition work the son had been *major domo* to the Percy Earl, whose morale was beginning to crack, and whose manors of Prudhoe and probably Walwick and Kielder were already in his subordinate's hands. Moreover Carnaby had superseded the current Keeper of Tynedale, Hodge à Fenwick, as Bailiff of Hexhamshire and was now in line for a farm of the Abbey lands.

The uprisings known collectively as the Pilgrimage of Grace did not begin around the Humber, as is popularly supposed, but at Hexham,[56] when on September 28th, 1536 agents sent to dissolve the Abbey were chased down the Corbridge road by armed monks and townsmen. It was not till October 1st, just before the Earl of Cumberland bolted home to Skipton after trying to stand in as Warden, that Lincolnshire rose, and on the 6th Robert Aske nailed a call to arms on the doors of York Minster.

Given that the highlanders were among the first and some quite the last in arms, the extent to which they shared the religious and mercenary motives of the Pilgrims at large has to be explored. First and foremost, everything in their history suggests that like countrymen everywhere they were resistant to religious change. Secondly, whereas for years past their Liberties of Wark and Harbottle had been run *de jure* or *de facto* by royal Keepers, they still 'claimed and used the old liberties of that country',[57] to which they were inveterately attached.[58] Thirdly, though for the customary majority the size of their rents did not yet add up to a substantial grievance, not a few of the senior heidsmen were freeholders, all the more often subject to the resented gressoms because from those holding in tenant right they had contracted the habit of frequent transfer of tenements. Finally all alike could only have welcomed a widespread anarchy which coincided with the classic raiding season.

Had they failed to notice this, there was a prompter close at hand. 'A sharp, wise man', and tall too if the nickname Little John is anything to go by,[65] John Heron of Chipchase was around sixty by the time of Sir John's belated death. After service in important capacities to the fifth Earl of Northumberland he had been forced to quit the household temporarily in 1520 for alleged complicity in murder,[10] but from 1528[59] probably into 1536 acted as the sixth Earl's Keeper of Redesdale. In the twenties his means had been modestly defined as of 100 marks *per annum* with forty horsemen but he had been sustained by hopes of succession not merely to Chipchase, but also to the Ford inheritance, which included such Tynedale properties as Chirdon, Snabdaugh and Simonburn Castle.[60, 61, 62] Nevertheless Little

John at Sir William's death was disappointed in this ambition when in June 1535 son George returned empty-handed from an audience with Cromwell, to which the younger Heron had been sped with a recommendation from the sickly Earl. Having learned from the fates of Ridley and Lisle that the race was not to the maverick, John Heron now sought allies in Sir Thomas and Sir Ingram Percy, who had just stepped aboard the same boat having been disinherited in the King's favour by their hostile and childless brother. The part of the joint task allotted to Little John was the raising of his own Western Northumberland, where he could rely for assistance on the Tynedale underworld, upon whose doorstep Chipchase was located. Not only had lands around Bellingham been in the family since the fourteenth century,[63] but Cuthbert Charlton, heidsman of Bellingham and nephew to Edward of Hesleyside,[65] had married Heron's daughter.

The laird of Chipchase conceived his initial objective to be a revival of the alliance between Tynedale and Hexhamshire which had taken such a battering in Wolsey's day. First of two obvious obstacles was Reynold Carnaby, Bailiff of Hexham, described by Sir Thomas Percy as 'the destruction of all our blood, for by his means the king shall be My Lord's heir'.[65] The problem was reduced by Carnaby's absence down south when Tyne- and Redesdales rose to arms in the second week of October;[64] when he did return it was to cut a poor enough figure, 'fleeing for the safeguard of his life' until cooped up in Chillingham Castle by the two Percys. However, in the sense of a base his father's house, north of Corbridge, still had to be neutralised. Moreover behind Reynold stood his friend the fifth Baron Ogle, of much sterner stuff, the watchword of whose family had always been loyalty to the Throne, whoever the occupant. The fact that Little John's grandmother had been a lady of the Ogles did not help him at all with the baron, whom at this juncture the ailing Earl, unable to reach his cure, appointed Vice Warden. Fortunately for Heron, however, the Ogle interest was strongest in eastern Northumberland, in contrast with at best certain traditional ties in Redesdale.

Then there were two potential allies, first of whom were the chapter of monks, fearful of what they had done and who 'before they joined with thieves' would adopt any other course 'if they could other wise save their lives'. Little John having overcome their scruples with the lying assurance that Carnaby intended to hang four of them anyway, Prior Edward consented to hire the Tynedalers for twenty nobles a year. The second was Keeper Fenwick, whose grievance against Carnaby augured well. However, support for rebellious Percys held no allure for a member of his royalist tribe, which was in any case paralysed by internecine feuds. Accordingly Hodge ignored an invitation from Cuthbert Charlton to join a tryst with Hexhamshire men at Chollerford on 16th October, to which Tynedalers had been summoned over their Keeper's head on pain of a fine of a noble apiece.

From the tryst the multitude rode over to St. John Lea near Hexham, where Heron left them to make for Halton in company with John of the Falstone, Head Surname man of the Robsons. It was now William Carnaby's turn to be bamboozled by Little John who on arrival mentioned that he was hungry. When they were all halfway through dinner Archie Robson of Yarrowhall burst in with the tidings that Tynedale and Hexhamshire had gathered and were heading that way, whereupon guest confided to host that 'they would do their worst' and 'if he remained in the house not all the goods in the world would save his life'. Having exclaimed at the tardiness of the warning — 'not like a friend' — Carnaby nevertheless agreed to take refuge in Chipchase Castle. On their journey a Halton servant managed to slip the fugitive a message that 'that traitor that rideth with you hath betrayed you', and that William on some pretext should make good his escape southwards to Langley. Thereupon Heron hurried back to Halton where he persuaded the Scottish Mrs. Carnaby to hand over her son's treasure chest for safe keeping. She was on the point of doing so when a well-wisher snatched it from her grasp and galloped off with it and seven retainers. Little John gave chase but abandoned it on perceiving that he was by himself, the reason being that John Robson and company were busy helping themselves to all the moveables in sight.' Putting a kercher as a pensell [i.e. pennant] upon his spear-point', Heron tried to rally them but to no avail. The casket came into the custody of the Ogles who subsequently also succeeded in fortifying Halton with an armed band, though at a later stage in the uprising it was to be occupied by Sir Thomas Percy's chaplain.

At the end of the month the Percy brothers came up from their lands in Yorkshire and, in full realisation that Tynedale and Hexhamshire formed the fulcrum of revolt, convened 'with all speed' a council of war at Prudhoe attended by Heron of Chipchase, Edward and Cuthbert Charlton, one Geoffrey Robson and an Errington out of Hexham. What aspired to be a county meeting held by the pair at Alnwick soon afterwards bracketed Redesdale and Durham too within the area of disaffection. Indeed it is clear *a posteriori* that the three senior conspirators had decided that operations in central Northumbria could safely be left in the hands of the Hesleyside Band; and that Heron had best plant his own banner within Redesdale, to which the Ford properties he had seized afforded ready access. By December he would be entertaining Sir Thomas at Harbottle[65] and still be regarded as *de facto* Keeper of Redesdale not only by the inhabitants[66] but even by the Court.[67] As for Durham, its Chancellor lamented that the highlanders were showing a vampirish propensity to convert those they devoured, since the inhabitants of the northern part of the diocese such as the Barony of Langley, besides having to be defended, had to be prevented 'from adhering to the said thieves and to become thieves as they be'.[68]

The Percys' deduction was that the same coercive technique could be applied with equal effect in Eastern Northumberland. When the gentry arrived at Alnwick Castle and ten days later attended another county meeting in Rothbury, it was under the impression that discussions would centre on the best means to crush Tyne- and Redesdales.[64, 69] Instead they saw the most notorious heidsmen 'cherished rather than rebuked', while John Lumley, Heron's brother-in-law from Durham, warned them that if they did not swear an oath of allegiance to the Pilgrimage within twenty days they could expect no mercy from the highland clans. Now Ogle's interest and what remained of Reynold Carnaby's ensured that the response from those under threat was largely negative.[65] The consequence was that, while the main body of Pilgrims farther south gradually foundered till the ultimate fiasco in mid-February 1537, the highlanders under Little John and the two Charltons devastated up to 60,000 acres of Northumberland,[70] 'to the utter undoing of four or five hundred of Your Grace's true subjects',[64, 67] 'spoiled so sore that many were weary of their lives,'[71] and the county through the 'evil acts of the Tynedale and Redesdale men clear out of frame'.[72] What compounded the treason was that they had brought in to help them Liddesdalers and others of the foreign enemy.[67] That at this stage the heidsmen were numbered by both sides amongst the foremost rebels is attested by the choice as delegates to the Doncaster 'Parliament' in December of John Hall of Otterburn for Redesdale, and Edward and Cuthbert Charlton for Tynedale, alongside Sir Thomas Percy for Northumberland;[73] and by the inclusion alongside Robert Aske of four from the two dales, as yet unnamed, in the King's list of exceptions to his general pardon.[74]

Yet in the immediate aftermath of the insurrection no punitive measures were undertaken, a design to pack Heron off to London to stand trial being postponed with the proviso that he be bound in 2000 marks.[67] Reasons were growing government uncertainty as to the true role of the highlanders in recent months;[75] reluctance to prosecute Northerners like Sir Robert Bowes, though indisputably compromised; and above all to give Redesdale leisure to settle down under a new Keeper.[67] However, by early April this condition had been satisfied,[76] and by early summer the dossier on Little John had grown so fat[65] that he was shipped south and imprisoned in the Fleet.

Meanwhile the hitherto dormant Hodge à Fenwick had been restored to the rule of Tynedale. His first act was to demand of his charges that they disgorge some of their loot, which was at once rejected by Edward and

D

Cuthbert Charlton unless exonerated for their dealings with the monks. Hodge's counter was to accuse the pair of a nice selection of capital charges,[67] though again in the interests of peace and quiet the Laird of Hesleyside was not arrested.[77] However, his dangerous feeling of insecurity was deepened through visits to the area by Sir Anthony Browne, personal emissary of the King, and by Norfolk the Lord Lieutenant at the end of February 1537. The former was beset by the clamour against the highlanders of 300 aggrieved Northumbrians,[78] while the latter having been similarly pestered descended on Hexham in baleful mood, declaring: 'I shall ere long so sing them such a song that the like was not heard among them sith any of them was born'.[79, 80, 81] By way of anti-climax, the Duke was in fact mollified by the contrite demeanour at a meeting of John Robson of the Falstone. Gyb Charlton of the Boughthill and John Hall of Otterburn, who could claim to represent a majority of the highlanders, and now proferred token compensation,[82, 83] which His Grace was disposed to accept. Having been left out of the talks, the chief of the Hesleyside Band now felt more isolated than ever, and determined to destroy evidence in the person of Hodge à Fenwick. Despite intelligence that his life was under threat, the Keeper rode from Newcastle to Bellingham on 3rd March to collect pledges for redress, when towards midnight near the Woodburn he was set on and killed by John Charlton of Blakelaw, Ninian Charlton of the Nuke, and John Dodd[61, 76] of the Hesleyside Band.

The Duke declared that he would be sorry to return home without punishing the murderers of a royal officer.[84] That it was to take him four months to appreciate that the crime had not been the work of mere freelances was the fault of the newly designated Keeper of Tynedale, Sir Reynold Carnaby, who, loth to stir the pot so soon after appointment, for weeks sat on evidence that incriminated Herons as well as Charltons.[85] When Carnaby did divulge the information to an exasperated Lieutenant, Cuthbert of Bellingham was executed;[86] Edward of Hesleyside with John Heron of the Hall Barns near Simonburn, Little John's bastard, outlawed; and his legitimate son George arrested and taken south by Norfolk for questioning.[87] Chipchase's own lands and goods were seized,[86] but the Duke could not make up his mind whether he should be kept in the Fleet or brought back north to be hanged. The question was settled for him on 22nd October when Little John was consigned to the Tower, the waiting-room for death, through whose portals Thomas Percy and Robert Aske had passed seven months before. 'Being well kinned', Carnaby gloomily opined of all these miscreants, 'they may still cause trouble.'[92]

Hodge's murder opened up a rift in Tynedale that was latent at the best of times. Accompanied by their herds and in strengths up to 100 men,[88] about the nucleus provided by the three strikers and their backers, the bitter-enders of the Hesleyside Band now bestrode the Borders, with one foot in England where they still sowed and harvested their crops,[89] the other in Scotland chiefly among the Armstrongs,[84] but occasionally in Teviotdale[90] or even the West Marches.[91] Thence they attacked lands south of Tynedale and between the Springs of 1537 and 1538 Tynedale as well, when relations with the majority there were strained to breaking point. But there was more to their activities than raids which inflicted damage to the tune of a mere £50 per month, because they were regarded as the forlorn hope from the Pilgrimage, always alluded to in Cromwell's correspondence as rebels rather than robbers.[92, 93] This was reasonable since Charlton of Hesleyside was maintaining a messenger service into the interior[94] devised to smuggle into Scottish sanctuary 'foxes and wolves put at large and let loose out of cloisters'; furthermore it was believed in responsible circles that if the Percy orphans had not been removed from a house near Durham, a mere sixteen miles from Tynedale,[95, 96] then the rightful seventh Earl would have been spirited away into Scotland by Edward Charlton.[97]

For the majority broadly rooted in the Robsons of the Falstone; the Charltons of Carriteth, the Bower and the Boughthill; Archie Dodd and Humphrey Milburn,[98] such politics were distasteful reminders of a past they wanted to live down. Cleverly they had manoeuvred themselves into a situation in which they had become debtors rather than traitors. Even on this matter of restitution they stalled endlessly, complying cheerfully with a royal demand that they surrender pledges as earnest of satisfaction, but the little that accrued left Norfolk still grumbling. He executed a few for fresh offences[99, 100, 101] which galvanised Redesdale into a modicum of redress,[86] but while more accommodating than Tynedale,[85, 100, 103] they fell back into equally bad ways, once His Grace's back was turned.[102]

The highlanders' recalcitrance was none the less kept within bounds, inasmuch as their behaviour towards both Carnaby and Sir John Widdrington, lately entrusted with Redesdale, remained correct.[86] The latter had some trouble with the Potts, one of whom was actually exacting protection money from a Widdrington toon,[89] and failed to hinder his charges from harbouring Scots thieves.[103] On the other hand the Tynedale majority stood aloof from the brisk hostilities, extending to demolition of houses, between Carnaby[93, 105, 106, 107] and the Hesleyside Band throughout 1537, and solemnly attended his Keeper's Courts.[104] In February 1538 Sir Reynold felt sufficiently sure of himself to start a six-month furlough in London, leaving as deputy his brother Gilbert, the Constable of Langley.[111]

It was during the Keeper's absence, and on the basis that my enemy's enemy is my friend, that the highland factions buried their differences, in the genuineness of which Carnaby mistakenly had never believed.[108] The catalyst was insistence, peremptory as never before, by the Council in the North that had succeeded Norfolk that the highlanders make adequate reparation, which in Norfolk's words was beyond them, 'the injured demanding so much and they having so little to make recompense withal'.[109] In the teeth even of an appeal from frustrated officials to King Henry to intervene,[110] the majority still made no move.[111] Instead, in this Spring of 1538, friction between the majority and the Band died down, to be replaced by a phase in which the former withdrew cooperation from their officers and so wrecked the machinery of justice. Clashes between 'the wild men of Tynedale and Redesdale' were staged in order to pretend meetings for redress, in reality designed 'to make conventicles and bonds against their Keepers'. While the Halls absented themselves from Widdrington's Head Court at Harbottle blatantly without excuse,[112] the Tynedalers 'dared not come [to the days of truce] for the feud that Redesdale hath against them'.[113] This was doubly unwelcome to government and convenient to themselves as coincident with many heavy raids from both Liberties into Teviotdate at this precise time[114] the upshot of which, as Gilbert Carnaby[113] and Widdrington concurred, was to destroy any prospect of Scottish cooperation in restraining Liddesdale and the outlaws of the Band.[115] While as yet the majority did not join with these openly in any operation, they did provide transit facilities for any excursions south.[116] On one such, in July 1538, a company of 120 Armstrongs, Nixons and exiles descended on Langley and kidnapped the Constable and acting Keeper, along with his cattle and twenty-six of his followers.[117] Pursuant to this 'break' upon the Borders,[115] a stampede to get out of the area started among the Northumbrian gentry[116] while William Carnaby, particularly hard hit, implored his son to curtail his London leave.[117]

Reynold Carnaby now rapidly became even for the majority the cynosure of hatred that he had always been for those in the Percy interest. As a defiant greeting on his return late in August the pledges escaped from Newcastle. The Keeper on September 12th summoned the majority heidsmen to meet him with other Northumbrian officers at a tryst in Chollerford where he ordered them to inlay new pledges, and upon refusal sent off to Warkworth under the guard the delegates themselves, to wit of the Charltons Gyb of the Boughthill, Gerard of Wark alias Topping,[118] and a kinsman of Tom of Carriteth; of the Robsons John of the Falstone; Eddie Dodd of the Crag; and John Stokoe of the Nuke. The response by the mass of Tynedale was twofold. First, 'openly in the face of the world, not remembering any part of their duty of allegiance', they assembled in great numbers, together with the three outlawed Charltons and some Liddesdale Scots; secondly they twice sent a Charlton and a Robson to Carnaby, proposing a further parley with ten or so of their fellowship, 'under assurance, safely to come and go', concerning the release of the seized pledges. This the Keeper rejected until their seditious assembly, 'so offensive to the King's Highness', had dispersed to their homes. To his demand that they renounce their united front[119, 120] 'with such persons as was proclaimed traitors,'[108] they retorted 'they could not do so for they were friends.[121] Their grievance that the safe conduct traditional on such occasions had been violated,[119] which Sir Reynold implausibly denied, was intensified in December when Stokoe succumbed to the plague in Warkworth. The survivors were shifted to Morpeth, except for Topping who was gaoled in Hexham Tower to await trial for sundry robberies.[122]

Among Gerard Charlton's fellow-prisoners were a prominent Armstrong and a couple of Dodds.[123] In addition there was Father Robert More, a priest from Chichester,[124] who divulged to Carnaby's patrol that had picked him up at Nunwick near Simonburn on 9th December that he was on his way into Scotland through the good offices of John Robson of the Falstone, presumably in control of the last lap on Edward Charlton's underground route. More would live to carry technically treasonable letters from Irish bishops to the Pope and Cardinal Pole.[125, 126] In short the gaol Tower became a prime target for Tynedale men of either stripe; it was a soft one, too, in view of Hexhamshire men's dislike for their Bailiff.

The highlanders had enough spies around to ensure that the priest's arrest did not go unperceived. About midnight on the same day, a candle having been pushed through the bars to alert Topping, a surge of horsemen from the surrounding woods broke the prison and took out the prisoners, as well as such of the watchmen as had not been dispersed on a fool's errand.[127, 128] While the outlaws and Liddesdalers had been particularly conspicuous, it was decided later that all Tynedale had been 'devisers of this act'. No hue and cry was raised by the townsmen.[122, 124]

That this 'traitorous dealing'[129] served to damn the Keeper rather than the highlanders was due principally to the international crisis with which Henry VIII was faced in the Spring of 1539.[130] Scotland for one had to be kept at bay through the mobilisation of Northumberland. On return to the North, Norfolk's first act was therefore to release the Morpeth prisoners, who had been subsisting on half rations for six months,[120] so that the list of 400 horsemen mustering for the King on 19th April was headed by John of the Falstone.[131] Commander Carnaby must have felt their 'grounded hatred'[132] scorching his back. His final ruin was accomplished in July when ambushed with nineteen followers by John Robson, Topping and a hundred men, who till the time came to get in their hay resisted every blandishment that the 'wits and policy' of Border officers could devise for his release.[88]

Disillusioned with Cromwell's gamekeeper, Henry VIII in September 1539 fished the chief poacher out of the Tower of London, where he had miraculously survived, and, with every confidence in his excellence proclaimed,[137] sent Little John back to police his old haunts. The initial appointment was as Constable of Harbottle[133] but the Tynedale Keepership followed in January 1540,[134] and after a spell *de facto* when Widdrington was ousted in his turn, the full Keepership of Redesdale seven months later.[135] Though the three assassins stayed beyond the Pale, amnesty also embraced Heron's old allies of the Hesleyside Band, notably Edward Charlton himself and Bastard John of the Hall Barns. With the still outstanding problem of the Tynedale majority a start was made when Hesleyside closed a deal with Topping on Carnaby's release, if at the high price of fifty marks each to the two chief captors and John Charlton of the Larederburn; retention of all horses and harness; and board and lodging for twenty unwilling guests.[88, 136].

Any tarnish on Heron's image from this one-sided arrangement was offset by his success in taking thieves from both dales,[137] and by an attack on the Robson strongholds of Falstone and the Belling just before entry into Keepership. Most of the clan and allied heidsmen made good their escape into the Head of Liddesdale, where unlike the Fenwick-slayers before them they took refuge not with the Armstrongs but with the Elliots and Croziers.[138, 139] Unfortunately for them their chief host, Clement Crozier, was captured on the West Marches in April, and they had to steal back two miles into England, building shiels in the inhospitable mosses of Lewisburn Holms.[140] As Little John had also got reciprocal justice moving with the Scots,[134] he felt he could boast that 'stealing and reiving is dead'.[138]

Having thus re-established his credentials, he was now free to pursue an ulterior motive, namely, after yet another interruption, to reunify Tynedale and set the tripartite league with Redesdale and Liddesdale on course again;[141] he was poor enough to be eager for booties from two sources — Scotland, and his English foes along the Marches. Fairly smooth collaboration with John Robson during the great rebellion meant the auspices were propitious, and in October 1540 he duly obtained from Norfolk, the new first minister, audience and pardon of the King for the offending heidsmen.[142]

Chief victims in the ensuing campaign were the Widdringtons, whose place at Haughton near Chipchase was stormed by Armstrongs with scaling-ladders in mid-May; the Fenwicks, seven more of whom were slain by Liddesdalers in mid-September while on 'hot trod' (i.e. pursuit of stolen property); and William Carnaby, who was rabbled and robbed at Corbridge Fair by Tyne- and Redesdalers probably under John of the Hall Barns in June,[143, 144] and whose places at Little Whittington[128] and Halton[145] were burned by the Elliots and the two Charlton 'strikers' in the late autumn. The Haughton incident and the slaughter of the loyal Fenwicks were stigmatised by Henry VIII as *casus belli*, as were by James V raids in the opposite direction, mainly into Teviotdale, by Heron himself and his two dales late in 1541.[114] This attitude on the part of the monarchs was according to growing and widespread suspicions precisely what Little John had been hoping to generate, in the belief that only all-out war would create the ideal conditions for an amassing of loot.

Pressure on Heron however intensified with the suspicions. Sir Robert Bowes and company were not twelve miles away from Halton on the crucial day, engaged upon the Survey that inspired this book. Upon news of the assault Bowes insisted that the Keeper retaliate immediately against Thorlieshope, which he did with extreme reluctance, and after which the league was never the same again. Next Sir Robert compelled Little John to go through the pantomime of a public reconciliation with Carnaby, at which 'true men' rejoiced, believing it to be a guarantee of better defence against Scots and thieves.[145] Thirdly, in March 1542, Sir Thomas Wharton, Vice Warden of the West Marches and friend of the Carnabys, lent a sympathetic ear to a tale from one of the Charlton outlaws' brothers, trying to rehabilitate him, that the Halton raid had been engineered by John Heron in order to cause war. The informant probably added — the source is cryptic — that the latter was also harbouring John Dodd, the third of the Fenwick-slayers. A harassed Duke of Suffolk, by then Lieutenant, declined to take any action,[146] but Little John's credit was melting fast enough during that summer of 1542 to ensure that he was closely watched. In the opinion of the new Warden General, the Viscount Lisle, 'surely this often riding thorough Tynedale could not be, if the Keeper did his partie'.[147]

The war with Scotland upon which Heron had set his hopes and helped to plan broke out in August and proved as great a disaster to him through Haddon Rig, where he was captured in company with Bowes, Widdrington and Sir Cuthbert Ratcliffe, as to King James through Solway Moss. The Keeper was to spend the rest of his life under house arrest, either in Edinburgh or Alnwick, but his spirit still hovered over the Middle Marches.

The main reason was that for practical reasons no better substitute could be found for the imprisoned Keeper than George Heron, always closely identified with his father's misdeeds. During his tenure there was a consensus that the state of Northumberland went from bad to worse, with pillage superimposed upon the famine of the 1542–3 winter.[148–158incl.] Lord Lisle declared that the enemies of 'unchristian' Tyne- and Redesdales were not the same as the King's enemies,[159] and singled out a Charlton and a Hall as thoroughgoing Scottish agents.[160] As important a prisoner as the

Earl of Bothwell had to be escorted past the 'dangers' of the two Liberties.[161] Of successive Lieutenants Suffolk laboriously patched up a truce with the Scots, only to see it immediately violated by the highlanders and their Liddesdale allies,[162, 163] while in September 1542 Norfolk deemed that a joint Anglo-Scottish expedition against the three dales would make more sense than a renewal of hostilities.[164, 165]

What made the authorities back away was, as in 1523, the military requirement. Even as a prisoner Little John had sent south intelligence on troop movements;[150] his Scots chaplain was a key intermediary between the Courts; and his son played an important role in warfare towards the end of 1542. Suffolk's successful[166] compromise consisted in the quartering of a large garrison on Tynedale between February and September 1543.'[168] 'And yet', murmured Warden General Lisle, 'you heard how much John Heron was against it.'[167]

Little John was indeed sinking in ever deeper water. Because currently attempting such subornation himself, the King was receptive to an allegation that King James had held discussions with the Keeper as prisoner of war just before Solway Moss. The grounds on which Henry was continually fobbed off by his officials were that John and George Heron, while guilty of receiving stolen property, harbouring rebels, and failing to prosecute theft, had never committed March treason.[169] At length the King resigned himself to the mere imprisonment of both, first at Newcastle, then at Alnwick, and finally in Bowes' household. On the eve of the King's death in 1546, when Little John was old, wasted and unfit to travel, Sir Robert interceded for them, 'being men of wit and experience and actively serving in all journeys when I rode into Scotland', and 'not so culpable as was reported'.[170]

Such was the epitaph of the Laird of Chipchase, marking the end of an era inasmuch as things were never again to be quite so bad. Meanwhile, in April 1543, the Keepership had fallen to Sir Ralph Eure who contrived[171] to procure yet another royal pardon for his charges, prompted perhaps by the cheerfulness with which they had turned King's evidence against Little John.[169] For the rest of Eure's tenure, the highlanders gave little trouble.[171]

NOTES

While no statement is made that cannot be authenticated, mainly from the Letters and Papers of Henry VIII, to give more than a selection of references is impracticable.

1. CBP, Vol. II Item 968, 15/7/1598.
2. PRO, SP I 2 fol. 89, October 1511.

3. *Ibid.*, 16 fol. 313–4, 25/6/1518.
4. *Ibid.*, 10 fol. 18, 27/1/1515.
5. *LP*, II(1) no. 1672, March 1516.
6. *Ibid.*, no. 2711, Christmas 1516.
7. *Ibid.*, III(2) no. 2328, 17/6/1522.
8. BL, Add. MSS 24965 fol. 35, 24/6/1523.
9. PRO, SP I 49.2 fol. 21–2, 2/9/1523.
10. *Ibid.*, 23 fol. 223–4, December 1521.
11. *Ibid.*, 7 fol. 281, 27/2/1514.
12. BL, Add. MSS 24965 fol. 41, 16/7/1523.
13. PRO, SP I 17 fol. 223–4, 23/12/1518.
14. BL, Add. MSS 24965 fol. 148, 8/1/1524.
15. *LP*, IV(1) no. 75, 30/1/1524.
16. BL, Add. MSS 24965 fol. 193, 1/4/1524.
17. *LP*, III(2) no. 3241, 15/8/1523.
18. *Ibid.*, IV(1) no. 313, 7/5/1524.
19. BL, Add. MSS 24965 fol. 226B, 13/5/1524.
20. *Ibid.*, fol. 126, c.3/12/1523.
21. PRO, SP I 30 fol. 334–5, 25/4/1524.
22. *Ibid.*, 31 fol. 123, 12/6/1524.
23. *Ibid.*, 34 fol. 113–4, 30/3/1525.
24. *Ibid.*, 31 fol. 196–7, 8/7/1524.
25. *LP*, III(2) no. 3576, 29/11/1523.
26. BL, Calig. B III fol. 6, 20/5/1524.
27. PRO, SP I 32 fol. 205, 30/11/1524.
28. BL, Add. MSS 24965 fol. 119, 11/12/1523.
29. BL, Calig. B I fol. 115, 23/6/1525.
30. *Ibid.*, B III fol. 158, 1/4/1525.
31. *Ibid.*, B VI fol. 407, 17/6/1525.
32. PRO, SP I 35 fol. 60–1, 8/7/1525.
33. *Ibid.*, fol. 22, c. 19/6/1525.
34. BL, Calig. B II fol. 260, 26/7/1525.
35. *Ibid.*, B I fol. 41, 27/4/1525.
36. *LP*, III(2) no. 3173, 12/7/1523.
37. BL, Add. MSS 24965 fol. 125, 24/9/1524.
38. BL, Calig. B VII fol. 236, 1/7/1525.
39. *LP*, III(2) no. 3218, 2/8/1523.
40. BL, Calig. B VI fol. 409, 13/5/1526.
41. PRO, SP I 44 fol. 32–3, 24/8/1527.
42. *Ibid.*, fol. 177–8, 16/10/1527.
43. *Ibid.*, 46 fol. 128–131, 18/1/1528.
44. *Ibid.*, 42 fol. 156–7, 4/7/1527.
45. BL, Calig. B III fol. 44, 17/8/1526.
46. PRO, SP I 46 fol. 105–6, 12/1/1528.
47. *LP*, IV(2) no. 3344, 12/8/1527.
48. PRO SP I 47, fol. 14–5, 25/2/1528.
49. *LP*, IV(2) no. 3370, 22/8/1527.
50. See p. 156 below.

51. *LP*, III(2) no. 2328, 17/6/1522.
52. *Ibid.*, IV(1) no. 448, 25/6/1524.
53. BL, Calig. B VII fol. 112, 28/1/1528.
54. *Ibid.*, B III fol. 209, 12/9/1527.
55. *LP*, IV(2) no. 3914, 11/2/1528.
56. The fullest narrative to date of the Northumbrian phase of the rebellion is to be found in M. H. & R. Dodds, *The Pilgrimage of Grace*, Volume II.
57. BL, Calig. B VIII fol. 128, 1551.
58. See *inter alia* p. 155 below.
59. BL,Calig. B III fol. 65, c. 27/12/1528.
60. PRO, S P I 116 fol. 217–8, 7/3/1537.
61. *Ibid.*, fol. 219, 7/3/1537.
62. PRO, Exchr. T. R. Misc. Books, Vol. 121 fol. 136, 20/4/1537.
63. Hedley, *Families*, Vol. II p. 48 ff..
64. BL, Harl. MSS. 289 fol. 32, c.15/10/1536.
65. PRO, SP I 119 fol. 94–104, end April 1537, which is the main authority for the preceding four paragraphs.
66. *Ibid.*, 69 fol. 54–5, 17/1/37 (not 1532 as calendared).
67. BL, Calig. B I fol. 133, 14/2/1537.
68. PRO. SP I 115 fol. 197, 5/2/1537.
69. *LP*, XI no. 68, 12/7/1536.
70. PRO, SP I 112 fol. 216, 13/12/1536.
71. *Ibid.*, 115 fol. 200, 6/2/1537.
72. *Ibid.*, 112 fol. 217–220, c. 13/12/1536.
73. *Ibid.*, 111 fol. 235–240, 24/11/1536.
74. PRO, Exchr. T. R. Books, Vol. 119 fol. 89, 2/11/1536.
75. See p. 167 below.
76. BL, Calig. B I fol. 128, 7/4/1537.
77. PRO, SP I 116 fol. 29, c. 15/2/1537.
78. *Ibid.*, fol. 180, 2/3/1537.
79. *Ibid.*, fol. 85–6, 19/2/1537.
80. *Ibid.*, fol. 89–91, 21/2/1537.
81. *Ibid.*, fol. 108–111, 24/2/1537.
82. *Ibid.*, 126 fol. 150–1, 13/11/1537.
83. *Ibid.*, 131 fol. 197–8, 24/4/1538.
84. *Ibid.*, 123 fol. 214–5, 20/7/1537.
85. *Ibid.*, 122 fol. 212–3, 8/7/1537.
86. *Ibid.*, 125 fol. 21–2, 23/9/1537.
87. *Ibid.*, 125 fol. 65–6, 28/9/1537.
88. *Ibid.*, 152 fol. 215–7, 23/7/1539.
89. *Ibid.*, 117 fol. 228–9, c. 1/4/1538 (wrongly calendared for 1537).
90. BL, Add. MSS 32646 fol. 100, 11/4/1537.
91. BL, Calig. B VII fol. 233, 7/11/1538.
92. PRO, SP I 125 fol. 120, 3/10/1537.
93. *Ibid.* 127 fol. 105–6, 21/12/1537.
94. *Ibid.*, 126 fol. 148–9, 13/11/1537.
95. *Ibid.*, 125 fol. 218–9, 15/10/1537.
96. *Ibid.*, 126 fol. 62–5, 2/11/1537.

97. *LP*, XII(2) no. 172, 30/6/1537.
98. BL, Calig. B III fol. 239, 17/3/1538.
99. PRO, SP I 124 fol. 232–3, 15/9/1537.
100. PRO, Exchr. T. R. Misc. Books, Vol. 119 fol. 137, (18/9/1537).
101. PRO, SP I 125 fol. 10–1, 22/9/1537.
102. *Ibid.*, 124 fol. 182–3, 5/9/1537.
103. BL, Calig. B VII fol. 224, 3/7/1537.
104. PRO, SP I 125 fol. 179, 10/10/1537.
105. *Ibid.*, 126 fol. 11–2, 24/10/1537.
106. *Ibid.*, 127 fol. 96–8, 18/12/1537.
107. *Ibid.*, 128 fol. 123–6, 19/1/1538.
108. *Ibid.*, 136 fol. 161–4, 15/9/1538.
109. *Ibid.*, 118 fol. 216–7, 18/4/1537.
110. *LP*, XIII(1) no. 1235, 12/6/1538.
111. BL, Calig. B III fol. 231, 31/3/1538.
112. PRO, SP I 132 fol. 25–6, 3/5/1538.
113. *Ibid.*, 131 fol. 167 & Exchr. T. R. Misc. Books, Vol. 121 fol. 22, 17/4/1538.
114. PRO, SP 49 5 fol. 29, December 1541.
115. PRO, SP I 132 fol. 91, 11/5/1538.
116. *Ibid.*, 134 fol. 140–1, 12/7/1538.
117. BL, Calig. B III fol. 246, 29/7/1538.
118. A to-name intriguingly interpreted by Godfrey Watson, *op. cit.*, pp. 48 & 185 as allusion to a startling tuft of hair, in which case the modern equivalent would be 'punk'.
119. BL, Calig. B III fol. 251–3, 17/9/1538.
120. PRO, SP I 136 fol. 217–8, c. 22/9/1538.
121. *Ibid.*, 137 fol. 1–2, 24/9/1538.
122. *Ibid.*, 140 fol. 77–8, 11/12/1538.
123. *Ibid.*, fol. 61–3, 8/12/1538.
124. BL, Calig. B III fol. 156, 19/12/1538
125. *LP*, XIV(1) no. 455, 7/3/1539.
126. *Ibid.*, no. 481, 9/3/159.
127. BL, Calig. B V fol. 36, 9/1/1539.
128. *Ibid.*, B III fol. 98, 9/1/1539.
129. PRO, SP I 140 fol. 131–3, 18/12/1538.
130. J. J. Scarisbrick, *Henry VIII*, p. 362. The Treaty of Toledo between Francis I and Charles V appeared to be the moment of truth for the English King.
131. PRO, E 36 Vol. 40 fol. 29, 29/3/1539.
132. BL, Calig. B III fol. 249, 12/6/1539.
133. PRO, SP I 154 fol. 96–7, October/November 1539.
134. BL, Royal MSS 7 cxxi fol. 136, 21/1/1540.
135. *LP*, XV no. 987, 19/8/1540.
136. PRO, SP I 153 fol. 86, August 1539.
137. BL, Arundel MSS 97 fol. 85B, Christmas 1539.
138. PRO, SP I 157 fol. 50–1, 13/1/1540.
139. *Ibid.*, fol. 67–8, 19/1/1540.
140. BL, Calig. B I fol. 131, 24/4/1540.

141. BL, Add. MSS 32646 fol. 259, 7/11/1541.
142. See p. 169 below.
143. BL, Add. MSS 32646 fol. 171, 9/7/1541.
144. *LP*, XVI(2) no. 1179, 14/9/1541.
145. BL, Add. MSS 32646 fol. 270, 2/12/1541.
146. PRO, SP I 169 fol. 203–5, end March 1542.
147. BL, Add. MSS 32649 fol. 135, 10/2/1543.
148. *LP*, XVII no. 681, 26/8/1542.
149. *Ibid.*, no. 682, 26/8/1542.
150. *Ibid.*, no. 695, 28/8/1542.
151. *Ibid.*, no. 719, c. 1/9/1542.
152. *Ibid.*, no. 753, 7/9/1542.
153. *Ibid.*, no. 808, 19/9/1542.
154. *Ibid.*, no. 828, 23/9/1542.
155. *Ibid.*, no. 1037, 5/11/1542.
156. *Ibid.*, no. 1069, 10/11/1542.
157. *Ibid.*, no. 1118, 23/11/1542.
158. PRO, SP I 176 fol. 107, 3/3/1543.
159. BL, Add. MSS 32648 fol. 201, 12/12/1542.
160. *Ibid.*, 32649 fol. 85, 19/1/1543.
161. *Ibid.*, fol. 76, 14/1/1543.
162. PRO, SP I 176 fol. 76, 25/3/1543.
163. *Ibid.*, fol. 107, 3/3/1543.
164. BL, Add. MSS 32647, fol. 238, 27/9/1542.
165. *Ibid.*, 32648 fol. 8, 2/10/1542.
166. *Ibid.*, 32650 fol. 16, 8/3/1543.
167. *LP*, XVIII(1) no. 291, 17/3/1543.
168. PRO. SP I 181 fol. 116, 9/9/1543.
169. BL, Add MSS 32651 fol. 247, 21/8/1543.
170. PRO, SP I 227 fol. 79, 13/12/1546.
171. *Ibid.*, 178 fol. 85, 24/5/1543.

CHAPTER EIGHT

The Heyday North of the Border

Just as Tyne- and Redesdales were counterpart to Liddesdale, so the two realms to which they respectively belonged seemed as designedly matched as black and white pieces on a chessboard. Each had an English-speaking majority, a Norman-veneered aristocracy, a Celtic hinterland, Angles on the eastern, and Welsh on the western, side of a common frontier that was divided into three March Wardenries or military districts. Though England was far richer and more populous, David did not always face Goliath because England's French connexion was a drain on men and treasure, whereas Scotland's was a source of strength.

Fitfully English Kings did divert some resources to the far more worthwhile objective of uniting the British Isles. Henry VII aspired to do this through a conciliatory marriage which would eventually bring his great-great-grandson to a joint throne; Henry VIII was more typical in so far as he preferred sporadic belligerence, funded by about one-sixth of what he squandered in Europe. Hence the Scots had generally to wrestle with St. Cuthbert rather than St. George, and as often as not it was not Scotland but England that sued for peace, even after inflicting the most grievous defeat in the island's history.

A further factor in Scotland's favour was the site of the actual frontier, so much closer to her centre of gravity than to England's. Due to the existence of great Abbeys, waxed wealthy out of sheep-farming, the northern was more heavily settled than the southern side.[1] The soldierly Duke of Somerset regarded the Merse and Teviotdale as 'the chief country of men in all Scotland'.

The improbably nice equilibrium that resulted could be disturbed at any time by the Borderers of, say, Ewesdale, Annandale, Gilsland or Bewcastledale. However, the difference in scale between these and the Tyne-, Redes- and Liddesdalers was as marked as that between gardeners and farmers in a more beneficent sphere. Because warfare entailed plunder, Tynedale and Redesdale in 1532[2] and 1538,[3] for example, and Liddesdale in 1543 and 1603, palpably lent themselves to calculated warmongering. Their instrument was the scathe, an archaism best retained because no modern term embraces a similar range of felonies with regard to both livestock and persons. Already familiar to the reader, 'scathes' with an international flavour are better documented because the stuff of diplomacy.

MAP 3

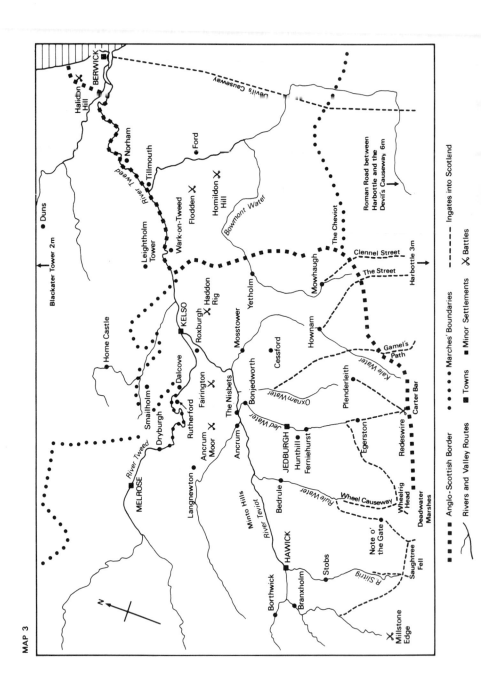

It was the international nature of the robbers' league that multiplied scathes. The clearing-house for damages was the day of truce ('trew') at which each Warden made the granting of redress conditional upon performance by the other side. Thus when Tynedale withheld redress,[4, 5] the Scots refused to answer for Liddesdale either; moreover, whenever both partners were simultaneously busy in a given area, the Warden opposite would disclaim any financial liability. Hence the Earl of Westmorland's comment on the Corbridge outrage, that 'it shall stop justice of Scotland'.[6 7] The best way to give one's partner a free hand was either to raid one's own compatriots in his company, or inflict scathes on *his* and deny redress: 'Tynedale and Redescale are mych glad that Liddesdale doth make this business. *They* had been minded to ride in Scotland'.[3]

Indifference to justice on the part of officials shaded into connivance with the malefactors, whom those with local lands found it undesirable to alienate. On this score Earls Maxwell and Bothwell in the forties had nothing to learn from Dacre and Heron. Indeed they outdid them with regard to the harbouring of fugitives ('reset'), more often villains than refugees for conscience like Father More. Frequently between 1521 and 1543[8] reset of Tynedalers on the run by Liddesdale or the aforesaid Earls[9] led to friction at government level.[10]

The main obstacle to carrying out scathes in Scotland was the foul weather in the high Cheviots, through which on the other hand ran eight Ingates,[11] affording access for deft horsemen on fell ponies over a broad front. From west to east these were:

1. up the river Slitrig to Kershopefoot;
2. along the upper Teviot from the bottom of Saughtree Fell;
3. from Saughtree Fell up the Note o' the Gate pass to Rule Water;
4. from Deadwater along the Wheel Causeway and over Wheelrig Head for Rule Water or the dense Jedforest;
5. from the Reidswyre on the Waste down Carter Fell to Jed Water;
6. Along Gammel's Path through the Waste to Coquet Head on to the Dere Street — for Redesdalers the highroad into Scotland;
7. From Harbottle over Clennel Street to Hownam and beyond;
8. Up the valley of the Tweed from Wark.[12]

Such were the factors pertaining in the four periods of Henry VIII's reign when there was a peace to disrupt. Henry VII's death had facilitated the re-emergence in the first of these of Bastard Heron as leader of robbers into the Scottish Middle Marches;[13] his patronage by Baron Dacre;[14] and his pardon by the new King,[15] which jointly provoked one clause in James IV's fateful ultimatum.[16]

The decade following the Flodden catastrophe saw Scotland with a dominant French party under the Regent Duke of Albany, who did not even send ambassadors to sue for peace; and an English party under the Chamberlain, Lord Home, and Archibald Douglas, Earl of Angus, brother-in-law to Henry VIII between 1514 and 1525, and destined to be great-grandfather to the first British King. After such a victory Baron Dacre found himself in the absurd situation of being driven, through lack of resources, to rely for support to the Anglophiles upon the highlanders and their Liddesdale cronies. These were of course compensated with more latitude than was proper within the English Borders, while Albany, too, for his part would castigate to Wolsey 'the evil mind of those who have the rule there'. In 1515, with the King's clandestine blessing, Dacre concocted a scheme for an expedition by Tyne- and Redesdalers under his brother Sir Christopher, Keeper of Redesdale, in order 'by excurses and robberies against the said Scots' to relieve pressure on Home, 'and compel the Duke to seek to Your Highness by sending of ambassadors'. To fend off subsequent claims for redress the Keeper was nominally outlawed.[17] Victualled for four days and joined by other Northumbrians, the expedition was cancelled on the point of departure at news that the Chamberlain had been beheaded. The Warden General had to resort to such expedients as in 1517 hiring the Armstrongs to raid on behalf of surviving Homes. Prelude to another outbreak of war in April 1522 was an acrimonious exchange on 9th January between the Regent and Dacre, concerning the default on redress for offences by each other's Borderers.

With the departure to France of the Duke of Albany in August 1524 Anglo-Scottish relations entered into nearly a decade of tranquillity. During the continuing minority of James V the Anglophile Angus became master of Scotland, while Francis I, soon to suffer a Flodden of his own at Pavia, was anxious to conciliate England. He recognised that the sole threat to British peace resided in the 'wild men' of the Borders.[18]

Because this was the period of the Ridley and Lisle revolts, the cordiality of the Scots regime was of signal convenience to England, especially in view of the loyal support given the rebels by Liddesdale. Vis-à-vis Ridley the Armstrongs were reckoned 'the greatest maintainers of the thieves of Tynedale' with whom 'they keepeth all company togidder',[19] while Lisle derived at least as much of his retinue from the Scottish dale as from 'your rebels and outlaws . . . being fled out of this your realm into Scotland'.[20] On assumption of wardenry in 1525 Angus was motivated as much by self-interest as by sentiment: Tynedale, he realised, was harbouring his master's traitors[19] and robbing widely in Scotland,[21] whereas the Englishmen who helped fight him at the Battle of Melrose[22] were probably Dodds and Charltons who after Ridley's collapse had taken refuge with the Armstrongs.[23]

On learning that Angus had fixed on that clan as his prime target, the Earl of Northumberland scoffed, in consideration of 'their great power . . . it is but a brag'. Undaunted, the Scots Warden between the Mays of 1525 and 1528 locked up their chieftains, executed others, and retrieved thousands of livestock. For these exertions he received scant thanks from the harassed English, who did not detect any deceleration in the rate at which their farms and garrisons were being destroyed.[24]

Barely sixteen, James V achieved his majority with three interrelated hatreds: at bottom one for his mother's England as bitter as any German Kaiser's; the others towards the provocative West Marchers and the step-father who menaced his realm with English domination. An aggravation was denial to him by his uncle Henry VIII of the lion's share of credit for Lisle's surrender upon which he had been counting. He dealt with the third of his problems in the autumn of 1528 when Angus was expelled south.

The other of James's domestic preoccupations was less tractable because in the light of Angus's hammering of the Liddesdalers they were toying with the possibility of secession to England. Feeling particularly insecure at Christmas, just after his Tynedale and Redesdale allies had lost many men and horses in a disastrous sortie into Teviotdale, Sym Armstrong, Laird of Mangerton, through the good offices of the Keeper of Tynedale met the Earl of Northumberland at Alnwick Castle. The possibility of a transfer of allegiance was ventilated and Sym set his hand to certain articles; Scots diplomats currently at Berwick confessed that Liddesdale was no longer in subjection to their King.[25] Three years later the Earl of Bothwell, one of two noblemen with strong Liddesdale links, in company with Robin Elliot of Thorlieshope, whose relations with the Tynedalers were peculiarly intimate, opened up similarly treasonable communications with the current Henry Percy at Dilston.[26, 27]

In parallel, Lord Maxwell, Warden of the West Marches, was maintaining a criminal connexion with Sym's Brother, Johnnie of Gilnockie, who had done a lot for Lisle during his rebellion and was now — in concert with the Elliots, Croziers and Nixons — in process of colonising the Threaplands and raiding both kingdoms therefrom.

Having arrested Maxwell and Bothwell, James V in May 1530 suddenly descended on Liddesdale to hang Gilnockie with thirty-five of his followers. Having thus disinfested the premises, the young King claimed Canonbie Holm, Johnnie's favourite Threapland haunt, with more stridency than any of his predecessors. He adduced the redress paid by the English in 1494 for the burning and plundering of the Priory by the Tynedalers, as proof that it was Scottish territory.[28]

With the Earls of Northumberland and Angus now in joint charge of the Northumbrian Marches, and equally bent on repair to their battered fortunes through renewal of war, they cheerfully added to the mounting *casus belli*. Behind them in full if still secret[29] support, King Henry enjoined the continuing subornation of Liddesdale and the incitement of Tyne- and Redesdales to back it in 'no small annoyance [to] the realm of Scotland'.[30] At one end of the 1532 summer 500 Tyne- and Liddesdalers attacked Clan Scott, slaying many, raising fire, and kidnapping the Laird of Buccleuch;[31] while at the other, Tynedale and this time Redesdale razed much of Kelso and surrounding abbeys,[29] to such purpose that even the Emperor got wind of it.[32] Having denounced 'z our lieges of Tynedale and Redesdale . . . accompanied with the Douglases our rebels' for murders and damage to the Kirk,[2] King James sent 5000 skirmishers to harry around Berwick on 20th November.

The norm for the decade after the war was the persistent league among the three dales, though it fluctuated in vigour and was impaired from time to time by Tynedale's internal dissensions.[33] Discontented with their share of the booty during hostilities, the highlanders tried to prolong them. Tynedale stirrings in January 1534 were reported by the Imperial ambassador,[34] and in March James V complained to his uncle about robbery and murder in Teviotdale by the Dodds, Charltons and Milburns.[35] What he omitted to mention was that the raiders flaunted the patronage of Maxwell, now his Keeper of Liddesdale as well as West Warden, in whose company they were descried at a day of truce in November 1535.[36] No less abetted by the Earl, Liddesdalers were engaged on reciprocal business in England, for which they laughingly offered redress at the Bells in Tynedale, 'where no true man dared to come'[37] and which was as big a joke on the Borders as Jeddart justice.[38]

Maxwell was a keen enough Catholic to lament his King's absence in France a-wooing when public order in Northern England collapsed in the autumn of 1536. The Liddesdale Keeper had to be satisfied with the measure of assistance vouchsafed by his charges during the rebellion to the hyperactive English highlanders. In the aftermath an inclination to see in exiles for the rebellion martyrs for the Faith may have accounted for the presence in his entourage of Edward Charlton of Hesleyside,[39] and, with a safe-conduct from James himself, of John Heron of the Hall Barns.[40] This was indicative of a new solidarity between the baron and a monarch whose conscience had induced him to condone the asylum offered the three 'strikers' of Keeper Fenwick by the Abbot of Jedburgh on Easter Day.[41, 42, 43, 44] A secondary motive for Maxwell was sensitivity to incursions into his own March, exemplified by an angry exchange with Norfolk,[45] and by his annoyance when a Scots freebooter on the run in Tynedale conducted his hosts around Scots targets.[40] Through preserving his understanding with the league, the Keeper aimed to divert such trouble away from the West Marches altogether.

The potentialities of the Tynedale/Redesdale/Liddesdale league as a nuisance to England were neutralised by the temporary secession of the Tynedale majority, and Maxwell may well have looked kindly on the coercive reaction of their opponents. Certainly the Warden Keeper was the particular target of King Henry's recriminations on the subject,[46, 47] and could not have been displeased when harmony was restored between the clans, especially as the upshot was a campaign to the particular detriment of the Hesleyside Band's enemies in England, and in Scotland to that of Andrew Kerr of Fernieherst, Warden of the Middle Marches, whom Maxwell disliked even more than he did the English. A series of assaults on Kerr's lands between Rule Water and the Dere Street was capped by a huge raid by 500 Tynedalers on Whitsunday 1538 against Sletrig of Clan Scott who lost two dozen horses, sixty head of cattle, twenty-eight prisoners, and 300 marks in property and ransoms.[48] Significantly, it was an attack in which the Charltons of Hesleyside and the Robsons of the Falstone collaborated.[49] An ironic feature was that the severely buffeted Sir Reynold Carnaby had personally to disburse £50 in redress upon which his Tynedalers had predictably defaulted.[50]

There is no direct evidence that on return to his cure John Heron aspired to share management of the Anglo-Scottish robbers with Lord Maxwell; the only thing to weigh against plentiful circumstantial evidence is a difference in rank that might have induced contempt. Little John found a flourishing concern. James V had just ridden to the Borders 'as for our pastime and solace of hawking', in reality to counter 'the greatest misrule and insolence . . . amongst z our subjects of Tynedale and Redesdale', in particular to pick up infiltrators guilty 'of slaughters and reifs'.[51] For contraflow there was a steady build-up to a total of thirteen Scots outlaws within the English highlands,[49, 52] most dangerous of whom was Robin Rutherford, harboured impartially near Bellingham, or by the four clans of Redesdale in concert.[53] English officers made no moves to arrest these miscreants, on the time-honoured grounds that the Scots were sheltering men as wanted as the Fenwick-slayers.[54, 55, 56, 57] These were massively reinforced in January 1540 when, in pursuit of his aim to bring the majority heidsmen to heel, the Keeper dropped on the Falstone. Either because the whole affair was a sham or because of a timely tip-off from Robin Rutherford who was right in the area,[52, 53] some forty scooted to Thorlieshope, including John and Cuddy Lion Robson, Topping and John Charlton of Larederburn.[58] Their hosts were sworn henchmen of Earl Maxwell, whose 'favours' towards the refugees were immediately solicited by the Elliots; overtures in the same sense were also being made on behalf of others of them by the Rutherford Laird of Hunthill to King James himself.[59] Clearly scenting collusion between the English and Scottish Keepers, Sir Thomas Wharton, observant Warden of the West Marches, addressed letters to both simultaneously, criticising the 'plain-ness' of reset to the latter,[60, 61] and chiding the former for not inviting Wharton's cooperation. Neither démarche elicited any positive response, even from Little John, whose 'great wisdom and experience' were flatteringly extolled by his colleague.[53] In significant conjunction the Scots and English Wardens of the Middle Marches then called on Maxwell and Heron to round up the fugitives,[62] which in Sir William Eure's estimation they were well capable of doing.[63] This plea too was ignored.

Little John having through the pardon reconsolidated Tynedale, there ensued a chain of explosions along the Borders from May 1541 onwards. While the offensive by the league against Heron's English foes proceeded apace, Wharton discarded smooth words for main force and attacked Maxwell on his West Marches with bands of up to 800 men,[49] whilst the baron at a conference with representatives from all the Liddesdale clans addressed them thus: 'Ye are the men that I can trust. I will have some notable act done to the Englishmen', with predictable results. For his part Heron in a score of scathes at the height of the raiding season steered his highlanders, either from the saddle or Harbottle, against Kerr of Fernieherst's lands in the placid valley between Hawick and Rule; the wedge of land between Jedburgh and the Dere Street; and even occasionally against mid-Tweeddale between Kelso and Melrose. Favoured Ingates were 3 and 7, with 2 and 6 as secondary routes. Most strenuous participants were the Charltons of Hesleyside, the Robsons of the Falstone, the Halls of Ellishaw, and as a native guide Robin Rutherford *alias* Cockback, leading bands of between forty and 800 men. Among 700 sheep and goats lifted, Fernieherst lost 100 ewes on Christmas Day, and other notable victims included the Sheriff of Roxburgh and the Homes of Egerston: damage in two of the raids was assessed at around £1000 Scots.[49, 64, 65]

The rise in the international temperature made all the more impact on King Henry because of his unique visit to York at around the same time, and he was shortly back in his 1532 position of urging on the Borderers 'three hurts for one',[66, 67] though still 'in secrecy',[68] and even putting out fresh feelers to Liddesdale. They for their part were boasting to Maxwell that they could start a war whenever they liked, and not idly, for shortly afterwards in reprisal for Halton the Elliot houses and garnered corn were set alight, albeit grudgingly, by Little John with a force of 500 Tynedalers, Redesdalers and Fenwicks who extracted 200 head of cattle, moveables and prisoners.[69] Whereas Wharton detected fresh evidence of collusion between Maxwell and Heron, King James felt he had to prepare for war.[49, 70] When in August 1542 France and the Empire fell to blows, Henry fulfilled his nephew's expectation, brushing aside one sensible proposal that instead of fighting one another James should quell Liddesdale and that Norfolk 'come upon those of Tynedale and Redesdale and so subdue them for ever'.[71] The war that was *mutatis mutandis* to dispose of Heron, Maxwell and King James himself went relentlessly ahead.

Defeat in the war should have sapped Scotland's will to survive, and indeed the Earl of Arran, from March 1543 Regent to the tiny Mary Queen of Scots, seemed at first as anxious as the repatriated Angus to serve England. Yet the French party led by Cardinal Beaton displayed a remarkable resilience in which they were assisted by two agents, of whom the major was Henry VIII: firstly through the brutality of the Treaty of Greenwich dictated to Scotland; secondly by another crazy declaration of war against France, whose aid to her partisans ceased to be lukewarm. Still substantial, even though the sun was fast setting on its heyday, the minor agent was the robber community on either side of the Border.

With the elimination of Heron and Maxwell, and the wound from Thorlieshope still raw, the tripartite league fell apart, a development which the two governments took some time to appreciate. During the honeymoon between the Regent and the King it was superfluously propounded that Tyne- and Redesdalers caught red-handed in Scotland should be punished by the Scots, and Liddesdale raiders given identical treatment in England, lest 'these evil-disposed persons . . . on both sides . . . breed strife and debate betwixt us'.[72, 73] Discovering the patronage of the peevish Bothwell no substitute for that of his predecessor; blocked by the warlike Wharton on the West Marches and by the huge garrison in Tynedale; and no longer provided by the English highlanders with a secure route south,[74, 75, 76] the Liddesdalers sought compensations in their own country. When this intensified pressure on them from the Scots authorities, the Armstrongs and the rest reverted to their policy in 1528 and sued to Sir Thomas Wharton and to the Keeper of Tyne- and Redesdales, by now Sir Ralph Eure, for the English allegiance, at least on a temporary basis.[77]

Meanwhile the highlanders selected the most sensitive period of all, between the armistice ('abstinence") in February and the Peace, to prolong warfare against Teviotdale. Noting 'they woll do the best they can to procure ill rule upon the Borders', the Warden General, Lord Parr, added he would rather they rode in Scotland than England. At the outset the Redesdalers lost forty prisoners in burning Ancrum up Ingate 6; as many Tynedalers were on the same warpath in March.[78, 79] After other counter-raids in May the Teviotdalers in July failed in a bid to rustle Eure's horses in Tynedale.[80] The highlanders retaliated first against the Kerrs,[81] then helped spoil the Scotts of Buccleuch of an enormous booty of horses, besides much else.[82] On receipt of that particular news Cardinal Beaton chuckled that the Englishmen should have begun it with the Scots.[83]

In fact by that September of 1543 the Homes, Kerrs and Scotts had long since rallied to the Cardinal. At a meeting with him[84] there had occurred an incident heavy with symbolism, and not merely because illustrative of the role of Tyne- and Redesdales in the approach to war. On being told that the new Keeper was a formidable adversary, Beaton with unclerical bravado had proclaimed he would fight the fellow himself. Though the hospitable[85] Clement Crozier was to be promised £100 for bearing the challenge south,[86, 87] and Henry VIII to manifest a lively interest,[88] Ralph Eure was never called on to assault the cloth. The truth was nevertheless that he and the Cardinal were already locked in a duel to the death.

NOTES

1. Jenny Wormald, *Court etc.*, p. 39.
2. PRO, SP 49 fol. 8, 20/11/1532.
3. BL, Calig. B III fol. 246, 29/7/1538.
4. PRO, Exchr. T. R. Misc. Books, Vol. 121 fol. 22, & SP I 131 fol. 167, 17/4/1538.
5. *Ibid.*, fol. 197–8, 24/4/1538.
6. BL, Add. MSS 32646 fol. 171, 9/7/1541.
7. *Ibid.*, fol. 209, 15/7/1541.
8. The English complained in the 1527 summer, October 1528, November 1529, the 1537 summer, the 1539–40 winter, the 1541 winter and the 1543 summer; the Scots in the 1522 summer, the 1525 summer, the three winters 1537–9, and the Spring of 1541.
9. BL, Add. MSS 32650 fol. 198, 18/4/1543.
10. Bl, Calig. B II fol. 43, 31/5/1525.
11. Scots Ingates into England are listed as such in *LP*, XVIII(2) no. 538, December 1543.
12. Hereinafter these Ingates will be referred to by numbers 1 through 8.
13. George Buchanan, *Scotland*, II p. 246.
14. BL, Calig. B VI fol. 50, 26/7/1512.
15. *LP*, I(2) (Kraus) no. 2222.10, 18/8/1513.
16. G. R. Ridpath, *(The) Border History (of England and Scotland)*, p. 332.
17. BL, Calig. B II fol. 187, 25/8/1515.
18. *LP*, IV(3) no. 5796, 26/7/1529.
19. PRO, SP I 34 fol. 205–6, 16/5/1525.
20. *Ibid.*, 42 fol. 156–7, 4/7/1527.

21. *Ibid.*, 35 fol. 244, 10/8/1525.
22. Armstrong, *Liddesdale*, p. 234.
23. BL, Calig. B VI fol. 409, 13/5/1526.
24. See p. 129 below.
25. BL, Calig. B II fol. 95, 14/11/1528.
26. *Ibid.*, B V fol. 216, 21/12/1531.
27. *LP*, IV(3) no. 609, 27/12/1531.
28. CDRS, Vol. IV App. I no. 34, 26/3/1494.
29. *LP*, V no. 1460, 22/10/1532.
30. PRO, SP 1 70 fol. 232–5, 23/8/1532.
31. See p. 218 below.
32. *LP*, V no. 1531, 10/11/1532.
33. See p. 138 below.
34. *LP*, VII(1) no. 83, 17/1/1534.
35. PRO, SP 9 IV fol. 18–9, 18/3/1534.
36. *LP*, IX no. 844, 18/11/1535.
37. *Ibid.*, X no. 1154, 17/6/1536.
38. A euphemism for execution without trial, allegedly characteristic of the species of justice dispensed in Jedburgh.
39. PRO, SP I 126 fol. 13, 24/10/1537.
40. BL, Calig. B VII fol. 233, 7/11/1538.
41. Ibid., BI fol. 128, 7/4/1537.
42. BL, Add. MSS 32646 fol. 100, 11/4/1537.
43. BL, Calig. B II fol. 6,25/4/1537.
44. *LP*, XII(2) no. 666, 8/9/1537.
45. BL, Calig. B I fol. 322, 27/4/1537.
46. PRO, Exchr. T. R. Misc. Books, Vol. 121 fol. 136, 20/4/1537.
47. PRO, SP I 119 fol. 130–3, 2/5/1537.
48. That killings and plunder were seldom attested in the same bill is a reminder that it was risky to disappoint one's visitors. Cf. the legend concerning the Robsons' raid on the Grahams, the subject of a waxwork in the Border Museum at Hexham, and described in Watson, *Reivers*, p. 29.
49. PRO, SP 49 5 fol. 29, December 1541.
50. BL, Calig. B III fol. 249, 12/6/1539.
51. BL, Royal MSS 18 B VI fol. 72, 19/12/1539.
52. PRO, SP I 157 fol. 108, 27/1/1540.
53. Ibid., fol. 98, 25/1/1540.
54. BL, Calig. B VII fol. 224, 3/7/1537.
55. *LP*, XIV(2) no. 689, 15/12/1539.
56. *LP*, XVI no. 356, 27/12/1540.
57. *Ibid.*, no. 426, 5/1/1541.
58. BL, Royal MSS 7 cxvi fol. 140–2, 22/1/1540.
59. PRO, SP I 157 fol. 138–9, (3/2/1540).
60. *Ibid.*, fol. 99, 25/1/1540.
61. *Ibid.*, fol. 168–9, 13/2/1540.
62. BL, Royal MSS 7 cxxi fol. 136, 21/1/1540.
63. BL, Calig. B I fol. 348, March 1540.
64. *LP*, XVI no. 1203, 25/9/1541.

65. BL, Add. MSS 32646 fol. 237, 14/10/1541.
66. *LP*, XVI no. 1202, 25/9/1541.
67. BL, Add MSS 32646 fol. 251, 20/10/1541.
68. *Ibid.*, fol. 240, 18/10/1541.
69. *Ibid.*, fol. 270, 2/12/1541.
70. *Ibid.*, fol. 282, 11/12/1541.
71. *Ibid.*, 32648 fol. 27, 6/10/1542.
72. *Ibid.*, 32650 fol. 6, 1/3/1543.
73. *Ibid.*, fol. 18, 7/3/1543.
74. *Ibid.*, 32649 fol. 135, 10/2/1543.
75. PRO, SP I 176 fol. 76, 25/3/1543.
76. *Ibid.*, fol. 107, 3/3/1543.
77. See p. 143 below.
78. BL, Add. MSS 32649 fol. 154, 15/2/1543.
79. *LP*, XVIII(1) no. 291, 17/3/1543.
80. BL, Add. MSS 32651 fol. 101, 17/7/1543.
81. *Ibid.*, fol. 38, 5/9/1543.
82. *Ibid.*, 32652 fol. 126, 22/9/1543.
83. *LP*, XVIII(2) no. 181, 13/9/1543.
84. *LP*, XVIII(1) no. 838, 7/7/1543.
85. See p. 92 above.
86. *LP*, XVIII(1) no. 886, 15/7/1543.
87. *Ibid.*, no. 914, 19/7/1543.
88. *Ibid.*, no. 937, 22/7/1543.

PART II: FROM CONTAINMENT THROUGH APPEASEMENT TO ELIMINATION

CHAPTER NINE

The Official Hierarchy

Ideally the highlands of the English Middle Marches were subject to seven echelons of government, from any of which a grapple might be extended but of which several might be missing. Concern at all levels was military, fiscal and judicial as well as a matter of police. There was plenty of what modern military jargon would term skip-echelon working; that is to say going over a superior's head, at which however only the imperious Norfolk ever took offence.

The topmost rung was the Court. As Lord of Tynedale and in process of becoming Lord of Redesdale also,[1, 2] Henry's personal stake in the region was comparable with Wolsey's. Nor did invigilation flag under Cromwell, who though not a property-owner along the Borders was the arch-centraliser. An innovation was the despatch thither of King's servants like Sir George Lawson and Sir Anthony Browne, as watchdogs on the Earl of Northumberland and the Duke of Norfolk respectively, not least in respect of dealings with the highlanders. The policy was informed by Henry VIII's inclination, especially after 1536, to resume the Northern Marches into his own hands, given the anarchy prevalent 'particularly in Tynedale and Redesdale'.[3]

Apart from emissaries *ad hoc* the Court continually invaded lower reaches of the hierarchy. Thus from 1515 onwards there were direct interventions by King or Cardinal right down as far as Vice Wardens and Keepers of Redesdale,[4] the normal provocation being Dacre's misgovernment, notably his failure to dragoon the robbers under his rule.[5, 6, 7, 8,] Ignoring the senior officers, Carnaby habitually harped on his dependence upon Thomas Cromwell.[9, 10] When Norfolk demanded this Keeper's dismissal and that of Widdrington, Henry angrily interpreted the aspersion as reflecting on his own judgment, since they were *his* nominees.[11] When the monarch set a thief, in the guise of Little John, to catch thieves, it was after Heron's man-to-man coaching from the royal council;[12] it was patently because the King felt personally let down that he was so vindictive towards him in disgrace. At the end of the reign correspondence between mere Keepers and the Privy Council[13] or Queen Regent[14] was routine.

---

* See Appendix.

The highest post in the field was the Lieutenancy, a crisis appointment once graced by John of Gaunt, and always by a high nobleman and a southerner at that, in order to ensure local independence.[15] He was expected to cow the highlanders by his mere proximity in 1537.[16] Like that of Richard of Gloucester, the Lieutenancy of the Earl of Hertford was prelude to the rule of all England. Until 1542 the office was practically monopolised by the Earl of Surrey who became third Duke of Norfolk in 1524. Till Bowes' advent he was regarded by the King as the expert on the highlanders, alone qualified to make their Keepers 'more able and meet to serve us',[11] and certainly their containment became an obsession with him.[17] He sent spies to size them up;[18] hunted Hodge à Fenwick's killers in person.[19] Naturally faced with a plethora of other problems, towards Tyne- and Redesdales he could claim no success at all, a fruitless confrontation in 1523 [20] being typical.

Consisting of canon and Chancery lawyers, the Yorkist Council of the North was restored in 1525, acquired an episcopal President in 1533, and eventually co-opted as members Wardens of the Marches. It busied itself assiduously with Tyne- and Redesdales, now drawing a Keeper's attention to his duties,[21] now recommending his dismissal.[22] Its clumsy meddling with Sir William Eure's plans during Lisle's revolt disappointed a King who could resist Dukes untold but never a committee. On balance, nevertheless, Lieutenants were justified in their reliance on it as a witan.[18]

At inception in the fourteenth century the Wardenry General for the co-ordination of all three Wardenries was thought fit only for a Prince of the Blood, and afterwards only for a Neville or Percy.[23] It was precisely in order to exclude the last-named that the Tudors appointed Baron Dacre of Gilsland to officiate between 1511 and 1525, except when Surrey's Lieutenancy in 1523 made him temporarily redundant.

Dacre was one of the best English soldiers alive: 'ye shall go next unto me into battle', declared the victor of Flodden, according to whom the Baron could catch more thieves in a day than anyone else in ten.[24] His deft handling of the Scots was praised repeatedly by Wolsey. On the other hand such successes were habitually ascribed to collusion with the highlanders, and not only by gentry,[25] clerics[26] and the Charltons of Hesleyside, all with axes to grind in the Percy interest, but even by the Lieutenant[27] and the Cardinal.[28] That he should have stooped to at least *ad hoc* arrangements with a military bloc adjacent to his own lordships of Burgh and Gilsland is hardly remarkable in view of the narrowness of the Northumbrian base upon which his 'ponderous burding' rested. According to Dacre's uncontested assertions he had received no wages for years, and his efforts to make good a consequent shortfall in friends and henchmen through the venial nepotism of appointing brothers Christopher and Philip were begrudged.[29] It was natural that in 1523 he should have sought demotion to Surrey's deputy, so as to daunt the 'misguided . . . inhabitants of Tynedale and Redesdale', as well as the Scots.[30]

Lessons drawn from Dacre's tenure were firstly to do without a Warden General altogether; secondly, if his co-ordinating role became indispensable, to avoid in the nominee any such distorting ties with one March as Cumbrian Dacre had had; thirdly that he should cohabit with a vigilant Lieutenant. After a lapse of seventeen years the conditions were satisfied in the persons of Lords Rutland, Lisle and Parr. These Southrons soon entered into the spirit of the thing: within a month of arrival Parr was employing Topping as intermediary with the Charlton assassins.[31]

By Henry VIII's reign individual Wardens for the East, Middle and West Marches never co-existed with a Warden General, while the first two were normally combined. Given the affiliation of Liddesdale to the West Marches and of their Tyne- and Redesdale allies to the Middle, the surviving hinge was awkward enough. In 1528 a pact was alleged between Liddesdale and the Cumbrian Warden to spare his territory at the expense of the Northumbrian, while intentions of the Warden's successors in 1536 and 1543 to aid their colleague against the highlanders stayed unfulfilled.[32]

Novi homines were as insistent as Dukes that a Warden's lineage be noble and indigenous.[33] According to a Durham Chancellor, whenever the Tynedalers 'be not in dread of some nobleman . . . they never desist to . . . do evil';[16] while peers in 1525 and 1542 concurred that to serve in Northumberland one needed to be related to all the local gentry. Yet of the Wardens before 1536 only the Earl of Northumberland measured up to both criteria simply because of the government's distaste for the second of them. Certainly the Henry Percy to whom the Court at length surrendered, though half the man, daunted the clansmen more than stranger Dacre had ever done. The Earl's success against the rebels in 1528 was psychological and the magic of his name continued to stand him in good stead in such negotiations as with the heidsmen at Hexham in 1535.[34]

Henry VIII's disgust with the conduct of the Percys in 1536 was aggravated by the refusal of the Neville Earl of Westmoreland to assume the Wardenry, lest he saddle himself with the hated Carnaby.[35] The sovereign reverted to his former principle that 'retaining all the gentlemen and heidsmen (sic), he shall not be ill served',[36, 37] and jettisoned both criteria. It was seven years until, acting on a recommendation from Wharton, he reappointed Wardens, to wit Wharton himself on the West, and the Eures father and son on the East and Middle Marches, ensuring continuance of a single Northumbrian command *de facto*. Probably also ratified was a further proposal that the Middle Warden spend one month per annum at both Harbottle and Chipchase, to keep an eye on the highlands.[32] Not only had knights — albeit soon ennobled — displaced earls, but when Sir Ralph fell in battle he was succeeded by Bowes, whose roots like Eure's were in Durham and Yorkshire, not Northumberland.[38]

One unchanging aspect was the rarity with which a Warden got paid. In the Earl's case this accelerated dissipation of the lordliest patrimony in England, so that he ended life wearing King Henry's cast-offs; while Bowes, lauded to the skies and ensconced in an independent Middle Marches, perforce risked a compromising dependence on the Herons.

For about half the reign the immediate rule of the Middle Marches was the responsibility of a knight dubbed Vice Warden or Lieutenant, whose significance was enhanced during a Warden's absence. Thus when the Earl of Northumberland in 1536 was stranded in the south, a contest for recognition as Vice Warden between his usurping brother and his nominee became critical. As Tyne- and Redesdalers primly explained, they opposed Ogle, supposing Percy 'to have the rule of the county under the King's Highness'.[39] Alternatively, his chief's absence afforded the Vice Warden an opportunity for insubordination, witness William Eure's journey to London in 1524 to pin upon Dacre 'the extreme desolation' caused by the highlanders.[26]

Normally friction arose over money. With inflation the salary climbed unsteadily from 100 to 200 marks p.a. between 1525 and 1537, insufficient to stifle Eure's moans about the expense of Lisle's revolt,[40] and the Earl's failure to defray even the 100 marks to which he had cut his deputy's salary. Consequent upon shortage of funds was inability to fee the gentry, essential when the incumbent was an outlander like Sir William, 'disdained' by Sir William Heron 'whose ancestors have been lieutenants here . . . and we [both Vice Wardens] be strangers in that country'.[41] In vain Eure fished around for someone to fill the Tynedale Keepership for the measly £10 p.a. 'besides profits' that he could afford.[42]

Pluralism was one solution for the impecunious Vice Warden. Dacre and Widdrington[2] each conformed to the principle that the governor of the Middle Marches, at whatever level, 'cannot well exercise his office unless he have the rule of the men of Redesdale'.[43] Eure indeed, who amassed jobs much as his master Wolsey did benefices, administered both Keeperships. Pluralism entailed neglect, and the sole incumbent ever praised during the reign was Roger Heron, then only posthumously. All his successors —

Edward Ratcliffe, Eure, Widdrington, and Cuthbert Ratcliffe — were branded incompetent.[44] Echoed later by Widdrington,[2] Eure confessed during Ridley's commotion that 'it lyeth not in the power of me and other your officers here to repress the said offences'.[26] Northumberland's sluggishness in designating a replacement becomes intelligible.

Apart from the monarchy, the Tynedale Keepership was the sole echelon never missing. Except between 1536 and 1543 the incumbent was at one level above, with the duties devolved upon deputies. Only Dacre's voice was ever raised against the hereditary element in the procession of Fenwicks and Herons, and then only because his own brother had been passed over.[29] Regarding the bias towards natives, Lord Howard de Walden was to remark in 1619: 'neither will any man which hath not been bred in those highland countries come from a more civil place to interpose himself on such a business for any reasonable means that can be given'.[45]

These reasonable means consisted of money and lands, the relative value of which with inflation is hard to compute.[46] Wages ran at £40-45 p.a. in the twenties;[47, 48] dipped to 40 marks for Hodge à Fenwick and Carnaby;[49] rose to 100 marks in 1541.[50] Little John received £5-10 for specific acts of thief-taking between 1539 and 1541,[51, 52] and 70 marks for rescuing Carnaby.[53] However, the major emolument came in the form of farms of lands. Between 1510 and 1514 the Keeper shared with the Vice Warden Northumbrian manors worth £70 p.a..[54, 55] Ralph Fenwick described Plenmellor, over which he quarrelled with Nicholas Ridley, as 'most principal thing and profit' pertaining to the Keepership.[56] Lands around Tarset were worth rather more to Carnaby than his salary;[2, 57] his farm of Hexham Abbey lands was not held *qua* Keeper but passed to John Heron as such.[58, 59]

The biggest subvention again came through a pairing with other jobs. Of three candidates — Redesdale, Hexhamshire and Langley — William Eure held the second if at one remove, Carnaby all except the first. Heron contended that all should reside with his Keepership, 'because they all join together'.[60] Once Widdrington had moved on the King, grouping similar terms, installed Heron[61] and eventually Ralph Eure in control of the whole highland zone, thereby anticipating Parr's query 'whedder one man or two . . . to keep such wild people in order'.[62] With regard to the lowlands in question, policy ebbed and flowed. Keeper Ralph Fenwick had managed Hexhamshire for nearly ten years, and during the Pilgrimage Norfolk had advocated that it should be assigned his successor, throwing in Langley[63, 64] and probably Corbridge[65] for good measure. When Carnaby the beneficiary died, the Duke of Suffolk as Lieutenant was keen that the arrangement continue[66] 'to make [the Keeper] to have more force and less to the King's charge to rule the wild people of Tynedale'.[59, 62] On the quixotic grounds that 'it would not be amiss to distribute some lands to others dwelling in those parts so that *they* can serve the Keeper',[67] the proposal was vetoed by Henry. However, he changed his mind again in 1545 when the omnicompetent Bowes was granted the lot.[68]

However abstruse to quantify the scale of funding was clearly designed to be lavish. Yet, to quote Carnaby, there was 'no profit in it'[69] since he had not received 20/- wages in 2½ years, while his farms were proving £300 less lucrative than expected.[70] The 'great expenses'[55] to be set against a largely notional salary for 'these troublous rooms'[71] were miscellaneous indeed. Sir Reginald could 'by no means attain any recovery'[72] for pledges' board and lodging; for the Hesleyside operation; nor for £80 paid the Scots for Tynedale depredations.[70] John Heron, too, was to be owed two months' pay for thirty soldiers quartered in Tynedale,[60] and had to defray redress to Scots out of his own pocket.[73]

In this connexion the personal liability of any steward was already operative by 1390, when William Swinburne, Keeper of Tynedale, entered into a bond of 500 marks with its Lord, the Duke of York, to guarantee the former's respect for 'Libertez et fraunchises de la dit Seignurie'.[74] Lord Dacre was virtually charged an insurance premium of 2000 marks before moving into Harbottle,[75] and in his turn levied a bond on the Keeper in 1514 for Tynedale's good behaviour.[29] Diplomats in 1540 described Heron as 'bound to warrant, relieve and keep scatheless [his Vice Warden] touching the bounds of Tynedale and Redesdale'.[73] Both Keepers in 1523[76] and Carnaby in 1538 similarly went bail.[77] There being no longer mention of stipulated sums, it seems that the sealed recognisance had been superseded by a tacit obligation to make good any losses.

It is not surprising, then, that *noli episcoparis* abounded. Following Lord Ogle [78] and most of the Northumbrian gentry a decade before,[79] the Lord Dacre of 1537 would 'rather lose a finger of each hand than meddle with Tynedale'.[64] Aside from the frankly dishonest, willing candidates tended to be desperately poor. Bastard Thomas Dacre, 'a quick sharp man brought up in the practices of such wild people', was ineligible because he would have required an extra £50 p.a..[11] The reluctance to press charges against John Heron becomes comprehensible: 'it would', averred the Council of the North, 'be hard to replace him'.[80]

Equally comprehensible is the stream of criticism[81] which those who did shoulder the burden attracted, and which underlay the constant harping on that paragon, the ideal Keeper: a true, hardy gentleman[1, 82] and captain with a stout heart,[83] independent[11, 64] and, as the Tynedale heidsmen sarcastically pointed out, an ability to think fast was indispensable.[84] On the one hand he must have no truck with thieves,[65, 85] on the other he should be popular with them[64] — somewhere between Carnaby, to whom none dared be friendly,[72] and Heron who figuratively as well as literally dwelled half a mile from Tynedale.[85] One fancied candidate had 500 marks p.a., 100 armed retainers and a good wit, and was related to half the county.[64]

In measuring up to the model, Keepers adopted either a confrontational or a permissive posture. The earlier Fenwicks belonged to the latter school. Sir Roger 'did ill'[47] while after Flodden Sir Ralph was implicated in the spoliation of Hexham market[86] and in up to 400 other offences.[25] However, the quarrel over Plenmellor set him on the opposite side from the highlanders during the Ridley revolt, in the course of which 'to his reproach'[87] he was repeatedly humiliated. It may be surmised that the Tynedalers did not exert themselves to prevent his capture in the Smailholm fray, sandwiched between the two repulses.[88] After a plea from Dacre to the Cardinal for a disciplinary letter to the Keeper, urging him to his duty, had been rebuffed on the grounds of the baron's own dereliction,[7] Sir Ralph was temporarily dismissed for failure to enforce redress.[47] Exponent of the permissive school, his replacement Sir John Heron, too, achieved in a brief tenure 'foul redress [which] . . . by maintenance and concealment . . . to the . . . thieves hath been the destruction of Northumberland'.[85] His resignation, however, was not out of sympathy with Lisle, but followed a reduction in wages of one third.[42] Although scepticism was voiced that Sir Ralph with less money would improve on previous incompetence,[85] he was not merely restored but eventually succeeded by what was presumably his son. Upon the outbreak of the insurrection, Hodge resumed the policy of confrontation that was to prevent the Fenwicks from hardening into a dynasty.

But it was Carnaby's career that most starkly exemplified the fate of the weak Keeper who essayed confrontation. He started with every advantage: lands shortly to be regarded as enough to underpin the rule of both dales, let alone one; intentions to govern Tynedale 'in fair and fearful manner';[9] ministerial, even royal favour, so that when his first steps excusably faltered, the King reminded Norfolk that 'young men must have a time to learn'.[11] Even when the Duke obstinately insisted he would rather see Reynold in Paradise than on his staff,[18] Henry mildly hoped that reproof would stir to new diligence.[19]

Though knighted for a military exploit, he was widely believed to be 'so afeared of his person that he does nothing but keep the house . . . having yet shewed no part of manhood'.[18, 63] His lack of stamina put resignation in his head no sooner than he had entered office,[89] 'because it was painful', then an exorbitant spell of leave, 'leaving the rebels at his back'.[69] Want of staying power generated two other weaknesses, firstly inattention to such details as the rickety state of Hexham gaol Tower 'and yet I can be bold to say and prove the same, not through any negligence in me . . . for since the time of the plague in Hexham I came not there'.[10] Secondly there was an abjectness of demeanour: he wished he had 'better news [for Cromwell] whereof I would be most glad',[9, 90] and that 'they whom I put in trust under me had been as earnest and as diligent in painstaking as I myself am'.[10] In short Sir Reynold laboured in the worst position conceivable, inspiring both dislike and contempt in his ruthless parishioners 'who neither love, trust, nor fear him';[91] 'they do not much esteem their Keeper, considered the quality of the man'.[16] Hence Ralph Eure's diagnosis to Cromwell: 'My Lord, they have no rules put to them . . . that is the great cause of their disobedience'.[92]

Had John Heron been honest the highlanders' predatory instincts would through the outbreak of war have found adequate scope at an enemy's expense. It was due to the crooked Keeper that their misdeeds spilled over into England as well. His two successors contrived to steer a nicer course between confrontation and indulgence. Thanks like Heron to a deplorable predecessor Ralph Eure had to serve a period of probation[93, 94] before final appointment. Rather eccentrically he had angled for the post for years, petitioning Cromwell 'to put the rule of Tynedale to me . . . I think good service might best be done amongst evil persons'.[92] In the event, having first meted out deserved punishments,[95] he backed heidsman Archie Dodd in his dispute with Hexham men about a deadly fracas,[96, 97, 98] then enlisted him with Giles, Little John's younger son, in a scheme of high skulduggery.[99, 100] After the death in action of this, the most intrepid and disastrous of the Tynedale Keepers, he was replaced by the highlanders' foremost anthropologist,[101] peculiarly aware that the incumbent was a King of the Wood destined for slaughter.[82] Accordingly the prestigious Bowes interposed a filial George Heron between himself and his charges,[102, 103] obtaining royal audience for him to plead his cause.[71] Reinstatement[68] of a family which for Tynedalers gloriously personified the good old days demonstrated that Bowes could get away with anything.

Until 1540, when married with that of Tynedale, the Keepership of Redesdale, too, was normally subsumed into the functions of a superior officer. Either because the dale was marginally less unruly or to emphasise that, although still technically a Liberty, it was firmly in royal hands, the appointment of deputies was less regular than with Tynedale. The record at whichever level was on a par with that of Tynedale colleagues, Edward Ratcliffe being reckoned the equal of Roger Fenwick,[47] and Widdrington that of Carnaby.[64, 104] The latter, according to one administrative bishop, was

E

'no fit Keeper for Redesdale . . . a man that lacketh both wit and goodwill', who did the opposite of any advice.[83] An extenuation was the usual paltry funding, forty marks p.a. remaining the standard rate for years,[2, 05, 105] plus farms of the Holystone convent, all of which John Heron by poetic justice had to spend to meet debts, and mortgage ancestral lands into the bargain.[71]

If Redesdalers 'little regarded their Keepers',[106] there was one exception. Before the two stints under Baron Dacre, Sir William Heron of Ford had served Henry VII in like capacity, on one occasion with fateful results.[107] Thanks perhaps to this long experience, his achievement in the segregation of Redesdale from the Ridley commotion was splendid. Yet in October 1524 and a year later[78] he made strenuous efforts to disengage and only to a minor extent because of ungracious criticism from Warden General[108] and Cardinal.[109] Once again the root cause was financial. Before entry he had jibbed at the emoluments, demanding half fees in advance and a £20 loan,[110] but eventually settled for a garrison assigned gratis.[111] Subsequently he realised that to perform the task satisfactorily he must either receive further concessions or perish, what with fees to the Constable, gaoler and watchmen of Harbottle, and 'substantial hospitality so as the people of the country may be entertained with meat and drink . . . Otherwise a true gentleman cannot have them at commandment ne know the secrets of their demeanour . . . The jeopardous and chargeable room of the Keeping of Redesdale [hath] greatly consumed my poor substance . . . Now being in miserable condition . . . I am constrained to sell my poor lands [which] lying on the Borders this late time of war be largely wasted, . . . and disherit my heirs for ever',[112]

NOTES

1. PRO, SP I 116 fol.219,7/3/1537
2. PRO, Exchr. T. R. Misc. Books, Vol.121 fol.15-48, c.12/7/1537.
3. BL, Calig. B VIII fol.44, c.25/1/1537.
4. *LP*, IV(1) no.1910, 20/1/1526.
5. PRO, SP I 17 fol.223-4, 23/12/1518.
6. BL, Add.MSS 24965 fol.35, 24/6/1523.
7. BL, Calig. B III fol.37, end February 1524.
8. BL, Add.MSS 24965 fol.259, 11/6/1524.
9. BL, Calig. B III fol.251-3, 17/9/1538.
10. PRO, SP I 140 fol.131-3, 18/12/1538.
11. PRO, Exchr. T. R. Misc. Books, Vol.119 fol.137, (18/9/1537).
12. PRO, SP I 46 fol.105-6,12/1/1528.
13. *LP*, XX(1) no.219, 19/2/1545.
14. *LP*, XIX(1) no.962, 22/7/1544.
15. *Patronage etc.*, ed.Ross, p.117, an article on Ruling Elites by M. M. Condon.
16. PRO, SP I 123 fol.214-5, 4/8/1537.

17. *Ibid.*, 117 fol.234-5, 1/4/1537.
18. *Ibid.*, 124 fol.182-3,5/9/1537.
19. *Ibid.*, 125 fol.21-2, 23/9/1537.
20. *LP*, III(2) no.3576, 29/11/1523.
21. PRO, SP I 136 fol.217-8, 22/9/1538.
22. *Ibid.*, 125 fol.10-11, 22/9/1537.
23. M. E. James, *Tudor Magnate*, p.16.
24. *LP*, III(2) no.3384, 1/10/1523.
25. PRO, SP I 16 fol.313-4, 25/6/1518.
26. *Ibid.*, 32 fol.205, 30/11/1524.
27. *LP*, III(2) no.3304, 5/9/1523.
28. *LP*, II(2) no.4547, end October 1518.
29. BL, Calig. B II fol.190, 17/5/1514.
30 BL, Add.MSS 24965 fol.110, 18/11/1523.
31. PRO, SP I 178 fol.53, 17/5/1543.
32. *Ibid.*, 179 fol.151, June 1543.
33. A matter in debate at least as early as Richard II's reign. Cf. J. A. Tuck in *NH*, Vol.III p.27.
34. PRO, SP I 96 fol.169-173, 15/9/1535.
35. *Ibid.*, 118 fol.148-9, 12/4/1536.
36. BL, Harl.MSS 6989 fol.68, 12/3/1537.
37. See p.170 below.
38. So I should somewhat antedate the trend towards appointment of inland men which Watson, *Reivers*, p.40 regards as an Elizabethan innovation.
39. PRO, SP I 69 fol.54-5, 17/1/1537 (not 1532 as calendared).
40. *LP*, VIII no.203, 12/2/1535.
41. BL, Calig. B I fol.41, 27/4/1525.
42. *Ibid.*, B III fol.209, 12/9/1527.
43. *Ibid.*, B I fol.133, 14/2/1537.
44. For the generally low level of competence in Border officials, see. M. L. Bush in *NH*, Vol.VI p.53 ff.
45. PRO, E 134, Michaelmas 1620.
46. See p.19 above.
47. BL, Calig. B VI fol.401 June 1525.
48. *Ibid.*, B III fol.65, c.27/12/1528.
49. PRO, SP I 122 fol.212-3, 8/7/1537.
50. BL. Calig. B VIII fol.63, 2/12/1541.
51. *LP*, XV no.1018, 30/8/1540.
52. *LP*, XVI no.1489, end of 1541.
53. BL, Royal MSS 18 B VI fol.72, 19/12/1539.
54. *LP*, I(1) (Kraus) no. 485. 26, 10/5/1510.
55. *LP*, I(2) (Kraus) no.2863, 5, 26/4/1514.
56. BL, Add.MSS 24965 fol.190, 1/4/1524.
57. *LP*, XIII(1) no.877, 24/4/1538.
58. *LP*, XVI(2), 1/9/1540.
59. PRO, SP I 178 fol.33, 15/5/1543.
60. PRO, E 36 Vol.121 fol.12 & 27.
61. *LP*, XV no.984, 17/8/1540.

62. BL, Add.MSS 32651 fol.247, 21/8/1543.
63. PRO, SP I 124 fol.232-3, 15/9/1537.
64. *Ibid.*, fol.234-7, 15/9/1537.
65. *Ibid.*, 116 fol.217-8, 7/3/1537.
66. BL, Add.MSS 32651 fol.108, 18/7/1543.
67. *Ibid.*, 269, 25/8/1543.
68. PRO, SP I 199 fol.161, late March 1545.
69. *Ibid.*, 129 fol.138-9, 27/2/1538.
70. *Ibid.*, 154 fol.96-7, October/November 1539.
71. *Ibid.*, 227 fol.79, 13/12/1546.
72. BL, Calig. B III fol.249, 12/6/1539.
73. BL, Royal MSS 7 cxxi fol.136, 21/1/1540.
74. Northumberland RO, Swinburne Charters, 1/81, 24/2/1390.
75. *LP*, I(1) (First Edition) no.380, July 1509.
76. BL, Calig. B VI fol.435, end August 1523.
77. PRO, SP I 136 fol.161-4, 15/9/1538.
78. *LP*, IV(1) no.1727, 29/10/1525.
79. PRO, SP I 45 fol.109, calendared 11/12/1527, but unlikely to have been written before 25/2/1528.
80. *Ibid.*, 169 fol.203-5, end March1542.
81. M. L. Bush, in *NH*, Vol.VI p.53.
82. BL, Calig. B VIII fol.106, 1551 (not 1542).
83. *Ibid.*, B VII fol.239, 11/1/1539.
84. *Ibid.*, fol.71, 22/11/1525.
85. PRO, SP I 45 fol.101-7, 2/12/1527.
86. *Ibid.*, 10 fol.18, 27/1/1515.
87. BL, Calig. B III fol.6, 20/5/1524.
88. PRO,SP I 31 fol.196-7, 8/7/1524.
89. *Ibid.*, 121 fol.169-170, 26/6/1537.
90. *Ibid.*, 139 fol.84-5, 14/11/1538.
91. *Ibid.*, 152 fol.215-7, 23/7/1539.
92. *Ibid.*, 126 fol.80-1, 6/11/1537.
93. *LP*, XIV(2) no.399, mid-October 1539.
94. BL, Calig. B III fol.262, 17/12/1539.
95. PRO, SP I 178 fol.85, 24/5/1543.
96. *LP*, XVIII(1) no.937, 22/7/1543.
97. PRO, SP I 180 fol.241, 27/7/1543.
98. *LP*, XVIII(1) no.964, 28/7/1543.
99. See p.184 below.
100. BL, Harl.MSS 1757 fol.292-302, c.5/8/1544.
101. BL, Add.MSS 32656 fol.195, 11/3/1545.
102. PRO, SP 49 5 fol.40, 19/11/1542.
103. BL, Add.MSS 32648 fol.224, 19/12/1542.
104. PRO, SP I 125 fol.25-6, c.28/9/1537.
105. BL, Calig. B VI fol.409, 13/5/1526.
106. PRO, SP I 132 fol.25-6, 3/5/1538.
107. See p.75 above.
108. BL, Add.MSS 24965 fol.193, 1/4/1524.

109. *LP*, IV(1) no.132, end-February 1524.
110. *LP*, III(2) no.3218, 2/8/1523.
111. BL, Add.MSS 24965 fol.52, 3/8/1523.
112. PRO, SP I 32 fol.127, c.14/10/1524.

CHAPTER TEN

The Keeper's Posse

The Ford letter reminds that an officer who was Sheriff, colonel, police superintendent and chief of Border Guards had to transmute funds, lands and influence into manpower, both amateur and professional. Thus a prime qualification for Keepership was the tally of one's household servants: Nicholas Ridley, for example, had forty and Reynold Carnaby nineteen.[1] Being tenant farmers, even such retainers could seldom be summoned 'suddenly without long tarrying'.[2]

Clearly the pool from which officeholders were selected, up to fifty of the Northumbrian gentry were feed to stand by for operations against the highlanders as well as the Scots. In 1528 typical such pensioners were Lord Ogle at twenty marks p.a., John Widdrington at ten, Cuthbert Ratcliffe and Sir John Heron at £5, partly rewards for service against Lisle.[3, 4] Subsequently their numbers were reduced but at larger fees, and in 1538 Carnaby nominated thirty who between them should raise 100 men to seal off Tynedale.[5] Unfortunately, however, they were over-insistent on the letter of their obligation. Thus after Carnaby's abduction they collectively protested an inability to sustain 'importunate pains and charges' 'for the resisting of the malice of the said Tynedales'.[6]

Between pensioners and a penumbra of roughly 100 Northumbrian gentry, exempt taxation for military service, the distinction was so threadbare that Wharton advocated the former's abolition. On one list the name of each gentleman was significantly followed by his distance from Scotland, then from Tyne- and Redesdales,[7] against whom the Earl of Northumberland took for granted that individual's obligation to collaborate.[3] A main objective in seeking lowland lordships for the Keeper was to enlist heartier cooperation from the South Tyne gentry.[8] As a class they were undependable, evacuating homes near the dales during trouble,[9, 39] and needing to be commanded to winter in 1540.[10] In Hertford's opinion 'one of them would see another's throat cut rather than they will go to their doors . . . That doth these thieves and outlaws know'.[11] 'Let the pensioners go', was a familiar disclaimer, while downright pacts with the highlanders to ignore hue and cry[12] may have accounted for passivity against Lisle[13] and that of a Vice Warden's own kinsmen in 1537.[14]

Equivalent of pensioners among the lower orders and run by them as

Setters and Searchers were pairs of watchmen in townships adjoining the highlands, who routinely watched fords over the Tyne and nearby toons.[2] Others would be set to confront such emergency threats as by Tynedalers to Hexham in 1514[15] and by Liddesdale and Charlton outlaws to Coquetdale in 1543.[16] Watchmen were paid — under protest — by local gentry, and subject to fines; Bowes saw justice in a contribution from remoter townships as well.[2] Normally vigilance was nocturnal[15] but Bowes favoured the posture described by martyred Bishop Ridley: 'In [South] Tynedale where I was born . . . my countrymen watched night and day in their harness . . . their spears in their hands . . . Like pretty men they defended their country'.[17] Clearly the system worked better in 1543 when their hue and cry saved Ralph Eure's horses[18] than during the Hexham fiasco in 1538.

To alarm or fray thus raised by horn or beacon responded the entire neighbourhood as spearmen or bowmen on horse or foot. A new bridge below Chipchase was projected in 1541 to facilitate approach for dwellers on either bank. Such bursts of activity carried no wage entitlement. That the ancestors of the Fighting Fifth were not martial material may be safely ruled out, but their handicaps were only too obvious: their acquaintance with the mosses was at best superficial;[2] 'labourers cannot be so soon in areadiness as the Tynedale men be';[5] and finally the impact of the gressum had since 1500 cut the numbers of armed men from five to one thousand, barely more numerous than the clansmen themselves. Resultant overall performance so disappointed Henry VIII as to evoke an extraordinary threat in 1543, that if this arriere-ban did not pull itself together 'the King woll look otherwise upon those that have offended them'.[19]

More practicable than to abandon the victim for the aggressor was however to meet the requirement for professional reinforcement formulated by Bowes, that for the Tynedale Keeper to be able to react promptly to incursions would be more 'surely achieved . . . by fifty or three-score active and well horsed men lying together in one house near . . . Tynedale, than by 500 . . assembled and gathered together by warning of the country', *a fortiori* because a great concourse 'be so evil kept secret in those parts'.

Most Border forts were on the flanks where the nations tended to fight their biggest battles. Any reorientation from Scots to highlanders would have been rated no distraction, since they were so often lumped together as a composite foe,[2, 20] the Marches being designated 'foreanempst Scotland, Tynedale and Redesdale.[21] Carnaby once wanted much of the Berwick garrison to be redeployed against Tynedale,[22] while from Carlisle it was feasible to keep the Liddesdale/Tynedale junction and even the Waste towards Redesdale under observation. However, Norfolk's dream of Bewcastle's becoming 'a marvellous great bridle to Liddesdale and Tynedale' never materialised.[23] Quite simply such strongholds were umbrellas too far from the clouds.

The Cheviots seemed to render forts on the Middle Marches superfluous until it was remembered that what excluded the Scots merely multiplied the highlanders' opportunities. Occasionally a safety-net along South Tyne was contemplated, with soldiers billeted at, among others, Haydon Bridge and Haltwhistle.[10, 24] In addition there were four fourteenth-century tower-houses, but by 1538 only one wall of Langley still stood, while Willimoteswick, though sound, was very much occupied by Nicholas Ridley. The two most commodious were in Hexham: firstly the rectangular gaol, whose three-score corbels supported battlements and where a vaulted ground-floor covered the basement housing the prisoners; secondly the Moot Hall, a gate-house in the shape of a letter T, the stem of which was likewise battlemented over corbels, while its bar, higher and topped with a turret, could accommodate soldiers no less than guards.[25] Hence the favour found by the town as an H.Q. for the surveillance of Tynedale in 1524,[26] 1525,[27] 1537,[28] and 1551.[20]

In the light of the Pilgrimage of Grace Carnaby,[29] Bowes[2] and the Council of the North[30] were unanimous that there was no substitute for a Keeper's stronghold inside each of the dales, 'as well for security of his own person'[8] as 'to reduce your misguided subjects'.[30] Within North Tynedale there were two sets of candidates, some five miles apart, of which the one downstream possessed the advantages of a still broad river and of proximity to headquarters. Haughton, the thirteenth-century hall-house of the Widdringtons, castellated in the fourteenth, found favour with Norfolk and others,[22, 24] but its walls and barmkin were flat,[22, 31] and it was too accessible,[2] witness the ease with which Liddesdale overwhelmed it. Not so Heron of Ford's thirteenth-century 'strongly builded tower' at Simonburn with a 'deep stayl' (i.e. steep) slope on three sides, and within hailing distance of Chipchase on the other bank, which would have been an asset had the intervening bridge ever been built. As matters stood, the old hulk needed £200-worth of repairs, inclusive of a barmkin wall,[2] so not infrequent recommendations that it should house a garrison[8, 32] were in the long run ignored. With its turrets and portcullis and spring-fed well in the cellar, the fourteenth-century tower at Chipchase to the east was in a good enough state of repair[2] to 'stand commodiously . . . for the safety of the whole country'.[33] It was advocated for a garrison in 1525[34] and 1539,[32] but was unthinkable as a Keeper's residence for anyone but a Heron. Completing this set, the motte-and-bailey castle at Wark-on-Tyne already belonged to the King but despite praise by Norfolk[28] had no stone of its fortifications standing by 1538, meriting dismissal by Bowes as an 'appearance of a fortress'.[2]

On the edge of the moors, where North Tyne is everywhere fordable and moss-hag the sole hindrance, the upstream set comprised a pair of fortresses, each visible from Hareshaw Common. Normally in lawless hands, the fourteenth-century tower at Hesleyside could accommodate fifty men or eight riders with mounts.[35] It was briefly garrisoned in 1525 and by Carnaby in 1537, but it was two centuries before the Charltons ceased to reside there. In its thirteenth-century prime Tarset Hall had been an oblong castle with four turrets.[34] Garrisoned between 1522[36] and 1525, the house was fairly flattened by the highlanders. Carnaby, who acquired the ruins,[22] seconded Norfolk[28] in pressing for reconstruction. Wharton, aiming subsequently to forage Tynedale Head, knew of nowhere for his horsemen to lodge.[37]

The Keeper of Redesdale had no such throng of crenellated derelicts to hesitate between as his colleague, given the highland-wide pre-eminence of Harbottle, the twelfth-century motte-and-bailey castle on the Coquet surrounded by a huge earthwork.[38] The dull Widdrington could dismiss it as too remote to guard anything beyond Redesdale,[39] but Dacre,[40] Norfolk,[41] Wharton[37] and Bowes all concurred on its pivotal importance for the defence of the whole Middle Marches, only enhanced by the untrustworthiness of the occupants of the strongholds in the Rede valley proper. Yet Bowes' aim to quarter 100 men there[42] was ambitious in so far as timber, lead and stonework had never recovered from the battering during the War of Independence. By 1537 there was no habitable room for the Keeper,[8, 41] no kitchen nor brewhouse,[20] nor stabling for the 100 horses required. It would have taken £443 and fourteen cartloads of lead to patch roofs,[42] the north tower, inner and outer wards, battlements and barmkin.[43] By 1543 no repairs had been effected for years,[44] though shortly afterwards Hertford did spend £100 on an iron postern, and to fill gaps in walls previously stuffed with thorn bushes.[42, 45] None of the artillery and ammunition considered an emergency requirement in 1537 ever arrived.[8]

The parsimony over against Scotland that informed English foreign policy implied that the King preferred to spend money at Guisnes than at Harbottle. Furthermore despite the 1535 Act and *de facto* control long before that of Liberty and castle by royal officers, commentators as late as 1546[31] obstinately insisted that responsibility for Redesdale, Harbottle and its dilapidations persisted with the absentee and uninterested Tailboys family.[42, 44, 45] It was only in 1538 when their heir became the King's ward that Henry himself became *de jure* occupant of the castle,[20,38] by which time for military purposes it no longer existed.

To man these haphazard barracks the plan was to procure 'sharp men chosen forth of places not nigh Tynedale,[32] always reckoned the major threat. In view of transportation costs, staple sources were Northumberland, the Durham Bishopric and the North Riding.[46, 47, 48] Under Little John's regime the point was startlingly stretched to embrace even his Redesdale cronies, 'such persons as he knows to be sharp and hardy men, such as he loves and trusts'.[10, 49] Indeed to justify his joint Keepership it was gullibly argued that whenever he rode in Tynedale he could call upon 'a hundreth well horsed men out of Redesdale to wait upon him'.[32] So much for the sources of what by the yardstick of the Berwick garrison of 500 men were termed the 'great garrisons' laid against Tyne- and Redesdales.[20]

Assignment of garrison was demanded by the Redesdale Keeper in 1523. During the Ridley revolt one company of horse archers was precariously ensconced at Tarset Hall with Fenwick; and a luckier one split between two petty captains at Hesleyside and Chipchase.[27, 34, 47] During Lisle's revolt Vice Warden Eure requisitioned the latter for another company.[50] The panic reaction of the Council of the North to the Pilgrimage and its aftermath, Hodge's murder, was to ask for a garrison of 300.[51] Not only was the plea rejected as excessive,[52] but Carnaby with Norfolk's backing[53] failed to obtain a single company for six months[28, 54] or even forty or fifty[22] for two.[5] The only force available to him for the attack on Hesleyside consisted of his own household.[35]

Contrasting with the shabby treatment meted out to Carnaby, that accorded his sinister successor was handsome, even if the garrison under six petty captains for distribution among the downstream and upstream sets, still prescribed by the Councillors, did remain asymptotic.[32] In the event Little John was allocated thirty men for Tynedale and twenty for Redesdale,[55] with a further 120 to ring the former for two months,[56] as 'standing with good policy'.[57] Thereafter he fell back on the previous contingents for each dale, 'the most active men', with the proviso that those discharged stand by 'ever . . . ready . . . with horse, harness and all things requisite'.[58] In 1541 a new norm for the Keepership was proposed by Bowes of fifty for Tynedale and thirty for Redesdale, 'since with any less number in a continual garrison . . . we doubt much that it cannot well be compassed'.[2] To confront the bad patch of disorder that followed Heron's second disgrace, Suffolk for six months installed garrisons totalling 500 men as 'a convenient number . . . to stay Tynedale and Redesdale'.[59, 60, 61] At curious pains to disguise the target,[62, 63] the Lieutenant spoke of a 'pretence' that they were there 'to keep good rule on the Borders' at large.[59] In his personal retinue Ralph Eure was therefore restricted at Chipchase to the same petty captain and fifty men as his predecessor.[64, 65]

As it cost nearly £7 p.a. to keep a soldier and his mount in the field,[2] the sums of money required to fund such troops predictably embarrassed an impecunious government. Neither Dacre during the Ridley affair,[66] nor John Heron needing £200 in wages at the outset of his Keepership,[55, 67] had the wherewithal to pay the garrisons. On the eve of Ancrum Moor the Lieutenant had to borrow 1000 marks in Newcastle to defray arrears in respect of those who would help fight it. That despite such difficulties officers exerted their utmost to maintain garrisons reflected the value they attached to them. Given fifty men, declared Carnaby, he would make Tynedale as peaceable as any other part of England;[22] according to Widdrington, without a garrison the tally of rebel highlanders would treble;[32] while the Council of the North, likewise in 1539, considered it vital to interpose one between both dales and the Liddesdalers and exiles.[58] The extent to which such testimonials were well founded has to be gauged from two particular incidents. In mid-May 1525 the government was warned that the only safeguard against still more damage at the hands of the Ridleyites was the garrison of 200.[34] As though to give the soothsayer the lie, 400 Scots and the Tynedale rebels a fortnight later attacked Tarset Hall whence they took fifty-five horses and prisoners; and then after a similar interval an even larger force added forty more of the latter, killing soldiers[68] and female camp-followers, though the loss of 'ane hundreth gelding' evoked the more fuss.[69] While one Hector Charlton was having a mass celebrated in liberated Tarset Hall,[70] a discomfited Vice Warden was pinning blame for the fiasco on Keeper Ralph Fenwick's shortcomings as a commander rather than on the horse-archers.[71] Shortly afterwards, however, the government adopted the opposing view, dissolving the garrison remnant that cowered behind the walls of Chipchase.[72]

This episode is counterbalanced by the indubitable success of the garrison planted by Suffolk which blocked any marauding expeditions into England, and satisfied the requirement postulated by Norfolk and the Council of the North that it should be big enough to stand on its own feet: even quiescent clansmen could never be trusted not to exploit any setback inflicted on a royal garrison.[48]

NOTES

1. PRO, E 36 Vol.40 fol.29, 29/3/1539.
2. BL, Calig. B VIII fol.63, 2/12/1541.
3. *LP*, IV(2) no.3689, 26/12/1527.
4. BL, Calig. B III fol.65, c.27/12/1528.
5. *Ibid.*, fol.251-3, 17/9/1538.

6. *LP*, I(1) (Kraus) no.1003, 23, 22/12/1511.

7. PRO, SP I 100 fol.1-2, end 1535.

8. *Ibid.*, 116 fol.217-8, 7/3/1537.

9. *Ibid.*, 42 fol.156-7, 4/7/1527.

10. *LP*, IV(1) no.2031, 18/3/1526.

11. BL, Add.MSS 32649 fol.135, 10/2/1543.

12. *Ibid.*, 32648 fol.201, 12/12/1542.

13. PRO, SP I 44 fol.177-8, 16/10/1527.

14. *Ibid.*, 117 fol.238-9, end March 1537.

15. *Ibid.*, 7 fol.281, 27/2/1514.

16. BL, Add.MSS 32651 fol.14, 8/6/1543.

17. Watson, *Reivers*, p.131.

18. BL, Add.MSS 32651 fol.101, 17/7/1543.

19. PRO, SP I 178 fol.53, 17/5/1543.

20. BL, Calig. B VIII fol.106, 1551.

21. PRO, Exchr. T. R. Misc. Books Vol.121 fol.15-48, c.12/7/1537.

22. PRO, SP I 140 fol.131-3, 18/12/1538.

23. BL, Calig. B VII fol.224, 3/7/1537.

24. PRO, SP I 152 fol.150-3, 21/9/1539.

25. T. H. Rowland, *Mediaeval Castles, Towers, Peles & Bastles of Northumberland*, pp.89-90.

26. *LP*, IV(1) no.726, 10/10/1524.

27. PRO,SP I 35 fol.60-1, 8/7/1525.

28. *Ibid.*, 124 fol.234-7, 15/9/1537.

29. *Ibid.*, 140 fol.77-8, 11/12/1538.

30. *Ibid.*, fol.61-3, 8/12/1538.

31. BL, Add.MSS 32651 fol.31, 2/9/1543.

32. PRO, SP I 152 fol.215-7, 23/7/1539.

33. PRO, E 36 Vol.121 fol.12 & 27, 6/4/1540.

34. PRO, SP I 34 fol.205-6, 16/5/1525.

35. *Ibid.*, 127 fol.105-6, 21/12/1537.

36. *LP*, III(2) no.1986, 24/1/1522.

37. PRO, SP I 179 fol.151, June 1543.

38. BL, Calig. B III fol.241, 7/4/1538.

39. PRO, SP I 134 fol.140-1, 12/7/1538.

40. *LP*, II(1) no.799, 12/8/1515.

41. PRO, SP I 132 fol.91, 11/5/1538.

42. BL. Calig. B VII fol.312, 27/5/1546.

43. *LP*,XIII(1) no.335, 22/2/1538.

44. PRO, SP I 178 fol.85, 24/5/1543.

45. *LP*, XX(1) no.1120, 5/7/1545.

46. *LP*, III(2) no.3378, 1/10/1523.

47. BL, Calig. B I fol. 41, 27/4/1525.

48. BL, Titus F III fol.97, 21/9/1539.

49. BL, Calig. B VII fol.228, 29/3/1539.

50. *Ibid.*, B III fol.209, 12/9/1527.

51. *Ibid.*, B I fol.133, 14/2/1537.

52. PRO SP I 116 fol.29, c.15/2/1537.

53. BL, Calig. B III fol. 207, c.2/10/1538.
54. PRO, SP I 117 fol.181-2, 31/3/1537.
55. Augmentation Office (E 323), Treasury Roll of Accounts, No.1 p.2, 29/9/1539.
56. *LP*, XV no.319, 9/3/1540.
57. PRO, SP I 155 fol.181-2, 27/12/1539.
58. *Ibid.*, 158 fol.72-3, 18/3/1540.
59. BL, Add.MSS 32649 fol.175, 23/2/1543.
60. *LP*, XVIII(1) no.209, 26/2/1543.
61. PRO, SP I 176 fol.107, 3/3/1543.
62. *LP*, XVIII(1) no.214, 27/2/1543.
63. *Ibid.*, no.291, 17/3/1543.
64. *Ibid.*, no.523, 11/5/1543.
65. *LP*, XIX(1) no.170, 6/3/1544.
66. *LP*, IV(1) no.75, 30/1/1524.
67. PRO,SP I 158 fol.72-3. 18/3/1540.
68. BL, Calig. B VI fol.407, 17/6/1525.
69. *LP*, IV(1) no.1427, 17/6/1525.
70. PRO, SP, I 35 fol.22, c.19/6/1525.
71. BL, Calig. B II fol.260, 26/7/1525.
72. PRO, SP I 35 fol.203-4, 30/7/1525.

CHAPTER ELEVEN

The Exaction of Securities

The highlanders could be summoned to stake, either personally or vicariously, something precious as earnest of reparation for the past or improved conduct in future.

Given the sinfulness of false swearing, one intangible possession that a man might venture was his soul. In 1523 the Tynedale heidsmen swore before Surrey's representative that they would banish or surrender Will Ridley and lieutenants, with their kinsfolk; commit no crime for six weeks(!); and release someone they had kidnapped. Subsequently they had to take the oath of allegiance, and to inform on any malefactor.[1] If notwithstanding 'they make any break', then 'we shall accuse them for breaking of their oaths'.[2] After the Pilgrimage this oath of allegiance became a shibboleth,[3] inability to pronounce which 'after this late busy time'[4] did more than denial of redress to separate Edward and Cuthbert Charlton from the rest of the highlanders. Oaths, then, were taken seriously, especially in the decade of the breach with Rome.[5] According to Bowes, Tynedalers were men of their word,[6] so it was natural that when Will of Bellingham tried to bind 200 of his fellows to Ridley his means was the administration of an oath.[7]

Yet there was wide recognition that 'whoever woll rob careth for none oath',[8] the Redesdalers being noted for perjury,[6] which was indeed an ingrained Border custom.[9] The aftermath of the 1523 solemnity was mayhem.

Secondly there were money bonds deposited by the principal or his 'surety' in guarantee of performance, failing which it became forfeit. Such was the bail fruitlessly intended to get Dodd of the Burnmouth to Newcastle assizes,[10] but which safely delivered Little John to London;[4] or the sureties for whom Widdrington mistakenly released Tom Pott.[11, 12] Another bond was the recognizance 'for good abearing'[7] of the type that double-banked the oaths in 1523. In mopping up after Lisle the Earl took recognizances from every heidsman and gentleman in Northumberland;[13] likewise from the Charlton heidsmen in 1535.[14] What might disrespectfully be called a little something on account was the third species, exemplified in 1523 by bonds exacted of the ten senior heidsmen 'to make redress . . . of all wrongs and robberies . . . according as Your poor subjects shall bring in their bills of complaint'.[15]

Bonds contributed effectively in 1527, but failed in 1523 and 1535. One factor was the quality of the sureties. Baron Dacre himself had in 1523 to undertake that reparation for the highlanders' offences be forthcoming.[15] 'Sufficient landed men' was the minimum requirement,[7] as when in 1524 the Herons of Chipchase and Ford jointly put up 200 marks for two Halls.[16] Heidsmen passed muster which is what Bowes meant by describing them as 'leading and answering for all the rest':[6] the five heidsmen of the Hesleyside Band who signed the bond with the Earl promised to hand over to the Keeper any delinquents from their grayne.[14] The drawback with such shady guarantors was readiness to forgo a bond the value of which was inferior to that of the loot. In 1524 Tynedale heidsmen cheerfully sacrificed their money when, 'having a part of any goods stole and reft', they declined to surrender the bailees.[7]

The third category of stake consisted not of verbiage or cash but of flesh and blood. The taking of hostages was still commonplace in international, especially Anglo-Scottish,[17] dealings, as when Francis I traded his children after Pavia, and the English surrendered 'pledges' in atonement for Sir Robert Kerr's murder. In law domestic to England, however, the levying of pledges was peculiar to the Borders. The periods in which pledges were exacted of the highlanders were the most turbulent: from Redesdale 1514-8,[18, 19] and from both dales 1523-4[7, 15, 20] 1526-8[21] and 1537-8.[22, 23] The aim looked back as well as forward, to secure redress[15, 18] and continuing good behaviour.[7, 23, 24] Despite continual reference to the pledges for Tynedale and Redesdale,[25, 26] this exaggerated the monolith so the true constituency has to be determined at the outset.

Rendezvous at which bonds of all types were collected were conducted according to hallowed protocol.[27] The presiding officer could be of any rank from Keeper to Lieutenant, and the venue Newcastle, Wark-on-Tyne or Chollerford.[28, 29] Whereas absence by any male from sixteen to sixty was reprehended,[22] it was equally axiomatic that 'if they and we agree not and that they wol or cannot find sureties for good rule[30] . . . they must needs depart again free, though they had slain my brother or friend'.[31] This principle of 'assurance' enunciated by Dacre was still normally respected in Elizabeth's reign,[32] so that Carnaby's protestations of 'honesty',[33] and contention that the highlanders arrived without assurance in September 1538, raised some eyebrows.[23, 34] In short the objective in such parleys was a pact 'of their own good will'.[35] Corollaries from individual bargaining were that none could represent a whole dale, and that pledge totals fluctuated. For Tynedale numbers were from six to twelve between 1523 and 1538,[15, 21, 22, 33, 36] and for Redesdale seven to ten between 1528 and 1537.[36, 37, 38] Frequency of rotation also varied from monthly in 1537[39] to four-monthly in 1526.[21]

If such totals suggest a unit of substitution between the Surname and the approximately four graynes that were its components, the arithmetic is not misleading. The pledges envisaged by Magnus in 1526,[21] Dacre in 1524,[35] the Earl in 1528,,[36] and Carnaby in 1537 were 'all Head Surname men as we call them here'.[22] Lord Dacre dealt with the Robsons *per se* in 1524,[7] and Northumberland with the Charltons in 1535. Andrew Hall of Redesdale stood for his entire Surname.[40] On the other hand there were circumstances under which the grayne became a more meaningful collective. A powerful grayne, like that of Hesleyside, might plump itself out into a Band which as after Ridley's revolt deserved its own representative.[25] At the end of Lisle's Edward Charlton was 'pledge for all his Band[41]' while in 1537 'Charltons that was in his Band dare not now pledge for him'.[42] Correspondingly whenever graynes within a Surname were at loggerheads, unitary representation became impracticable. In 1528 Charlton pledges were drawn from three graynes, whereas Milburns, Robsons and Dodds were content with one apiece.[41] In 1537 the regular Charlton pledge jibbed at standing for Edward[42] and, with the Dodd, for Fenwick-slaying namesakes.[43] The reason why on balance the Surname level seemed preferable was a desire to avoid pledges that were 'nothing meet',[23, 44] such as a tenant proposed by Edward Charlton.[42] It was, however, felt to be overdone when a for the moment conciliatory John of the Falstone and Gyb of the Boughthill turned up at York, 'who of all others had been most meet to have been at home to resist the coming in of the rebels'. Carnaby's retort that 'he trusted not these men' was ill received.[39] In the Council's opinion the ideal pledge was a heidsman's kinsman held long term.[45]

To revert to procedures. Within the week the Keepers, having collected the pledges,[22, 30] escorted them to Hexham or Newcastle,[25, 28] which the Redesdale Keeper was in a particular hurry to reach because of cramped quarters at Harbottle.[46] Next day[28, 47] they pressed on to Pontefract[48] or Sheriffhutton,[25, 26] when Norfolk[24] or the Council were in charge, but under Dacre[7, 18] or the Earl[41] stayed at Hexham or passed to Morpeth or Warkworth. Ultimately it was Newcastle that was preferred due to staff-shortages at York and to dislike there for 'pledges coming to the knowledge of Yorkshire . . . They learn all the by-ways . . . which makes them more bold . . . to steal, when they know which way to escape with their prey'.[39] At whichever destination hostages were intermediate between prisoners and guests, Dacre[7, 18] and later the Council wanted them 'straitly looked on and surely kept as well in their diets as otherwise',[23] whereas Cromwell and Northumberland lest replacements be frightened off favoured a more lenient custody.[49, 50] Eventually those in Yorkshire boarded with a sergeant, reporting daily to the Sheriff.[39] They were allowed such generous rations that when there was a shortage at Harbottle Redesdalers in transit were shifted promptly to more abundant pastures.[46] Carnaby was not the only offical to jib at the 1/6d-2/- per week, half a soldier's wages, that was the going rate.[21, 33] Bemoaning the expense right up to 1544,[50, 51, 52] the Council of the North contemplated the sale of goods of attainted persons to defray the cost of the highland hostages.[53]

For these the system held other consolations as when in 1537 it was observed of John Robson and Gyb Charlton that 'they have offered themselves as pledges . . . to be honestly . . . quit of their promise to My Lord of Northfolk and to bear no blame of that that should be done in their absence.[39] Moreover that Duke was so alive to opportunities for intelligence-gathering that he had Heron brought from London to Newcastle by nights and 'with an hood on his head', lest the pledges at Sheriffhutton alert those on the wanted list back home.[54] The stock advantage, however, was the immunity purchased for kinsfolk. Having seized as pledges the heidsmen of Bellingham and Carriteth, Dacre proclaimed that no royal officer would molest 'their wives, children, goods or cattle, nor also their friends, Surname or part-takers.[35]

But none of these lures outweighed the repugnance with which the highlanders surrendered pledges. That bonds were the preferred option underlay Dacre's summons in 1524 to those 'that has found no sureties yet . . . come in and speak with us . . . to find surety by pledges'.[30] Occasionally individual heidsmen pushed to dangerous lengths non-compliance with an accord subscribed at a tryst by the rest of the Surname. Dacre reported to Wolsey in that same May how 'Robert Robson, being the fourth heidsman . . . of the Robsons in Tynedale who are in great numbers . . . held out and . . . no sureties or pledges answered . . . I sent my servants with a part of the King's garrison . . . at night . . . who fortuned to take four persons . . . of the Surname . . . whereof the said Robert was one, whom I arraigned afore me . . . and justified [i.e. hanged] . . . for the fearful example of all others'.[7] The Cardinal passed on Henry VIII's congratulations to the baron, with a fatherly injunction to string up any who withheld pledges in future.[55] However, Charlton of Larederburn and Cuddy Lion Robson were spared that fate when in 1537 they denied Norfolk.[56]

Undoubtedly in a clannish society hostages were regarded as the most hampering tie of all, which was why the classic signal for armed resistance was for pledges to decamp as they did at the outset of Lisle's revolt and in throwing down the gauntlet to Carnaby. Pledges were liable to victimisation: when a Hall disobeyed the Redesdale Keeper his pledge was consigned to the cells,[40] while the heidsmen conscripted by Sir Reynold were deprived of food.[23] More starkly, as in contemporary Scotland,[57] it was widely accepted that 'if any Surname and friendship . . . do offend . . . the pledge forthwith may be executed'.[25] On recall, the Percy Earl's first act was to take pledges from both dales as an earnest of willingness to 'speir' [i.e. track down] offenders.[36] When in due course heidsmen proved loth or unable to deliver four malefactors, all of them 'accused by name',[58] the Warden lost no time in hanging six pledges with the appropriate Surnames.[59] Norfolk in 1537 spoke of the ten Tyne- and Redesdale pledges in his hands as 'lying upon their lives if their countrymen do not well'.[60]

Enthusiasm for pledges was not untempered on the offical side. Unlike their Scottish equivalents,[53] equity lawyers at York had intermittent qualms about the execution of one man for the crimes of another, and also about the system's efficacy in obtaining the desired result. Possession of pledges did not procure redress for either the Dacre brothers in 1514[18] or Norfolk in 1537,[61] while the Duke's conciliar successors assured Cromwell that the highlanders never ceased to rob out of solicitude for their hostages.[53] Yet Dacre reckoned that their retention provided indispensable protection for Tyne- and Redesdale's neighbours,[7] while the Council of the North in fits of optimism even regarded them as the key to a perpetual reformation.[63] The crisis in 1536 did nothing to invalidate the system because none was in custody at the outbreak, so there was instinctive[64] and hopeful[65] recourse to the device afterwards. Carnaby had the Council with him in the judgment that his detention of Topping 'was special occasion of stay of a great part of Tynedale'.[23, 30, 66]

NOTES

1. BL, Add.MSS 24965 fol.126, c.3/12/1523.
2. *Ibid.*, fol.148, 8/1/1524.
3. *LP*, XII(1) no.98, c.16/1/1537.
4. BL, Calig. B I fol.133, 14/2/1537.
5. J. J. Scarisbrick, *Henry VIII*, pp.299 & 324.
6. BL, Calig. B VIII fol.106, 1551.
7. *Ibid.*, B III fol.6, 20/5/1524.
8. *Ibid.*, fol.241, 7/4/1538.
9. Tough, *Last Years*, p.32.
10. PRO, SP I 23 fol.223-4, December 1521.
11. *Ibid.*, 124 fol.234-7. 15/9/1537.
12. *Ibid.*, 125 fol.10-1, 22/9/1537.
13. *LP*, IV(2) no. 3689, 26/12/1527.
14. PRO, SP I 96 fol.169-173, 15/9/1535.
15. BL, Calig. B III fol.255, 16/4/1523.
16. BL, Add.MSS 24965 fol.125, 24/9/1524

17. *LP*, XVIII(1) no.795, 30/6/1543.
18. PRO, SP I 7 fol.281, 27/2/1514.
19. *Ibid.*, 17 fol.223-4, 23/12/1518.
20. *LP*, III(2) no.3615, 3/12/1523.
21. BL,Calig. B III fol.44, 17/8/1526.
22. PRO, SP I 125 fol.179, 10/10/1537.
23. *Ibid.*, 136 fol.217-8, c.22/9/1538.
24. *Ibid.*, 118 fol.216-7, 18/4/1537
25. *Ibid.*, 36 fol.55, 10/10/1525.
26. BL, Calig. B VII fol.224, 3/7/1537.
27. PRO, SP I 45 fol.101-7 & (1-3) P.S., 2/12/1527.
28. *LP*, XII(1) no.918, 12/4/1537.
29. PRO,SP I 136 fol.161-4, 15/9/1538.
30. BL, Add.MSS 24965 fol.255B, 16/6/1524.
31. PRO, SP I 30 fol.334-5, 25/4/1524.
32. CSPF, (ed.1865) Item 299, 19/11/1559.
33. PRO, SP I 140 fol.77-8, 11/12/1538.
34. BL, Calig. B III fol.251-3, 17/9/1538.
35. BL, Add.MSS 24965 fol.226B, 13/5/1524.
36. PRO, SP I 46 fol.128-131, 18/1/1528.
37. *Ibid.*, 115 fol.200, 6/2/1537.
38. *Ibid.*, 118 fol.54-8, c.7/4/1537.
39. *Ibid.*, 126 fol.180-1, 13/11/1537.
40. *Ibid.*,127 fol.96-8, 18/12/1537.
41. *Ibid.*, 47 fol.25, 28/2/1528.
42. BL, Calig. B III fol.197, 18/7/1537.
43. PRO, SP I 116 fol.219, 7/3/1537.
44. *Ibid.*, 137 fol.1-2, 24/9/1538.
45. *Ibid.*, 131 fol.56-7, 7/4/1538.
46. *Ibid.*, 118 fol.223, c.18/4/1537.
47. *Ibid.*, fol.148-9, 12/4/1536.
48. *Ibid.*, 46 fol.105-6, 12/1/1528.
49. *Ibid.*, 125 fol.218-9, 15/10/1537.
50. *Ibid.*, 126 fol.62-5, 2/11/1537.
51. PRO, Exchr. T. R. Misc. Books, Vol.121 fol.15-48, c.12/7/1537.
52. *LP*, XIX(2) no.239, 16/9/1544.
53. BL. Calig. B III fol.98, 9/1/1539.
54. PRO, SP I 124 fol.113-4, 27/8/1537.
55. BL, Add.MSS 24965 fol.259, 11/6/1524.
56. PRO, SP I 117 fol.228-9, c.1/4/1538 (calendared a year earlier).
57. Macdonald Fraser, *Steel Bonnets*, pp.226, 229 and *passim*.
58. BL, Calig. B VII fol.112, 28/1/1528.
59. *Ibid.*, B III fol.146, 2/4/1528.
60. PRO, SP I 120 fol.146-7, 18/5/1537.
61. *Ibid.*, 118 fol.52-3, 7/4/1537.
62. BL, Calig. B VII fol.71, 22/11/1525.
63. PRO, SP I 116 fol.178-9, 2/3/1537.
64. *Ibid.*, 125 fol.21-2, 23/9/1537.
65. *Ibid.*, 140 fol.131-3, 18/12/1538.

CHAPTER TWELVE

Embroilment

One expedient in this land of deadly feud was to set the highlanders at one another's throats. Generally there was a measure of solidarity throughout the bloc. On Redesdale the Halls ex Harles imposed the same unity as the Umfravilles before them from a loftier level; 'if it be for a quarrel or matter of any one of theirs against a true man . . . [the Tynedalers] will all take the one part';[1] Liddesdale and Tynedale 'have always been . . . great friends and buddy fellows in all their thefts and murders';[2] and all three dales 'been so combined, confederated and knot in one that . . . they woll not infringe . . . their bond and amity'.[3]

There existed none the less hair-cracks that could be coaxed to yawn. Whilst the Armstrongs and the clans of Liddesdale Head collaborated jointly with rebel Lisle, they usually kept their distance from one another. Even in harmonious Redesdale murderous dissensions among the Hedleys were reported in 1551, and the two English Keepers regularly held days of truce for redress as between the kingdoms.[4] However, the fulcrum for potential strife lay within Tynedale, where the tradition of discord set during the Scottish War of Independence died hard. After Flodden Charlton of Carriteth, Dodd of the Burnmouth and a Milburn heidsman conspired 'ilk one to take oder partie',[5] manifesting at least a faction. Less transient, the most divisive element was the numerous grayne of Charltons within an equilateral triangle overlapping the middle reaches of the river. One side of the triangle stretched three miles from Newton via Charlton to Blakelaw on the north bank; the other two via Hesleyside and Bellingham *cum* the Bower[6] respectively down to Shitlington south of the river. 'Chief stirrer of sedition'[7] in 1536, the Laird of Hesleyside in the long run ruled the roost[8] but there were periods in the twenties when due to age or personality he was overshadowed by his brother at Bellingham[9, 10] and the Shitlington heidsman.[11] Edward Charlton was credited with a Band of his own,[5] the additive to the grayne primarily comprising those Dodds[12, 13, 14, 15] who according to Bowes were under the Charltons' rule.[4]

Peculiarities of the Hesleyside Band were special relationships with the Armstrongs,[12, 13] also with the Percys, where tenurial roots had been reinforced through marriage into the Heron family, the Earls' standard-bearers in Western Northumberland. Hence the disaffection of the Band towards Dacre and attendant Fenwicks, Mistrust hardened into hatred when Will of Bellingham swung for Sir Ralph's discomfiture,[16] so that Hodge's murder was naturally ascribed to 'old propensed malice'[17] and 'old grudges of deadly feud'.[18] What set the Band apart from the Tynedale majority was that the Charltons of Carriteth, the Boughthill, Leehall and Wark; the Robsons to the west; the Milburns to the north; and even such insiders as the Bowery Charltons never wholeheartedly shared these loyalties and enmities.

To obtain eminence a heidsman did not have to belong to the Band. William Charlton of the Leehall after Flodden was jointly spokesman for Tynedale with Edward of Hesleyside, and all the clans marched to their rescue when imprisoned in the gaol Tower.[5] Tom of Carriteth in Ridley's day was rated one of 'the most principal heidsmen and captains',[9] in which capacity indeed he narrowly escaped execution.[19, 20] None the less the corporate supremacy of the Band was incontrovertible. Will of Bellingham, Ridley's right-hand man, was sent to London to be interrogated by the Cardinal as 'privy to all the secrets of both Tynedale and Redesdale'.[10] His execution was seen as an awful warning to 'all oder malefactors pretending to be Heid herafter'.[9] Standing in a similar relationship to Lisle, Will of Shitlington was described to the King as 'head rebel of all our outlaws',[12, 13] with the implication that he too was aspiring to the sort of hegemony exercised by Hall of Otterburn. Certainly when he was slain Lisle immediately threw in his hand. Hector Charlton, probably of Hesleyside[21] and brother to Gerard of the Bower,[22] was reckoned 'one of the principal captains and felons of all the felonies and murders lately done by Tynedale men'.[23] However, the arrogance that was to stir up so much internal discord was best exemplified by Edward of Hesleyside himself. That there was already tinder in the uplands had been demonstrated by Armstrong attacks on Tynedale targets when Lisle collapsed,[24, 25] and by the presence of Tailboys tenants, i.e. Redesdalers, in the doomed Tarset garrison.[26]

What set things alight was the arrival as Warden of the sixth Earl of Northumberland which coincided with Will of Shitlington's last throw. On return from a raid into Durham he and eight followers were cornered at Haydon Bridge between trail-hounds and Tyne in flood. Among the pursuers was Charlton of the Leehall with other Tynedalers, whose 'forwardness in oppressing of malefactors' was unprecedented and no doubt deeply offensive to the Hesleyside Band, especially as the leader was killed and his Dodd and Armstrong companions subsequently executed. More serious was the escape of the rest[27] since it precipitated the hanging in April 1528 of six pledges, including two sons of Tom of Carriteth and a brother of Gyb of the Boughthill.[28] Henry of the Falstone was spared because there was no Robson among the raiders, but what caused outrage was similar leniency extended by Northumberland to his vassal Edward Charlton, to whom the Earl had already accorded special treatment in the matter of board and lodging.[29] Presumably the specious grounds were that Shitlington had expiated his own crime, but the fact remained that he had been a prominent member of the Band, for which Edward stood pledge.

With a show of impartiality the Warden, after the waves from the Lisle storm had subsided, appointed William of the Leehall as well as Edward of Hesleyside to his household.[30] Furthermore the Earl in the early thirties was bent upon involving the whole of Tynedale, as well as Redesdale and Liddesdale, in his war with Scotland, but even so a schism could still be sensed. After the war was over certain heidsmen of the majority sought to prolong it, notably the Dodds of the Crag, Christie Milburn and Topping. With a Percy in command Edward Charlton and the Band proclaimed their devotion to law and order, undertaking 'to do their diligence . . . for the apprehension . . . of such notable offenders . . . being rebels apparent'.[8]

Harmony was seemingly restored during the Pilgrimage. Whereas the Band gladly threw in their lot with the Percy brothers, who with the Earl comatose had come to incarnate the family interest, the majority joined them for the pickings. Little John could draw on the services of the resurgent Robsons,[31] while Edward of Hesleyside effortlessly arrogated to himself the Heidship, his final accolade being selection by Henry VIII himself as candidate for arrest and despatch under guard to London.[32] Nothing dissolves a partnership more effectively than a bankruptcy.[33] Even before Hodge's murder the authorities were drawing a distinction between the Band and heidsmen 'willing to take oaths upon their Keepers to be loyal subjects'.[7] These 'persons of Tynedale of good estimation'[18] included Bowery Charlton, who had changed sides, Tom of Carriteth, Topping, Gyb of the Boughthill, John Robson of the Falstone, and Dodd of the Crag.[34] John Charlton of Larederburn and Cuddy Lion Robson still wavered,[35] but the rest pressed pledges on the government,[36] in the collection of which Hodge met his death at the hands of the Band's agents. When delivery did materialise it was with the proviso that they did not stand for any bitter-enders.[18] Simultaneously the majority paid back the Band for the undertaking given the Earl in 1535: 'John Robson of the Falstone . . . promised My Lord of Northfolk . . . that he would do much against the rebels . . . Gyb of Charlton . . . made like promise'.[37]

The civil war thus declared could have been avoided had not the authorities left suspect Herons and Charltons at large for several months. As it is, flickers are still discernible of a year-long free-for-all which aligned

Hesleyside, Armstrongs and Little John's followers in Redesdale against the majority and Liddesdale Head. For instance Armstrongs and Fenwick-slayers lifted £40-worth of moveables from Carriteth and the Falstone,[38] and 200 of them 'violently spoiled' Charltons from outside the Band;[39, 40] Redesdalers raided the Milburns, a thing 'not heard of heretofore'.[41, 42] Such incidents were by June 1537 reckoned weekly events,[43] so that even Maxwell pretended to take action.[44] On the other side Liddesdale clamoured for redress from Tynedale in the successive Aprils,[45, 46, 47] while Potts and Halls accused Elliots and Croziers of stealing horses, silver and gold.[38] On balance, however, the majority faction fared worse, because the Band had more Scots friends.[46]

It was through no fault of Topping's that Edward Charlton was left till September to ride out the storm in his own home,[43] for it was the Wark heidsman who as early as April had laid the damning evidence about the Fenwick murder[48] before the new Keeper.[49] When belatedly in a position to act upon it, Norfolk in October commanded Carnaby to seize Hesleyside and hand it over to William Charlton of the Leehall[50] 'as a mean and ready way to have sown dissension and mortal debate between their kin and friends'. Having fulfilled the mission in company with most of the Northumbrian gentry,[51, 52] Sir Reynold consigned the little tower to the beneficiary who however 'durst not keep it for fear of his life'.[53] Edward promptly inserted his own 'folks' again who by moonlight around Christmas[52, 54] were once more ousted by a small garrison.[55] For some months the owner commuted between Liddesdale; a shiel at Bellesburn shared with the assassins; and finally the reoccupied tower with Heron's henchmen,[56] 'all minded to do the most mischief they may'.[52] Their opponents, by contrast, spent a blameless winter[55] without persuading Carnaby to accept the Duke's analysis of a rift: 'there is', the Keeper asserted, 'such ways amongst them they woll not fall out'.[53] With memories perhaps of how John Robson had robbed his father after dinner at his table, Reynold adopted the hard line towards the majority that made his own words come true. Whereas Hodge á Fenwick had set at loggerheads, so this Keeper equally inadvertently became the great healer, until a situation was restored in which 'the inhabitants of Tynedale . . . had promised together . . . if one were meddled with, all to be in like'.[57]

Before return northwards Little John had probably received a slightly out-of-date briefing from Norfolk about divide and rule. Since all Heron's ties were with the Band, his Keepership at first naturally involved confrontation with the majority, especially as Edward Charlton was his relative and assistant. The latter was free with ironic advice that there would never be peace 'so long as any of the sort that dwell there . . . shall remain there'; that a noble captain be sent 'to war against them';[58] that 'to make mischief among them' virtuous Tynedalers be incited to purloin recalcitrants' goods;[59] and that traps be set for Carnaby's kidnappers.[60] Such was the prevalent climate when John Heron struck at the Falstone, symbolising that the centre of gravity had shifted away from Hesleyside. Soon the Keeper came to realise that Edward Charlton had become as much an irrelevance as the Percy interest he had so long served. Two of the Fenwick-slayers were dwelling together with the Carnaby-takers in the dens of Thorlieshope,[61] while Hector Charlton, probably of Hesleyside, had ridden in Scotland with Topping, Carriteth and the Robsons as early as the rapprochement of 1538. Any obstacle Edward might have presented to a full-blooded revival of the Tynedale-Redesdale-Liddesdale league was removed by his death in 1541.[1]

This league was in fact on its last legs. Henry VIII's fury at the slaughter of still more Fenwicks almost under the royal nose in York[62] coincided with the arrival on the Borders of Bowes' team of Surveyors.[63] While Sir Robert still harboured a few illusions about Heron, he had none about the highlanders and resolved to unhook the link with Liddesdale, their most vulnerable hinge. On the subject's being broached with Little John he protested that Tyne- and Redesdales 'would [not] commit any slaughter of any of the notable Surnames of Liddesdale for fear of deadly feud', against which he unguardedly conceded only his own presence as Keeper could immunise. Moved less by Heron's prediction that he would be unlikely to return alive[64, 65] than by loud grumbles from the monarch at the 'untowardness' of Tyne- and Redesdale men,[66] Bowes after the attack on Halton in November became irresistible in his insistence on a raid against Thorlieshope. Although thirteen houses were demolished, the English authorities commented sourly on the invaders' failure to inflict casualties.[68] Whilst deadly feud had been avoided on a technicality, the victims did resent such requital of former hospitality, and declared that it was not they but the Tynedalers who had set alight the Carnaby's corn.[67] Conclusive rupture was however postponed for eighteen more months, when in a descent on Capheaton the Liddesdalers and Charlton outlaws despoiled a widow, probably a Milburn,[69] who afterwards asked her Tynedale kinsfolk for reprisal. The outcome was that 'they rose . . . to the fray and rescued the goods, and many sore hurt so that there is like to grow . . . deadly feud between Liddesdale and Tynedale'.[2]

The upshot was desultory fighting between the pair that continued throughout 1543. The Earl of Bothwell, who had replace Maxwell as Keeper of Liddesdale,[70] had been imprisoned after Solway Moss and felt no affection for Henry VIII's subjects. Furthermore his influence was greatest among the neighbours to his Hermitage Castle, the clans of the Head most antagonised by Thorlieshope and Capheaton.. The great garrisons, which according to Viscount Lisle had 'clean stopped the passage of the Scots through Tynedale',[71, 72] had not likewise slammed the door upon incursions into the Liberty itself. In May Bothwell's men carried fire into Tynedale, to which Sir Ralph Eure, the fierce new Keeper, responded by ravaging Liddesdale from Mangerton right up to the Head.[70] His guide had been Barty Young, 'as proper a man as is within all Tynedale' who soon afterwards was killed, together with one Percy Robson, by the Nixons and Armstrongs, leading to still further retaliation by Eure.[73] None of this deterred plans by the Charlton outlaws and their hosts in June to cross Redesdale and raid down the Coquet.[74]

Meanwhile English officers were striving to reclaim the traitors responsible for so much havoc. As keen as Heron had been to reconstitute the tripartite league, though for patriotic not selfish purposes, Keeper Eure envisaged the Charlton assassins as a bridgehead into Liddesdale. With support from Suffolk he put out feelers through that seasoned go-between, Topping. In the tradition of the Hesleyside Band, the two exiles refused to have anything to do with him, causing the Duke to swear 'they shall shortly repent their proud refusal'.[75] Next year Sir Ralph angled fruitlessly again for the survivor of the pair.[76] The reason was that the Fenwick-slayers were in Bothwell's pocket, now at Jedburgh, now at the Hermitage. When summoned by Arran[77, 79] to disgorge 'such abominable murderers', the Scots Keeper 'made it very strange as though he had never heard of the said outlaws',[80] for he had no desire to remove thorns from England's flesh.

More crucially for Bothwell, however, the control of Liddesdale itself was slipping away, since yet again the clans were wavering in allegiance. That the tender of Nixons and Armstrongs to Eure quickly aborted,[70, 75] to be meaningfully resumed with Wharton, indicated a reorientation of forces along the Borders due to the breach between Liddesdalers and their English neighbours. Another sign was that an increasingly isolated Charlton exile, from being courted by Eure, became his suitor.[76] There is a remarkable difference in tone between Bowes' 1541 Survey, describing the Tynedale/Redesdale/Liddesdale league as indissoluble;[1] and that of 1551 which declared the coercion of the third could be safely left in the hands of the first two.[4]

NOTES

1. BL,Calig. VIII fol.63, 2/12/1541.
2. BL, Add.MSS 32649 fol.146, 12/2/1543.

3. *Ibid.*,32646 fol.259, 7/11/1541.

4. BL, Calig. B VIII fol.106, 1551 (not 1542 as calendared).

5. PRO, SP I 7 fol.281, 27/2/1511.

6. Modern Ordnance Survey maps show a Bower four miles to the west of Bellingham. However, there is still a farmstead called by the same name immediately north of the town, and in Queen Anne's reign a Bower adjoined Redesmouth district, so I am assuming the correctness of the latter identification

7. BL, Calig. B I fol.133, 14/2/1537.

8. PRO, SP I 96 fol.169-173, 15/9/1535.

9. BL, Calig. B III fol.6, 20/5/1524.

10. PRO, SP I 31 fol.123, 12/6/1524.

11. BL, Add.MSS 24965 fol.126, c.3/12/1523.

12. BL, Calig. B VI fol.409, 13/5/1526.

13. PRO, SP I 46 fol.162-3, 28/1/1528.

14. PRO, SP 9 IV fol.18-9, 18/3/1534.

15. BL, Calig. B I 128, 7/4/1537.

16. See p.161 below.

17. PRO, SP I 116 fol.215-6, 7/3/1537.

18. *Ibid.*, fol.219, 7/3/1537.

19. BL, Add.MSS 24965 fol.226B, 13/5/1524.

20. PRO, SP I 31 fol.196-7. 8/7/1524.

21. See p.142 above. A Hector Charlton of Hesleyside was raiding in Scotland early in 1538(68) but if identical with this heidsman the intervening deep silence would be difficult to account for.

22. BL, Calig. B I fol.41, 27/4/1525.

23. PRO, SP I 35 fol.22, c.19/6/1525.

24. BL, Calig.B II fol.427, 28/10/1525.

25. *LP*, IV(2) no. 3914, 11/2/1528.

26. BL, Calig. B II fol.43, 31/5/1525.

27. *Ibid.*, B VII fol.112, 28/1/1528.

28. *Ibid.*, B III fol.146, 2/4/1528.

29. PRO, SP I 47 fol.25, 28/2/1528.

30. BL, Calig. B III fol.65, c.27/12/1528.

31. PRO, SP I 115 fol.200, 6/2/1537.

32. *Ibid.*, 116 fol.29, c.15/2/1537.

33. Despite close familiarity with the documentation M. H. & R. Dodds, *Pilgrimage of Grace* (*inter alia* Vol.II p.238) failed to detect any lack of solidarity in Tynedale.

34. BL, Calig. B III fol.239, 17/3/1538.

35. PRO, SP I 117 fol.228-9, c.1/4/1538 (wrongly calendared to a year later).

36. *Ibid.*, 116 fol.178-9, 2/3/1537.

37. *Ibid.*, 126 fol.150-1, 13/11/1537.

38. *Ibid.*, 134 fol.142-153, 12/7/1538.

39. PRO, Exchr. T. T. Misc. Books, Vol.121 fol.136, 20/4/1537.

40. PRO, SP I 118 fol.235-6, 21/4/1537.

41. *Ibid.*, fol.54-8, c.7/4/1537.

42. *Ibid.*, fol.223-4, c.18/4/1537.

43. *Ibid.*, 121 fol.169-170, 26/6/1537.

44. BL, Calig. B I fol.322, 27/4/1537.

45. PRO. SP I 117 fol.273-4, 6/4/1537.

46. PRO, Exchr. T. R. Misc. Books, Vol.121 fol.22 & SP I 131 fol.167, 17/4/1538.

47. *Ibid.*, fol.197-8, 24/4/1538.

48. See p.88 above.

49. PRO, SP I 140 fol.61-3, 8/12/1538.

50. Though never vying in social status with the Catholics at Hesleyside, the Charltons of the Leehall came in the fullness of time to be regarded locally as the principal Protestant grayne within the Surname.

51. PRO, SP I 125 fol.179, 10/10/1537.

52. *Ibid.*, 126 fol.11-12, 24/10/1537.

53. *Ibid.*, fol.13, 24/10/1537.

54. *Ibid.*, 127 fol.96-8, 18/12/1537.

55. *Ibid.*, fol.105-6, 21/12/1537.

56. *Ibid.*, 117 fol.181-2, 31/3/1537.

57. *Ibid.*, 136 fol.161-4, 15/9/1538.

58. *Ibid.*, 153 fol.86, August 1539.

59. BL, Calig. B III fol.262, 17/12/1539.

60. BL, Titus F III fol.97, 21/9/1539.

61. BL, Royal MSS 7 cxvi fol.140-2, 22/1/1540.

62. See p.92 above & *LP*, XVI no.1207, 26/9/1541.

63. *Ibid.*, no.1206, 26/9/1541.

64. BL, Add.MSS 32646 fol.237, 14/10/1541.

65. *Ibid.*, fol.235, 15/10/1541.

66. *Ibid.*, fol.251, 20/10/1541.

67. *Ibid.*, fol.270, 2/12/1541.

68. PRO, SP 49 5 fol.29, December 1541.

69. Newly arrived on the Borders as Warden General, Lord Lisle referred to them as the Middlemoors, which sounds like a Southron's mishearing of a Northumbrian name.

70. PRO, SP I 178 fol.85, 24/5/1543.

71. BL, Add.MSS 32650 fol.16, 8/3/1543.

72. *LP*, XVIII(1) no.291, 17/3/1543.

73. *Ibid.*, XIX(1) no.170, 6/3/1544.

74. BL, Add.MSS 32651 fol.14, 8/6/1543.

75. PRO, SP I 178 fol.53, 17/5/1543.

76. *LP*, XIX(1) no.190, 11/3/1544.

77. BL, Add.MSS 32648 fol.228, 21/12/1542.

78. *Ibid.*, 32649 fol.85, 19/1/1543.

CHAPTER THIRTEEN

Swords Spiritual and Temporal

The government could reach for one of two swords, the first designed to afflict in this world, the other in the next. Because the two Liberties marched with so many episcopal lands, the Church was never slow to place the latter at the disposal of the State. So comical was the obsession of clerics with property that the Bishop of Durham construed Flodden principally as punishment for the battering of his Norham Castle — 'that cruel deed is well requited'.[1] Resort to spiritual sanctions was far rarer after than before the Reformation because bishops were less frequently ministers. What is at issue is excommunication, not of named individuals as in 1498, but of the whole community 'wherefore they nor their wife nor childer shall not come within any church'. According to both Dacre[2] and the Earl of Northumberland,[3] such interdict was 'a fearful thing' to the highlanders. When in Ridley's day the Cardinal laid his ban on Tynedale churches, Redesdale's being specifically exempted,[4] the pariahs were literally brought to their knees after six months 'with weeping tears'.[5] Lisle's uprising too was arguably snuffed out when 400 from Redesdale and 500 from Tynedale 'humbly and lowly submitted them' pursuant to the 'dreadful sentence of the Church'.[3]

Like that of their King, the highlanders' veneration was reserved for the mass, not extending to the celebrant hierarchy which as in 1313 they were prepared to ignore or even to cheat. In 1525, all Tynedale churches having been interdicted, Hector Charlton took the Blessed Sacrament out of Bellingham Church in the form of a ferkin of wine and 800 'breads', 'then caused a Scots friar[6] . . . to minister them their communion of his fashion . . . yeving the Sacrament to a great number of evil-disposed persons'.[4,7] The readiness of Scots to provide bolt-holes for the souls no less than the bodies of Tyne- and Redesdalers was indeed a source of frustration to English prelates, perhaps only aggravated by hearty collaboration against the Tynedale thieves in 1525 from the Archbishop of Glasgow[8] which showed what they could do when they tried. In a despatch the English ambassador enclosed the text of this tremendous Glaswegian curse which fell like a thunderbolt on those 'who had part murdered, part slain, brynt, harried, spoiled and reft openly on daylicht and under silence of the nicht . . . I think proper to strike them with the terrible sword of Halykirk . . . I curse them wakend, I curse them sleepand, I curse them risand, I curse them lyend, I curse them at hame, I curse them frae hame . . . I take frae them and cries doon all the gude deeds that ever they did or sall do . . . I declare them partless of all matins, masses, evensongs, dirges or other prayers on book or bead'.[9] Normally, however, the ancient jealousy with the See of York precluded such co-operation.

To conclude, even ecclesiastics were cynically aware that for maximum effect spells and incantations ought to be coupled with dragonnades,[10] the hangman's rope[11] or invasion.[3]

The ideal window for invasion, defined as the 'breaking of all their hearts', was envisaged as during and immediately after the harvest, preferably before Michaelmas (29th September),[12, 13] certainly no later than Martinmas (11th November).[14] Carnaby's outer limit of Candlemas[15] was derided by Little John 'because there is neither meat nor reliefs for horse and man'.[16] The strike, then, must be made 'before they have the chief of their hay, corn and straw eaten, which time past they fear no man';[17] and also when the moon was brightest, a factor to which Heron alone attached less importance than to the weather.[18, 19, 20] Consensus was that, come the Spring 'and new grass sprung up when they go on shieling . . . unto the latter end of summer there can be no harm done unto them'.[15] The fact that the Tyne- and Redesdalers themselves operated within a far wider window was a tribute to their horsemanship.

The invasion concept has to be reconstructed from plans rather than events, the most complete being that drafted in 1539 by the Council of the North, over which the Bishop of Llandaff presided and which included Bowes. While taking no direct part in the 'enterprise', the garrison assigned would first spread a net along the south of Tynedale.[21] Next a blockade would be imposed on either Liberty as necessary, with the markets at Hexham and Carlisle, and either Penrith[22] or Morpeth,[13] closed for trading to all the highlanders' wives or servants, a measure actually enforced in the case of Tynedale during the Ridley affair.[4] One refinement proposed in 1539 was that only the menfolk be banned from the markets, but that any outlaws' wives who attended be 'spoiled and robbed'.[16]

Like the blockade, the battle-plan depended on co-ordination along all three Marches. The nucleus of what Norfolk termed 'a good company'[23] and Llandaff ambitiously 'Your Majesty's power royal'[24] would be the Keeper's posse, since the convention persisted throughout the reign that that officer had to be present at any such penetration,[25] although the Vice Warden would be in command. In the Spring of 1525 both East and West Marchers were considered for participation[4] but in the event Sir William Eure led into Tynedale 300 of his Durham 'friends'.[26] Under

Carnaby's regime two incursions, one by 400 Northumbrian horse, indeed materialised, in the wake of which he recommended a third in concert with the Constable of Langley and Sir Thomas Wharton, lying in ambush on the southern and western edges of Tynedale respectively.[14] Subsequently[13] this blueprint was transformed into three-pronged and simultaneous invasions by the Vice Wardens, 'then all three companies to meet and lodge all togidder there'.[24] That such an assault never happened was not the fault of the Cumbrian officers: in 1539, for example, the Earl of Westmorland offered his sword against Tynedale just as soon as he was over the gout;[27] while Wharton complained to Cromwell that his offers of advice and reinforcement had been rebuffed by John Heron who declined to 'make me privy to any of his doings there'.[28] Only a Warden General could synchronise invasion, and as often as not none was in post.

Invasion was visualised in two phases and the only controversy was about their relative order. Thus outlaws would be caught and executed, their wives and progeny gaoled in Newcastle,[13] harbourers and backers distrained of all property,[15, 29] which would be handed to their victims.[3] In parallel 'the superfluous number of people, more than sufficient to labour . . . the said country of Tynedale [should] be . . . dispeopled in other countries far distant from Tynedale',[30] 'their wives and children . . . shipped into strange regions'.[3] More positively, they should be replaced by God-fearing planters, 'to be sorted and divided into sundry townships and . . . build their houses near together in some plain and open spaces'.[21] Once again it has to be remarked how spontaneously such social engineering occurred to English officialdom. With the convenience in mind of having the more blameless population out of the way before starting military operations, Sir William Eure in 1539 wanted the evacuation to come first, those resisting the proclamation to be summarily executed.[13] On the other hand in 1525 it was judged that 'whensoever we begin our war (sic) with Tynedale, the thieves shall avoid and flee the country',[4] and it is relevant that Carnaby, who shone more as a policy-maker than as an executive, estimated that extradition belonged to a second stage.[31] Of course the debate was academic because, whether or not there had been a supplementary plantation by his Plantagenet ancestor, Henry VIII had not the remotest intention of supplanting the toughest of his frontiersmen with a bunch of market-gardeners.

The Duke of Norfolk,[29] Carnaby,[17] and Sir William Eure[32] all assumed a sequel to invasion in which the garrisons of up to three companies would remain *in situ* until 'those that flee out were compelled to be of good . . . rule'.[15] In 1525[4] and 1539 fortnightly or monthly incursions were contemplated under the six petty captains, in order to wear down the rebels through attrition.[24] All this was tantamount to confession that no invasion was likely to accomplish its objectives, would in fact be no more than the opening salvo in an ongoing campaign.

Of five factors informing this gloom, the first was a realisation that funds would not be forthcoming, since the Court repeatedly disclaimed Treasury liability.[21] There was anxiety in 1525 that any Durham men conscripted would demand bonuses,[4] and in 1537 that the longer an invasion was postponed, the more it would cost.[12]

The occasion for the heaviest expenditure lay in the nature of the defences already familiar, entailing in Tynedale at least the subjugation of many inaccessible bastles, 'in which natural strength . . . the said Tynedales do much rejoice and embold themselves and do rather trust in the strength of such places without their houses than to the defence of their houses'. Even so, the little forts themselves were 'very hard without great force . . . to break', the great timbers of walls and roofs being incombustibly covered with turfs and earth.[30] When Carnaby managed to demolish the three Fenwick-slayers' houses he prided himself on a *tour de force*.[19, 33] Nor were the stout peles of the older Liberty an easy proposition, even though 'not set in so strong places as they been in Tynedale, nor the passages unto the same so . . . dangerous to convey a number of men in order'.[30]

The mention of fire brings us to the third factor since that element was deemed the only viable device by authorities as varied as John Heron,[20] the Durham Chancellor,[4] the Earl of Northumberland,[3] the Duke of Norfolk,[29] and Llandaff.[21] Whatever turfs might do for the bastles, they could not save harvested hay and corn,[15] so 'any other punishment generally they fear not, nor yet that but only this time of the year'.[14, 17] Unfortunately, however, the raising of fire within the realm, like the flesh of the sturgeon and the swan, was so much a royal prerogative as to render it for practical purposes taboo. When Norfolk applied for an indulgence, Henry VIII sharply reminded him that 'they be our subjects though evil men . . . We do rather desire their reformation than their utter destruction'.[34] When the Northumbrian gentry a year later jibbed at invasion without licence to burn, they were told 'in no wise to do [it] . . . [without] further auctoritee',[14] and that 'the King's pleasure was there should rather be used honest secret policy'.[15] To the frustration expressed by Heron in 1540 at similar inhibition, the King retorted: 'Ye shall not commonly use in your exploits upon the said rebels of Tynedale to raise incontinent fire and burn their houses like as in extreme war between strange realms'. The torch remained strictly a last resort.[35, 36]

There was as scant chance of taking by surprise as by fire because the highlanders' intelligence network was so sensitive. Not only did news spread like wildfire through the houses, but as in the assault on Hexham Tower they were well served by 'espials and other their secret feats and confederacies'.[21] During the hiatus between Carnaby and Heron an ambush attempted by the Sheriff of Northumberland at Waterfall Rig between Redesdale and Tynedale miscarried, when herdsmen alerted the fugitives to ignore the bait of cattle.[24] Even those inhabitants who abode the law 'woll always in time of night and other secret times be more favourable and kind to the . . . rebels than to the garrison'.[21] During Ridley's commotion 'privy and politique' plans to invade Tynedale[37] were being blown in Edinburgh four days beforehand, allegedly because a Charlton outlaw had been given the nudge by one of Dacre's brothers.[38] Lastly, no more than six persons could assemble for any mission, let alone an invasion, averred Bowes, 'but their purpose shall be discovered and warning thereof given'.[30]

Linked with poor security, the fifth factor was the adjacency of Scotland and Liddesdale, whose succour to Sir William Lisle the English believed to have been 'the chief and principal cause of all the misorder'.[39] It was in their opinion as vital to deny highland families access to Hawick and Jedburgh as to any English market.[13] According to Viscount Lisle, Redesdale and Tynedale could never be effectively policed until the Scottish Lowlands had been annexed.[40] However, there was continual recognition that the control of the three confederate dales furnished the kingdoms with their one common interest: proposals for bilateral action wafted to and fro in 1525,[4] 1528,[41] 1532,[42] 1539[13] and 1541[43], as well as in 1542–3. 'The time doth fast come upon to chastise the rebels and indisposed persons of Liddesdale and Tynedale, which woll not be done', Norfolk assured Cromwell, 'unless both Princes concur together'.[44] In exaggerated tribute to the highlanders' influence it was remarked later that 'those naughty people . . . take all the ways they can to let the said meeting'.[45] In any case all such schemes for joint encirclement aborted, if only because of the arrogance behind Henry VIII's demand to discipline Liddesdale while refusing reciprocal facilities to the Scots, inasmuch as Redesdale and Tynedale 'were great countries and far within the realm'.[46]

What anyway reduced talk of invasion to huffing and puffing was trepidation at the highlanders' retaliatory powers. Officials in 1525,[4] 1537,[29] 1538 and 1539 recommended that before invasion by other forces the garrison keep their horses 'lusty and fresh to resist the malicious incurses of the rebels of North Tynedale'[21] that would surely follow.[15] After his Falstone sortie Heron indented for twenty bows and sheaves of arrows and half a bushel of gunpowder since 'I could scarcely pass Tynedale without danger unless I had bows and handguns'.[20, 35] Bowes had the last word about both dales in 1551, that 'incurses [have been] made against them and by them, even as it were between England and Scotland in time of war, and ever at such times have they done more harm than they have received'.[47]

The classic instance had occurred during Ridley's rampage, when after the expulsion of the Keeper and the liquidation of the garrison, Sir William Eure invaded Tynedale as Vice Warden. 'Sir Rafe of Fenwick went up o side of Tyen Water and I of tother side and . . . I put my nuncle Eustace to him and fourscore archers and John of Ogle with fifty spears . . . The thieves set upon [Rafe Fenwick] . . . and . . . hath taken mine uncle and ten of my servants and slew one.'[26] A month after this fiasco Sir William negotiated a conditional surrender[48] of which he was patently ashamed,[49] although the concessions, wrung perhaps for the sake of Uncle Eustace, were to be inexplicably abandoned by Ridley.[5] Invasion was never tried again.

NOTES

1. PRO, SP I 5 fol. 229–230, 20/9/1513.
2. BL, Add. MSS 24965 fol. 148, 8/1/1524.
3. PRO, SP I 46 fol. 128–131, 18/1/1528.
4. BL, Calig. B I fol. 41, 27/4/1525.
5. PRO, SP I 36 fol. 55, 10/10/1525.
6. Watson, *Reivers*, p. 179 surmises that he would have been one of the itinerant and usually disreputable priests known along the Borders as 'book-a-bosom parsons', from the Mass books stowed in their clothing.
7. PRO, SP I 35 fol. 22, c.19/6/1525.
8. BL, Calig. B II fol.43, 31/5/1525.
9. Armstrong, Liddesdale, p. 223.
10. PRO, SP I 34 fol. 205–6, 16/5/1525.
11. BL, Calig. B VII fol. 71, 22/11/1525.
12. PRO, SP I 124 fol. 113–4, 27/8/1537.
13. *Ibid.*, 152 fol. 215–7, 23/7/1539.
14. *Ibid.*, 136 fol. 161–4, 15/9/1538.
15. *Ibid.*, 140 fol. 131–3, 18/12/1538.
16. BL, Calig. B III fol. 262, 17/12/1539.
17. *Ibid.*, fol. 251–3. 17/9/1538.
18. PRO, SP I 126 fol. 11–12, 24/10/1537.
19. *Ibid.*, fol. 148–9, 13/11/1537.
20. PRO, SP I 157 fol. 50–1, 13/1/1540.
21. *Ibid.*, 152 fol. 150–3, 21/9/1539.
22. *Ibid.*, 34 fol. 113–4, 30/3/1525.
23. BL, Add. MSS 32647 fol. 238, 27/9/1542.
24. BL, Titus F III fol. 97, 21/9/1539.
25. See p. 154 below.
26. PRO, SP I 35 fol. 60–1, 8/7/1525.
27. *Ibid.*, 153 fol. 198, 30/9/1539.
28. *Ibid.*, 157 fol. 106–7, 27/1/1540.

F

29. *Ibid.*, 124 fol. 234–7, 15/9/1537.
30. BL, Calig. B VIII fol. 63, 2/12/1541.
31. *Ibid.*, B III fol. 207, c. 2/10/1538.
32. PRO, SP I 157 fol. 108, 27/1/1540.
33. *Ibid.*, 127 fol. 105–6, 21/12/1537.
34. PRO, Exchr. T. R. Misc. Books, Vol. 119 fol. 137, (18/9/1537).
35. PRO, SP I 157 fol. 67–8, 19/1/1540.
36. For King Henry's not entirely irrational sympathy with the English highlanders see Chapter 15 below.
37. BL, Calig. B II fol. 109, 19/6/1525.
38. *Ibid.*, fol. 260, 26/7/1525.
39. PRO, SP I 144 fol. 177–8, 16/10/1527.
40. BL, Add. MSS 32648 fol. 201, 12/12/1542.
41. *LP*, IV(2) no. 4298, 27/5/1528.
42. *LP*, V no. 1054, 29/5/1532.
43. BL, Add. MSS 32646 fol. 259, 7/11/1541.
44. *Ibid.*, 19401 fol. 1, 27/8/1537.
45. *Ibid.*, 32648 fol. 8, 2/10/1542.
46. BL, Calig. B III fol. 91, 17/12/1528.
47. *Ibid.*, B VIII fol. 106, 1551 (not 1542).
48. *Ibid.*, B VII fol. 236, 1/7/1525.
49. PRO, SP I 35 fol. 203–4, 30/7/1525.

CHAPTER FOURTEEN

Due Process of Law

Concerning the more discriminant castigation meted out in courts of law one infers from the wealth of amazed comment that the crime rate, overlap of jurisdictions, and avoidability of justice in Tyne- and Redesdales were higher than elsewhere, and Bowes for one was convinced of the need to let no offence go unpunished.[1]

Divergence between the Court's view of justice as the brightest jewel in the Crown and the low priority assigned to it by Lord Dacre generated endless friction. Incensed at the highlanders' comparative impunity, the King once impressed upon Surrey that the arrest of Redesdale ringleaders[2] would do the Warden more good than 5000 marks.[3] Under-resourced and overworked, Dacre was blamed from the Cardinal downwards,[4, 5] not merely for indifference,[6] but for collusion,[7] so that when in 1512 his adversaries clamoured for redress against Tynedale and Redesdale it was partly to blacken *his* reputation.[8] While Dacre's downright guilt remains dubious, a grand justiciar widely suspected of shielding felons[4, 9] could scarcely be regarded as a lion under the Throne. That said, he was not unique in subordinating justice to expediency. Because internationally inconvenient an English ambassador in 1525 objected to Eure's hunt for highland malefactors,[10] while in 1523 Henry himself blew cold on their prosecution when required for campaign.

Yet the rules though bent were seldom disregarded, there being a creditable fastidiousness about hard evidence, in default of which, for example, no-one would have dreamed of arresting the Herons in 1537[11] and 1543.[12] When Tynedalers brushed with Hexhamshire men in that year Lieutenant and Warden General agreed that Sir Ralph Eure's testimony be taken with reserve, given a partiality to his charges. Wrote Suffolk: '[Sir Cuthbert Ratcliffe's] son . . . rode the fair with ane hundreth persons and saw all the misorder of it, wherefore [he] taking unto him another J.P. next adjoining . . . shall better know the truth than by Mr. Eure'.[13, 14] Though presumably the brand-marks on livestock at times proved useful reference points, the staple of evidence, then, consisted in statements of one or another sort.

One often unforthcoming source was any surviving victim, who might well prefer to settle for partial refund of his property than risk deadly feud with a hanged man's ruthless relatives.[1] Slightly more productive, because prior to Habeas Corpus a prisoner could be held long enough for him to crumble, were alleged culprits. Among assorted Herons left to languish in this way were Little John[15] and George;[16] Bastard John of the Hall Barns; and Roger of Corbridge detained at Darlington 'with all such further proofs and matter as ye can get to lay unto his charge' concerning an escape from the Chollerford tryst.[17] Confession being even more dangerous than denunciation, suspects, too, tended to a reticence that does not seem habitually to have been overcome by torture along the Borders.[18] Least productive were third parties such as young Ratcliffe or the gaol Tower watchmen.[19] Even those in less good standing were not ignored, an example being the Charlton who albeit unsuccessfully informed against Little John, by 'throwing out this bone' to Wharton and the Carnabys.[20] By contrast it was a declaration by Tynedalers that all Heron's conspiracy had been with themselves, not King James, that got their old crony off the sharper hook of March treason.[21]

However, most arrests in Durham or Northumberland outside the Liberties were effected not in the light of such collated evidence, but after red-handed detection followed by immediate pursuit *alias* 'hot trod'. All fit men were expected to participate from the watchmen censured for under-performance in Lisle's day;[22, 23] through the gentry[1] who failed to detain Halls and Tynedalers caught on their lands after breaking into Morpeth Castle;[24] to the Bailiff of Hexham who hounded Will of Shitlington to his death.[25] Then up through Vice Warden Sir William Eure who patrolled around Felton for twenty-five days with forty men looking for Lisle;[26] the Warden whose posse surprised his council of war at a nearby house, bagging Hedleys and Armstrongs;[27] the Warden General who took Tom Charlton of Carriteth with sixty followers at the Colwell bridle;[28] to the Lieutenant who arrested Dodd of the Burnmouth and four 'very tall men'.[29]

Due to time-lag arrests stemming from collated evidence were routinely executed within the Liberties by their Keepers. Ralph Fenwick was sent into Tynedale to fetch Will Ridley;[28] Robert Dodd 'Lowshorn' was killed in resisting arrest by the Keeper in 1528;[30] and Dacre exacted a bond of the Redesdale Keeper for the surrender of two Halls.[31] In 1511,[4] 1518[32] and 1525[33] Wardens were scrupulous about having Keepers with them during arrests in either Liberty.[34] Of two sets of exceptional circumstances, the first was a Keeper's absence. During the hiatus between Sir John Heron and Ralph Fenwick's second term Dacre's brothers attempted to arrest offenders;[35] during Carnaby's furlough, then abduction, the Constable of Langley, then the Sheriff of Northumberland, were pressed from above to execute his warrants.[36, 37] The second type of emergency arose whenever the Keeper was clearly incompetent, as was Ralph Fenwick for most of the time. When in 1514 he summoned Christie Milburn, James Dodd and Tom of Carriteth to surrender to custody at his court, he was ignored. Thereupon the Dacre knights slipped in with a six-day ultimatum, equally ignored, although they did inveigle another wanted heidsman, Edward Charlton of Hesleyside, into Hexham gaol Tower.[8] When in 1524 the baron unguardedly complained about Fenwick's ineffectiveness,[38] Wolsey's 'wholesome and friendly admonition' was to make good any shortfall himself,[39] and in particular to round up six named Tynedalers, a command that Dacre characterised as 'the like whereof hath not heretofore been seen',[40] arguing that 'for malefactors inhabitant either in Tynedale or Redesdale, being under the rule of Sir William Heron and Sir Ralph Fenwick . . . Keepers . . . reason and good conscience would they should answer to the same . . . I beseech Your Grace that [Fenwick] according to his grant and promise may be charged with the apprehending of them.[40, 41] Eventually the Warden General had to climb down, as one still had to do with the Cardinal, himself arresting the Charltons of Bellingham and Carriteth, and the four Robsons.[28, 42] The next year also the baron had to implement warrants against the Ridley gang that Sir Ralph had allowed to remain dead letters.[43]

The universal assumption was in other words that arrests within the Liberties were the proper business of the Keeper, so that John Heron's cold shoulder to Wharton was more correct than Dacre's enforced interventions. If a Keeper was weak or crooked, the corollary was a virtual immunity from prosecution for the highlanders that they prized highest among their privileges as denizens of a soken; by conscientious officials it was by contrast rated the most pernicious feature of the ancient franchise.[5] Hence William Eure's counsel to Wolsey that 'good rule shall never be there till the countries of Tynedale and Redesdale may be brought in to answer unto the King's laws . . . without making any untrue excuses . . . cloaking or colouring any old customs or pretended privileges . . . better to be neglected than . . . so great countries . . . be brought to utter ruin and destruction'.[26]

This is tantamount to saying that the 1504 statute, purporting to give the Sheriff of Northumberland the same powers of arrest in Tynedale as in the county at large[1] was as inoperative as that of Henry V. Even after the 1535 Act what G. R. Elton has termed the suppression of the troublesome Tynedale franchise[44] was still scouted, with the clans in 1551 'claiming always the old liberties of that country, as it was before the making of that statute'. In serving writs the Sheriff still stopped short at South Tyne.[1]

Far into the century, in fact, a Keeper's reputation depended on his success with arrests, to effect which Sir William Heron paid £10 p.a. to the Constable of Harbottle as compared with £7/13/4 retained for himself.[45] Heron was congratulated by the Court for one arrest he made.[46] Contrarywise Widdrington's slackness in apprehending Redesdale robbers, Carnaby's cowardly inertia[47, 48] and Little John's suspiciously low score[21] became proverbial. The Keepers' near-monopoly was seldom envied, let alone challenged. *Mutatis mutandis* arrest was fraught with the same obstacles as invasion, particularly in the matter of masking intentions. Henry VIII set the tone after the Pilgrimage when he enjoined 'dexterity, secrecy and foresight' in running to earth the Charlton ringleaders.[49] By the same token, lest George Heron and Cuthbert Charlton learn from their incarcerated kinsman that they were in danger of arrest for the murder of Hodge à Fenwick, Norfolk wanted Little John either 'put in some comfort to be shortly at liberty' or simply 'so kept that he sends no knowledge thereof to these parts'.[50] When on the track of Heron junior the Duke surpassed himself in elaborate subterfuge. Having summoned George 'on a feigned matter',[11] he subjected him to a couple of tests in the mistaken belief he would give himself away: Heron was appointed foreman of the jury that found true bills against the Fenwick-slayers, then despatched to Chipchase to seize an unnamed 'arrant traitor'. 'If he do', quoth His Grace, 'I shall have in my hands two false harlots.'[51] Another surprise that could be sprung was rearrest in court after acquittal on another charge, as once happened to Tom of Carriteth.[52]

What made for slippery customers was that the highlands were so replete with bolt-holes. Lewisburn Holms in which the Ridleyites skulked was 'a marvellous strong ground of woods and waters',[118] while Norfolk explained that he could not capture Charlton outlaws because 'with their cattle, friends and servants in so strong a ground'.[50] Wharton wished to fell underwoods in Tynedale Head 'where any strength is for keeping of offenders'.[53] To trap fugitives in the Waste required a military operation, and William Eure related how he 'went to the rebels of Tynedale . . . and set upon them at break of day. *And by reason we had no good guide* the thieves escaped themselves but we gat divers of their horses and their plate coats, and four-score or more of their milk-kie and more than ten-score milk-ewes'.[54]

As usual, however, the biggest hole in the net was the road north. Provided fugitives were not wanted for offences in Scotland, Scottish officers normally indulged their reset. Even King James, while claiming credit for Lisle's surrender,[55] denied he had ever been in Scotland at all.[56] The asylum afforded Edward Charlton and the Fenwick-slayers, 'some time with one friend of theirs, some time with other',[57] was a standing provocation to Norfolk.[58] Even when they did remove into England they were poised to dart irretrievably into Liddesdale at short notice.[50] The same problem arose two years later with regard to the Carnaby-takers who 'fed their horses and laid watches as men being always in dread . . . for sudden enterprises to be on them made for their apprehension, and always ready to start and flee into the wastes of the realm of Scotland'.[37] Sure enough, when Heron shortly afterwards assaulted the Falstone all he accomplished was to bounce the offenders into Teviotdale and the Head of Liddesdale.[59] The Council of the North urged the new Keeper 'by some secret espial' to establish their exact whereabouts so that their extradition could be demanded,[60] but John Heron's own preference was to snatch the quarry by a swoop over the Border with 300 men.[61]

As with pledges, the next problem after arrest was custody. Nearest home were Harbottle,[62] the staff for which cost the Redesdale Keeper more than six marks p.a., and Hexham gaol Tower,[1] which housed Edward Charlton of Hesleyside and Topping from time to time.[8, 35, 63] Little John lodged James Robson, his single catch from the Falstone, at Newcastle, 'trusting to God he shall have more company not long unto',[64] and that gaol was a favourite resort for most of the reign.[26, 65, 66] The heidsmen pledges in 1528 spent their last forlorn hours in Morpeth, while it was to Alnwick Castle that ironically its erstwhile Constable surrendered in his shirt, with a halter around his neck.[25] The Tower of London was reserved for wayward gentlemen like Little John.[67] Not only do ramshackle fortresses make poor prisons, but in an age of ferocious punishments standards of imprisonment were surprisingly lax. Widdrington was criticised for holding Redesdalers in Harbottle 'where they cannot be kept strong'.[68] As for the gaol Tower deterioration set in between 1514, when leg shackles were in place,[8] and 1537 when 10/- for repairing doors and locks were begrudged by Carnaby. The watchmen who drifted away at midnight to tend their cattle were so many Dogberries, and there were no piles of stones to drop on intruders.[19] Anyone could converse casually with prisoners through the gate,[1] while inmate Topping was left free to saunter round the town and attend Mass in the Abbey.[69]

Escapes were numerous enough to be used as argument for frequent gaol delivery.[70] Even before Lisle had been sprung, twelve highlanders had absconded from Alnwick and Newcastle.[71] The success of the Dacre knights in defending the gaol Tower in 1514[8] showed up Carnaby's failure in face of the same threat in 1538. Blaming subordinates for what he called 'mine unhappy chance',[63] he adduced as an excuse for incompetence what was an aggravation, namely 'neither the Bailiff [i.e. himself] nor any other officer was with the men to give them suitable orders'.[19] Lord Dacre's reputation fared little better in 1518, when 'the highlandsmen of Redesdale had such espial around Rothbury that from an ambush they scattered an escort of eighty horsemen to rescue important prisoners into Scotland, killing his Bailiff of Morpeth in the process'.[62]

Prisoners were not tried in the Keeper's head courts or law-days[72] at Wark[73, 74] or Harbottle,[75] which had shrunk to the status of baronial courts with jurisdiction in such quasi-civil cases as related to redress, sureties or tenure — a far cry indeed from the twelfth century when his writ had run in Tynedale to the exclusion of the King's.[76] Keepers like Sheriffs had come down in the world,[77, 78] and their commissions contained no reference to judicial functions at all,[79] so when they swore to chastise highland offenders,[80, 81] they were speaking not as magistrates, but as police officers.

Since the jurisdiction of a Warden of the Middle Marches stemmed from a military commitment, the gravest offence within his province was March Treason, that is, treacherous intercourse with Scots.[82] Outside warfare, transactions with Scotland had since the thirteenth century been regulated by that amalgam of dooms and treaties known as the *Leges Marchiarum*, the sole corpus of Anglo–Scottish law that has ever existed.[83] For international offences by those who had eluded arrest the forum in which the Warden officiated was a day of truce jointly with his Scots equivalent, convened at Gammel's Path or Hexpethgatehead,[1] where Wardens exchanged culprits after conviction by an Anglo–Scottish jury.[84] A hampering factor was a traditional claim by the Liddesdale Keeper to a day of truce all to himself.[1]

The Warden — in his absence the Vice Warden — dealt with domestic offenders, or Scots taken *in flagrante delicto* within England, at sessions of the Marches in his own Warden Court. One such court condemned a Robson and two Charltons simply for being men of bad character.[28] During the Pilgrimage the ability of the Percys to disrupt Lord Ogle's court,[85] but inability to stage one of their own,[86] became a political barometer: had the court ever met, depredations by Redes- and Tynedalers would have topped the agenda.[87] Another Warden court in Newcastle tried some Armstrongs netted by the Tynedale Keeper,[88] and the Scottish Warden of course enjoyed similar powers with regard to English highlanders taken in Scotland.[89]

As was emphasised to Lord Parr by the Duke of Suffolk, a Warden had no authority *qua* Warden to try any felony that did not involve March Treason. The problem was however skirted by his regular inclusion in the Commission of the Peace or even in that of Oyer et Terminer,[90] thereby rendering him competent for offences at Common Law. The development dovetailed with that by which the 1414 Act had belatedly become effective, in so far as the franchises still hindering arrest no longer affected trial.

Indeed in one respect practice already outstripped the old statute, since felonies committed within the Liberties, too, had been brought under the Common Law: Cuthbert Charlton was condemned at the ordinary sessions for a murder in the middle of Tynedale,[51] and the original proviso, that before such prosecution a highlander had first through outlawry to be deprived of the Liberty's protection,[91] had fallen into abeyance.

Occasional involvement of Wardens in the administration of the Common Law has led some historians to imagine that highland offenders were still tried nowhere but in the Warden Courts.[92] In fact most of them — like Ridley's heidsmen followers,[93] Little John,[94] Tynedale fugitives in 1539,[37] and participants in the Hexham fray[90] — ended up before justices in eyre at sessions of Oyer et Terminer or gaol delivery. If it suited them, these judges would co-opt, among other J.P.s, of whom there was a great shortage in Northumberland, the Wardens and Vice Wardens.[32, 95] There was never any pretence, however, that these officers did not fetch and carry for the visitors, for whom they rounded up those suspected[28] or indicted.[4, 32] The King even commanded the itinerant justices to report on a Warden's performance on his own bench.[96]

Given the overlap, it is remarkable that until Elizabeth's reign[97] jurisdictions so seldom clashed. The explanation lies in attitudes that were often the opposite of what might have been expected. So far from trespassing, the Earl of Northumberland was probably typical in leaning thankfully on any lawyer in sight.[35] As to the courtly Janus, what they particularly prized was short shrift. Charlton ringleaders were to be 'there ordered [i.e. hanged] without delay',[49] and Dacre to hustle Tom of Carriteth to the gallows, with forty others if necessary. King and Cardinal were careless as to which body of laws was enlisted to achieve the desired result: Dacre should not tarry an instant for the coming of the justices,[98] the Herons condemned under 'either the laws of the realm or of the Borders, as best may serve'.[12] That Lisle was arraigned for treason, his heidsmen for March Treason was a matter of indifference.[99] In fact Warden Courts and Border laws were distinctly preferred because so expeditious: as an equity lawyer Wolsey evinced no tenderness for the Common Law anyway, while time would be lost awaiting the arrival of justices itinerant. Barely two days elapsed between the arrests of Lisle's retinue and their trials in Northumberland's court,[27, 100] while it was reckoned extraordinary that Hall Barns' case should have been ignored by two successive Warden's Courts.[66] So we have the strange spectacle after the Pilgrimage of a centralising administration embarked on urgent recodification of the archaic *Leges Marchiarum*.[82, 101]

To resume ascent of the hierarchy, a Lieutenant was *ex officio* senior of all justices of assize.[1] Norfolk presided over sessions at which the Herons were indicted as accessories to murder,[15, 47] and it was once mooted that he hold sessions twice or thrice yearly to deal specifically with Tyne- and Redesdales.[82] However, other pressures ensured that legatine activity was confined to months when rebellion or mistrust of Dacre peaked.

Most awful of all was London justice but normally reserved for the likes of Sir William Lisle. Bringing harbourers of highland thieves before Star Chamber was pondered in 1523,[102] and it was there that a Northumbrian delegation denounced Lord Dacre as the robbers' patron.[5] A project in 1514 to despatch Charltons of Hesleyside and the Leehall for trial in the capital came to nothing.[8]

Any forensic proceedings commenced with the collation of bills of complaint. Not content in 1517 with a huge number already filed to lay before the justices, bailiffs and parish priests of 'toons adjoining to the highlands' lobbied for still more.[32] One month's notice was proclaimed of the meeting of a court of oyer et terminer, presumably much less for a Warden Court. In due course the judge empanelled a jury of presentment which pursuant to an inquest on the bills presented indictments.[1] Probably nothing had changed since the mid-fifteenth century when nearly all suspects along the Borders were so arraigned.[103] Should the accused stay out of reach, then they could be declared rebels[104] or outlaws[51] — the distinction is unclear. If the accused were accessible, the Keeper would be expected to secure them.[32] Once in custody, prisoners were tried by jurymen, fifteen to twenty-four at the Warden Court, a dozen before an assize judge. At the former none could be challenged.[1]

The jury system is inappropriate to violent and clannish societies. Always faint, the public-spiritedness of the Northumbrian gentry, from whom juries of presentment were composed, tended to vanish altogether under intimidation. Amazement was voiced when they behaved exemplarily at the 1526 sessions. Despite the King's confidence that all that was required to secure the conviction of the Herons in 1543 was a jury of 'indifferent' gentlemen, properly briefed, Suffolk halted the trial because of their transparent determination to acquit.[105] Indeed the chances of obtaining the conviction of 'either gentlemen or men of great Surname' inspired him with gloom. When Ede Robson patently slew a witness on his way to the Duke of Norfolk, the jury found 'he did it in his own defence'. It was still received wisdom around 1600 that jurors failed in their duty through fear of feuds, and witnesses ('talesmen') likewise, so that 'many evil-doers were quit for lack of evidence'. The same applied to plaintiffs 'in this wild country' who at 'open trial at the bar . . . will not show their faces'.[21] The high rate of acquittal observed by Mr. C. J. Neville for the mid-fifteenth century still provoked comment in 1523,[71] 1543 and 1600[106] with regard to the highland dales.

When the highland offender did evade the judicial net, there were still two penalties that he might incur through administrative action. While there *was* provision for imprisonment in the *Leges Marchiarum*, there is no trace of such sentences, but after Heron's conviction had aborted, Suffolk committed him to ward during pleasure.[21] Less rare were proclamations of outlawry, the abolition of which as a judicial sentence had been demanded by the peasants in 1381. Lisle's accomplices were outlawed in all three Border counties,[6, 22, 104] and the Fenwick-slayers similarly anathematised, with the gentry enjoined to take advantage of their plight.[107] Though Henry VII in a technical sense had treated his debtors in this way, 'to bear the wolf's head' was more normally an invitation to shoot on sight.[108]

To turn now to sentences of death passed by the courts: decapitation for March Treason; hanging for felony; the same plus drawing and quartering for high treason. The cull was frightful,[109] especially in the first half of the reign. Alone in not escaping in the Rothbury ambush, Tom Pott was hanged almost immediately; James Dodd of the Burnmouth and associates went the same way late in 1523;[110] Will Charlton of Bellingham, similarly accompanied, was treated likewise by Surrey;[52] sixteen of the Head Surnames of Tynedale and especially Redesdale perished in a bloody assize in 1526;[93] several again after the first Felton swoop at the end of 1527, the Scots ambassador being present;[26, 100] another fourteen beheaded or hanged after the second;[27, 111] a regular holocaust in the Spring of 1528 devoured not only Lisle and his closest friends, but also five Redesdalers, the Tynedale pledges and Will of Shitlington and his crew;[25] six more Tynedalers went to the gallows in Newcastle while Lisle's quarters were still dripping.[99] In comparison, the mopping-up after the Pilgrimage was rather tame: a Hall and Hedley hanged in chains, that is slowly asphyxiated;[112] six highlanders merely hanged;[47] and of course Cuthbert Charlton.

A penalty which at least thinned out the troublemakers enjoyed predictable support. After one execution of Charltons and Robsons the Cardinal urged more of the same as 'a great furtherance to the . . . restfulness of those parties',[98] whereas Norfolk assured Dacre that the hanging of Will of Bellingham was the best thing he had ever done.[113] The King trusted that when Will's son Cuthbert trod the same path this would indirectly save the lives of many others.[16] Those in the North from the Council downwards[114] were no less devoted to capital punishment. On suspicion of complicity in a Teviotdale raid south, the Earl threatened Tynedale with terrible execution.[115] Wharton held that sheer body count was the least

fallible criterion of an efficient Keeper,[116] while Widdrington confessed
that 'unless . . . part of [Tynedale] . . . be put in execution, with a part
of the inhabitants of Redesdale', the Vice Wardenry was beyond him.[117]
Lastly, though they used to face death earlier and more painfully than
most, nowhere was faith in the effectiveness of the death penalty stronger
than among the highlanders themselves. In his negotiations with Ridley's
followers the Tynedale Keeper was assured they would consent to anything,
'their lives reserved'.[54, 118] After one spate of executions 'Redesdale men in
great numbers submitted themselves in their shirts with halters about their
necks, upon bare knees, unto the King's mercy'.[119] Rattled by Little John's
despatch south, ostensibly scaffold-bound, the Hesleyside Charltons were
'in a dread now and fear for their lives'.[120]

Yet advocacy of the rope and the axe was not unanimous, it being
sporadically recognised that desperate men would resist to the death arrest
that spelled no less, while third parties were not invariably 'encouraged'. It
was in trying to seize Ridley that Ralph Fenwick was put to flight. The Earl's
effort to soften the Cardinal's heart about Lisle[121] was born of reluctance to
alienate 'allies and friends on the Borders to whom I must trust my life'. Parr
feared that the sequel to executions in 1543 would be the flight of many
highlanders 'knowing themselves semblably . . . culpable'.[122]

Tyne- and Redesdale freeholders condemned for felonies outside the
Liberties or for March treason were liable to confiscation along with the
death sentence. Exemption of the customary majority from this additional
pain[123] was greatly prized by them, inspiring the jingle 'the father to bough
[i.e. hang], the son to plough.[124] As for punishment by fines as such, admiss-
ible under the Common Law, they were never imposed on the highlanders
by assize justices, which was why stern Durham churchmen preferred their
courts to the Warden's.[4, 32]

Most pecuniary penalties were in the field of redress and were inflicted in
the Warden's courts. In Anglo-Scottish litigation each Warden forwarded to
his opposite number a sheaf of complaints, personal details in which reveal
the Borderers of either nation as familiar to one another as members of the
same club.[125] Come the day of truce, each bill was filed or cleared by the
accused's Warden on his honour, or by the man's compatriots on the jury.
For a filed bill the penalty was 'double and sawfey',[1] i.e. thrice the value of the
plunder, but in an inflationary age[126] beasts were ridiculously underpriced,
often leaving the thief comfortably in pocket.

Regarding domestic robberies it would appear[127] that after indictment
by the presenting jury the defendant was tried by another. The usual shoals
between justice and a conviction having been negotiated, anyone found

guilty was sentenced by the Warden, whose function, except on capital charges, consisted in the 'cassing' of damages through collation of the plaintiff's sworn claim with the same inadequate tariff of going rates as applied at days of truce. Distraint was consigned to the Keepers, so it was, for example, from Roger Fenwick that his parishioners concealed their booty in 1514;[8] Ralph Fenwick who guaranteed collection of redress in 1523;[128] exclusively to those whom they irregularly recognised as their Keepers that the highlanders pretended to offer restitution in 1537.[87]

The wrangle over the out-of-court bargain struck on redress between the Lieutenant and the majority heidsmen shows how fast and loose could be played with the rules. According to a petition signed by fourteen of them, they were 'commanded to make restitution of the third part of all such goods as we had, by our oaths'.[129] This double and sawfey turned inside out was grudgingly accepted by the Council of the North[130, 131] and even the despoiled,[132] pending realisation that the marauders 'wol pay a great part . . . with their oaths and small with their purses',[133] Widdrington's court broke up in confusion when it dawned on the aggrieved that they were to be denied even the measly ninth of what by tradition they were entitled to expect.[120] Eight months later, when really in control, the Council put a more equitable gloss on Norfolk's arrangement that it would not truly bear, assigning precedence to the proofs of robbery and values of property stated in their bills by the plaintiffs, and permitting the accused to clear themselves on oath only when the proofs were judged 'insufficient'.[130, 133] While appeals reached the King and Cromwell for endorsement,[131, 132] the heidsmen would not 'bide' this new decree, 'marvelling what is the cause thereof'.[129] Despite the procession of pledges in and out of Newcastle like manikins on an ornamental clock, the acting Keeper returned from Tynedale empty-handed,[131] and the cry from Durham in 1524 that to get a bill filed against Tynedalers was as far as one ever got,[38] again rang true.

To be fair to Norfolk, even the Council of the North admitted[37] that ill-gotten gains had been so improvidently squandered as almost to rule out payment of even the token compensation envisaged by the Duke.[134] Only Parr, however, was astute enough to detect the self-perpetuating element outside villainy in the highlanders' situation, that 'they having no goods to live by would for necessity fall to their accustomed theft'.[122] To live down the past was beyond their means.

NOTES

1. Bl, Calig. B VIII fol. 106, 1551, not 1542 as calendared.
2. BL, Add. MSS 24965 fol. 35, 24/6/1523.

3. *LP*, III(2) no. 3304, 5/9/1523.
4. PRO, SP I 2 fol. 89, October 1511.
5. *Ibid.*, 32 fol. 205, 30/11/1524.
6. *LP*, II(2) no. 4547, end October 1518.
7. *LP*, IV(1) no. 701, 3/10/1524.
8. PRO, SP I 7 fol. 281, 27/2/1514.
9. *LP*, III(1) no. 347, June 1519.
10. BL, Calig. B II fol. 109, 19/6/1525.
11. PRO, SP I 121 fol. 169–170, 26/6/1537.
12. *Ibid.*, 177 fol. 68 & 73, 21/4/1543.
13. *Ibid.*, 180 fol. 241, 27/7/1543.
14. BL, Add. MSS 32651 fol. 178, end July 1543.
15. PRO, SP I 125 fol. 65–6, 28/9/1537.
16. *Ibid.*, fol. 25–6, c.28/9/1537.
17. See p. 90 above.
18. PRO, SP I 47 fol. 248, 6/6/1528.
19. BL, Calig. B V fol. 36, 9/1/1539.
20. PRO, SP I 169 fol. 203–5, end March 1542.
21. BL, Add. MSS 32651 fol. 247, 21/8/1543.
22. *LP*, IV(2) no. 3370, 22/8/1527.
23. PRO, SP I 44 fol. 177–8, 16/10/1527.
24. BL, Add. MSS 24965 fol. 41, 16/7/1523.
25. BL, Calig. B VII fol. 122, 28/1/1528.
26. PRO, SP I 45 fol. 109, c.11/12/1527 (more probably after 25/2/1528).
27. *Ibid.*, 46 fol. 105–6, 12/1/1528.
28. BL, Calig. B III fol. 6, 20/5/1524.
29. PRO, SP I 49.2 fol. 21–2, 2/9/1523.
30. *Ibid.*, 47 fol. 14–5, 25/2/1528.
31. BL Add. MSS 24965 fol. 125, 24/9/1524.
32. PRO, SP I 16 fol. 313–4, 25/6/1518.
33. *Ibid.*, 35 fol. 60–1, 8/7/1525.
34. In the two episodes involving Dacre he was himself nominal Keeper, but the Fenwicks father and son were *de facto* Keepers.
35. PRO, SP I 47 fol. 25, 28/2/1528.
36. *Ibid.*, 131 fol. 167 & Exchr. T. R. Misc. Books, Vol. 121 fol. 22, 17/4/1538.
37. BL, Titus F III fol. 97, 21/9/1539.
38. BL, IV(1) no. 28, 14/1/1524.
39. BL, Calig. B III fol. 37, end February 1524.
40. PRO, SP I 30 fol. 334–5, 25/4/1524.
41. BL, Add. MSS 24965 fol. 193, 1/4/1524.
42. *Ibid.*, fol. 226B, 13/5/1524.
43. PRO, SP I 34 fol. 113-4, 30/3/1525.
44. *England under the Tudors*, p. 175.
45. PRO, SP I 32 fol. 127, c.14/10/1524.
46. *Ibid.*, 31 fol. 123, 12/6/1524.
47. *Ibid.*, 124 fol. 232–3, 15/9/1537.
48. *Ibid.*, 125 fol. 10–11, 22/9/1537.
49. *Ibid.*, 116 fol. 29, c.15/2/1537.

50. *LP*, XII(2) no. 291, 20/7/1537.
51. PRO, SP I 125 fol. 21–2, 23/9/1537.
52. *Ibid.*, 31 fol. 196–7, 8/7/1524.
53. *LP*, XVIII(1) no. 799, June 1543.
54. BL, Calig. B VII fol. 236, 1/7/1525.
55. *LP*, IV(2) no. 4116, 30/3/1528.
56. BL, Calig. B III fol. 209, 12/9/1527.
57. PRO, SP I 126 fol. 11–12, 24/10/1537.
58. *Ibid.*, 117 fol. 181–2, 31/3/1537.
59. *Ibid.*, 157 fol. 99, 25/1/1540.
60. *Ibid.*, fol. 67–8, 19/1/1540.
61. PRO, E 36 Vol. 121 fol. 12 & 27, April 1540.
62. PRO, SP I 17 fol. 223–4, 23/12/1518.
63. *Ibid.*, 140 fol. 77–8, 11/12/1538.
64. *Ibid.*, 157 fol. 50–1, 13/1/1540.
65. *LP*, IV(2) no. 3344, 12/8/1527.
66. *LP*, XVI no. 1179, 14/9/1541.
67. *LP*, XIII(1) no. 627, 31/3/1538.
68. PRO, SP I 118 fol. 223–4, c.18/4/1537.
69. BL, Calig. B III fol. 98, 9/1/1539.
70. *Ibid.*, fol. 262, 17/12/1539.
71. *LP*, III(2) no. 3240, 14/8/1523.
72. BL, Calig. B VIII fol. 63, 2/12/1541.
73. BL, Add. MSS 24965 fol. 255B, 16/6/1524.
74. PRO, SP I 125 fol. 179, 10/10/1537.
75. *Ibid.*, 132 fol. 25–6, 3/5/1538.
76. Reid, *Council in the North*, pp. 8 & 300.
77. *LP*, III(1) no. 1225, 12/4/1521.
78. Elton, *England under the Tudors*, p. 58.
79. PRO, SP I 115 fol. 45–6, late January 1537.
80. *Ibid.*, 126 fol. 80–1, 6/11/1537.
81. *Ibid.*, 127 fol. 105–6, 21/12/1537.
82. *Ibid.*, 116 fol. 217–8, 7/3/1537.
83. The main source for the *Leges Marchiarum* is the Bell MSS in Carlisle Cathedral, compiled by the last Warden Clerk of the West Marches. These have been subjected to collation and analysis — but not alas clarification — by D. L. W. Tough, *Last Years of a Frontier*, Chapters VI through IX. Cf. also J. A. Tuck, in *NH*, Vol. III, pp. 32–3.
84. Watson, *Reivers*, p. 57 ff. gives a good summary of procedure at a day of truce.
85. PRO, SP I 119 fol. 94–104, end April 1537.
86. BL, Calig. B III fol. 264, 24/1/1537.
87. PRO, SP I 69 fol. 54–5, 17/1/1537 (not 1532 as calendared).
88. *LP*, XVII no. 650, 22/8/1542.
89. BL, Add. MSS 32650 fol. 18, 7/3/1543.
90. *LP*, XVIII(1) no. 964, 28/7/1543.
91. *Rot. Parl.* IV 21A, 1414.
92. Rachel Reid (*op. cit.*, pp 8 & 117) describes the two dales as Liberties

where the King's writ did not run till the 1535 Act. Tough seems unaware that the Common Law impinged on the Borders at all.

93. BL, Calig. B III fol. 44, 17/8/1526.

94. PRO, SP I 124 fol. 113–4, 27/8/1537.

95. *LP*, IV(3) no. 5954, 23/9/1529.

96. PRO, SP I 96 fol. 169–173, 15/9/1535.

97. Tough, *Last Years*, p. 160 ff..

98. BL, Add. MSS 24965 fol. 259, 11/6/1524.

99. BL, Calig. B III fol. 146, 2/4/1528.

100. *LP*, IV(2) no. 3914, 11/2/1528.

101. Tough, *op. cit.*, p. 98.

102. BL, Calig. B VI fol. 435, end August 1523.

103. C. J. Neville, in *NH*, Vol. XIX, p. 48.

104. PRO, SP I 44 fol. 32–3, 24/8/1527.

105. BL, Add. MSS 32651 fol. 269, 25/8/1543.

106. Reid, *op. cit.*, p. 286; Tough, *op. cit.*, p. 162; and Neville, *op. cit.*, p. 56.

107. *LP*, IV(2) no. 3689, 26/12/1527.

108. *Peasants* etc., ed. Hilton, pp. 229 & 260.

109. It was too on the Welsh Marches. Cf. Penry Williams, *Council of the Marches of Wales*, Chapter 1.

110. *LP*, III(2) no. 3545, 19/11/1523.

111. *LP*, IV(2) no. 3796, 12/1/1528.

112. *LP*, XII(1) no. 919, 12/4/1537.

113. *LP*, IV(1) no. 530, 23/7/1524.

114. PRO, SP I 136 fol. 217–8, c.22/9/1538.

115. *Ibid.*, 70 fol. 232–5, 23/8/1532.

116. *Ibid.*, 179 fol. 151, June 1543.

117. *Ibid.*, 134 fol. 140–1, 12/7/1538.

118. BL, Calig. B II fol. 260, 26/7/1525.

119. PRO, SP I 47 fol. 248, 26/4/1528.

120. BL, Calig. B III fol. 197, 18/7/1537.

121. M. E. James, *Tudor Magnate*, p. 14.

122. PRO, SP I 178 fol. 85, 24/5/1543.

123. PRO, E 134, 18 James I Easter No. 13, 1620.

124. Gray, *Chorographia*, p. 118 ff..

125. PRO, SP 49 5 fol. 29, December 1541.

126. G. R. Elton, *England under the Tudors*, p. 224.

127. Tough, *op. cit.*, p. 161, which does not however elucidate several obscurities.

128. BL, Calig. B III fol. 255, 16/4/1523.

129. *Ibid.*, fol. 239, 17/3/1538.

130. *Ibid.*, fol. 241, 7/4/1538.

131. PRO, SP I 131 fol. 197–8, 24/4/1538.

132. *LP*, XIII(1) no. 1235, 21/6/1538.

133. BL, Calig. B III fol. 231, 31/3/1538.

134. *Ibid.*, B VII, fol. 224, 3/7/1537.

CHAPTER FIFTEEN

Indulgence, Oblivion and Salary

Implicit in the diagnosis by the later Earl of Essex was a prognosis that the poverty in which highland lawlessness was rooted could be assuaged only by injections of money, even if only negatively in the cancellation of debts. Was there perhaps another side to the record of Tyne- and Redesdalers that had created the requisite climate of indulgence?

While the clansmen's services to the King against Scotland were plain enough, that they had been of any assistance to him during a great rebellion, when they had bludgeoned seditious oaths out of the gentry, might at first blush seem preposterous. What lent plausibility to the notion, nevertheless,[1] was the dichotomy in the larger Liberty between the majority and the Hesleyside Band that manifested itself from November 1536 onwards. Whereas the loyalty of the latter to the Percys persisted, the unalloyed self-interest galvanising their rivals counselled abandonment of a lost cause. For the Court it became defensible, as well as expedient, to treat the Band as scapegoat and the majority heidsmen, not the Doncaster M.P.'s, as representative of Tynedale. During the Pilgrimage Norfolk accused the highlanders of every crime under the sun, except treason,[2, 3, 4] while the Court blamed even those on what were vaguely termed their officers.[5] By the Duke of Suffolk Tyne- and Redesdales were grouped with Carnaby as the soundest prospects for restraining Northumberland 'in good stay and quiet';[6] and by Norfolk's marching orders, with Cumberland and Westmorland as faithful subjects.[7] The sole dissentient voice was that of Lord Darcy, who till unmasked was feeding a stream of disinformation south, but doing his not unjustifiable utmost to keep the highlanders in Henry VIII's bad books.[8, 9]

What dismayed Aske's ally and thrilled the Court was that, albeit 'for their own lucre',[10] they had pinned down a population, adherence by whom to the insurrection could have tipped the balance.[11, 12] Perceiving that the Northumbrian threat had evaporated and that Tyne- and Redesdales had been preying on the inhabitants, the monarch reasoned that the former had resulted from the latter. The talk among his potential enemies in the shire was of taking up arms not against himself, but into the highlands: the Privy Council remarked that if Northumbrians 'would attempt to stir . . . amongst the rebels, the Tynedale and Redesdale men should be ever ready to spoil them at their pleasure'.[13] The 'poor folks' thought only of vengeance,[14, 15, 16]

167

vainly lobbying the Percys' meetings for redress.[17, 18] Elsewhere the very
stuff of insurrection, churchmen from the Prince Bishop, who lost 70% of
his tithes from plundered tenantry,[19] down to the Hexham monks, donors
of protection money, had been the highlanders' main victims. The upshot
was that Northumberland did not enter into Wharton's calculations as a
centre of disaffection in the still troubled January of 1537.[20] So much for
Sir Thomas Percy's saucy pledge not to reappear at Doncaster without 500
Northumbrian spearmen at his back.[17]

Circumstances were then conceivable under which the King would
make excuses for the highlanders, as when in 1541 he ascribed Scottish
raids by them to 'extreme sorrow and rage' at what they had themselves
suffered.[21, 22] Excuses are next door to pardon which indeed fell thicker
and faster during the reign of this fellow Marcher's grandson on the Tyne–
and Redesdalers, than on any other segment of his subjects. While Henry
VIII never dealt as ferociously with rebels as Catholic mythology would have
it,[23] his clemency towards the inhabitants of the two Liberties was unique.

Earlier pardons were seals on royal triumphs, with strings attached. After
Ridley's collapse clemency to Tynedale was akin to a stay of execution;[24, 25]
after Lisle's, it was only after hangings that offenders from both dales were
allowed to submit to mercy.[26, 27] On each occasion pledges were surrendered
for good behaviour.[25] The anonymity of the quartet excepted from the
general pardon in 1536[28] indicated they were to die on the representative
principle of military decimations. When Norfolk was enjoined to execute
all northerners who had robbed since the pardon, it was the highlanders
whom everyone had in mind.[29]

It was after reappraisal of the clansmen's recent role[30] that the Court
now began to smudge its hard line. Whereas the Tynedale majority were
being shepherded back into the fold, the cut-off date for amnesty left only
the Fenwick-slayers out in the cold.[31] The breaking of Hexham gaol was
the next offence requiring absolution which, with a Papal crusade against
England seemingly imminent, duly materialised. The Duke of Norfolk bus-
tled north yet again to dish out pardons to all Tynedale offenders, though
the former exception was maintained.[32] The response to this kindly gesture
was Carnaby's abduction, coupled with an insolent demand for pardon wide
enough to embrace both its perpetrators and the assassins.[33] Swallowing the
camel of Little John and Edward Charlton, the Court still strained at the
kidnappers and Fenwick-slayers.

The new Keeper now endeavoured to reclaim as many of the outlaws
as possible. To obtain Carnaby's release he prematurely promised the
kidnappers their pardons.[34] Having failed to deliver, he had no better

luck in persuading twelve of them to give themselves up. After a fortnight's seclusion they replied that 'unless they might have Your Highness's pardon they would in no wise agree'; and that even if pardoned would not pay the redress to Scotland being called for. The sequels were an abortive ambush and the punitive expedition[35] against the Falstone. Meanwhile the Court was relapsing into the position that would leave only the assassins beyond the Pale.[36] Contributory were a deterioration in relations with Scotland which made hitherto deplorable activities positively meritorious; and the elevation of Thomas Cromwell, patron of the highlanders' foes from Lawson to Carnaby, to an earldom and the scaffold in rapid succession.

If in what ensued Little John played the lead and Norfolk was the producer, the script was Henry VIII's.[37] On August 18th 1540 a Privy Council at Windsor discussed how to get representative Tynedalers to London without loss of face. The outcome was letters to Heron and the Vice Warden supplemented, at the King's instigation, with a message 'by mouth'[38] 'as though without the King's knowledge' that 'the King will undoubtedly pardon them'.[39] Six to eight of the chiefs should travel as suppliants to London, while their henchmen made their submission to the Vice Warden on the spot.[40] The Duke, who was by way of being an expert on pardons — once, northward bound, he had put in for a dozen blanks under the Great Seal — waited for the delegation in Norfolk, whence he reported on 16th October the arrival of 'five of the principal offenders of every Surname one of Tynedale'. He advised them to throw themselves at the royal feet and ask for pardon, adding that one of them, John of the Falstone, 'a principal offender', was very sick.[41] In due course they set off through an upholstered countryside as novel as the sort of English they heard on all sides, to audience of Henry VIII at Windsor four days later. Concerning this singular encounter between one of the ornaments of the Renaissance and the wildest of his frontiersmen, Privy Council minutes preserve a deplorable discretion. Of the outcome, however, there is no doubt, to wit pardon for forty outlaws[42] and yeomen in respect of all treasons committed before 1st November. The list included, of the Robsons John and Henry of the Falstone, and Cuddy Lion (Coeur de Lion) of Yarrowhall; of the Charltons Gerard of Wark alias Topping and old Brade John of Larederburn.[43, 44]

Whatever the impression they made on the monarch, the reciprocal effect of his own imperious presence did not take long to fade. Upon Ralph Eure's arrival three years later to sweep up the mess accruing from Heron's infamous stewardship, the national military requirement demanded another pardon. Cheerfully complying with the rituals, Tyne- and Redesdalers confessed lèse-majesté 'both in favouring his rebels and also in damaging his subjects', and were 'pardoned conditionally so as they live henceforth honestly and truly and in due obedience to His Majesty'. A sanguine project of Parr's that they also compensate 'to their uttermost powers' was watered down by a more fatalistic Suffolk into a lame compromise whereby the wealthiest offenders should vouchsafe whatever they could afford.[45, 46]

Even the 'unforgiveable' Fenwick-slayers were never brought to book. Probably tucked under Little John's wing shortly after recall, this John Dodd may have figured in the 1539 musters[47] or served Hertford as a captain in his 1544 invasion.[48] Ninian Charlton vanishes in June 1543[49] while his fellow exile, John of the Blakelaw, having changed his tune,[50] eventually submitted in the English camp before Pinkie to Hertford become Protector Somerset, who pardoned him for all offences from Fenwick's murder onwards.[51]

Local reactions to bountiful clemency ranged from the scepticism of officials to the outrage of the population at large. The Durham Chancellor would admit only the highlanders' womenfolk to his markets even after pardon, else 'after their accustomed manner' they would boast that 'for their evil deeds they always obtain mercy'.[36] Bald amnesty according to Bowes made them 'very bold in doing evil',[52] so that 'they have always newly perpetrated . . . heinous and detestable offences',[53] whereas Parr enlarged on the sense of injustice engendered in their victims, 'who raised a slanderous rumour of too much favour born by me unto the said thieves'.[54]

The subsidy of a clean slate was insufficient as a palliative. There were in addition rewards for services to, even offices under the Crown, which must have seemed to contemporaries to be drying itself on a very damp towel. First there were casual sweeteners like a £10 Christmas box shared by Heron of Chipchase and Charlton of Hesleyside,[55] the latter of whom received another £1 in 1540;[56] or £5 to Bastard John of the Hallbarns for despatch-riding to London;[55] or income out of Customs to namesake of Crawley in 1519.[57, 58] More germane was the hiring as his under-Keepers by the Earl of Northumberland for £3/6/8d p.a. of the two Charltons, and for £2 p.a. of Hall of Otterburn,[59] which probably continued *mutatis mutandis* till April 1540.[60] By that time Edward Charlton was almost certainly acting as Little John's under-Keeper, to be eventually replaced under Ralph Eure by Archie Dodd. The evidence, however, is purely circumstantial.

Feeing the highlanders excited as little general delight as remission of their sins. A dispute on the topic between the King and Lieutenant was one occasion when someone dared to stand up to the tyrant. Just before the Fenwick murder Henry directed that every heidsman be paid £5 twice yearly, on a par with the Cumbrian gentry, having first sworn fealty to himself as new Head of the Church of England.[61] Described as gentlemen,[16] beneficiaries would include John Hall of Otterburn and two other Halls; Edward and

Cuthbert Charlton, not yet fatally compromised; Henry Robson of the Falstone and Geoffrey: and John and David Milburn[30, 62] The Duke's scorn was unbridled: 'More arrant thieves and murderers be not in no realm than they have of long time been . . . and now those ungracious persons to be taken into the King's fees'.[2] Against a nominal list he inserted unflattering entries such as 'not only a thief but a principal maintainer of all mischiefs' against Hesleyside, and 'no more arrant thief living' against the Falstone. Although John Hall was technically a 'true man',[63] 'yet few thefts done in . . . Redesdale but . . . he hath part thereof and might have let much theft if he had list'.[3] Rather than give them fees, he upbraided Cromwell, 'it shall be more convenient to hang up a good number'.[64] In rebutting this tirade 'the King marvelled he should be more earnest against . . . murderers and thieves than such as have been traitors. These men rather did good in the late trouble . . . and . . . the King's money will be well spent'.[10] Having protested, Norfolk distributed the fees[65] to John and one other Hall, and Geoffrey Robson who were the only ones to report. Allegedly the rest 'will not come in by cause of their evil deeds', but just conceivably it was the novelty of the oath.[16] Subsequently the monarch grumpily withdrew the entire scheme when the Council of the North endorsed the legatine strictures on it as a positive incitement to malefactors to misbehave in future.[66, 67]

It was not long before the Duke underwent a change of mind, due in general to the Tynedale schism, but more particularly to the favourable impression wrought on him by the majority heidsmen at the conciliatory meeting in November 1537. In retrospect Norfolk was to commend the calibre of John Robson of the Falstone and John Charlton of Larederburn as 'men as ye shall well perceive of a very rude fashion, and yet of their sort, right expert and wise men'.[41] And to be fair, it has to be conceded that a government that could hire John Heron of Chipchase could hire anyone.

NOTES

1. M. H. & R. Dodds, *Pilgrimage of Grace*, Vol. I p. 196 were the first to observe that the behaviour of the Tyne- and Redesdalers had served to discredit the religious insurrection.

2. PRO, SP I 115 fol. 178–9, 2/2/1537.

3. *Ibid.*, 129 fol. 275, end May 1537.

4. BL, Calig. B VII fol. 224, 3/7/1537.

5. *Ibid.*, B VIII fol. 44, c.25/1/1537.

6. PRO, SP I 112 fol. 53–4, 30/11/1536.

7. *Ibid.*, 118 fol. 125, 4/12/1536.

8. *Ibid.*, fol. 216, 13/12/1536.
9. *Ibid.*, fol. 217–220, c.13/12/1536.
10. BL. Harl. MSS 6989 fol. 64, February 1537.
11. *LP*, XI no. 759, 17/10/1536.
12. *Ibid.*, no. 993, 6/11/1536.
13. BL, Harl. MSS 6989 fol. 60, 2/12/1536.
14. PRO, SP I 69 fol. 54–5, 17/1/1537 (not 1532 as calendared).
15. BL, Calig. B III fol. 264, 24/1/1537.
16. PRO, SP I 115 fol. 200, 6/2/1537.
17. *Ibid.*, 119 fol. 94–104, end April 1537.
18. *LP*, XII(1) no. 1062, 29/4/1537.
19. PRO, SP I 116 fol. 188–9, 4/3/1537.
20. *LP*, XII(1) no. 185, 21/1/1537.
21. BL, Add. MSS 32646 fol. 240, 18/10/1541.
22. *Ibid.*, fol. 243, 22/10/1541.
23. Compared with Alva, Norfolk was as mild as a modern probation officer. The Spaniard *boasted* of having burned 18,600 Protestants during his rule in the Netherlands, whereas only 216 persons were put to death for participation in the Pilgrimage of Grace (Cf. G. R. Elton, *Policy and Police*, p. 388–9).
24. BL, Calig. B II fol. 260, 26/7/1525.
25. *Ibid.*, B VII fol. 71, 22/11/1525.
26. PRO, SP I 46 fol. 128–131, 18/1/1528.
27. *Ibid.*, 47 fol. 248, 26/4/1528.
28. See above, p. 87.
29. *LP*, XII(1) no. 98, c.16/1/1537.
30. BL, Harl. MSS 6989 fol. 63B, 30/1/1537.
31. *LP*, XII(2) no. 291, 20/7/1537.
32. BL, Calig. B VII fol. 228, 29/3/1539.
33. PRO, SP I 152 fol. 215–7, 23/7/1539.
34. *Ibid.*, 154 fol. 96–7, October/November 1539.
35. BL, Titus F III fol. 97, 21/9/1539.
36. BL, Calig. B III fol. 262, 17/12/1539.
37. *LP*, XV no. 1021, 31/8/1540.
38. BL, Harl. MSS 6989 fol. 87, 28/8/1540.
39. *Ibid.*, fol. 88, 2/9/1540.
40. *LP*, XV no. 1018, 30/8/1540.
41. PRO, SP I 163 fol. 121–2, 16/10/1540.
42. *LP*, XVI no. 172, 18/10/1540.
43. *Ibid.*, no. 780, c.30/4/1541.
44. BL, Add. MSS 32646 fol. 274, 3/12/1541.
45. *Ibid.*, 32651 fol. 247, 21/8/1543.
46. *Ibid.*, fol. 269, 25/8/1543.
47. PRO, E 36, Vol. 40 fol. 29, 29/3/1539.
48. See pp. 175 and 198 below.
49. BL, Add. MSS 32651 fol. 14, 8/6/1543.
50. See p. 143 above.
51. William Patten, *The Expedition into Scotland (of Edward, Duke of Somerset)*.
52. BL, Calig. B VIII fol. 106, 1551 (not 1542 as calendared).

53. *Ibid.*, fol. 63, 2/12/1541.
54. PRO, SP I 178 fol. 85, 24/5/1543.
55. BL, Arundel MSS 97 fol. 85B, Christmas 1539.
56. *LP*, XVI no. 2, 1/9/1540.
57. *LP*, III(1) no. 347, June 1519.
58. *LP*, IV(1) no. 693, early October 1524.
59. BL, Calig. B III fol. 65, c.27/12/1528.
60. *LP*, XV no. 465, 6/4/1540.
61. PRO, Exchr. T. R. Misc. Books, Vol. 121 fol. 32, 28/6/1537.
62. *Ibid.*, fol. 15–48, c.12/7/1537.
63. See p. 44 above.
64. PRO, SP I 115 fol. 175–7, 2/2/1536.
65. *Ibid.*, fol. 45–6, January 1537.
66. BL, Calig. B I fol. 133, 14/2/1537.
67. PRO, SP I 116 fol. 29, c.15/2/1537.

CHAPTER SIXTEEN

The Alternative Occupation

The fundamental quandary of the Tyne- and Redesdalers could never be solved by occasional largesse to their upper crust. With reference to the Waziris and Afridis, likewise dwelling on high and barren ground, Arnold Toynbee wrote that 'for the rulers of the plains the alternative to being at war with the highlanders is to provide them with some alternative occupation'.[1] The solution in the Cheviots, as on the North-West Frontier, was to go for a soldier.

For the clansmen here was no novelty since, if our surmise is correct, that is why their original settlement had been fostered. That such a raison d'être had never been lost sight of is attested by Wharton's recommendation in 1543 that 'every year no more women nor old and disabled men be allowed to remain there than cultivable ground for the maintenance of men to serve the King His Majesty woll bear'.[2] The question was whether Henry VIII would add hire to Edward III's tenures, which though privileged had become inadequate to sustain abundant life. Under the Tudor, as under Edward IV, the only effective foreign warfare was waged against the British neighbour, which brought the highlanders into the picture as possessors of a relevant military capability. Hence one moves away from peculiarities to characteristics shared with a select class of English soldier.

In any emergency against the Scots the men of the Liberties must answer within the hour[3] the Warden's summons via hill-top beacons.[4] For a planned operation their Keepers, in common with barons and Sheriffs,[5, 6] received from above letters under the signet.[7] Having mustered through the heidsmen,[4] the Keeper led his men.[8] Thus in July 1542 joint Keeper Heron ordered them, having got in their hay, to stand by for the Earl of Rutland.[9]

The short engagement envisaged made it unsuitable not merely for overseas service, but even for lengthy campaigns in Scotland. Although no standing force was ever set up, what was recruited from the Border shires from 1523 onwards[10] was a Band of Northern Horsemen, to which the large minority of Tyne- and Redesdalers who were horsemen came to belong. 'Band' was only less vague than the modern 'unit', so that in 1552 the two dales were described as 'inhabited by certain Surnamed Bands of men, each . . . containing more than a good number'.[11] By 1546 the King's Band of Northern Horsemen numbered 2500[12] under command of Sir Ralph

Ellerker. Such a Captain General[13] was assisted by a second-in-command —
Lord Ogle the next year[12] — and a standard-bearer.[14]

Each of the variable number of companies in the Band was one
hundred strong and under such captains as Robert Bowes[15] and Richard
Manners,[16] future Wardens of the Middle Marches, and in 1544 heidsman
John Dodd.[17] Since prominent heidsmen were commonly referred to as
captains of Redesdale or Tynedale,[18] merging with this structure must have
been smooth. Each captain had a petty captain and often a trumpeter as
well.[14]

The highlanders were accustomed to war-leaders as familiar as their own
cousins, and Keeper Heron informed Cromwell in 1540 that, though eager
to serve the King anywhere, Tyne- and Redesdalers would be reluctant to go
abroad 'except I send one of my friends with them'.[19] Without popularity an
officer could find service as risky as Ralph Fenwick in 1524.

The uniform of the Band was that of the highland raider, with the pious
addition of St. George's Cross on a white sleeveless shirt.[20] Armour was so
costly that the most serious loss at Haddon Rig was in 'harness'.[21] The lance,
which could run a foe through, was the stock weapon, supplemented by a
dagger or bow[22] and sometimes substituted by a stubby javelin.[5, 23, 24]

Mounts, which became a trooper's property on enlistment unless so
already,[25] were 'small light horses . . . of the Middle Marches . . . for the
ground is soft and all mosses'.[19] Much as the jack recalled the hacqueton,
so these were reminiscent of the 'hobbies' of the Hundred Years War.[26] A
'sufficient' horse was one that could transport its spearman[27] from either
Liberty unto Teviotdale and back within twenty-four hours.[28] The Band
was derived almost equally from the Cumbrian and Northumbrian Marches,
amongst which the Middle Marchers preponderated in the ratio 5:3.[29, 30]
Statistics for the reservoir represented by the highland majority of the
last-named are highly erratic. Of horsemen the numbers for Tynedale
and Redesdale respectively were 403 and 445[31] in 1528,[32] which had
fallen lopsidedly to 391 and 188 by 1539,[33] and 180 and 140 by 1540.[19] In
addition there were potential riders classified as 'foot thieves', computed for
Tynedale in Edward VI's reign at 400 against 200 horsemen.[4] Taken with
Liddesdale in 1541, the entire league was credited with 2000 horse and foot.[34]

It was at that time that the reservoir began to be tapped for continental
over and above Scottish service. The long wait had been partly due to a
burning local conviction that the Crecys were for Southrons to fight.[35]
When Wolsey tried to enlist Northern Horsemen for France in 1525 there
was dogged resistance from the Redesdale Keeper downwards.[36] From a
buyer's standpoint, too, scoundrels who had rebelled thrice in fifteen years
were unprepossessing recruits, for it took a long time to sink in that these

were the strongest grounds for their enlistment. Indeed a Prince Bishop had been a lone voice after Flodden in declaring they should be hurried to France where 'they would do much good, whereas here they do none but much harm'.[37] Later Widdrington attributed Northumbrian failure to produce half again as many horses as the highlanders to *their* horse-thefts: 'The more men that is taken forth of Tynedale and Redesdale it shall be the better'.[38] Apparently they did not join the first drafts of the Band to France in 1523[10] and 1524,[39, 40] nor yet a company for Ireland in 1540.[41] It was only when Henry VIII cleared his throat for a swansong in France that London began to trawl for them. With other schemes in mind for his charges, the joint Keeper grudgingly conceded that twenty out of each dale 'may well be spared'.[19] Heron and Wharton on the West Marches jointly received conduct money — essentially travel allowances — for a captain and sixty horsemen.[42] The exodus thus commenced was interpreted both by the Emperor Charles V[43] and by James V as a sign that Henry meant business against the French.[44] On June 30th 1543 three companies, one of which was drawn equally from the East Marches and from Tyne- and Redesdales,[45] embarked on eight ships at Hull. With seventeen French men o' war on the lookout, the English hugged the sands till meeting convoy at the North Foreland. Thence to Guisnes via Calais,[46, 47] for the defence of the Emperor's Low Countries.[15]

In the following Spring the King expressed a wish for more Border horsemen in France, partly from the West Marches, partly from the two Liberties.[48] Since the highlanders, unlike the Cumbrians, were currently involved in the invasion of Scotland, Hertford urgently consulted Ralph Eure[49] as to how many 'picked and chosen men' Tynedale and Redesdale might provide.[48] His response took shape as the backbone of two companies[50] bound for Dover on 31st May.[51] After fifteen nights in Scotland without blankets[52] and five more journeying south by road and ship,[50, 53] they must have found arduous the instruction laid upon them to keep their mounts fresh for immediate service upon disembarkation.[54] Having been split between elements of the Band in the rearguard[55, 56] and the main body or Battle,[57] they joined Norfolk before Montreuil until the capture by the King of Boulogne,[58] which they then helped to garrison.[59] Soon afterwards Henry turned his attention towards 'many good horsemen of the Borderers come now into such poverty as they . . . have no horses of their own',[54] and directed that two companies be sent south to be mounted.[60] The shortage of horses proving to be as acute as that of riders, the project had to be countermanded in May 1544,[61] too late however to stop fifty highland 'foot thieves' already set out for France.[53] Another company of Middle Marchers joined the Band of Northern Horsemen at Calais in 1546,[62] but owing to recent losses at Ancrum Moor the proportion therein of Tyne- and Redesdalers may have been reduced. After Ralph Ellerker's death in action, the size of the continental Band slumped to 160.[63]

NOTES

1. From *The Observer* of Sunday, 12th May 1957.
2. *LP*, XVIII(1) no. 799, June 1543.
3. *LP*, IV(2) no. 4882, 28/10/1528.
4. BL, Calig. VIII fol. 106, 1551 (not 1542 as inscribed).
5. PRO, SP V fol. 184, c.30/1/1541.
6. *LP*, XVI no. 497, end January 1541.
7. According to Mr. Clifford Davies the best treatment of this subject is a London University Ph.D thesis of 1955 by J. J. Goring inadequately summarised in Cruikshank, *Army Royal*. See also J. D. Mackie, 'The English Army at Flodden', in *Miscellany of the Scottish History Society*, Vol. VIII concerning Letters Patent.
8. BL, Calig. B II fol. 43, 31/5/1525.
9. PRO, SP I 169 fol. 192–8, 28/7/1542.
10. *LP*, III(2) no. 3363, 26/9/1523.
11. BL, Calig. B VII fol. 440, 1552.
12. Patten, *Expedition into Scotland*.
13. *LP*, XX(1) no. 1049, 28/12/1545.
14. *LP*, XIX(2) no. 524, end October 1544.
15. *LP*, XVIII(1) no. 832, c.7/7/1543.
16. BL, Add. MSS 32657 fol. 47, 19/8/1548.
17. PRO, SP I 187 fol. 232–7, 23/5/1544.
18. *Ibid.*, 34 fol. 205–6, 16/5/1525.
19. BL, Calig. B I fol. 131, 24/4/1540.
20. *LP*, III(2) no. 2525, 9/9/1522.
21. *LP*, XVII no. 750, 6/9/1542.
22. BL, Calig. B IV fol. 258, January 1558.
23. *LP*, XX(1) no. 772, 19/5/1545.
24. (J. W.) Fortescue, (*History of the*) *British Army*, Vol. I, p. 114.
25. BL, Harl. MSS 643 fol. 169, c.1/8/1557.
26. Fortescue, *op. cit.*, Vol. I, p. 27. Cassell's *History of the British People*, p. 456.
27. *LP*, XVIII(1) no. 342, c.31/3/1543.
28. *LP*, XVII no. 1069, 10/11/1542.
29. *LP*, XIX(1) no. 596, 29/5/1544.
30. *Ibid.*, no. 601, 30/8/1544.
31. They included 54 Charltons, 62 Robsons, 53 Dodds, 30 Milburns, 70 Halls, 64 Hedleys and 39 Reeds.
32. *LP*, IV(2) no. 4336, 6/6/1528.
33. PRO, E 36 Vol. 40 fol. 29, 29/3/1539.
34. BL, Add. MSS 32646 fol. 259, 7/11/1541.
35. *LP*, XIX(1) no. 252, 27/3/1544.
36. BL, Calig. B I fol. 41, 27/4/1525.

37. PRO, SP I 5 fol. 229 & 230, 20/9/1513.
38. *Ibid.*, 159 fol. 255–6, 3/5/1540.
39. *LP*, IV(1) no. 615, 2/9/1524.
40. *Ibid.*, no. 662, 15/9/1524.
41. *LP*, XV no. 849, 6/7/1540.
42. *LP*, XVI no. 661, 27/3/1541.
43. *Ibid.*, no. 785, 1/5/1541.
44. *Ibid.*, no. 832, 14/5/1541.
45. PRO, SP I 179 fol. 1, c.10/6/1543.
46. *LP*, XVIII(1) no. 729, 18/6/1543.
47. *Ibid.*, no. 676, 9/6/1543.
48. *LP*, XIX(1) no. 227, 21/3/1544.
49. *Ibid.*, no. 259, c.28/3/1544.
50. BL, Add. MSS 32654 fol. 98, 14/4/1544.
51. *LP*, XIX(1) no. 545, 21/5/1544.
52. *Ibid.*, no. 531, c.18/5/1544.
53. BL, Add. MSS 32654 fol. 207, 25/5/1544.
54. *Ibid.*, fol. 54, 25/3/1544.
55. *LP*, XIX(1) no. 271, end March 1544.
56. *Ibid.*, no. 276, end March 1544.
57. *Ibid.*, no. 275, end March 1544.
58. *LP*, XIX(2) no. 223, 12/9/1544.
59. *LP*, XX(1) no. 929, 4/12/1545.
60. *LP*, XIX(1) no. 501, 14/5/1544.
61. BL, Add. MSS 32654 fol. 196, 18/5/1544.
62. *LP*, XXI(1) no. 300, c.8/3/1546.
63. *Ibid.*, no. 1092, July 1546.

CHAPTER SEVENTEEN

Scorched Earth

The military sphere in which the highlanders made their heaviest contribution was in the tradition of the fourteenth-century chevauchées, and of the flaying of Northern England by the Bruce. Either as irregulars under their Keepers, or as part of the Band of Northern Horsemen, their readily accessible targets were Teviotdale and the Merse, as rich in agriculture as in warlike populations, forming a cockpit within an arc through Home, Kelso, cliff-girt Jedburgh and Hawick. Scathes which were officially sponsored differed from those privately undertaken in extra emphasis on the wasting of hay and corn, this being an age when provender for men and horses was as essential to an army's mobility as petrol nowadays — witness the lamentations from English Border commanders about victual shortages between 1543 and 1545. Given the primitive technology, destruction was not easy, Dacre having once to indent for 300 sixpenny axes for wrecking.[1] Arson was unpopular as courting reprisals, and difficult anyway against a population adept at fire precautions and in a climate so damp that when Tyne- and Redesdalers set Leighton Tower alight it was saved by a heavy shower.[2] For all the gunpowder expended, Cessford had to be 'destroyed' twice in one year,[3, 4] while it took two bloody assaults in ten days and 'scumfishing'[5] to deal with Buccleuch's Moss Tower.[6, 7]

Once under command, the highlanders had to obey ground rules, because non-indigenous commanders insisted on amenities the natives could dispense with. Cumbrian Dacre was in all senses afraid of the dark, while invasion after invasion was cancelled due to rain. Contrast the clansmen's exploit in the 1532–3 winter when they cut sixty miles through snowdrifts to sack a toon.[8] Furthermore outlanders generally stuck to open and close seasons for raids, with a preference for the sowing and the harvest. Although the highlanders favoured the final quarter of the year, the legend of the Charlton spur symbolises a readiness to sally forth whenever the cupboard was bare.[9] Acceptance by Tyne- and Redesdales of petty restrictions was the price of admission to wider stamping grounds. In return they contributed to the havoc that Wolsey boasted about, and that enabled Dacre to assert he had done more in one raid than the reigns of Edward IV and Henry VII put together.[10] How did the highlanders' performance in four particular campaigns measure up to such statements?

After Flodden the Warden General was commanded to assail the enemy along the whole frontier, but being starved of funds restricted targeting to Teviotdale and the Merse, which had survived the disaster intact. Having neutralised the latter through a compact with Lord Home, Dacre brought his fire to bear on Teviotdale.[11]

Around Michaelmas the highlanders reconnoitred Ingate 6 to burn around Ancrum Castle, bringing out sixty prisoners, cattle and other plunder.[12] Heartened by a royal commendation, the baron then summoned all Northumberland to follow him up the same route, but the rendezvous was boycotted by Percy tenants, leaving him only 1000 horse. Once over the leafy Kale, he extended two forays, each 300 strong and one of highlanders, which veered west through Jedforest as far as Rule Water. Having raked both banks, these rejoined the stale or main body and retired to the Belling via Deadwater Marshes after a running fight. Having been joined next morning by the West Marchers, they pursued Ingate 1 over high moors towards Hawick to harry Clan Scott, and driving herds despite the enemy at their heels, re-entered via Harbottle. Sir Christopher Dacre spent the night with the Halls at Otterburn Tower.[11]

After a winter similarly employed, Dacre claimed devastation of 75,000 acres[13] on the Scottish Middle Marches. Special targets of the highlanders were Buccleuch lands between Slitrig and Borthwick.[14] While the campaign fell dismally short of ramming home the recent victory, it did at least pin the Teviotdalers down.

Bogged down in France, Henry and Wolsey in 1522 proceeded to exhibit their lack of means to make headway in Scotland either. Surrey and Dacre having as realistic soldiers dissuaded this pair of amateurs from a lunge at Edinburgh, the English as usual had to make do with the Merse, which had forfeited previous immunity, and Teviotdale, objectives which immediately restored the two Liberties to the front line. The following comrades in arms were to receive royal letters of congratulation: the Tynedalers under Sir Ralph Fenwick; the Redesdalers under Sir Philip Dacre; Sir Ralph Ellerker, future Captain General of Northern Horsemen; Sir William Lisle and Sir William Percy, indicative that the House of Percy was wending its way back.[15]

Until the summer of 1523 operations were desultory, though by up to 4000 men. For example both Leighton[2] and Blackater[16] Towers were attacked from Ingate 8, Will Hall of Otterburn being wounded.[2] On Surrey's arrival the assault on the Merse intensified, when Cessford Castle was taken out with gunpowder and scaling-ladders,[3] and in June another thrust by 6000 men up the same Ingate was aimed at towers along Tweed and Eden Waters, to the very fringe of Lammermoor. Without heavy ordnance and harassed by

3000 Scots skirmishers,[1] they shied away from Home and Duns Castles but ingloriously knocked down Eccles Convent instead. Tynedale rode in the rearguard with the Percy tenants, and the Herons of Chipchase and Ford with the van. Since Lord Dacre was directing operations from Harbottle,[17, 18] the Redesdalers should have been participant too, but there are no longer traces. Three more such blows, averred the baron, would destroy the enemy Borders.[1] In one such, with highlanders and light artillery in the rearguard, he stabbed at Kelso, flattening the Abbey Gatehouse and the Moss Tower, then, having scoured the steep red banks of the Lower Teviot, arrived home at sunset via Kale and Bowmont Waters.[19, 20]

Late in September, with Ridley's revolt well ablaze, the Court's demands for Jedburgh as a consolation could no longer be resisted. Surrey and Dacre with 10,000 men, including Tyne- and Redesdalers in the vanguard, combined the mission with burning the Michaelmas corn, 'on which most of their living depends'.[10] The eve of the successful three-pronged assault[21] was spent in a laager of carts, whence Dacre reported having sighted the Devil all of six times.[22] When the Duke of Albany struck back at Wark-on-Tweed, he was foiled by an intrepid Sir William Lisle. Whether the highlanders were with the army that emerged to the rescue from the Ford woods is uncertain, but their Keepers were thanked by the Cardinal shortly afterwards.[23]

In April 1524 the Warden General coordinated an assault from all three Marches, himself leading 1200 Middle Marchers, including Tyne- and Redesdalers, up Ingate 5 or 6 to harry slopes above Oxnam and moorland up to the Jed.[4] In July his brother Christopher took Tynedale and 1000 other Marchers by Ingate 8 to pillage around Smailholm, in the fighting withdrawal from which the Tynedale Keeper was captured.

By this time, with the English prey to the Ridley paroxysm, the conflict was simmering down. As for the Scots, the English asserted for enemy Borderers within reach that nothing remained but the walls of their houses, the ultimate raid being by Tynedale and Gilsland on what even Sir William Eure dubbed the poor men of Jedforest.[24]

To fight the war of the early thirties primarily with regular forces was beyond Henry's means. Hence there seemed every likelihood that the highlanders would be as prominent in prosecuting the war as they had been — at the King's urgent instigation — in causing it. However, Sir George Lawson, Cromwell's paymaster in Newcastle, was resolved that the Earl of Northumberland should not be permitted to run hostilities indefinitely through letters of marque to a bunch of rogues.[25]

Initially, all the same, Tyne- and Redesdales were encouraged to prolong into the war their vendetta with Buccleuch,[26] leaving the Douglas and the Percy free to cope with the Homes and Kerrs. In the snowy February of 1533[27] they formed part of a force of 1500 men that raided Branxholm from Ingate 4 through a maze of hills, burning buildings and taking fifty horses, 500 head of cattle and prisoners including a Scott of Buccleuch.[8] Shortly afterwards the highlanders raided Oxnam on foot up Ingate 5 at which the Earl of Northumberland marvelled; they also lent a hand with a fire-raid on the Kerrs of Cessford via Ingate 6 or 7.[28] The unwonted alacrity with which fire was used was a retort to Buccleuch's boast that 'he would like to see who durst burn *him*'.[8] Unimpressed, Lawson's reaction to Keeper Ralph Fenwick's proposal that his men join the regular whitecoats against Kelso,[29] a garrison town replete with granaries, was to drop Tynedale altogether from the order of battle. By contrast Redesdale, who enjoyed the distinction of having just been harried by James V in person,[30] were suffered to follow Lord Ogle in a strike up Ingate 7 to Kale Water, and a clash with a Scots army.[31]

So far by then was Henry VIII from taking the war seriously that he forbade operations so long as his heir presumptive[32] was in the war zone. Teviotdale had been softened up for a blow that never fell. Only domestically did the conflict assume any importance through expediting the financial ruin of the Earl of Northumberland, who now traded the Percy estates for a pension, a park for his horses and the promise of a free funeral.

The last real war between England and Scotland began on St. Bartholomew's Day 1542 when Bowes pierced Ingate 8 with 3000 horsemen, including Heron with Tyne- and Redesdales. Having sped two forays, one of highlanders, towards Teviotdale, the Warden wasted enough time on cattle in the bow of the Tweed for the Scots to assemble who won Haddon Rig.[33] Sensing a counter-stroke, successive English commanders first launched a pre-emptive incursion, then sent George Heron, acting joint Keeper,[34] to harry and burn around Jedburgh, whence the highlanders retired with prisoners and over 400 beasts under the nose of the Lieutenant of Scotland.[35, 36] Royal congratulations by return of post[37] would have been better reserved for Wharton's illustrious triumph at Solway Moss a few days later. During Advent Heron hit at West Teviotdale up Ingate 4 first with 100, then with 200 Tynedalers who destroyed toons and granaries and brought off beasts and prisoners.[38] With Redesdale they also rendezvoused with 1200 horsemen whom Viscount Lisle intended to lead against East Teviotdale and the Merse, but the expedition aborted by order of the King on James V's death of shame or poison.[34] That the ensuing armistice lasted a bare six months, and that at its conclusion the Northumbrian not the Cumbrian remained the key command, despite Wharton's victory, owed as much to the highlanders as to anybody else.

When fighting flared up again in July 1543 everything was visualised as prelude to the march on Edinburgh on which the King had now immovably set his heart. The actual operations might otherwise seem a mixture as before. The contribution looked for from Sir Ralph Eure, *de facto* Northumbrian Warden, was the employment of 5000 men in small troops of horse to pound fifty toons in the Merse and between Jedburgh and Hawick.[39] Immediate command of the Middle Marchers was at various times delegated to Lord Ogle, and of Tyne- and Redesdales to Giles Heron, once George had followed Little John into disgrace. In a score of raids between October and April 1544, with peaks in November and March, the highlanders, occasionally leavened with garrison whitecoats, destroyed £2000-worth of corn,[40] and took 100 prisoners, 120 horses and 1550 head of cattle, besides untold sheep and goats. Because unremunerative, only thirty-three defenders were butchered. Losers included Buccleuch by Ingate 3, and by Ingate 6 both sorts of Kerr and the outskirts and Abbey of Jedburgh.[41]

The overture concluded, the Lieutenant's plan was to bring the Northumbrians overland to meet his disembarked army at Leith, while Wharton feinted at the West Marches. On the morrow of the landing[42] the Eures' 5000 horsemen broke camp at Berwick,[43] penetrated the Lothians and burned Haddington as a diversion[44] before covering fifty miles to the bridgehead.[45] Thence, whereas the Lieutenant attended to the capital, the overlanders 'left neither pele, village nor house unburned nor stacks of corn and brought in daily great numbers of cattle' from seven miles in all directions.[46, 47] On May 16th Hertford reformed ranks and harried his way south to Kelso, with 8000 out of the Merse and Teviotdale dogging the withdrawal. He re-entered England through the Cheviots.

Sir Ralph Eure now became chief instrument of a design for the creeping conquest of Scotland, to begin with the detachment of the Teviotdale clans from their allegiance in the wake of Liddesdale. Through seizure or demolition the Jedburgh citadel and possibly Melrose, at either end of Dere Street, must be denied to Scottish garrisons. On June 9th Eure and his recently ennobled father stormed Jedburgh with the Northumbrian Marchers in a three-pronged assault, driving out the garrison, of whom 160 besides civilians were killed, and returned with 500 horseloads of spoil. The skeleton of Greyfriars Abbey still stands reproachfully on the road into the town as memorial to that day. On re-entry through Cessford the invaders became bloodily engaged with Scots who had been reciprocating against the English East Marches.[48]

Normally with other Northumbrian Marchers or whitecoats, in numbers up to 2300 men, the highlanders thereupon resumed the pulverisation of East and Central Teviotdale. In the high summer they took spoils, prisoners, 100 horses, 1200 head of cattle and around 1600 sheep from the Cheviot slopes carved into ravines by the Bowmont headwaters; the steep sandstone banks around the Nisbets; and the glorious country between Ancrum and Dryburgh. Such significant lairds as Mow, Bedrule, Rutherford and Bonjedworth were among the losers.⁷ Even these scarcely rated in comparison with Andrew Kerr of Fernieherst who was defeated and captured with his eldest son when trying to intercept the raiders on Bedrule on July 19th.⁴⁹ Superimposed upon the retreat of their garrison from Jedburgh to Melrose, the loss of their Warden was doubly demoralising to the Teviotdalers because followed by his defection to Henry VIII, with client Kerrs, Rutherfords and Turnbulls in his train. An aggravation was painful awareness that the English already had the ripening oats and barley in their sights. Not only did the turncoats reinforce with up to 600 men the East and West Marchers riding with the highlanders and other Middle Marchers, but through their good offices Ingates 3 through 6 became negotiable beyond the Minto Hills, to the Ancrum Knoll, and farther still to the wooden flats between Ale and Tweed; through Ingates 7 and 8 the Merse cornfields became as accessible to the Middle, as they had always been to the East Marchers. Throughout the autumn and into November scores of toons were smashed, some beyond Melrose, others into Lauderdale. Notable actors included John Hall of Otterburn, Sir Ralph Eure's priest and Fernieherst's son;⁵⁰ notable victims the Abbot of Glasgow, a royal bastard the Lord James, and most portentously the fourth Laird of Buccleuch. Damage inflicted comprised enormous spoils; about 400 prisoners; over 150 killed; nearly 500 horses and over 2800 cattle driven off; and at the harvest 'much corn threshen and unthreshen'⁷ — counting only those raids mounted from the Middle Marches. The hither parts of Scotland were reported to the Emperor as being utterly wasted.⁵¹

Buccleuch was to prove the stumbling block. Lately, as in 1532, he must have sighed for the nine and twenty knights of fame sung by his illustrious descendant, but meanwhile, to save his corn, pretended to apply for 'assurance' to the English. In fact he schemed revenge, his hatred of the highlanders in particular being intensified on intelligence that they were plotting to kidnap him. Scornfully Buccleuch divulged to Wharton, who was implicated, that 'he did know of the coming of Giles Heron and Archie Dodd unto me at Carlisle to draw a purpose . . . against himself'.⁵² What ended Sir Walter Scott's isolation in suborned Teviotdale was a volte-face by the Earl of Angus, alienated by English attacks on his manor of Coldingham and by those of the highlanders on the Laird of Bonjedworth, who bore the Douglas name.[53] Having been reconciled with Cardinal Beaton, Angus was appointed Lieutenant on the Borders, while Buccleuch was sufficiently encouraged to besiege some of Fernieherst's English gunners, garrison Hawick, and turn on the renegades.

On 21st February 1545 Archibald Douglas marched with his standard into Melrose, similarly inclined to punish the traitors who had belatedly followed his example and gone in with England. Simultaneously the Warden Keeper led his Marchers down Till towards Jedburgh,[54] then switched likewise to Melrose,[55] from which Angus deceptively retired to contemplate from the Eildon Hills smoke rising around the bones of his illustrious ancestor, victor of Otterburn. He too now changed his mind, resolving to snuff out Eure on Agricola's Dere Street, which he had made the highway for so much rapine. Out of his pursuit developed the Battle of Ancrum Moor.[56] The exultation in which Governor Arran afterwards kissed the ambiguous Angus twenty times is understandable, for the fight on Penielheugh was the second sweetest that Scotland ever won. When Arran conducted a prisoner to identify the corpse of his commander on a mound of others, it was with the obituary: 'He was a fell, cruel man, and over-cruel, which many a man and fatherless bairn might rue . . . [Angus] had done a great good day's work for Scotland'.[57]

The replacement as Warden Keeper for the vanquished of Ancrum Moor was the vanquished of Haddon Rig, whose stern judgments of Tyne- and Redesdales in the 1541 Survey may have been softened by the comradeship of the King's Band overseas, and by their obvious suitability for the rough wooing of the infant Queen of Scots that impended. On resumption in September the conflict acquired a more international character, with the arrival of a French garrison in the Merse, and through the enlistment by Hertford, the new Lieutenant, of Mediterranean mercenaries with modern techniques. When Hertford invaded from Berwick on the 7th the Earl of Cumberland's vanguard comprised Bowes with 1000 Middle Marchers and thrice as many foreign cavalry. Two days later Kelso Abbey was stormed, though by Spanish hackbuteers,[58] and it was three days before Sir Robert's horsemen came into their own when they took vengeance on Melrose town and abbey, and cast down the Abbey of Dryburgh and Dalcove Castle, removing cartloads of lead.[59] While Hertford burned Jedburgh yet again, Bowes forayed for ten hours with 1500 horse along the Teviot and Rule beyond the town, destroying many toons and corn from an abundant harvest,[60] and even spilling into the Merse.[61] Partly for want of targets, Bowes did not resume operations until April 1546 when a force including the highlanders under another Roger Fenwick, as deputy joint Keeper, by Ingate 8 took 1000 sheep and 100 oxen from around Ale Water. They were overtaken by the Scots, but there any parallel with Haddon Rig ended,

Fairnington Crag being the last of all the victories won by the bowmen of England. [56, 62]

Though James IV's ghost was still destined to play Banquo to Henry VIII's Macbeth, the pounding given the Merse and Teviotdale was construed by the Scots as a threat to their nationhood. Andrew Kerr had set a pattern for March treason that lasted into the next reign, [63–6 incl.] so that the allocation of his pledges testifies to the prominent contribution made by the highlanders in the final five years of the old King's reign: of fifteen, ten to the Warden Keeper and one to Hall of Otterburn. [67] On September 4th, 1547 Henry's *de facto* successor, the former Earl of Hertford, breached the Pease Strait at Dunglass with a dangerous little army. Bowes' contribution was to have spread a banquet before the Duke at Alnwick, but Tynedale and Redesdale rode with the van. [68]

NOTES

1. *LP*, III(2) no. 3098, 12/6/1523.
2. *Ibid.*, no. 2402, 23/7/1522.
3. *Ibid.*, no. 3039, 21/5/1523.
4. *LP*, IV(1) no. 278, 25/4/1524.
5. I.e. suffocating the inmates by setting fire to damp straw heaped against the walls. Cf. Watson, *Reivers*, p. 126.
6. *LP*, XIX(2) no. 191, 6/9/1544.
7. *Ibid.*, no. 625, 17/11/1544.
8. BL, Calig. B VII fol. 222, c.7/2/1533.
9. It was reputedly presented to the Laird of Hesleyside on a charger by his wife whenever they were out of food.
10. *LP*, III(2) no. 3134, 26/6/1523.
11. BL, Calig. B VI fol. 37, 13/11/1513.
12. *Ibid.*, B III fol. 1, 23/10/1513.
13. In Dacre's own words, 42 miles and land for 630 ploughs. Traditionally a plough was the amount of land that could be ploughed by one team of eight oxen in a year, equal to one hide or 120 acres.
14. BL, Calig. B II fol. 190, 17/5/1514.
15. PRO, SP 49.2 27 fol. 11, 15/4/1523.
16. *LP*, III(2) no. 2852, 24/2/1523.
17. BL, Add. MSS 24965 fol. 10, c.12/6/1523.
18. *LP*, III(2) no. 3096, 12/6/1523.
19. *Ibid.*, no. 3135, end June 1523.
20. *Ibid.*, no. 3147, 1/7/1523.
21. *Ibid.*, no. 3349, 21/9/1523.
22. *Ibid.*, no. 3363, 27/9/1523.
23. *Ibid.*, no. 3509, 4/11/1523.
24. BL, Calig. B III fol. 209, 12/9/1527.

25. *LP*, VI no. 16, 2/1/1533.
26. According to the *Dictionary of National Biography*, the third Laird of Buccleuch died in 1504, the fourth in 1552, the fifth in 1574, and the sixth — who was a Lord as well — in 1616. All were named Sir Walter Scott.
27. *LP*, V no. 1638, 17/12/1532.
28. *LP*, VI no. 143, 9/2/1533.
29. *Ibid.*, no. 113, 3/2/1533.
30. *Ibid.*, no. 185, 27/2/1533.
31. BL, Calig. B VII fol. 264, April 1533.
32. Through the illegitimisation of the Lady Mary.
33. BL, Add. MSS 32647 fol. 162, 16/9/1542.
34. *Ibid.*, 32648 fol. 224, 19/12/1542.
35. PRO, SP I 174 fol. 133–7, 13/11/1542.
36. BL, Add. MSS 32648 fol. 148, 19/11/1542.
37. *LP*, XVII no. 1104, 20/11/1542.
38. BL, Add. MSS 32648 fol. 179, 6/12/1542.
39. *LP*, XVIII(2) no. 236, 30/9/1543.
40. In the eyes of contemporaries of the order of £1m today.
41. BL, Harl. MSS 1757 fol. 292–302, c.5/8/1544.
42. *LP*, XIX(1) no. 463, 4/5/1544.
43. *Ibid.*, no. 467, 5/5/1544.
44. *Ibid.*, no. 223, 20/3/1544.
45. *Ibid.*, no. 497, 12/5/1544.
46. *Ibid.*, no. 483, 9/5/1544.
47. *Ibid.*, no. 533, c.19/5/1544.
48. *Ibid.*, no. 684, 12/6/1544.
49. *Ibid.*, no. 945, 20/7/1544.
50. Hardly any of the many despatches sent to the English Court by Ralph Eure, or by the Laird of Fernieherst after his defection, have survived.
51. *LP*, XIX(2) no. 105, 18/8/1544.
52. BL, Add. MSS 32655 fol. 203, 25/9/1544.
53. George Buchanan, *Scotland*, Vol. II, p. 345.
54. *LP*, XX(1) no. 264, 25/2/1545.
55. *LP*, XIX(2) no. 185, 5/9/1544.
56. See p. 191 below.
57. BL, Add. MSS 32656 fol. 180, 3/3/1545.
58. *LP*, XX(1) no. 347, 11/9/1545.
59. *LP*, XX(2) no. 633, 22/10/1545.
60. *Ibid.*, no. 400, 18/9/1545.
61. *Ibid.*, no. 432, 23/9/1545.
62. BL, Calig. B V fol. 1, June 1544–July 1546.
63. BL, Harl. MSS 353 fol. 58, 5/8/?1549.
64. BL, Add. MSS 32657 fol. 56, 20/1/1549.
65. BL, Calig. B VII fol. 396, 24/7/1549.
66. BL, Titus F XIII fol. 215, 1552.
67. *LP*, XIX(2) no. 603, 29/10/1544.
68. Patten, *Expedition into Scotland*.

CHAPTER EIGHTEEN

Combat

As to the formations, numbers of ranks, and spacing in which Northern Horsemen fought no information survives. Yet to the contemporary connoisseur their array was so familiar that Charles V could in 1543 compliment Bowes on the marshalling of the Band 'after the fashion of the Scottish Border'.[1] One can nevertheless be confident that they did not transplant to Europe their domestic practice of dismounting for combat.

Regarding their tactical employment during the attack there is less obscurity. Elusiveness and mobility made them in Henry VIII's last years the mainstay of the scout. During the Picardy campaign it was upon their 'avant-courriers' that the Emperor relied to reconnoitre and report the withdrawal of the French cavalry before Landrecies;[2] who brought in prisoners, news on morale and cattle from the besieged inhabitants of Boulogne;[3] and who hampered the French scout on reciprocal missions out of Montreuil.[4] When Somerset's army crossed the Border for the Pinkie campaign its scout consisted of 400 Northern Horsemen, who continually updated the Duke on the Scots assembly along the Esk[5] and on the safest places to bivouac.[6]

But if in Fortescue's estimation the eyes and ears of the army,[7] the Northern Horsemen were some of the claws as well, as when they skirmished to drive the French back to their trenches before Cambrésis,[1] drew bows at enemy horsemen under Thérouanne walls,[8] cut off Italian hackbuteers,[9] or came to grief themselves in an ambush by 250 French cavalry near Hardelot.[10] Nearer home their comrades were inflicting casualties on enemy skirmishers, Frenchmen out of Home Castle in a running battle, and Scots out of Melrose.[11, 12] In the advance to Pinkie the King's Band helped the future Duke of Northumberland[13] to extricate himself from an ambush, and brushed aside Scottish attempts to impede the army's smooth passage of the Pass of the Pease.[5]

The Northern Horsemen were skilled, too, in feints and diversions. Before Lord Lisle launched an attack on Duns in the Merse in 1542, he distracted the Teviotdalers from thoughts of rescue by sending against them 1200 light horsemen from Northumberland, including the two dales.[14] The mission of Eure's overlanders in 1544 was 'in skirmishing, to [i.e. until] such time as great part of the army were landed, with 2000 of our best horsemen . . . whereof . . . 800 archers and demi-hakes, and the rest spears . . . to keep 2000 of the best Scots horse occupied for one whole day'.[15, 16] In October 1548, in order to mask the recapture of Jedburgh by Lord Grey de Wilton, the Tyne- and Redesdalers 'went to Ancrum where a power lay . . . and drove the enemy to the strong houses'.[17]

Another trick was the ambush, of which the King's Band were adept practitioners and occasional victims, so that the more significant name for the stale from which their forays detached themselves was the bushment. One unsuccessful aspect of the highlanders' raid on Branxholm in 1533 was that it failed in its design to entice either the notoriously rash Buccleuch, or the Earl of Moray, Lieutenant of Scotland, into Wharton's bushment.[18] Returning from Jedburgh in 1544, the Warden Keeper sighted fires around Tillmouth lit by 1000 Scots, on either side of whom Eure set up ambushes of 270 and 200 men respectively. A foray of thirty horsemen then 'gave such an onset' that the invaders 'fled upon their spurs' into the larger bushment.[19]

That men on ponies could even contemplate the charge was basically due to their always picking on someone their own size, never for example hurling themselves at a mass of pikemen. Additionally they aimed to compensate for lack of weight by 'wightness', that is to say bold swiftness. Classic encounters were Solway Moss where the Cumbrian 'prickers' hunted a Scottish army into the marshes, and that on the eve of Pinkie, when the English from Fawside Brae and the Scots along Edmonstone Edge could each observe the camp of the other in the Esk valley below. In a bid to deny their enemy his high ground the Scots sent 1500 skirmishers to assail it on the landward side, but once on top were surprised and chased back three miles to their own camp, mainly by the Northumbrian light horse 'with good speed and order'. Ancrum Moor, where the Scots had offered no quarter, was later adduced to justify the scale of carnage, between 800 and 1300 slain, as variously estimated by Bertheville[6] and Patton. The Borderers had never taken kindly to the divine monopoly on vengeance.[5]

Sequel to a successful charge was the pursuit, which could also commence or, if rash, culminate in an ambush; it was a logical development of the sort of hot trod launched by the Tynedalers against the interlopers in quest of Sir Ralph Eure's horses.[20] Out of an ambush around Tillmouth in 1544[21] Eure went in pursuit of Scottish infiltrators with eighty men, and later claimed to have killed more than a hundred. To a lucrative total of 170, up to nine prisoners apiece were taken by Charltons, Halls, Milburns, Robsons and Potts.[19, 22, 23] Probably with Bicocca in mind,[24] Somerset at Pinkie reserved the Northern Horsemen for the end-game as well as the opening. For five hours they concentrated on the exodus into Edinburgh, but this time with forbearance, aware that more could be made from a fleece than a carcase. Time and again Patton spotted them bargaining for ransoms while swopping sham strokes with the quarry.[5]

A basic role for Northern Horsemen in defence was as pickets. Thus a company sent to Calais in 1543 was as 'scowlt' for 'defence of the high country in the harvest'.[75] At the siege of Boulogne one sentinel was hanged for failure to report a French penetration from Hesdin.[26]

Defensive diversions were another natural field for them. When in 1523 Surrey hesitated between Carlisle and Berwick as Albany's probable objective, he commanded William Heron and Ralph Fenwick with Redes– and Tynedale respectively to invade Teviotdale, whose chiefs had rallied to the Duke,[27] mainly to mask another feint along the East Coast.[28] In what the Earl termed 'two very good roads', the Keepers inflicted sufficient damage to delay the Governor's offensive for three weeks.[29] After Haddon Rig Hertford tried to prevent the Scots from exploiting their victory by getting the highlanders to raid the Jedburgh area,[30] but unhappily for James V failed to disrupt his preparations for Solway Moss.

Once a threat had developed, its nature conditioned the highlanders' response. Whereas the Tillmouth incursion was met head-on, a penetration of Coquetdale in 1533 was countered through retaliation against the raiders' home base.[31] In face of the offensive of November 1542 the joint Keeper was ordered to Harbottle at speed to watch the beacons,[32] so that Tyne- and Redesdales slotted into the line of defence like everybody else. That the blow fell elsewhere would not have surprised Bowes, in whose opinion the warlike and mobile highlanders rendered the Ingates south between Cheviot and Kershope an uninviting prospect.[33]

Another task was the relief of gains under threat. On Fernieherst's defection in 1544 he requested of Henry VIII 1000 Northumbrian horse, mainly from Tyne- and Redesdales. Loth to trust a traitor, the King sent him £100 instead.[34] During the next month the Middle Marchers did however move to the relief of Coldingham.[35] When in 1545 Wharton pleaded shortage of horsemen to save previously captured Carlaverock Castle,[36] 600 Northumbrian Marchers rode to the rescue up Ingate 2,[37] only to be trapped and worsted by the Scots in the fells around Millstone Edge, north-west of the Hermitage, although the scale of the reverse was exaggerated to the Emperor.[38] In operations around Haddington in 1548 one company of the King's Band convoyed 400 hackbuteers into the town to relieve the English garrison, while another afforded cover through a feint against the French besiegers.[39, 40]

Even a successful English army had usually to fight its way out of Scotland, and such rearguard action devolved primarily upon Northern Horsemen. In November 1513 they had to hold at bay for hours with spears and arrows Teviotdale prickers who 'bickered with us and gave us hard knocks and there came three standards to back them'. Next day the

Dacres returned through the Robson country and Liddesdale with 2000 horse and 400 foot 'with bows for safeguard of those in straits', but beat another retreat via Carter Bar in face of the Chamberlain of Scotland with seven standards. It must have been a diverting spectacle to watch Scots pursuing Englishmen within a bare month of Flodden.[41] Less tame was the withdrawal from Smailholm in 1524, when 2000 Scots inserted themselves between the invaders and England, whereupon both sides dismounted. The English repulsed their assailants, slaying thirty and taking prisoners, but in a counter-attack their rear was scattered with the loss *inter alia* of Bastard John Heron. Lastly the rest of the English rode back and the Scots retreated, leaving the enemy 200 prisoners and an optimistic claim to have slain Kerr of Fernieherst, but bearing away the Tynedale Keeper.[42] When the Redesdalers and others in 1533 withdrew from Kale Water towards Yetholm, their march discipline was tight enough to fend off the Jedburgh garrison that was tailing them.[43] When in 1544 400 Tyne- and Redesdalers again penetrated the same area, it was on foot because they were sparing mounts for the Edinburgh campaign: 'the Scots to the number of 500 horsemen gave them a proud onset, yet the Englishmen made them recule and hurt divers of their horses and them'.[44] Shortly afterwards a force of highlanders fought the rearguard action that netted them three basses[45] as well as the Kerr chieftains. At Fairnington Crag in 1546 Bowes with 2000 Northumbrian Marchers was confronted by like numbers of pursuers out of Tweed- and Teviotdales. After preliminary brushes between the skirmishers both sides dismounted. Sir Robert, upon whom the lessons of Haddon Rig had not been wasted, sent his worst-equipped men back over a Tweed ford driving the livestock, while the dwindling bridgehead was shielded by the remainder including 300 archers in two echelons. Exhorted by their gentry, 'well hindmost of the company', the Scots 'with great shouts and cries came upon us and gave a very sharp onset', while half the English horses were into the river. Thereupon 'the archers so hailed them with sharp shot of arrows that the multitude was abashed and began to flee', 200 being slain and as many taken prisoner. Casualties could have been heavier, had not the defenders been parted from their mounts.[46, 47]

Just how wrong rearguard actions *could* go had already been demonstrated on Ancrum Moor, as well as at Haddon Rig. On the earlier occasion the Earl of Huntly had adroitly interposed between Little John's foray of highlanders and Bowes' stale[48] and thrown the withdrawal of each into confusion, with the loss of much equipment[49] and, if the French ambassador is credible, 800 dead and 2000 prisoners.[50] When Sir Ralph Eure quit smouldering Melrose for home in February 1545, Angus and Buccleuch were lying in wait to his south in Langnewton Forest. Dismounting and sending their horses to a hilltop, the Scots hid themselves in a fold in the moor. Mistaking the horses for the main army, Eure's men charged uphill, only to discover the phalanx arrayed beneath. Dismounting in their turn, they attacked in disordered ranks and, their banners trodden underfoot, were broken on the Lowland spears. Among the 180 or so killed were the Warden Keeper himself, his second-in-command, Lord Ogle, and a disproportionate number of captains.[51, 52] 'Concerning the great loss and damage that is happened unto us,' lamented the Captain of Norham, 'we might as well have been slain ourselves, for our great friends is gone.'[53] Some prisoners were killed, notably by Angus and Buccleuch, but the 1200 who survived comprised much of the Northumbrian gentry. The half of the invaders who escaped did so with the loss of all their horses[54] and draught animals,[55] two culverins and cartloads of hackbuts and arrows.[51, 52] Whereas after Flodden[56] and Haddon Rig[48] the Northern Horsemen had been criticised for not alighting, this time they were blamed for having done so.[54, 57] In short, the lesson from the continental experience was that they should behave invariably as light cavalry, without ever lapsing into the mounted infantry of Saxon tradition.

NOTES

1. *LP*, XVIII(2) no. 345, 6/11/1543.
2. *Ibid.*, no. 291, 21/10/1543.
3. *LP*, XIX(1) no. 949, 20/7/1544.
4. *LP*, XX(1) no. 929, 4/12/1545.
5. Patten, *Expedition into Scotland.*
6. (Le Sieur) Bertheville, (*Récit de*) *l'expédition en Écosse* (*l'an MDXLVI*).
7. Fortescue, *British Army*, Vol. I, p. 114.
8. *LP*, XVIII(2) no. 13, 4/8/1543.
9. *Ibid.*, no. 321, 29/10/1543.
10. *LP*, XXI(1) no. 682, 26/4/1546.
11. *LP*, XX(2) no. 347, 11/9/1545.
12. *Ibid.*, no. 432, 23/9/1545.
13. Then Viscount Lisle, penultimately Earl of Warwick.
14. BL, Add. MSS 32648 fol. 224, 19/12/1542.
15. *LP*, XIX(1) no. 335, 14/4/1544.
16. *Ibid.*, no. 531, c.18/5/1544.
17. BL, Calig. B VII fol. 323, 4/10/1548.
18. *LP*, VI no. 143, 9/2/1533.
19. BL, Add. MSS 32655 fol. 26, 12/6/1544.
20. *Ibid.*, 32651 fol. 101, 17/7/1543.
21. See p. 195 below.
22. *LP*, XIX(1) nos. 555 & 556, 22/5/1544.
23. *Ibid.*, no. 684 ii, 12/6/1544.

24. A closer parallel, surely, than Ravenna, which C. W. Oman, *Art of War (in the Middle Ages)*, p. 360 believed particularly influenced the Protector.

25. *LP*, XVIII(1) no. 967, c.28/7/1543.

26. BL, Calig. E IV fol. 57, 19/8/1544.

27. *LP*, IV(1) no. 662, 15/9/1524.

28. *Ibid.*, no. 685, 26/9/1524.

29. *LP*, III(2) no. 3515, 7/11/1523.

30. PRO, SP I 49.5 fol. 40, 19/11/1540.

31. BL, Calig. B VII fol. 264, end April 1533.

32. *LP*, XVII no. 1115, 22/11/1542.

33. BL, Calig. B VIII fol. 106, 1551 (not 1542 as inscribed).

34. BL, Add. MSS 32656 fol. 65, 28/11/1544.

35. *LP*, XIX(2) no. 692, 1/12/1544.

36. *LP*, XX(2) no. 676, 28/10/1545.

37. *Ibid.*, no. 795, 15/11/1545.

38. *LP*, XXI(1) no. 58, 13/1/1546.

39. BL, Add. MSS 32657 fol. 7, 9/7/1548.

40. *Ibid.*, fol. 14, 10/7/1548.

41. BL, Calig. B VI fol. 37, 13/11/1513.

42. PRO, SP I 31 fol. 196–7, 8/7/1524.

43. BL, Calig. B VII fol. 264, April 1533.

44. BL, Add. MSS 32654 fol. 74, 6/4/1544.

45. I.e. barces or very small cannon.

46. *LP*, XXI(1) no. 700, 29/4/1546.

47. BL, Calig. B V fol. 1, June 1544–July 1546.

48. BL, Add. MSS 32647 fol. 50, 25/8/1542.

49. *LP*, XVII no. 750, 6/9/1542.

50. *Ibid.*, no. 729, 2/9/1542.

51. BL, Add. MSS 32656 fol. 195, 11/3/1545.

52. *LP*, XX(1) no. 1046, 26/6/1545.

53. BL. Add. MSS 32656 fol. 172, 28/2/1545.

54. *LP*, XX(1) no. 332, 10/3/1545.

55. *Ibid.*, no. 395, 20/3/1545.

56. PRO, SP I 5 fol. 229–230, 20/9/1513.

57. BL, Add. MSS 32656 fol. 183, 5/3/1545.

CHAPTER NINETEEN

Value for Money

Just how soldierly, then, were Northern Horsemen in general and the highlanders in particular? The basic aspersion was of indiscipline, a natural tendency in skirmishers who under the right circumstances do have to break ranks. The Earl of Angus's strictures on their conduct at Haddon Rig — 'it was not [the enemy][1] that won the field, but we that lost it with our disorder'[2] — were variously amplified by Lawson,[3] Shrewsbury[4, 5] and the Privy Council[6] in respect, for example, of Ancrum Moor and Millstanes.

Obsession with loot was considered a contributory cause. To clear the decks before Haddon Rig Bowes ordered that the livestock collected by the forays be sent back ahead into England, but 'als soon as Tynedale and Redesdale saw the gudes gone they galloped forth of ane wing of our host[2] . . . Those of Redesdale . . . was the first that fled'.[7] At Fairnington Crag the Warden handled the problem differently: 'lest . . . Tynedale and Redesdale . . . minded after their accustomed fashion . . . to run away with the prey . . . leave the residue of the company in the danger of the enemies with a more greater discourage because of the departing'.[8] On the belated arrival of the Northern Horsemen before Edinburgh it was observed that they were weighed down with booty,[9] the amassing of which according to the Imperial ambassador had almost disrupted Hertford's timetable.[10]

The suspicion was widespread that the highlanders were apt to plunder even their own comrades. In a commentary on Flodden to Wolsey the Prince Bishop accused them of rifling tents, taking oxen from gun-teams and spiriting away a fantastic 5000 horses once battle was joined.[11, 12, 13] After Haddon Rig Scottish envoys declared that as much gear had fallen into highland as into their own hands.[14] In a spasm of fury Henry VIII commanded his officers in future to enlist as few Tyne- and Redesdalers as possible 'considering the pageants lately played by these Borderers . . . with their natural desire to stealing'.[15]

Charges of March treason of course abounded. Typical, in connexion with a raid south by 400 Teviotdalers, was the 'jealousy' in which the Earl of Northumberland held the 'inhabitants of Tynedale . . . for being privy to the conveyant of the said Scots into this Your Highness' realm'.[16] Of treachery on the battlefield on the other hand, there was one allegation only, from that same Bishop Ruthall regarding Flodden, according to whom the highlanders had killed English sentries, sold back prisoners to the Scots, and in general done more damage to their own side than had the enemy.[12]

Whether lions or not, Northern Horsemen were often led by donkeys. Thus Bowes displayed deplorable judgment before Haddon Rig in concealing plans from his staff.[7] Like Prince Rupert Sir Ralph Eure tended to charge too far, casting away most of the fruits of victory at Tillmouth by losing through carelessness great numbers of horses.[17] A heavy price was paid on Ancrum Moor for his obtuseness regarding the genuine conversion to England of the Laird of Bonjedworth, whose Surname was Douglas and whose lands had previously been ravaged by the Tyne- and Redesdalers.[18] On the battlefield Bonjedworth rejoined his fellow-countrymen with dire effect; perhaps knowledge of his intentions accounted for the boasts circulated abroad by the Scots of an English defeat even before it happened. In any case Eure should have awaited promised reinforcements before probing to Melrose, and not led breathless men into the assault with the sun in their eyes.[19] Shrewsbury ascribed the 'overthrow' to overmuch 'adventure and forwardness' of a man 'who forgat . . . Fortune is not always one woman'.[20, 21] The commander defeated at Millstanes was characterised as 'lacking in wit and authority'.[6] When the Band and some Albanian stradiots were ambushed by the French before Boulogne, the foreigners extricated themselves but not the English, astonishment being expressed that an officer of Ellerker's experience could have been so trapped. In July 1548 Bowes out of Berwick ignored urgent advice from Spaniard Gamboa to refrain from pursuing certain French cavalry, and had to be rescued by the mercenary captain. Obdurately bent on pursuit, Bowes dropped into a second ambush, with the loss of sixty dead and many horses and prisoners, including himself.[22]

One is left, then, with Ruthall's Flodden denunciation as one slur that cannot be extenuated by incompetent leadership. However, the credibility of his account is weakened by the hearsay and the animosity towards the Warden and the highlanders that informed it. Demonstrably a lion, not a donkey, Dacre might assert that his 'folks' had been too occupied in salvaging Lord Edmund Howard's right wing[11] for any horse-thieving.[23] Since the East Marchers had run away,[24] these 'folks' consisted of 1500 Middle Marchers, among whom Tyne- and Redesdalers bulked large, which dovetails with the tradition that the day was saved by the intervention of Bastard John Heron of Crawley with a band of fierce outlaws.[19] If the highlanders had disgraced themselves on the battlefield, they would never have been allocated so prominent a role in the follow-up operations; nor would their commander have received a royal commendation.[25] Ruthall ate his words.[26]

Other verdicts differed radically from his. Fortescue wrote that 'the most

remarkable of the mounted men in [Henry VIII's] army were the Northern
Horsemen who, called into being . . . by the eternal forays of the Scottish
Border . . . were light cavalry . . . probably the very best in Europe'.[27] That
authoritative work, *The King's Council of the North*, describes the Tyne- and
Redesdalers in particular as 'the most able defenders of the frontier against
the Scots from the Middle Ages onwards'.[28]

Contemporaries were hardly less complimentary. Dorset described the
highlanders in 1523 as 'men which may evil be spared',[29] while Dacre felt
compelled to parley with Albany because of his rift with Tynedale.[30] After
a raid by Redes- and Tynedalers had ended in fiasco, the Borders were said
to be 'mych the weaker thereby'.[31] In 1540 it was reckoned that a hundred
'English spears Northern on horseback', with as many archers and gunners,
would be more use than the thousand in Irish garrisons.[32] The Queen of
Hungary was assured that Northern Horsemen were 'skilful and wary and
experienced men',[33] 'the flower of the youth here'.[34] The restraint of
Tyne- and Redesdalers before an offensive in operating on foot for their
horses' sake was admired by Hertford,[35] and the dash for Leith by the
overlanders rated the height of daring.[36] Recounted in detail to Charles
V,[37] Fernieherst's reverse earned warm praise from the Queen Regent.[38]
When a London alderman refused a benevolence, Henry VIII attached him
to Eure's horsemen, so as to assimilate 'the sharp discipline militair of the
northern wars'.[39] The standing of the Redes- and Tynedalers in particular
was symbolised by that of Little John, whose services against the Scots,
whatever his misdemeanours, had in Bowes' estimation been valiant and
continual; and by the back-handed compliment to the Reeds of Troughend
in Elizabeth's reign that 'a ruder and more lawless crew there needs not be; yet
if well tutored they might do Her Majesty good service'.[40] In short Northern
Horsemen were reckoned the pick of English troops, being preferred to the
horse archers of Yorkshire by the Council of Ireland in 1523, and by Ralph
Lord Eure in 1597, as 'better at handling spears on horseback . . . better
prickers in the chase'.[41] In Surrey's judgment the highlanders excelled others
in endurance and daring;[42, 43] in Wallop's the King's Band were worth more
than thrice the number of unseasoned troops;[44] in that of Hertford, later
Duke of Somerset, far above inlanders as raiders,[45] and a match for half
again as many infantry.[34] The favouritism shown them by Lord Grey de
Wilton, as a *corps d'élite*, was resented by the rest of the army.[46, 47]

The key to prestige was the central importance of horseflesh, loss of
which at Edinburgh[48] and Ancrum[49] was considered disastrous, and by
the Scots at Solway Moss a bigger calamity than that of their earls.[50] The
grounds for Dacre's quarrel with the highlanders in 1523 was his denial of any
prize money, because at Jedburgh they alone[51] had hung on to their horses.[52]

Their equestrian proficiency had improved since 1279, when inquests were held on residents who had tumbled off their horses into the Tyne, sometimes when drunk.[53] Crucial was what by national standards[54] was a lavish supply of high-quality mounts. Whereas only one-fiftieth of the Army Royal was mounted in 1551, one-third of the highlanders were so equipped, and that after a decline from one-half during the forties.[55] The Keeper was almost the only Border officer whose men were decently horsed.[56] By the same token they were better furnished with carts, without which no army could move, than most of their compatriots.[57, 58, 59] In 1523 Tynedale had twenty, four more than the remainder of Northumberland.[60] With so many horses to spare, small as they were, they could also in an emergency yoke them to the guns,[61] as was in fact done by the worst mounted of the overlanders on arrival before Edinburgh.[62]

The other enhancement to their status was due to the obsolescence of the rest of the English army, now deep in the trough between Verneuil and Marston Moor. With no pikemen and no handguns ('hackbuts') till around 1544, it relied largely on battle-axes ('bills'), like the Saxon host at Hastings, and on archers. The sole arm reckoned up-to-date was the light horsemen, of which the army still had too few in 1519 and as late as 1544. Even though scarcely a revolutionary concept in view of the antecedent hobelars, the King's (or Queen's) Band continued to be regarded as modern and viable till around 1550,[63] and contrasted favourably with fellow-exponent Flemings[64] and Albanian stradiots.[65] When in Picardy the English cavalry commander, Wallop, boasted to Charles V that the Northern Horsemen 'would do as well as any Albanians and Arabs or any other nation [and] the Emperor saw them hurl up the hill so lightly he said: *Par ma foy, voilà des gens qui vont de grand courage, et ils semblent très bien les Alarbes d'Afrique'*.[66] Within the polyglot camp the reputation of the Band was as being among the cream of the skirmishers.[67]

Even if the Tyne- and Redesdalers had not fully shared in this martial esteem, their enlistment would still have been highly attractive, because for the Scottish operations that remained the primary commitment their logistic demands were so much less than those of other troops, thanks to a domicile along the front and intimacy with the enemy's forward areas.

What was the going rate for the military capability attributed to the highlanders in common with other Northern Horsemen? In the first place there was a widespread[68, 69] and tenacious conviction[70] that the sole remuneration to which Borderers were entitled for British service was tax immunity,[15, 71] a limitation compounded in the case of the two dales by tenures akin to knight service. Henry VIII in 1544 pronounced them to be out of place on the payroll,[72] and even their right to mounts and armour out of commissariat was disputed.[73] In practice, however, only intermittently did the Court overlook that the obligation to serve *gratis* extended to defence only,[74] or to offensive service for one day between two nights.[75, 76] Even such restriction was ignored by the highlanders and other Marchers, ever insistent on the rate for the job.[77, 78] Surrey paid them for two nights' provisions brought to an attack on Cessford;[79] Dacre distributed wages except when Spring grass was there for the horses;[80] the Tynedale Keeper was given 300 men's wages for a pounce on Kelso.[81] Insistence on the book would leave the King 'far underpeopled of the number of men armed to serve'.[73] And in any case 'sudden raids' were becoming only a minor aspect of sixteenth-century campaigns.

Between 1522 and 1544 the daily rate of pay for a foot-soldier in Scotland was 6d; a cavalryman 8d; a petty captain 2/-; and a captain 4/-, out of which a man bought his own rations. After Edinburgh John Dodd drew wages for what was presumably a Tynedale company, less a deduction of nearly £34 for twenty days' victuals,[82] about 4d per diem per head.[83] During this 1544 highlanders joined the garrisons in large numbers, it being admitted that otherwise 'neither so many, nor yet so notable exploits had been done within Scotland as hath been'.[45] Though often in arrears, garrison wages opened prospects of a steadier income altogether. A less remunerative system had been mooted in 1526, involving assignment of the dozen Redes- and Tynedale pledges to the Berwick garrison just for their keep, with the economy of five or six soldiers' wages.[84]

Apart from salary there was the occasional windfall, firstly in the shape of prize money: after a storming of Cessford in 1519, £10 to each Keeper and £4 to Heron of Chipchase, some of which may have filtered down;[85] £122/14/4 shared among all Northumbrian Marchers in 1523, and £835 likewise after a descent on Teviotdale;[86] £1745 among the overlanders in 1544.[87] Much in evidence after the Tillmouth clash and the Battle of Pinkie, ransoms, like plunder, were massive but fitful, and to be set against reciprocal loss such as that incurred by the highlanders at Ancrum.[88]

However, it was enrolment for service in France that was for the highlanders the critical juncture. Except for plunder on the hoof, ruled out by remoteness of front from home base, overseas service was more lucrative because more protracted. Pay-days were at intervals of from two to six weeks. Being in the government's opinion for a higher priority, the enhanced rates of 6/-, 4/- and 9d for a captain, petty captain and horseman respectively[61] were not grudged. There were also supplementary benefits, firstly conduct money as far as Calais at 9d *per diem* for board and lodging — Admiral Stanhope charged three companies £13 for food and provender out of Hull; secondly, coat money at 4/- per head for uniform. Typical recipients included a petty captain and sixty highlanders in 1541;[89] 300 Marchers including Tyne- and Redesdalers in 1543;[90] and fifty highland 'footmen' in 1544.[91] Once paid, allowances were irrevocable, which was why a company of Northern Horsemen and these footmen were not countermanded when the need for their expedition lapsed.[92] Finally miscellaneous bounty was apt to find its way from a generous commander like Sir Ralph Ellerker to 'such as will venture their bodies to serve the King'.

Unquantifiable with precision, the resultant flow of honest money into the two dales was obviously considerable. Hundreds of men must have been on the payrolls by 1544, creating a modest boom that fleetingly transformed the clansmen's conduct. Parr in the Spring of 1543 reported 'no complaints of any of them by Englishmen',[93] and in the autumn the great garrison was moved out, 'for about Tynedale and Redesdale we think that now they shall not need to lie'.[94] Early in Edward VI's reign Somerset was assured that their offences were trivial,[95] while Bowes forgetfully affirmed they had been behaving themselves throughout the forties.[96] That the treacle was working better than the brimstone had ever done was reflected in a novel tendency on the authorities' part to side with the highlanders in controversy. Thus after the clash at Hexham fair Suffolk's concern was lest they take the law into their own hands in the quest for vengeance, a thing which in normal times would have been regarded as a matter of course.[97] By 1546 offences against them by the Scots were treated as *casus belli*. During the night of July 7th the Teviotdalers attempted to lure the Tynedalers from their summer shiels into two ambushes laid in the Waste by up to 100 men, through firing some Milburn houses and 'cruelly murthering' Geoffrey Robson, 'one of the heidsmen and best ordered of all the Tynedales'.[98] Yet in 1537 this same Geoffrey had been denounced to the Duke of Norfolk as one of the most arrant thieves alive,[99] so his reformation symbolised that of his countrymen. On news of these attacks the old King swore a revenge that was to be no less terrible for being posthumous.[100, 101]

During the next two reigns most other heidsmen, too, teetered on the edge of respectability. Commissioners for Enclosures in 1552 included besides the Keeper the Halls of Otterburn and Monkridge, Reed of Troughend, a Hedley,[102] Charlton of Hesleyside and three others — a Milburn, a Dodd and John Robson of the Falstone,[103] who was also appointed Setter and Searcher.[104]

NOTES

1. He was English on this occasion.

2. BL, Add. MSS 32647 fol. 50, 25/8/1542.
3. *LP*, VI no. 16, 2/1/1533.
4. BL, Add. MSS 32656 fol. 180, 3/3/1545
5. *LP*, XX(1) no. 465, 19/3/1545.
6. *LP*, XX(2) no. 1049, 28/12/1545.
7. BL, Add. MSS 32747 fol. 48, 24/8/1542.
8. BL, Calig. B V fol. 1, June 1544–July 1546.
9. *LP*, XIX(1) no. 483, 9/5/1544.
10. *Ibid.*, no. 497, 12/5/1544.
11. *LP*, I(2) (Kraus) no. 2246, 9/9/1513.
12. PRO, SP I 5 fol. 229 & 730, 20/9/1513.
13. Oman, *Art of War*, pp. 317–8.
14. BL, Add. MSS 32648 fol. 17, 5/10/1542.
15. *Ibid.*, 32647 fol. 162, 16/9/1542.
16. PRO, SP I 70 fol. 232–5, 23/8/1532.
17. BL, Add. MSS 32655 fol. 26, 12/6/1544.
18. *LP*, XIX(2) no. 625, 17/11/1544.
19. (Sir Herbert) Maxwell, (*History of the*) *House of Douglas*, Vol. II, p. 62.
20. BL, Add. MSS 32656 fol. 170, 1/3/1545.
21. *Ibid.*, fol. 183, 5/3/1545.
22. *CSPF* (ed. 1871), Item 917, 28/1/1567.
23. PRO, SP I 5 fol. 240, c.22/10/1513.
24. Oman, *Art of War*, p. 313 follows Letters and Papers in stating that it was Tyne*dale* that fled, but the original letter says Tyne*mouth*.
25. BL, Calig. B VI fol. 37, 13/11/1513.
26. *Ibid.*, fol. 40, 24/10/1513.
27. Fortescue, *British Army*, Vol. I p. 114.
28. Reid, *Council of the North*, p. 14.
29. BL, Calig. B III fol. 255, 16/4/1523.
30. *LP*, IV(1) no. 21, 12/1/1524.
31. BL, Calig. B II fol. 95, 14/11/1528.
32. PRO, E 36 Vol. 121 fol. 12 & 27, April 1540.
33. *LP*, XVIII(1) no. 685, 11/6/1543.
34. *Ibid.*, no. 759, 23/6/1543.
35. BL, Add. MSS 32654 fol. 74, 6/4/1544.
36. *LP*, XIX(1) no. 348, 17/4/1544.
37. *LP*, XIX(2) no. 105, 18/8/1544.
38. *LP*, XIX(1) no. 962, 22/7/1544.
39. *LP*, XX(1) no. 98, c.27/1/1545.
40. Hodgson, *Northumberland*, Pt II, Vol. I, p. 137.
41. (*The State*) *Papers* (*and Letters of Sir Ralph*) *Sadler*, Vol. II, p.16.
42. PRO, SP 49.2 27, fol. 11, 15/4/1523.
43. *LP*, III(2) no. 3509, 4/11/1523.
44. *LP*, XVIII(1) no. 786, 28/6/1543.
45. *LP*, XIX(1) no. 293, 1/4/1544.
46. *LP*, XXI(1) no. 819, 13/5/1546.
47. BL, Add. MSS 32657 fol. 12, 10/7/1548.
48. *LP*, XIX(1) no. 596, 29/5/1544.

49. *LP*, XX(1) no. 332, 10/3/1545.

50. Scotland certainly had Earls and to spare. Cf. A. Grant, *Earls and Earldom (in late mediaeval Scotland 1310–1460)*, p. 25 ff.. A given earldom lasted on average four years and was then replaced.

51. *LP*, III(2) no. 3363, 27/9/1523.

52. *Ibid.*, no. 3395, 5/10/1523.

53. *Iter de Wark*, 1279.

54. Cf. Queen Mary's letter to gentlemen in every shire in January 1558: 'The more horsemen, the more thankful shall be your service' (PRO, SP 11 12 6).

55. *LP*, XVII no. 750, 6/9/1542.

56. *LP*, XVII no. 1083, 13/11/1542.

57. *LP*, III(2) no. 3115, c.17/6/1523.

58. *Ibid.*, no. 3349, 21/9/1523.

59. *LP*, XIX(1) no. 223, 20/3/1544.

60. *LP*, III(2) no. 3110, 16/6/1523.

61. *LP*, XIX(1) no. 273, end March 1544.

62. *Ibid.*, no. 387, 23/4/1544.

63. BL, Harl. MSS 643 fol. 169, c.1/8/1557.

64. *LP*, XVII no. 619, 13/5/1542.

65. *LP*, XXI(1) no. 682, 26/4/1546.

66. *LP*, XVIII(2) no. 291, 21/10/1543.

67. *Ibid.*, no. 345, 6/11/1543.

68. *LP*, III(2) no. 3574, 29/11/1523.

69. *LP*, VI no. 144, 9/2/1533.

70. BL, Harl. MSS 643 fol. 267, 19/9/1558.

71. *LP*, III(2) no. 3282, 30/8/1523.

72. PRO, SP I 199 fol. 161, late March 1545.

73. *Ibid.*, 124 fol. 67–72, 20/8/1537.

74. *LP*, XX(2) no. 95, 11/8/1545.

75. BL, Calig. B VIII fol. 63, 2/12/1541.

76. *LP*, XVII no. 957, 17/10/1542.

77. *LP*, III(2) no. 3515, 7/11/1523.

78. PRO, SP I 30 fol. 334–5, 25/4/1524.

79. *LP*, III(2) no. 3040, 21/5/1523.

80. *LP*, IV(1) no. 161, 15/3/1524.

81. *LP*, VI no. 113, 3/2/1533.

82. PRO, SP I 187 fol. 232–7, 23/5/1544.

83. *LP*, IV(1) no. 132, end February 1524.

84. BL, Calig. B III fol. 44, 17/8/1526.

85. *LP*, III(1) no. 573, end 1519.

86. *LP*, III(2) no. 3177, 13/7/1523.

87. *LP*, XIX(1) no. 476, 7/5/1544.

88. BL, Add. MSS 32656 fol. 195, 11/3/1545.

89. *LP*, XVI no. 1489, end April 1541.

90. *LP*, XVIII(1) no. 729, 18/6/1543.

91. *LP*, XIX(1) no. 545, 21/5/1544.

92. BL, Add. MSS 32654 fol. 207, 25/5/1544.

93. PRO, SP I 178 fol. 85, 24/5/1543.
94. *Ibid.*, 181 fol. 116, 9/9/1543.
95. BL, Add. MSS 32657 fol. 47, 19/8/1548.
96. BL, Calig. B VIII fol. 106, 1551 (not 1542 as inscribed).
97. BL, Add. MSS 32651 fol. 178, end July 1543.
98. PRO, SP I 226 fol. 142, 21/11/1546.
99. *Ibid.*, 220 fol. 275, end May 1537.
100. *LP*, XXI(2) no. 443, 25/11/1546.
101. *Ibid.*, no. 457, 29/1/1546.
102. Hodgson, *Northumberland*, Pt II, Vol. I, p. 71.
103. William Nicholson, *Leges Marchiarum*, p. 335.
104. Pease, *Wardens of the Marches*, p. 155.

CHAPTER TWENTY
Relapse

In reality Fawside Brae had signalled not the dawn of prosperity but the climax of a fleeting career as professional soldiers. In an age of military innovation obsolescence now overtook even the Northern Horsemen. From 1547 onwards the cavalry requirement was increasingly for the stubby demi-lance and the heavier horses appropriate to its wielders, whose superiority to light horsemen by the end of Mary's reign was regarded as axiomatic.[1, 2] Signs of an impending collapse in prestige might have been detected as early as the defeat at Millstanes, woundingly attributed to the absence of mercenaries in winter quarters.[3] With the intensifying enlistment of foreigners *qua* exponents of modern techniques, the English army under Edward VI began to resemble a foreign legion. Usually short of funds, the government lavished what it did have on such as the stradiots, whose receipt of thrice the pay of a Northern Horseman according to Paget killed the Englishman's heart.[4] Without the cushion of high wages against tearaway inflation the once proud King's Band could be described to Somerset in 1549 as among the refuse of men.[5] As for the expanding majority of clansmen with no alternative to foot service, their sole skill was certified as late as 1580 to be as bowmen,[6] already in 1557 bracketed with billmen as 'for the wars now used [standing] to very small purpose'.[1]

Even within their native Northumberland the highlanders' plight was aggravated by shortage of official funds, for there was renewed insistence on the supposed traditional obligation to serve against the Scots *gratis*, Henry VIII 'liking very well [Bowes'] resolution that there should be a lesser number of Tynedale and Redesdale men kept in wages'.[7] The proportion of Borderers overall in the garrisons sharply declined,[8, 9] a development dangerously resented locally: in 1597 a Warden was to warn the Redesdale Keeper that if he 'kept none of them in pay, but stranger soldiers only . . . [the Redesdalers] will betray him'.[10]

Occasionally the highlanders' hopes of a military livelihood might be rekindled as when after James I's accession 320 Tynedalers were recruited under a Charlton of Hesleyside to fight in Ireland,[11] joined in 1607 by '100 men from any of the outlaws of Redesdale and Tynedale, except the ringleaders'.[12] However, the obstacle was insurmountable that, apart from the odd scuffle, from 1560 onwards wars with Scotland for good, and with

France for over a century, had become things of the past. The ban imposed in 1605 by the Commissioners of the new Midland Shires on 'all Borderers, notably including those of Tynedale and Redesdale, from keeping jack, spear or other weapon, or a horse worth more than 50/- sterling' had the ring of finality about it. [13]

As fast as the newer tap was closed, the highlanders naturally strove to turn the old one back on again. Any superficial inspection of events during the late sixteenth century, and even beyond, would leave the impression that nothing had really changed since Wolsey's day. Memoranda to Edward VI's inaugural Lieutenant spoke of Tynedale as 'now plenished with wild and misdemeaned people', [14] and confirmed that both dales were still 'allied and confederated together', and their heidsmen influential enough to suborn the rest into 'disorder or disobedience'. [15] Tynedale bade farewell to the reign of the Spanish Tudor with such violence [16] that the unanimity of observers persisted well into the reign of the great Queen. According to Sir Ralph Sadler, her first Northumbrian Warden, the Redes- and Tynedale thieves were 'naughty, evil, unruly and misdemeaned, no better than very rebels and outlaws', screwing blackmail and protection money out of law-abiding neighbours. [17, 18, 19] His astute and unscrupulous successor, Sir John Forster, fell out rapidly with the Redesdalers, who were beginning to outstrip the Tynedalers in power and who, led as usual by the Halls, attempted in the winters of 1566 and 1567 to break Harbottle gaol and spring the prisoners. Before being overpowered, the assailants wounded some of the guards, [20, 21, 22] and six of them were subsequently beheaded, [23] while surrounding prisons were crammed with the remainder. [24] On entry into the Wardenry of the Middle Marches towards the end of the reign, Sir Robert Carey certified that 'the thieves did domineer and do what they pleased, and . . . the poor inhabitants were utterly disabled and overthrown'. [25] Notorious robbers like John Charlton of the Bower and murderers like a latter-day Will Ridley in Tynedale, [9] and the fierce and numerous Halls of Otterburn in Redesdale [26] lorded it with impunity. A contemporary *Description of Britain* was at a loss to decide, with regard to Redesdale, Tynedale and for that matter Liddesdale, 'whether thieves or true men do most abound in them'. [27]

Apparently the advent of the United Kingdom had no perceptible effect. According to a Redesdale vicar in 1606 murderers, thieves and outlaws lived blatantly there and 'there were twenty outcries for things stolen every Sabbath day'. [28] In 1618 Anthony Hall and John Reed were indicted for sheltering felons and fugitives, including Dodds and Milburns from Tynedale. [29] In the very year of Charles I's execution a commentator on the Northumbrian scene explained that 'these highlanders are famous for thieving; they are all bred up and live by theft. They come down from these dales into the low countries and carry away horses and cattle . . . There is many every year . . . at the assizes . . . condemned and hanged, sometime twenty or thirty'.[30]

There were of course religious rumblings in this age of the Protestant earthquake, since the Tyne- and Redesdalers tarried longer than most Englishmen on the Roman side of the fence. That they still manifested an awkward tendency to flock to banners of rebellion was demonstrated during the uprising of the Northern Earls in 1569. Sadler affirmed that throughout Northumberland 'the common people be ignorant, full of superstitions and altogether blinded with the old Popish doctrine'. According to Elizabeth's general, the Earl of Sussex, most of the 700 horsemen among the 3000 rebels were Liddesdalers, Teviotdalers and 'outlaws of Tynedale and Redesdale . . . English and Scottish thieves together'.[31] One quarter of 2000 light horsemen brought to Raby by the Percy Earl were 'after the order of Redesdale'.[32] Yet strangely enough, after the commotion had subsided, no Tyne- or Redesdalers figured on the roll of attainted persons.[19]

The government tackled the problem by the propaganda route instead. The Anglican drive along the Borders had started in 1560,[33] culminating in the visitation of 1578 which brought the larger into line administratively with the smaller Liberty, inasmuch as the vast Simonburn parish sloughed off Bellingham for the north banks of the Wark and Shitlington burns, and Falstone for the west side of Tarset Water.[34] At a pastoral level the main drive was imparted by the intrepid Bernard Gilpin, a County Durham vicar and preacher of notable power, who undertook annual missions in Redes- and Tynedales.[35] Thanks to him, it was written in 1586, the inhabitants 'have been called to some obedience and zeal unto the Word . . . At the present their former savage demeanour is very much abated, and their barbarous wildness and fierceness so much qualified that there is hope left of their reduction into civility and better order of behaviour'.[27, 36] Upon discovery that horses he had stolen were Mr. Gilpin's, a thief was in a mighty hurry to return them, lest he 'be thrust down quickly into hell', so 'adored was he by that half barbarous and rustic people'.[37]

Sadly, the conversion was barely skin deep, Gilpin himself perceiving during a visit to Redesdale that 'there was neither minister nor bell nor Book, [but] there was a red hand put on a spear point in defiance of deadly feud'. And as Dr. Rowse also reminds us, when once the saintly vicar thundered against breaches of the eighth commandment, an ancient Tynedaler cried out in dismay: 'Then the deil I give my sall to, but we are all thieves'.[36] Recommended to Simonburn in 1596, even in its reduced state still a most lucrative living,[38] Mr Crackenthorp of The Queen's College, a less muscular but more prudent Christian, declined, 'deeming his body unable to live in so troublesome a place, and his nature not well brooking the perverse nature of so crooked a people'.[39, 40] Lord Eure's remedy in 1596 for low church attendance was more Bible-readers and repairs to church roofs.[41] Eventually, whether through conviction or apathy, the Reformation was to prevail among the highlanders as in the rest of England. Only the top families possessed the means and fortitude to abide in the old ways: the fidelity to Rome of the Charltons of Hesleyside has endured to the present, while the then Hall of Otterburn died a Catholic on Tyburn Tree for his part in the rebellion of 1715.[42] The influence of such pundits remained strong among the clans.

Although religious irridentism was more objectionable to the English government than predatory behaviour, that too was doubly unwelcome in the half-century preceding the union of the Crowns. If, as was asserted in 1569, '[the whole life and delight of] the bush country of Tynedale is only in robbing and spoiling their poor neighbours',[43] those included Scots as well as Englishmen. The resultant resentment exacerbated the international ill-will due to the Catholic and Francophile sentiment widespread along the Scottish Borders, particularly before 1568 when Mary, Queen of Scots misguidedly took refuge in England. Long after that, however, the cumulative grudge against the English highlanders continued to fester. Among other pinpricks inflicted by them in some pretty sensitive spots were raids undertaken by both dales in concert in 1565;[44] and by Tynedalers in 1567 against the Laird of Fernieherst, 'taken by him in very evil part';[45] against the Earl of Angus's Jedforest clients in 1575;[46] and repeatedly against a selection of targets in 1583.[47, 48, 49] Close to Elizabeth's death 400 Tyne- and Redesdalers 'bodden in jacks and spears in most warlike manner',[50] set on a party of half as many huntsmen who had entered from Teviotdale in quest not only of venison, but also of timber to house their burgeoning population. Numbers of them were killed by men of Surnames in deadly feud with them, and three eminent Lairds captured for ransom.[51] According to the Scots their men had been carrying only hunting pieces, whereas the English allegation was that they were armed with full-blown culverins.[50]

More fraught with eventual peril were assaults on two other targets. Four hundred Redesdalers under Hall of Otterburn and the Constable of Harbottle in 1563 relieved Liddesdale of 100 head of cattle and prisoners, sacking sixteen houses,[52] and in 1596 Tynedalers did the same by Elliots of Larriston in particular.[53] In the same year, in two separate episodes, highlanders from both dales took first 300, then 1000 sheep from their neighbours, some of whom they ambushed in hot trod into the bargain.[54] Eighty Tynedalers in 1597 purloined still more cattle from the Elliots of

Larriston, killing two of them.[55, 56, 57] Riskiest of all was a humiliation administered by Tyne- and Redesdalers to the fifth Laird of Buccleuch in 1569, when they made him and 260 of his clansmen prisoner, slaying and wounding many besides.[58] In 1597, 700 Tynedalers on horseback took 1000 head of cattle from the sixth Laird.[59]

Still more of an embarrassment were clashes associated with official business, notably at days of truce, occasions so ticklish that in Mary's reign both nations had agreed on a joint suppression of 'bawling and reproving' exchanged there between Borderers.[60] When the international atmosphere was bad, the arrangement still tended to break down, as at the Reidswyre in 1575. For three years past Sir John Forster, his joint Keeper Sir George Heron, and Robson heidsman John of the Stonehouse, with whom Forster was on compromisingly good terms,[61, 62] had been harbouring Kerr of Fernieherst, by then on the run from the Scottish authorities.[63] *Inter alia* he had been plotting with the Tyne- and Redesdalers on ways and means of raiding the Jedburgh area.[64] Around the same time Stonehouse guided certain Fenwicks into Liddesdale to murder sundry Croziers, with whom they were at feud. To the English Warden's ill-concealed rage, Heron surrendered John Robson to the Scottish Warden for punishment, for which Forster went so far as to suspend the Keeper from office,[46] proof surely that Sir George was less unsavoury than Sir John. By contrast the rule of Liddesdale resided with an unprecedentedly conscientious Keeper, Sir John Carmichael,[62] who duly arrived at the tryst all the less disposed to give the English the benefit of any doubts, because Forster was standing in for his displaced junior,[65] who however still attended.[66]

Nevertheless all proceeded smoothly for the first three hours during which the highlanders and Liddesdalers gambled, drank and jested together, while their officers dispensed justice. The latter then took a pause for refreshments, affably toasting one another.[67] However, when they resumed the mood quickly turned ugly upon Carmichael's discovery that young Henry Robson of the Falstone, against whom a true bill had been found, was not present to answer it.[46] Dissatisfied with Forster's promise to produce him next time, the Scot reproached him with yet again covering up for 'fugitives, rebels and traitors', which the Warden provocatively rebutted by drawing attention to his own superior rank. Thereupon the clansmen started to fight with a flight of arrows, discharged either by the Croziers at the Fenwicks with fatal results; or by the Tynedalers standing around their Warden against every Scot in sight, according to the English or Scottish account of events respectively. 'Then was there naught but bow and spear, and every man pulled out a brand.'[68] Carmichael had temporarily left the field, but only to fetch horse and foot out of Jedburgh,[67] who duly arrived 'with three pencils [i.e. banners] and a drum'. Either because they had come to the tryst without armour, or because too busy plundering stalls set up by the Jedburgh hucksters, the Tyne- and Redesdalers swiftly got the worst of it, inasmuch as George Heron and a score of others were killed in a pursuit,[69] and old Forster was captured in England after a chase and handed over to the Scots Lieutenant in Jedburgh.[70] In the course of their brief invasion the Scots rounded up 300 head of cattle in Redesdale.[71]

In ascribing the affair to bilateral loss of temper,[70] the Earl of Huntingdon did not fall far short of the mark. Through attempts to swindle redress much in excess of their losses by false claims, Tynedale in the aftermath did nothing to assuage the residual bitterness.[72] However, the rage that really counted was that of the Queen who admonished the Scots Regent that 'so foul an act as . . . the detaining of our Warden . . . wounds our honour'.[73, 74] So perturbed by the episode were both that same Earl of Morton and Sir John Forster that the latter, despite personal loss of face, averred it should never be allowed to hinder the amity between the realms;[69] while the former sought to mollify Elizabeth with an offer to surrender Carmichael.[75] Secretary of State Walsingham was advised that 'peace or war hangs now by a twine thread'.[76]

A decade later there erupted at Cocklaw between Forster and Fernieherst, now rehabilitated as Scots Warden, yet another menacing day of truce. Shortly beforehand the current Charlton of Hesleyside had intercepted a messenger from Kerr and his master the Earl of Arran, head of a temporarily ascendant Catholic party, and removed from his pouch an encyphered message. From Fernieherst's consternation one might surmise a content connected with the exiled Queen of Scots. Charlton dutifully consigned the missive to Lord Francis Russell, Forster's son-in-law, who forwarded it to the Privy Council. Catching sight of the peer at Cocklaw, the Scottish Warden either incited or suffered his followers not merely to assail Hall of Otterburn's Redesdalers, but also to shoot dead Lord Russell, with whom he was 'in great grief'.[77] Given that Mary Stuart's execution and the Spanish Armada were already imminent enough to be foreshadowed, this second fracas exploded at a juncture even less opportune than the first, and it was fortunate that Arran was ousted shortly afterwards, with the result that the two Protestant establishments could wholeheartedly collaborate in damage limitation.[78, 79]

The lack of control responsible for the anarchy was largely due to the chronic impotence of the officers at one echelon down from Forster, 'being but mean gentlemen and of small living'.[15] Memories were disquietingly green of 'other times when the Keeper of Tynedale . . . with small power or parties have been resisted and sometimes overthrown and slain and taken prisoners'.[14] To avoid such eventualities roughly the same gamut of expedients remained available as in the past.

In the first place, especially at mid-century, there was occasional recourse to the Keepers' superiors. At the end of Mary Tudor's reign the Earls of Westmorland and Northumberland, as Lieutenant and Warden respectively, were congratulated on efforts to bring Tynedale to heel: the latter was advised, 'if they will not be brought to order by gentleness then to use extremity unto them',[80, 81] and the former to consult the Bishop of Ely and the Master of the Rolls, just arrived on the Borders with an agenda topped by both dales.[2] It was Forster as Warden who in 1559 commanded the Tynedale heidsmen to meet him at Chipchase and hand over nine named 'bandsmen', who subsequently threw themselves on the Queen's mercy.[82] At the other end of Elizabeth's reign an ex-Keeper praised the then Warden Lord Eure for having 'used all his godly wits to amend the wicked life of these people',[26] while his successor Sir Robert Carey personally superintended the hanging or beheading of nearly twenty highlanders during his inaugural year.[83]

All the same for everyday business the Keepers had to rely on their own resources, to augment which efforts were fitfully made. In Edward VI's time Dorset recommended for 'each of the Keepers a garrison or retinue of thirty light horsemen to be continually and daily attending upon them' to facilitate arrests.[15] To man Harbottle Forster wanted twenty soldiers in 1565[20] and years later a hundred and twenty,[77, 84] together with fifty 'shot' (i.e. marksmen) for up to four months.[85] In a curious footnote to the Rising in the North, Robert Constable offered to undertake the joint Keeper's job if assigned 300 men by the insurgent Earls.[86]

Having annexed the Redesdale Keepership, Forster was just as keen to ensure recognition of Harbottle as indispensable to it, as that the castle be adequately garrisoned: 'if I be not worthy of the credit of the one, I desire not the other'. Amounting to 40% of the Keeper's salary, the fee of twenty marks p.a. could not in any case be foregone.[87] The Tynedale Keeper was even worse served for accommodation than his colleague. Since the escape of several Charltons from Hexham in 1559, taking their gaoler with them, the reputation of the towers there had declined,[88] with Sadler scoffing at their imperfections. Lady Carnaby having refused to cede Halton to the Keeper for more than three weeks, Tarset Hall and Haughton once more came up for examination, but the problem had not been solved by 1561.[89]

One traditional method of protecting the Keeper was the taking of hostages for good behaviour. Thus on arrival on the Middle Marches as Warden Sir Ralph Sadler levied pledges from each grayne of the Head Surnames of Tynedale.[47] Just prior to the 1569 insurrection Forster not merely expelled 'rebels' from Redesdale, destroying their houses, but also took ten pledges from the remainder.[22] Exemplifying another species of surety, bonds were taken in 1597 by Lord Eure from the then Bowery Charlton, 'a great thief'.[9]

Another device available to an astute Keeper was embroilment for which there was as much scope as ever. Even collaboration between one dale and another could end in a quarrel, as when in 1559 some Liddesdalers, having despoiled Sweethope in Cumberland, split into two parties on the way back, one overnighting in Tynedale with their prisoners, the other in Redesdale with the cattle. Tynedalers returning through Redesdale from a reciprocal errand in Scotland promptly collected the beasts from their new owners while 'in shiels . . . at fires'. Lending the invaders a trail-hound for the pursuit, the Redesdalers appear to have sided against their compatriots.[90] As for Redesdale itself, it was as prone to internal discord as Tynedale had once been, Bowes remarking in 1551 'two or three malicious displeasures raging among the Surnames there for slaughters done and not agreed for'.[14] For one thing the paramount Halls were now what the Hesleyside Charltons had once been, and the Campbells of the Scottish Highlands were destined to become, obnoxious to some neighbouring clansmen. Witness the legend from Elizabeth's reign that three false Ha's of Girsonfield betrayed Percy Reed to murder by the Croziers. Bowing courteously to anyone kind enough to notice him, Percy's ghost still haunts the banks of the Rede.[91]

As formerly, there were carrots as well as sticks, which it was often risky to apply anyway, as Lord Eure gloomily observed in the nineties: if any 'Keeper of Redesdale shall be severe with extremity of law and prosecute the heidsmen for offences before his time, neither he nor any other Keeper shall live long to serve there'.[9] Having perused the state of Redesdale at Elizabeth's accession, Sadler prescribed in conjunction with the sterner measures of garrison and law enforcement 'the gentler means of a general pardon for all past offences'.[18] In 1561 the Queen pardoned all Tynedale offenders who were penitent.[92]

Jobs could still be distributed to blunt temptation. Hall of Otterburn was the Percy Earl's Keeper of Redesdale in 1558.[93] Despite, perhaps because of, a vicious record Bowery Charlton was hired in 1597[9] as one of eighty horsemen allotted the Keepers, along with other famous robbers such as Hall of Otterburn and Robsons from Harbottle, whither the clan had been migrating over the past half-century.[94] When Burghley wore a 'heavy countenance' at the Redesdale Keeper's habit of enlisting local reprobates rather than virtuous strangers, Eure protested there was scarcely a man able to find his way through the Waste who was not at odds with the law,[95] and added he held it 'politic' by doling out employments to draw heidsmen of the Fenwicks, Erringtons and Robsons, for example, from friendship with the Scots.[9]

The danger in such an attitude was that it could bring an official to within a stone's throw of connivance, reinforcing the tacit recognition in many quarters that without a modicum thereof the wheels would just not go round. The proclivity to collaborate in felony is tellingly illustrated from the ongoing saga of the Herons. Sir George, who apparently stayed as joint Keeper till the eve of the Reidswyre fray, lived up to Little John at every turn. In 1558 he had fallen under suspicion of making away with a rival claimant in the re-emergent question of the Ford inheritance. Outlawed, arrested and shipped south for interrogation, the Keeper was ultimately cleared after a fashion, not least because his brother-in-law, Sir John Forster, though suspected of complicity himself, stood in the high esteem of the Marian regime.[96] On taking up the reins as Warden under Elizabeth soon afterwards, Sadler certified that Heron had been bribed by the Tyne- and Redesdalers to ignore their offences, which was 'an encouragement to those naughty and misdemeaned persons . . . to rob and spoil'.[97] Although eventually turning against John Robson of the Stonehouse, Sir George at one time came under a cloud for harbouring him.[98]

Eventually Heron was to be succeeded, if in the Redesdale Keepership only, by a son and namesake, despite involvement in 1587 in the misdeeds of Will Armstrong of Kinmont.[99] By 1595, however, Lord Eure was petitioning the Queen for his dismissal, together with that of his Tynedale colleague William Fenwick, and their replacement by inland gentlemen.[100] The Warden's case included the latter's illicit dealings with Kerr of Cessford and other Scots,[101, 102] and the difficulty he had had in persuading young George to hang twelve of the biggest thieves in Redesdale.[26]

Not that performance at the Warden level was any more impressive. On Elizabeth's accession the Earl of Northumberland sent his two Keepers to London to defend his reputation,[103] while towards the close of the reign Carey said of Lord Eure that for all his good intentions every one of his five years was worse than its forerunner.[25] In post most of the time between 1560 and 1595, and conveniently related to most of the Northumbrian gentry, Forster was praised for his 'good skill and service' under Mary and as 'an active and valiant man' under her successor. Yet this Methuselah of the Middle Marches, a very reincarnation of Dacre of Gilsland, was unique in history for having been sacked for misbehaviour at the age of ninety-four. In 1586–7 he was suspended from duty[104] on such charges as the maladministration of Redesdale;[105] taking bribes from the highlanders;[99] and condoning murder.[26] That a Warden should so demean himself as to wage deadly feud against the Halls of Redesdale was disgraceful: once he sold

John of Otterburn to the brigand Elliots for £1000 Scots, and superintended in his own garden the payment of ransoms by the English to the Liddesdale clan.[106] Latterly he was delegating most of the work to a bastard son who was a notorious drunkard.

In fact men who were sober and honest fought shy of appointments on the Middle Marches. When told to be Warden, Sadler 'thought he had great wrong, having neither men, horse nor money and having necessarily in that charge to entertain many gentlemen'.[18] Sir Robert Carey wriggled to as little avail, 'the government of the Middle Marches being too hard a task for me[94] . . . one where neither honour, profit, pleasure nor contentment can be reaped'.[107] Even Sir George Heron, who in the long run was to manipulate the Keepership to gross personal advantage, initially turned it down because there was no money in it. When he did reluctantly agree it was for a short period only, and as a personal favour to Sadler.[108]

NOTES

1. BL, Harl. MSS 643 fol. 165, 11/7/1557.

2. *Ibid.*, fol. 258, 25/6/1558.

3. *LP*, XXI(1) no. 58, 13/1/1546.

4. *Ibid.*, no. 691, 28/4/1546.

5. BL, Add. MSS 32657 fol. 52, 17/1/1549.

6. CBP, Vol. I Item 50, 2/5/1580.

7. PRO, SP I 199 fol. 161, late March 1545.

8. *LP*, XVII no. 1048, 8/11/1542.

9. CBP, Vol. II Item 652, 8/6/1597.

10. *Ibid.*, Item 650, 6/6/1597.

11. Watson, *Reivers*, p. 195.

12. *Calendar of State Papers Domestic Series of the Reign of James I, 1603–1610* (hereinafter *CSP J I*), Vol. XXVII, p. 358, 24/5/1607.

13. Pease, *Wardens of the Marches*, p. 239.

14. BL, Calig. B VIII fol. 106, 1551 (not 1542 as inscribed).

15. *Ibid.*, B VII fol. 440, 1552.

16. BL, Harl. MSS 643 fol. 225, 1/3/1558.

17. CSPF, (ed. 1863) Item 1409, 30/9/1559.

18. CSPF, (ed. 1865) Item 213, 8/11/1859.

19. *Sadler Papers*, Vol. II p. 16.

20. CSPF, (ed. 1870) Item 1323, 26/7/1565.

21. CSPF, (ed. 1871) Item 110, 19/2/1566.

22. CSPF, (ed. 1874) Item 180, 20/3/1569.

23. CSPF, (ed. 1871) Item 917, 28/1/1567.

24. *Ibid.*, Item 1990, 7/2/1568.

25. *Memoirs (of Robert) Carey, (Earl of Monmouth*, ed. H. Powell), p. 55, late 1597.

26. CBP, Vol. II Item 763, 24/9/1597.

27. *Op. cit* by William Harrison, p. 91.

28. *CSP J I* Vol. I p. 316, 3/5/1606.

29. Northumberland RO, DE/7/63, List of Fugitives 1618.

30. Gray, *Chorographia*, p. 118 ff..

31. *Sadler Papers*, pp. 38–55.

32. *Arch. Aeliana*, Vol. III, p. 366.

33. Trevelyan, *Social History*, p. 154.

34. *Arch. Aeliana*, Vol. VIII p. 82.

35. D. Marcombe in *NH* Vol. XVI, pp. 26–32.

36. Cited in A. L. Rowse, *Expansion of Elizabeth England*, p. 15.

37. Carleton, *Life of Galpin*, cited in M. E. James, *Family, Lineage and Civil Society*, p. 55.

38. W. W. Tomlinson, *Life in Northumberland during the Sixteenth Century*, p. 141.

39. *CBP*, Vol. II Item 357 (p. 183), 1/9/1596.

40. *Ibid.*, Item 421, 24/10/1596.

41. *Ibid.*, Item 268, 18/5/1596.

42. Hodgson, *Northumberland*, Pt II Vol. I, p. 113.

43. Tomlinson, *op. cit.*, p. 128, quoting Tate, *History of Alnwick*, Vol. I, p. 271.

44. *CSPF*, (ed. 1870) Item 1532, 28/9/1565.

45. *CSPF*, (ed. 1871) Item 1592, 10/8/1567.

46. *Calendar of State Papers relating to Scotland*, ed. Joseph Bain (hereinafter C Scot P), Vol. V Item 226, 15/3/1575.

47. *Sadler (Papers: The State Papers and Letters of Sir Ralph Sadler)*, Vol. I 613, 1559.

48. *C Scot P*, Vol. VI Item 678, 23/10/1583.

49. *Ibid.*, Item 680, 25/10/1583.

50. *CBP*, Vol. II Item 992, 9/9/1598.

51. *Ibid.*, Item 974, 4/8/1598.

52. *CSPF*, (ed. 1869) Item 602(5), 10/4/1563.

53. *CBP*, Vol. II Item 239, 23/3/1596.

54. *Ibid.*, Item 245, 1/4/1596.

55. *C Scot P*, Vol. XII Item 412, 21/4/1597.

56. *Ibid.*, Item 420, 28/4/1597.

57. *Ibid.*, Item 421, 28/4/1597.

58. *CSPF*, (ed. 1871) Item 2594, 14/10/1568.

59. *C Scot P*, Vol. XIII Item 24, 21/6/1597.

60. BL, Harl. MSS 6811, 4/12/1553.

61. *CSPF*, (ed. 1880) Item 274, 4/8/1575.

62. *Ibid.*, Item 309, 24/8/1575.

63. *C Scot P*, Vol. V Item 238, August 1576.

64. *Ibid.*, Vol. IV Item 64, 19/7/1572.

65. Most of the ensuing account is based on n. 62 and on Hodgson, *Northumberland*, Pt II Vol. I p. 155 ff., except where other sources are specified.

66. *CSPF*, (ed. 1880) Item 222, 10/7/1575.

67. *Ibid.*, Item 275, August 1575.

68. 'The Raid of the Reidswyre' ballad is quoted at length in Pease, *Wardens of the Marches*, p. 133.

69. *CSPF*, (ed. 1880) Item 223, 11/7/1575.

70. *Ibid.*, Item 290, 17/8/1575.

71. Watson, *Reivers*, p. 64.
72. C *Scot P*, Vol. V Item 228, 27/5/1576.
73. *CSPF*, (ed. 1880) p. 244, July 1575.
74. *Ibid.*, Item 311, 29/8/1575.
75. *Ibid.*, Item 297, 24/8/1575.
76. *Ibid.*, Item 216, 8/7/1575.
77. CBP, Vol. I Item 341, 23/8/1585.
78. *Ibid.*, Item 330, 28/7/1585.
79. Watson, *Reivers*, pp. 67–9.
80. BL, Harl. MSS 643 fol. 312B, 4/11/1558.
81. *CSPF*, (ed. 1863), Vol. I Item 209, 6/1/1559.
82. *CSPF*, (ed. 1865) Item 299, 19/11/1559.
83. *Carey's Memoirs*, p. 58, late 1597.
84. CBP, Vol. I Item 50, 2/5/1580.
85. *Ibid.*, Item 529, 18/8/1587.
86. *Sadler Papers*, Vol. II p. 128.
87. CBP, Vol. I Item 398, 27/12/1585.
88. *CSPF*, (ed. 1865) Item 449, 17/12/1559.
89. *CSPF*, (ed. 1866) Item 342, July 1561.
90. *CSPF*, (ed. 1865) Item 426, 15/12/1559.
91. Hodgson, *Northumberland*, Pt II Vol. I p. 110 & 'The Ballad of Percy Reed'.
92. *CSPF*, (ed. 1866) Item 429, 22/8/1561.
93. C *Scot P*, Vol. VIII Item 653, July 1586.
94. CBP, Vol. II Item 913, 27/2/1598.
95. *Ibid.*, Item 660, 16/6/1597.
96. BL, Harl. MSS 643 fol. 219, 221, 225, 229, & 275, all 1558.
97. *Sadler Papers*, p. 64.
98. Hodgson, *Northumberland*, Pt II Vol. I p. 156.
99. Pease, *Wardens of the Marches*, p. 99.
100. CBP, Vol. II Item 131, September 1595.
101. *Ibid.*, Item 267, 18/5/1596.
102. *Ibid.*, Item 292, 2/7/1596.
103. *CSPF*, (ed. 1863) Item 311, 10/2/1559.
104. Many items between 453 & 556 in CBP, Vol. I.
105. *Ibid.*, Item 453, 27/9/1586.
106. C *Scot P*, Vol. VIII Item 351, 16/4/1586.
107. CBP, Vol. II Item 1105, 16/9/1599.
108. *CSPF*, (ed. 1865) Item 349, 30/11/1559.

CHAPTER TWENTY-ONE
The Final Solution

The preceding chapter illustrates how by selection of facts the historian can leave a wrong impression. So far as there had been within the Northumbrian highlands any harking back to the past during the late sixteenth century, it was to the reign of Edward II rather than to that of Henry VIII. An irreversible upheaval had taken place that was to enable English and Scottish individuals, in unconscious collaboration, to settle for good the problem presented by the highlanders. What lay behind that upheaval was an impoverishment which paralysed where once it had stimulated.

To start with, there was little chance of making up for the loss of military pay through resort to the old brigandage. There is no more practical method of quenching a forest fire than felling the sound timber thereabouts, and the highlanders' English neighbours were less and less worth stealing from. The reign of Elizabeth was not the golden age in economic that it was in artistic or naval terms, and in pastoral areas the position was aggravated, when after 1550 the tendency in the earlier phase of the fourth demographic period for meat and wool prices to outstrip those of corn went into reverse:[1] nor were the enclosures that were getting into their stride devoted to the tillage that would have made sense. By 1587 complaints to Burghley about food shortages in Northumberland were incessant. In consequence such nationwide epidemics as the plagues of 1586 and 1597–8 hit the Border counties hardest of all.

Naturally the Tyne- and Redesdalers suffered directly as well as indirectly from the sheep slump, and could no longer afford the expensive new weaponry that had become indispensable to soldiers and bandits. At the 1580 musters none appeared with any firearm,[2] while only a few Redesdalers carried petronels in 1595.[3] Lord Eure was alarmed at their appearance, 'starved, unarmed either with shot or bow or any warlike weapon', apart from the occasional spear. Some had only a steel cap, for all the world like a little boy in aeons to come wearing his father's 'tin hat'.[4] More serious still was the extent to which a legendary mobility had been impaired, since few could afford a horse.[5, 6] Whereas in 1558 Redesdale had fielded 300 light horsemen, Hall of Otterburn on his own contributing fifty,[7] the corresponding number for 1580 was ninety-one, many with inadequate accoutrements,[2] and for 1586 barely a score.[7] The tally of eighty in 1595 included Coquetdale, and of those 70% disallowed for poor quality.[3] In 1580, 134 horsemen mustered for North and South Tynedale taken jointly, many again without proper harness.[2] In

215

the mid-nineties North Tynedale produced a lamentable twenty-one, 75%
of which were rejected for quality,[3] and Ralph Lord Eure was shocked at
their response to a call 'to watch my front in arms' upon a false alarm
of invasion.[8, 9] During a later emergency he reiterated to Burghley 'with
sorrow . . . the weak estate of Tynedale, for there was not six able horse to
follow the fray upon the shout . . . and whereas reported to me there were
300 able foot or better, there was not one hundred'.[10]

This Warden pinned the blame on gavelkind which formed with tenant
right a composite system originally devised to produce a swarm of decently
armed horsemen, but which through excessive fragmentation now had the
opposite effect 'so that neither elder nor younger can keep horse . . . the
parts being so divided . . . Tynedale hath neither horse nor bow among the
common people, and Redesdale not much better'.[4] Various remedies were
propounded, firstly that individual portions of a customary tenement never
be reduced to a size worth less of 'the ancient yearly rent' than 6/8d or not
big enough to site a proper house;[11] alternatively any customary tenant —
or freeholder for that matter — without 'a sufficient light horse and armed
for service' should forfeit his estate;[4] finally a proposal from Sir John Forster
in 1561, never acted upon,[12] that tenant right be confiscated in return
for leases of twenty-one years, 'without fine or gressum . . . to be laid in
sufficient tenements that the tenants live and serve the Queen with horse
and armour'.[13] Such a surrender would of course rule out gavelkind as key
to a permanent inheritance.

These idle projects did nothing to assuage a situation in which a society
that had for centuries preyed on others was no longer capable of defending
itself. In both 1583[14] and 1596[4] Berwick whitecoats were lodged at Harbottle,
Chipchase and Hesleyside but for the reverse of the old reasons, viz. 'to be
the help and stay of our Borders of Redesdale and Tynedale, which with a
little aid, encouragement and maintenance would soon lay the pride of the
Elliots and Croziers'.[14] Perhaps the decline in military capability reflected in
these developments had been foreshadowed in Edward VI's reign, when the
Threapland Grahams had begun to oust the highlanders as an obsession of
governments,[15] as a bone of contention with Scotland, and as surreptitious
favourites of the sovereign.

In fact the new impotence placed the Scots in a position to exact
a vengeance for past affronts as thorough as, if on a smaller scale
than, that of their forefathers after Bannockburn. The economic base
that partly explains their success was the mixed farming of the Merse
and Teviotdale, which benefited sufficiently from the rise in the price of
corn to fund the purchase of expensive horseflesh and guns. Furthermore
as the Scottish Borders thrived they became relatively more populous.[9]

The upturn helped to convert the Laird of Buccleuch, for example, into a minor warlord. However, it would not seem to explain the resurgence of Liddesdale at this time: perhaps the clans there enjoyed the psychological advantage over their English neighbours of never having in the recent past come to rely on ephemeral soldiers' pay.

Liddesdale was indeed the spearhead of an assault that was concentrated in the years 1578–98, but ran on for years beyond that. The Elliots, of whom the Larriston grayne was the most active, were engaged throughout, the Armstrongs of Kinmont Willie more sporadically. Pursuant to appointment as Keeper of Liddesdale in 1590, the sixth Laird of Buccleuch assumed command in the later phase 'with sound of trumpet and ensigns displayed'. Between 1582 and 1586 bands of raiders numbered from one to five hundred; between 1593 and 1596 commonly between one and four thousand, the peak being attained by Elliots and Armstrongs in October 1593 when they harried Tynedale in four 'companies'. Most attacks between 1578 and 1590 were on Redesdale; between 1590 and 1598 Tynedale bore the brunt. [16–22 incl.]

Even hard-bitten officials were appalled at the scale and persistence of the raids which they continually depicted as big[23] or grievous.[24, 25] The English Warden certified in 1596 that the spoils by Scots on the Middle Marches over the past twenty years totalled in value £16,000.[8, 26] In one decade Redesdale lost £2460 equivalent, as well as two hundred prisoners — half of them in one disastrous hot trod[7] — as a consequence of 'great robbery, burnings and hereships'.[27] One sortie by Buccleuch against both dales in June 1595 'took up the whole country and did very near beggar them for ever'.[28] The heaviest loss in livestock was of 6000 head incurred by Tynedale in October 1593.[16, 17]

An additional dimension was furnished by shock at the sheer savagery of the transactions. 'Those poor wretches of Tynedale', who had 'lost the whole wealth they had',[17] were for once in a way exciting pity. The vocabulary of reference freely included such epithets as heinous,[20] outrageous,[16, 29] and intolerable, both the last being applied to a breaking of Bellingham Fair by the Elliots of Larriston in 1595.[30] The earliest intimation of what lay in store probably reached back to 1560 when it was reported that Tynedale prisoners in Liddesdale were 'very evil handled'.[31] After slaying four Charltons of the Boughthill in 1595, 'very able and sufficient men',[32, 33] Buccleuch proclaimed 'he would come back soon and kill more of them'. Six months later he was as good as his word.[17] Among thirty-five despatched on that occasion, he 'cruelly burned in their houses seven innocent men and murdered with the sword fourteen which had been in Scotland and brought away their booty'.[10] He spared neither age nor sex, cutting some in pieces with his own hand, burning others and drowned others . . . This odious act was done on the Holy Sabbath'.[34] Of eight Dodd and two Robson victims,[10] three children were burned alive in their houses,[33, 35] and seven adults stabbed to death in their beds. To sum up, it was estimated that three hundred English had been 'horribly murdered' since the accession of Elizabeth.[36, 37]

What injected the venom into such exploits was 'the evil-disposed persons having deadly feud in their hearts', to whom the Reidswyre encounter had been attributed. One of these feuds was that raging around 1586 between the Elliots and the Halls of Otterburn, which Forster had initially authorised the latter to pursue, then virtually betrayed them to their foes, in a move denounced as 'an utter overthrow and bondage to the said John Hall and the whole country of Redesdale'.[7]

Chiefly, however, there was Buccleuch's feud with Tynedale at large which, in the light of repeated clashes between those clans and his ancestors — in 1514, 1523 and during 1541-4 *inter aliis* — he had come to regard as his hereditary enemy. The grudge that particularly 'stuck in Buccleuch's stomach' was against the Charltons and was resonant enough for Burghley to enquire about it. 'Being the sufficientest and ablest men upon the Borders', the Secretary was informed, they had heartened their fellow Tynedalers to retrieve from Clan Scott property that the latter had stolen from them, in the teeth of the Laird's boast that they would never dare do it. Furthermore he was enraged that the sword purloined from his grandfather by the Charltons in 1532[38] had since been treasured at Hesleyside — as it still is by the way in the late twentieth century. 'This saith he is the quarrel'.[28] It would seem, then, that however much the family rancour had been slaked by the Laird's grandfather's triumph at Ancrum Moor, it had been stoked up again by his father's discomfiture in 1568. His nomination as Liddesdale Keeper was accordingly a godsend, in so far as it presented him with a command independent of any Scottish Warden, despite English protests that it should be as subordinate as those of Tyne- and Redesdales;[29] and it also aligned him with the experienced and cooperative Elliots and Armstrongs. From the outset Sir Walter never hid his intentions, 'acknowledging his feud with Your poor subjects of Tynedale which he had at other times sealed with many of their bloods'.[36]

The third deadly feud embroiled the Elliots of Larriston, and the Armstrongs of Mangerton and Kinmont with the Robsons.[39] One can only surmise that it was rooted in what for Liddesdalers was the treacherous attack on Thorlieshope half a century before, and inflamed more recently by the Sweethope incident.

By 1595 it had become so obvious that the English parties to these feuds were getting so much the worse of resultant exchanges that the

English Warden attempted to negotiate a pact between the Liddesdalers on the one hand; and the Tyne- and Redesdale clans, plus Ridleys, Ogles and Fenwicks who were also involved, on the other hand. The pious aim was to outlaw their 'deadly and detestable feuds . . . the original offenders being slain or justified [i.e. executed], the innocents unborn when the quarrel began cruelly murdered'.[40] Although all assented to this 'doom', the extent to which it remained a dead letter can be gauged not only from Buccleuch's untrammelled campaign, but equally from the subsequent fate of the Robsons. For one thing both John of the Stonehouse and Henry of the Falstone were finally paid out for their roles at the Reidswyre, when slain by Liddesdalers they were pursuing in lawful trod towards the close of the century.[41] In 1611, furthermore, there took place an episode reminiscent of the massacre on St. Valentine's Day in the Chicago of 1929. In what was viewed as 'the most horrible and grievous outrage that e'er hath been done in my time', seventy of the Armstrongs and Elliots, armed with long spears, pistolets and lances surprised at Lionel Robson's house in Leaplish a pow-wow of the clan. Before hacking down the walls with axes they killed or wounded eleven of the heidsmen, including besides the host those of the Falstone, the Belling, Croshels and Yarrowhall. A typical casualty was 'Thomas Robson, shot with one quarter shot in the fillets of his back, another quarter shot in his haunch and another great bullet shot through his breeches and missed his skin'. Four wives were likewise killed or maimed, including Elizabeth, 'great with child . . . hurt very sore in the head with the stroke of a piece'.[42]

To revert to the previous reign, Buccleuch in the thick of his atrocities had expressed confidence that 'they would not offend Her Majesty, being done upon feud and no way in contempt of Her Majesty'.[43] In fact the Queen continued to contemplate incidents along her middle frontier with no more equanimity than in 1575, so his optimism was misplaced. She protested via her ambassador, Sir William Bowes, about the slaying of Stonehouse, whom she dignified as 'Mr Robson of Tynedale',[44] and declared after a second attack on Bellingham that she might even break off relations with Scotland 'to revenge these insolences, so full of pride and treachery'.[30] However, given the persistent delicacy of England's international situation, the threat was unlikely to materialise. Elizabeth was still haunted by the ghost of the defeated Armada, leading her to assume that Anglo-Scottish dissension could be turned to advantage by the forces of the Counter-Reformation, a conviction in which she was strengthened by a stream of intelligence southwards from Bowes about the Catholic faction of the Earls of Errol, Angus and Huntly by which he felt surrounded. He was urging his Protestant hosts that 'these outrages are not committed for pickery . . . but . . . seeking to bring in foreign foes for alteration of this religion and estate, and to break the Borders for the more ready compassing of their practices'.[45] In the heavy raids of the 1597 Spring he 'detected Spanish and Catholic practices',[46] not altogether implausibly since Buccleuch favoured the Old Religion, though hardly an advertisement for it. Forster shared whatever paranoia there was, diagnosing the peak of the Tynedale devastation in 1593 as 'drawn on by the Papists, agreeable to their own ployte [*sic* — plot?]'.[47] Bowes remarked to King James on the high degree of cooperation between the marauding clans, which in his opinion argued an overall coordination by the three Earls 'for their advantage and with the advice of the Jesuits'.[48]

Only rarely did the English officers take reprisals. Lord Hunsdon planned punitive measures against 'the King's lewd subjects' in 1584, and in 1597 Lord Scrope, probably in a limited response to Elizabeth's annoyance at the Stonehouse and other killings, laid waste Liddesdale 'with great barbarity'.[22] In 1601 the Warden of the Middle Marches went so far as to cross the frontier and abduct his opposite number, Kerr of Cessford, and Buccleuch, but neither was held for long.[30] That said, the tactlessness of warlike operations against the subjects of a monarch about to become their own was not lost on English officers. The devious Forster can be left out of account. No redress had been demanded by him for injuries to Redesdalers since his entry, so when some of them in 1583 ventured to recover a few beasts from the Elliots after their massive raid on Elsdon, the Warden handed them back:[7] his motive, however, is more likely to have been complicity with the Liddesdalers than fear of King James. But even honest Wardens like Eure were no less restrained. When a poor Widow Milburn was robbed in 1595, Tynedalers could muster only slow-moving foot for her relief, and stood helplessly on a hill watching the Scots divide the spoils. Yet Lord Eure felt constrained to hope that this idle demonstration would not offend the Queen,[49] pathetically adding that 'the poor hungry thieves of our country may not retaliate, but we are straightway threatened with breach of peace',[8] a clear glance at policy handed down from above.

Appreciative of English weakness, the Scots adopted, not always without warrant, a system of representing most of their enormities as reprisal. Thus Larriston's 1593 sweeps were justified by him with a bill against Tynedale;[48] those of 1596 by Buccleuch with a reference to Tynedale scathes,[49] ignoring Eure's contention that an ambush in question was pure fiction;[8] those against the Laird and the Elliots in 1597 by Buccleuch himself with a lengthy reciprocal bill, and with an allegation that 700 Tynedalers had lately stolen 1000 head of cattle, in the teeth of an English counter that the true figures were thirty and seventy-four respectively.[35] When the Laird chased eighty Tynedalers out of Liddesdale, killing some, he pointed out not unreasonably that they were 'trespassers taken with a red hand' from murder and that he was performing 'what lawfully became a Keeper'.[46, 50] King James lent support, dwelling on wrongs recently endured by Martin Elliot of Larriston, which the English by contrast asserted to have been provoked through two descents on Tynedale by his own clan,[51] and maintaining that Buccleuch had set fire to Tynedale houses only when not admitted to search for his own property. The English rebuttal was that invasions by one hundred men could hardly be characterised as hot trod.[36]

With the stronger party resolved to avoid war at any cost, the debate never rose above mere bickering, nor action undertaken above an even-handed trade in hostages. Thus in 1597 thirteen pledges were extracted from the highland Head Surnames in return for like numbers out of Liddesdale and Teviotdale;[44] while Buccleuch formed part of another barter also involving three Robsons, one of whom however was rejected as inappropriate and the other two absconded during a scuffle.[52]

That no effective means were jointly devised on the very eve of the United Kingdom to stem Liddesdale's unremitting onslaught upon Tyne- and Redesdales had a double outcome. From the Scottish ability to stall with impunity the English caught not for the last time the whiff of Stuart duplicity. For instance, after the terrifying raids in 1593 Burghley deprecated James's failure to arrest Larriston, charitably blamed by Elizabeth on 'evil councillors', as well as the way the Elliot heidsman had been forewarned to make himself scarce. A second result was that the English Liberties edged unimpeded to the brink of ruin.

They were propelled over that brink by landlords, not so much a new breed as an old one reacting to the new circumstance of devastation by the Scots. A commission in 1593 recognised 'great decay [i.e. depopulation] through spoiling and burning in Tynedale',[53] where 127 tenancies had been evacuated.[27] In 1596 it was singled out as the Border district where wastes were most spacious,[8] one upshot being the near-collapse of the manorial structure. To judge from the 1604 Survey, such Wark members as Shitlington, Simonburn, Haughton and Humshaugh had as such vanished. Only Charlton, Tarset Hall and Bellingham survived as manors, probably because held by an earl and two baronets. Under Harbottle the changes were analogous, since of eleven members only Troughend, Elsdon and Otterburn retained their ancient status. Indeed over a relatively short period manors had come to be rated almost an irrelevance. Half the Tynedale freeholders sat on tenements that had never been so labelled,[54] while Redesdalers were hazy as to whether Otterburn of all places was a manor or not,[55] though classified as such along with Monkridge, Woodburn and Corsenside as recently as

1568.[56] Although manorial decay had been gathering momentum all over Europe since 1300,[57] the proclivity was accentuated in the highlands by the gravitational pull of the heidsmen's chief houses such as Hesleyside, no less than by Scottish ravages.

Not only were there less honeycombs in the two old hives around the turn of the century, but the queen bees were no longer the same. The Crown was now eager to unload its commitment upon noblemen deemed suitable, who would for some years yet co-exist with the Keepers. While Warden, Lord Eure probably functioned as Lord of Redesdale, where in any case there were family lands.[58] In 1613, upon marriage with a Scottish lady of the Homes, Lord Howard de Walden, great-grandson of the third Duke of Norfolk, was presented by the first British King with the Head Manors of Wark and Harbottle in return for a hefty fee farm. Bent upon recovery with interest of his investment, the young baron discerned at the outset that the military ingredient in the tenurial obligation of all tenants had become meaningless. Accordingly it appeared reasonable to maximise the financial ingredient instead.[59]

Initially Howard's fire was directed at the freeholders, of whom there were only eight in North Tynedale but over one hundred in more prosperous Redesdale.[55] Why he did not address himself to the paltry rents these highlanders paid — despite gross inflation £1/18/- to Elizabeth latterly as against the £7/11/1d jointly subscribed by Tynedale ancestors under Henry VII[54] — is a puzzle. Instead he targeted the fines for which they were liable, a move for which the climate was propitious: nationally, because elsewhere they had started to increase at the Queen's accession, and continued to do so; locally, inasmuch as Lord Eure had been criticised, then exonerated, for the big fines levied on Redesdale freeholders in the best lands in 1597,[58] while Heron of Chipchase had been fining his tenants at entry the equivalent of three years' rent. After five enquiries between 1619 and 1622 Lord Howard sued the Halls of Otterburn and the Charltons of Hesleyside for refusal to pay any extra fines. They had disputed his right on the grounds that as denizens of royal Liberties they were tenants-in-chief, a quaint defence in view of the creeping dissolution of the Liberties signalled nearly a century ago, and one which the baron lost no time in refuting as 'a lewd and pretended custom', seeing that 'Tynedale and Redesdale are not Liberties . . . but were disfranchised by Act of Parliament'. In a significant sidelight on Stuart justice, he deemed it worthwhile to request of the King 'direction to the judges'.[55] However, this litigation is as likely as not to have ended in a vindication of the freeholders, who were presumably in the midst of restocking the farms that had undergone such inroads in the previous generation. No certain information survives, but the presence in their ranks of the Earl of Northumberland in Tynedale, and of the Earl of Rutland in Redesdale,[54] left Lord Howard de Walden with a high mountain to climb.

A softer target altogether were the customary tenants from whom the bulk of the rents derived. Though the amounts were nominally fixed by ancient custom, the Crown while principal landlord had always taken an indulgent view of ability to pay, which despite unremitting inflation progressively declined during Elizabeth's reign. Thus from Redesdale she was in receipt of 'rents diminished . . . by reason of the hostility between England and Scotland'. Highlands at Otterburn, High Carrick and Bindhope were 'laid waste and taken again at half rent', while other summer grounds, upon which a fearful tenantry no longer dared to pasture beasts, yielded no rents at all.[55] Roland Robson of the Reins near Bellingham, a typical customary, paid 5/- rent per annum instead of the 6/8d by his grandfather at the end of the fifteenth century.[54] One Nicholas Ridley possessed a rental showing that the Crown in Edward I's time had received £1700 in yearly rents as against £30 in that of the Queen.[9] Even then it was still contended that rents had been maintained at such an uneconomic level as to cause almost as many wastes as the Scots.[53, 55] Accordingly, when in the first year of the new dynasty, with the usual Stuart aim of raising the wind, an official commission recommended after inspection of the two Head Manors that all rents be put up, a scornful minority report objected that 'those of the commission who best know the nature of the country . . . with no fertility to recompense the charges . . . finding their proceedings ridiculous refuseth to set their hands to the same.[54]

So far from scaling down rents, the regime of private landlords which largely displaced the Crown under James I was similarly bent upon putting them up. Less tolerant than Elizabethan officialdom of the underlying military fiction, they concluded that the most promising approach must be an attack upon tenant right. The provocative behaviour of some customary tenants, who pushed that 'pretended custom' to the lengths of denying they owed anything at all for their tenements, did not help their case.[60] The assault was unleashed in 1611 by the Earl of Northumberland as lord of the manor of Charlton, shortly to be followed by Howard de Walden in respect of the Head Manors of Wark and Harbottle. For the time being, though, the Court of Exchequer ruled in favour of the anachronism. However, by 1620 the King himself, vexed with the same tenure within his manor of Kendal, was proclaiming that 'tenant right be extinguished and abolished, being but dependencies of former hostility between England and Scotland'. Nevertheless even the monarch had to wait five years for ratification by the Court of Star Chamber.[61]

In view of the inability of most Wark and Harbottle tenants to produce documentary proofs that they held their customary estates of inheritance, and of their being too 'miserably poor' to hire lawyers to plead defects in the court rolls, the two noblemen themselves did not generally have to wait that long. The Court of Exchequer in 1622 ruled that claimants to tenant right in Redesdale must settle for either tenures at will or leaseholds, while the Earl in 1614 was able to impose leaseholds on his tenants at Charlton. Customary tenants of Heron of Chipchase followed suit, while others elsewhere actually applied for leases in Charlton.[55] Moreover the difficulty of finding outsiders to farm inhospitable country induced Howard de Walden to relent to the extent of a compromise with his Harbottle tenants in 1630, whereby they surrendered one third of their tenements, retaining the residue as tenants at will for the whole of the ancient rent. Over in Wark customary tenants were offered eighty-year leases.[62]

In better standing through Surname status, a smaller minority among the customary tenants strove to fend off the onslaught by securing reclassification of their tenements as freeholds. Such were Charlton of Hesleyside for Hazelhurst, William Charlton for the Leehall and Henry Dodd for the Riding, who claimed as freeholds at exiguous rents what had long been regarded as customary holdings at larger ones.[54] An enquiry in 1620 decided against the Nuke, the Blacklaw, Chirdon, Hazelhurst, and certain lands around Wark and Bellingham, but endorsed the claims of the Eales, the Reins and the Leehall.[55]

So much for the customary tenants in the two Liberties who managed to dig in. The unlucky majority, however, 'being for the most part very poor men',[54] fell within the terms of a regulation in 1622, according to which default on payment of rents incurred expulsion from one's tenement.[62] What escape routes were available for these victims of what were in effect English highland clearances?

The dispossessed might in the first place procure a plot on a manor by entry into a condition of bondage, pledged to perform defined farm labourer's tasks for the remainder of his life. According to an ex-Keeper of Redesdale in 1597, this near-serfdom was a 'great oppression to the poor commons in the said Middle Marches': many Ogle and Widdrington tenants, for example, would, if they had the means, 'give double their rents for their farms if only relieved of bondage'.[58]

The other two categories followed at long last in the wake of those who had deserted Tyne- and Redesdales in the fourteenth century. Some ventured no farther afield than downriver, to join the Durham and Northumberland coal industry that was dramatically expanding between 1560 and 1620. According to a standard work on the subject, the pitman was 'a member of a despised

and suspected group, recruited from the marginal and drop-out elements —
the decayed husbandmen and wandering poor, immigrants from Scotland or
from the over-populated Border dales whose half-savage inhabitants had a
reputation for thieving and cattle-raiding'.[63]

The more enterprising or desperate drifted south, some as far as the
capital, and the lot of such exiles is epitomised by the account given
of himself by the London beggar in William Bulleyn's play. Written in
1564, this *Dialogue*[64, 65] shows that the effects of the agrarian crisis were
making themselves felt long before the débâcle at the end of the sixteenth
century. Even though devastation by Scots was not to attain its apogee for
another fifteen years, the vagrant xenophobically attributes his misfortunes
to that rather than to the impoverishment which had exposed him to it. 'I
was born in Redesdale in Northumberland, and came of a wight [i.e. bold
and swift] riding Surname called the Robsons, gude honest men and true,
saving a little shifting for their living, God and Our Leddie help them, puir
selie men.' He claims to 'have brought many a Scot to ground in the North
Marches and gave them many grisly wounds. Nae man for man durst abide
my like, I was so fell. Then the limmer [i.e. rascally] Scots harried and
burned my gudes, and made deadlie feud on me and my bairns that I have
naething but this sarie bag and this staff and the charity of sic gude people
as you are, gude maistress . . . I have many of my Surname here in this city'.
Some apparently had made good: 'I came in nae place but either the parson,
baillie, constable or chief of the parish is of our countryth born . . . among
them the beadle of the beggars, being a Redesdale man born'.

The speaker encapsulates much of the destiny of Tyne- and Redesdales
in his own person, condition and experience. He is the typical product
of a 'miserable, distressed and wretched country', as Lord Eure described
Redesdale;[66] 'this wretched March', as he lamented to Burghley.[4] A less
sentimental onlooker was edified to observe 'how God should have laid
his heavy scourge on the said wicked country'.[58] Because life had become
nastier, more brutish and shorter than ever, many like him had forsaken the
land of their fathers: by 1604 only three of the Tynedale freeholders still bore
the ancient names, and not one of the customary tenants was a Robson,[54]
which at the 1528 musters had been as common as Jones in Wales.[67] In the
intervening period overall numbers of able-bodied men had slumped hugely.
Gone for ever was the situation in the middle of the sixteenth century when
the astute Bowes had ascribed lawlessness to over-population, and when the
pundits concurred to press for the extradition of all highlanders who through
age, infirmity, poverty or perversity were failing to win sustenance from the
soil. In 1596, by contrast, it was seriously contended that 'if it might be so
convenient, some colonies [should] be transferred thither from other parts

of the kingdom, where it laboureth of the abundance of people'.[9] As till the age of Malthus at any rate depopulation was reckoned symptomatic of a society in its death throes, it now seemed plain to all and sundry that at Fawside Brae the clansmen had laid a wreath not only on King Harry's tomb, but also on their own.

Most of this history has covered the span of nearly three centuries between two blighted generations, whose trials were similar but whose ultimate fates widely differed. Hence the reasons why the Scottish assault during Elizabeth's reign was so much more decisive than that which followed Bannockburn, are worthy of recapitulation. Because the earlier catastrophe had guaranteed an independent and formidable Scotland, the highlanders were viewed by English Kings as indispensable pieces in the jigsaw of defence, so that the rehabilitation of the two Liberties attracted a lofty priority. Thus Edward III through a conversion of tenures, possibly accompanied by a measure of plantation to replenish population losses, provided the military basis upon which Henry VIII could still rely centuries later for abundance of light horsemen. Largely through their agency the Scots breadbasket on the Borders came closer to conquest during the 1540s than at any time since 1300. Positively or negatively the Tyne- and Redesdalers accordingly continued to be subsidised for many years, despite such attendant drawbacks as the privileges of a liberty, the *esprit de corps* of the clans, and the nefarious opportunities they offered malcontents of gentle birth, all of which had to be tackled by numerous legal, political and military devices. That none of these ever really worked was due to the asylum and succour offered the English highlanders by their allies in Liddesdale. Only when that friendship had turned to hatred were the Tyne- and Redesdalers exposed naked to the blast.

By 1580 they were generally regarded by their own government as a mere nuisance, their military justification having disappeared in the climate of Anglo-Scottish amity that normally prevailed. With a Scots sovereign in prospect, English officials dreaded such threats to that amity as were twice posed through the highlanders' activities during the captivity of Mary, Queen of Scots. What rendered these doubly obnoxious was their tendency, whether deliberate or accidental, to serve the Catholic interest in the era of the Armada. When from motives of deadly feud the Liddesdalers opened their reprisals against Tyne- and Redesdales at around the same time, they were in consequence suffered to apply remorselessly to an impoverished and therefore defenceless community the brute force from which English governments had usually shied away. Furthermore there was no chance, as sporadically in the fifteenth and early sixteenth centuries, of appeals by the highlanders to a sympathetic and mighty House of Percy. By contrast the local nobility, including the latest scion of that House, put the finishing touches to the ruin begun by the alien marauder. In short it was not the advent of the first British monarch, so much as the anticipation thereof that finally dispelled the power of Tyne- and Redesdales. With the national enemy in his new guise of fellow-subject, any prospect of highland resurgence was ruled out. Whatever Ralph, Lord Eure's fantasies about the Middle Marches in 1596, the sole plantations of concern to British administrations henceforward would be of Scotsmen in Ulster and of Englishmen in Virginia and New England.

NOTES

1. For the meat/wool price scissors see Bowden, in *Agrarian History 1500–1640*, (ed. Joan Thirsk).
2. *CBP*, Vol. I Item 50, 2/5/1580.
3. *Ibid.*, Vol. II Item 168, 24/11/1595.
4. *Ibid.*, Item 267, 18/5/1596.
5. *Ibid.*, Item 131, September 1595.
6. *Ibid.*, Item 652, 8/6/1597.
7. *C Scot P*, Vol. VIII Item 653, July 1586.
8. *CBP*, Vol. II Item 245, 1/4/1596.
9. *Ibid.*, Item 323, July/August 1596.
10. *Ibid.*, Item 591, 18/4/1597.
11. Finberg, *Agrarian History*, Vol. IV, p. 24, which refers specifically to Tyne- and Redesdales.
12. See p. 224 below.
13. *CSPF*, (ed. 1866) Item 440, August 1561.
14. *CBP*, Vol. I Item 162, June 1583.
15. Particularly for their ultimate suppression under James I & VI, see Trevelyan, *Social History*, p. 154; BL, Calig. B VIII fol. 59; and Macdonald Fraser, *Steel Bonnets*, *passim*.
16. *CBP*, Vol. I Items 174, 668, 900, 903, 904 & 915, August 1583 through November 1593.
17. *CBP*, Vol. II Items 77, 80, 189, 190, 209, 211, 239, 299, 968 & 974, June 1595 through August 1598.
18. *C Scot P*, Vol. VII Item 271, 26/8/1584.
19. *Ibid.*, Vol. VIII Items 351 & 653, 16/4 and July 1586.
20. *Ibid.*, Vol. IX Item 145, 6/10/1593.
21. *Ibid.*, Vol. XI Items 155, 164, 170 & 527, October 1593 through April 1595.
22. *Ibid.*, Vol. XII Items 420, 421, 425 & 437, April and May 1597.
23. *C Scot P*, Vol. VIII Items 459–681 *passim*.
24. *Ibid.*, Vol. VII Item 36, 15/3/1584.
25. *Ibid.*, Item 204, 6/7/1584.
26. This sum would have made the same sort of impression upon contemporaries as £5M upon us nowadays.

27. CBP, Vol. I Item 998, December 1594.
28. Ibid., Vol. II Item 80, 2/7/1595.
29. C Scot P, Vol. IX Item 45, September 1586.
30. Ibid., Vol. XIII Item 49, 23/7/1597.
31. CSPF, (ed. 1865) Item 755, 21/2/1560.
32. CBP, Vol. II Item 521, 4–19/2/1597.
33. C Scot P, Vol. XII Item 425, April 1597.
34. CBP, Vol. II Item 602, 23/4/1597.
35. C Scot P, Vol. XIII Item 24, 21/6/1597.
36. Ibid., Vol. XII Item 437, 11/5/1597.
37. Ibid., Vol. XIII Item 25, 22/6/1597.
38. See p. 104 above.
39. CBP, Vol. I Item 197, December 1583.
40. Ibid., Vol. II Item 228, March 1596.
41. C Scot P, Vol. XIII Item 333, February 1599.
42. PRO, Londesborough, 28/5/1611.
43. C Scot P, Vol. XI Item 527, 24/4/1595.
44. Ibid., Vol. XIII Item 31, 25/6/1597.
45. Ibid., Vol. IX Appendix, 12/2/1590.
46. Ibid., Vol. XII Item 420, 28/4/1597.
47. Ibid., Vol. XI Item 155, 12/10/1593.
48. Ibid., Item 170, 12/11/1593.
49. CBP, Vol. II Item 239, 23/3/1596.
50. C Scot P, Vol. XII Item 421, 28/4/1597.
51. Ibid., Item 412, 21/4/1597.
52. CBP, Vol. II Item 784, 9/10/1597.
53. Ibid., Item 133, 7/10/1595.
54. PRO, SP 14 9A, 1604.
55. PRO, SP 14 109, 1619 & E 134, 18 James I, Easter No. 13; and Michaelmas 1620, 1621 & 1622.
56. Hodgson, Northumberland, Pt II, Vol. I, p. 75.
57. Margaret Spufford, Contracting Communities, p. 65.
58. CBP, Vol. II Item 763, 24/9/1597.
59. For a discussion on the friction between landlord and tenant, particularly in Co. Durham, due to the falling into abeyance of military service, see James, Family, Lineage etc., pp. 80–2.
60. Chancery Proceedings Series, ii 340/37, cited in M. H. Dodds, History of Northumberland, Vol. XV.
61. S. J. Watts, in NH, Vol. VI, pp. 72–8.
62. Ibid., pp. 79–81.
63. J. V. Nef, The Rise of the English Coal Industry, Vol. I, p. 146 ff., cited in James, Family, Lineage etc. p. 95.
64. CBP. Vol. II Item 357 (p. 183), 1/9/1596.
65. There are two copies of The Dialogue in the Bodleian Library. Its main theme is a plague in the capital and what medicines to take.
66. CBP, Vol. II Item 660, 16/6/1597.
67. LP, IV(2) no. 4336, 6/6/1528.

APPENDIX

Officers to whom Tyne- and Redesdales were subject under Henry VIII

(a) Lieutenants (General) in the North

August 1513: Earl of Surrey
Aug./Sept. 1522: Earl of Shrewsbury
Feb./Nov. 1523: Earl of Surrey
Jan./Aug. 1537: Duke of Norfolk
Feb. 1539: Duke of Norfolk
Aug./Oct. 1542: Duke of Norfolk
Nov. 1542: Earl of Hertford
Jan. 1543/Feb. 1544: Duke of Suffolk
March/June 1544: Earl of Hertford
June 1544/May 1545: Earl of Shrewsbury
May/Oct. 1545: Earl of Hertford

(b) Wardens General

1511–25: Lord Dacre
Aug. 1542: Earl of Rutland
Sept. 1542: Duke of Suffolk
Dec. 1542: Viscount Lisle
April 1543: Lord Parr
July 1544–July 1545: Earl of Shrewsbury

(c) Wardens of the East & Middle Marches

1509–11: Lord Darcy
1523: Marquis o Dorset
1526: Earl of Westmoreland
1527–36: Earl of Northumberland

(d) Wardens of the Middle Marches

1544–5: Sir Ralph Eure
1545–7: Sir Robert Bowes

(e) Vice Wardens of the Middle Marches

   1503–14: Sir Edward Ratcliffe
   1523–9: Sir William Eure
   1536–7: Lord Ogle
   1537–40: Sir John Widdrington
   1540–3: Sir Cuthbert Ratcliffe
   1543–4: Sir Ralph Eure

(f) Keepers of Tynedale

   1503:14: Sir Roger Fenwick (*de jure* 1511–? Lord Dacre)
   1514–25: Sir Ralph Fenwick
   1525–7: Sir John Heron (*de jure* 1526–7 Sir William Eure)
   1528–35: Sir Ralph Fenwick (*de jure* 1528–36 Earl of Northumberland)
   1535–7: Roger (Hodge à) Fenwick
   1537–9: Sir Reynold Carnaby
   1540–3: John Heron
   1543: Sir Ralph Eure (assistant Giles Heron)
   1545: Sir Robert Bowes (assistant George Heron, then Roger Fenwick)

(g) Keepers of Redesdale

   1511–23: Sir William Heron (*de jure* Lord Dacre)
   Sir Philip Dacre
   1523–6: Sir William Heron
   1526–8: Sir William Eure
   1528–36: Probably John Heron (*de jure* Earl of Northumberland)
   1537–40: Sir John Widdrington, as Vice Warden
   1540–7: jointly Keepers of Tynedale, *q.v.*.

Bibliography

(a) Sources

Bell MSS — In Carlisle Cathedral. See note [83] to Chapter Fourteen.

BL — MSS in the British Library, mainly in the Caligula I–VIII and Additional-MSS 24965 & 32647–57 series. See *LP* below.

George Buchanan, *History of Scotland*. Three volumes, translated from the Latin by James Aikman, Glasgow 1827.

Cal. Chart. R. — *Calendar of Charter Rolls from Henry III onwards.* Six volumes, London 1903 ff..

Cal. Inq. Misc. — *Calendar of Inquisitions Miscellaneous in Chancery.* Three volumes, London 1916 ff..

Cal. Inq. PM — *Calendar of Inquisitiones post mortem.* Sixteen volumes for Henry III through Richard II, London 1904–74.

William Camden, *Britannia, A Chorographical Description*. Innumerable editions from 1586 onwards, the first in English being dated 1610.

Carey's Memoirs — *Memoirs of Robert Carey, Earl of Monmouth*, ed. H. Powell. London 1905.

CBP — *Calendar of Letters & Papers relating to the Affairs of the Borders of England & Scotland*, ed. Joseph Bain. Two volumes, London 1894.

CCR — *Calendar of Close Rolls from Henry III onwards.* Sixty-one volumes, London 1902 ff..

CDRS — *Calendar of Documents relating to Scotland*, ed. Joseph Bain. Four volumes covering 1108–1509, Edinburgh 1881 ff..

F. J. Child, *English and Scottish Popular Ballads*, London and Boston 1905.

CPR — *Calendar of Patent Rolls for Henry III through Elizabeth.* Seventy-four volumes, London 1901 ff..

C. Scot. P. — *Calendar of the State Papers relating to Scotland*, ed. Joseph Bain & W. K. Boyd. Thirteen volumes, Edinburgh & Glasgow 1898 ff..

CSPF — *Calendar of State Papers Foreign Series for Elizabeth* ending at 1593. Twenty-five volumes. London 1863–1901.

CSP James I — *Calendar of State Papers Domestic Series of the Reign of James I*. Four volumes, London 1857–9. (References only, not transcripts).

Foedera — *Foedera Conventiones Litterae inter Reges Angliae et alios quosvis*, from 1066, ed. Thomas Rymer. Four volumes, London 1816.

Bishop Fox's Register — Surtees Vol. 147, Durham & London 1932.

William Gray, *Chorographia or a Survey of Newcastle-on-Tyne*, Newcastle & London 1649.

Edward Hall, *Chronicle, being the Union of the two Noble & Illustre Families of Lancaster & York*. First published London 1548: the London edition of 1809 has been used.

William Harrison, *An Historical Description of the Island of Britain*. One volume, London 1908 (originally 1577 in four).

John Hodgson, *History of Northumberland*, of which Part III Vols. 1 & 2 contains transcriptions of original documents. See (b) Commentaries below.

Iter de Wark — From the Reign of Alexander III. In *Historical Antiquities of Northumberland*, Archaeological Institute of Great Britain & Ireland, London 1858.

LP — Letters & Papers Foreign & Domestic of Henry VIII, ed. J. S. Brewer, J. Gairdner & R. H. Brodie. Twenty-one volumes, London 1862–1932. Also reprint by Kraus, Vaduz 1965, which omits some letters in the original editions. For the present purpose the two volumes of Hamilton Papers, Edinburgh 1890, contain nothing extra. See p. 76 above concerning the extent to which originals have been consulted in preference to the *Calendar*; also BL above & PRO below.

J. G. Nichols (ed.), *Chronicle of the Rebellion in Lincolnshire*. Camden Society, Vol. I, London 1847.

William Nicholson, *Leges Marchiarum*, London 1747.

Northern Petitions — Surtees Vol. 194, *anno* 1981.

N & D Deeds — Northumberland & Durham Deeds from the Dodsworth MSS in the Bodleian Library, Newcastle 1929.

Northumberland De Banco Rolls — Surtees Vols. 158 & 159, *anno* 1943.

Northumbrian Petitions — Surtees Vol. 176, *anno* 1961.

Palgrave Docs. — Documents & Records illustrating the History of Scotland preserved in H. M. Treasury, London 1837.

Paston Letters — Introduction by James Gairdner to Vol. II of the three-volume edition of the Letters 1422–1509, Westminster 1896.

William Patten, *The Expedition into Scotland of Edward, Duke of Somerset*, London 1548. Reprinted in *Tudor Tracts*, ed. A. E. Pollard.

Plumpton — The Plumpton Correspondence, Camden Society Vol. IV, London 1839.

Priory of Hexham — Surtees Vol. 44, *anno* 1863.

PRO — Many MSS in the State Papers 1 series bear on the subject, as well as a few in the State Papers 9, 11 & 49 series.

Reg. Pal. Dun. — Registrum Palatinum Dunelmense, ed. Hardy. Four volumes in the Rolls series.

Rot. Parl. — *Rotuli Parliamentorum ut et Petitiones et Placita in Parliamento.* Seven volumes for 1278–1503, the last of which was published London 1832.

Sadler Letters — *Letters & Negotiations of Sir Ralph Sadler, Ambassador in Scotland 1540 & 1543.* Edinburgh 1720.

Sadler Papers — *State Papers & Letters of Sir Ralph Sadler,* ed. A. Clifford. Two volumes, Edinburgh 1720. Especially a Memorial covering 1559–69 in Vol. II.

John Stowe — *Three Fifteenth Century Chronicles with Historical Memoranda,* ed. James Gairdner, Camden Society, London 1880.

Swinburne Charters — Seven Volumes in the Northumberland County Record Office.

John Warkworth — *Chronicle of the First Thirteen Years of Edward IV.* Camden Society's Vol. X, London 1880.

(b) *Commentaries*

S. Armitage-Smith, *John of Gaunt,* Westminster 1904.

R. B. Armstrong, *History of Liddesdale,* Edinburgh 1883. Only one of the intended two volumes was published.

Cadwallader Bates, *History of Northumberland,* London 1895.

J. M. W. Bean, *The Estates of the Percy Family 1416–1537,* London 1958.

Caroline Bingham, *James V, King of Scots,* Glasgow 1971.

J. B. Black, *The Reign of Elizabeth,* latest reprint Oxford 1965.

P. Hume Brown, *History of Scotland.* Three Volumes, Cambridge 1905.

A. H. Burne, *The Agincourt War,* London 1956.

A. H. Burne, *The Crecy War,* London 1955.

Edward Charlton, *Memorials of North Tynedale and its Four Surnames,* Newcastle 1871.

D. C. Coleman, *The Economy of England 1450–1750,* London 1977.

M. H. Dodds, *History of Northumberland,* Vol. XV, which is concerned with Tynedale.

M. H. & R. Dodds, *Pilgrimage of Grace 1536–7.* Two Volumes, Cambridge 1915.

G. R. Elton, *England under the Tudors,* London 1974.

G. R. Elton, *Henry VIII.* An Historical Association pamphlet, London 1962.

G. R. Elton, *Policy & Police. The Enforcement of the Reformation in the Age of Thomas Cromwell,* Cambridge 1972.

G. R. Elton, *The Tudor Revolution in Government,* Cambridge 1953.

English Historical Review — Published London, New York & Toronto, 1886 onwards.

H. P. R. Finberg (ed.), *The Agrarian History of England & Wales*. Four Volumes, Cambridge 1967.

J. W. Fortescue, *History of the British Army*. Eight Volumes, London & Edinburgh 1910.

C. M. Fraser, *History of Antony Bek*, Oxford 1957.

G. Macdonald Fraser, *The Steel Bonnets*, London 1971.

James Gairdner, *The Houses of Lancaster & York, with the Conquest and Loss of France*, London 1874.

A. Grant, 'Earls & Earldoms in Late Mediaeval Scotland 1310–1460'. One article in a book of essays presented to Michael Roberts, Belfast 1976.

A. Grant, *Independence and Nationhood. Scotland 1306–1469*, London 1984.

W. Percy Hedley, *Northumberland Families*. Two volumes, Newcastle 1968.

H. J. Hewitt, *The Organisation of War under Edward III*, Manchester 1966.

R. H. Hilton (ed.), *Peasants, Knights & Heretics*. Past & Present Series, Cambridge 1976.

T. Hodgkin, *The Wardens of the Northern Marches*. A lecture delivered in 1907 and published in London 1908.

John Hodgson, *History of Northumberland in three parts*. Those bearing on the subject in hand are all three volumes of Part II, Newcastle 1827–40; and the first two volumes of Part III, London 1820 & Newcastle 1828 respectively (see under (a) Sources). Part II, Vol. 1 comprises a history of Redesdale. Hodgson did not write a history of the larger Liberty, but a synopsis of mediaeval events there is contained in the Introduction to Part II, Vol. 3.

Edward Hughes, *North Country Life in the Eighteenth Century*, Oxford 1952.

Philip Hughes, *The Reformation in England*. Three volumes, London 1950 and a single volume, London 1963.

E. F. Jacob, *The Fifteenth Century 1399–1485*. In the *Oxford History of England*, Oxford 1961.

M. E. James, *A Tudor Magnate & the Tudor State*, York 1966.

M. E. James, *Change & Continuity in the Tudor North*, York 1965.

M. E. James, *Family, Lineage & Civil Society*, Oxford 1974.

M. H. Keen, *England in the Later Middle Ages*, London 1973.

H. G. Koenigsberger & G. L. Mosse, *Europe in the Sixteenth Century*. Open University, undated.

Andrew Lang, *History of Scotland*. Four volumes, Edinburgh 1900–4.

N. Macdougall, *James III, A Political Study*, Edinburgh 1982.

J. D. Mackie, *The Earlier Tudors 1485–1558*, Oxford 1952.

J. D. Mackie, *The English Army at Flodden*. In *Miscellany of the Scottish History Society*, Vol. VIII.

Sir Herbert Maxwell, *History of the House of Douglas*. Two volumes, London & Edinburgh 1902.

Edward Miller, *War in the North. The Anglo-Scottish Wars of the Middle Ages*, Hull 1960.

Margaret Moore, *Lands of the Scottish Kings in England*, London 1915.

Northern History — Twenty volumes so far, Leeds 1968 ff..

C. W. Oman, *Art of War in the Middle Ages*. Two volumes, London 1924.

C. W. Oman, *Warwick the Kingmaker*, London 1891.

Ordnance Survey of Great Britain — Sheets 70, 71 & 76 in the old edition; in the new metric 1:50,000 Sheets 80, 86 & 87.

Howard Pease, *The Lord Wardens* (sic) *of the Marches of England and Scotland*, London 1913.

Procs N/C Antiq. — Archaelogea Aeliana. Miscellaneous tracts published by the Society of Antiquaries of Newcastle-on-Tyne, published in various series since 1806. The current series started in 1904.

Thomas Rae, *The Administration of the Scottish Frontier*, Edinburgh 1966.

Sir James Ramsay, *Lancaster & York*. Two volumes, Oxford 1892.

Rachel Reid, *The King's Council of the North*, London 1921.

G. R. Ridpath, *The Border History of England & Scotland*, Berwick 1848.

Charles Ross, *Edward IV*, London 1974.

Charles Ross (ed.), *Patronage, Pedigree & Power*, Bristol 1979.

J. Horace Round, *Peerage & Pedigree*. Two volumes, London 1910.

T. H. Rowland, *Mediaeval Castles, Towers, Peles & Bastles of Northumberland*, Morpeth 1987. An invaluable compendium.

A. L. Rowse, *The England of Elizabeth*, London 1950 & 1953.

A. L. Rowse, *The Expansion of Elizabethan England*, London 1962.

J. J. Scarisbrick, *Henry VIII*, London 1968.

Margaret Spufford, *Contracting Communities*, Cambridge 1974.

Sir Frank Stenton, *Anglo-Saxon England*, Oxford 1943, last printed in 1971.

R. L. Storey, *The End of the House of Lancaster*, London 1966.

Joan Thirsk (ed.), *The Agrarian History of England and Wales*, Vol. IV 1500–1640, Cambridge 1967.

W. W. Tomlinson, *Life in Northumberland during the Sixteenth Century*, London & Newcastle 1897.

D. L. W. Tough, *The Last Years of a Frontier*, Oxford 1928.

Sir G. M. Trevelyan, *English Social History*, London 1946.

Sir G. M. Trevelyan, *The Middle Marches*, Newcastle 1976.

P. F. Tytler, *History of Scotland*. Four volumes, London 1873–7.

Godfrey Watson, *The Border Reivers*, Bury St. Edmunds 1974.

J. C. Wedgwood, *The History of Parliament 1439– 1509*, London 1936.

T. D. Whitaker, *An History of Richmondshire*, London 1823.

Jenny Wormald, *Court, Kirk & Community. Scotland 1470–1625*, London 1981.

Jenny Wormald, *Lords & Men in Scotland*, Edinburgh 1985.

INDEX

Because of continual recurrence Scotland, Northumberland, (North) Tynedale and Redesdale have been omitted. Battles or Frays are grouped under the general heading Battles.